TRANSFORMING

THE APPALACHIAN

COUNTRYSIDE

Transforming the

RAILROADS,

DEFORESTATION,

AND SOCIAL

CHANGE IN

WEST VIRGINIA,

1880–1920

Appalachian Countryside

RONALD L. LEWIS

THE UNIVERSITY OF
NORTH CAROLINA PRESS

CHAPEL HILL & LONDON

This book was set in Monotype Bulmer

by Keystone Typesetting, Inc.

Book design by April Leidig-Higgins

Manufactured in the United States of America

The paper in this book meets the guidelines for perma-

nence and durability of the Committee on Production

Guidelines for Book Longevity of the Council on Library

Resources.

Library of Congress Cataloging-in-Publication Data

Lewis, Ronald L., 1940–   Transforming the Appalachian

countryside: railroads, deforestation, and social change in

West Virginia, 1880–1920 / Ronald L. Lewis.

p. cm. Includes bibliographical references (p.) and index.

ISBN 0-8078-2405-4 (cloth: alk. paper).

ISBN 0-8078-4706-2 (pbk.: alk. paper)

1. West Virginia—Economic conditions. 2. West Virginia

—Social conditions. 3. West Virginia—Environmental

conditions. 4. Industrialization—West Virginia. I. Title.

HC107.W5L39   1998   97-36616

338.9754—dc21   CIP

02 01 00 99 98   5 4 3 2 1

TO SUSAN AND JENNIFER

CONTENTS

ILLUSTRATIONS

TABLES

MAPS AND FIGURES

ACKNOWLEDGMENTS

Authors of scholarly books publish their work only with the assistance of a multitude of generous people, and I am no exception.

I have incurred my greatest debts at West Virginia University, where I have been fortunate to receive support from all levels of the institution. A sabbatical leave allowed me the time to write much of the first draft of this manuscript. An Eberly Family Professorship provides me with funds to support my research activities, and I am indebted to the Eberly College of Arts and Sciences, particularly the former dean and current provost Gerald Lang, for making these resources available to me.

The Regional Research Institute at West Virginia University provided me with a forum for presenting my ideas before colleagues from several disciplines at seminars and workshops. As a faculty associate in the institute and member of institute delegations to joint seminars abroad, I have presented sections of this book at the University of Glasgow in Scotland and at the Institute of Industrial Economics in Ukraine. I also presented a paper drawn from this research at a Southern Regional Science Association meeting in San Antonio and at several local conferences and symposia sponsored by the Regional Research Institute. For three years the institute greatly facilitated the completion of this work by funding a graduate research assistant to gather, collate, and tabulate census data and to plow through mounds of state government documents. I wish to acknowledge my gratitude to Andrew Isserman, until recently the director of the institute, and staff members Mary Lou Myer and Carla Uphold for their assistance over the years.

Several scholars commented on portions of this book in manuscript, and I would like to thank them for taking time from busy schedules to provide this professional courtesy. Altina Waller of the University of Connecticut critiqued a paper I presented at a Southern Historical Association meeting, and John A. Williams of Appalachian State University commented on another paper presented at an annual Appalachian Studies Association conference. Both are excellent critics, and I have taken their advice. The environment chapter was read by colleagues in the West Virginia University Division of Forestry, Stephen Hollenhorst and Cedric Landenberger. On several key points their comments were important in keeping my nonscientific conclusions accurate, and I am thankful for their advice. The chapter on the law was read by Thomas Carney, a lawyer who is also a Ph.D. candidate in the Department of History at West Virginia University. His advice on several legal points prevented me from committing uninformed errors.

It has been my blessing to have served as adviser for several outstanding graduate students and, while I hope I have helped them to become professional historians, I acknowledge that I also have learned a great deal from them. Nothing clarifies one's thoughts so well as having to explain them to others. I am grateful for the conscientious persistence of two graduate students whose assistance on this project was funded by the Regional Research Institute. Barbara Rasmussen compiled a detailed database from manuscript census schedules on over thirteen thousand households. Rebecca Bailey collected data from the West Virginia Incorporation Reports, entered the data into a machine-readable format, and collated the data for use in tables. Her research in West Virginia government documents unearthed a trove of previously unused information relating to this subject. I also wish to thank Paul Rakes for making the graphs that are reproduced in this book and his careful reading of the manuscript. Debra Benson, a drafting specialist in the Geography Department, created the maps. Undergraduate research fellows sponsored by the Regional Research Institute Jonathan Byrne and John Kamorados gathered valuable data on environmental legislation and railroad court cases.

I cannot overemphasize the helpfulness of the library staff at West Virginia University, a uniformly professional group who labor under difficult conditions. In particular, I want to thank our Appalachian librarian, Jo. B. Brown, and the staff at the West Virginia and Regional History Collection. Christelle Venham, David Bartlett, and David Ware have provided invaluable assistance for many years in locating materials in our special collections. Nathan Bender, curator of special collections, also has my thanks for his cooperation not only with this project but with other initiatives emanating from the Department of History. Also, I would like to thank the staff at the West Virginia State Archives in Charleston, particularly Debra Basham whose knowledge of the collections and courteous service are appreciated. Scholars have created an entire repertoire of horror stories about researching in county courthouses, but my own experience in the Tucker and Randolph County courthouses contradicts this folklore.

I have had extended conversations about segments of this book with friends and colleagues who have helped me to formulate my ideas, but I particularly want to acknowledge the insights of Dwight Billings, Durwood Dunn, John Inscoe, Mary Beth Pudup, and Paul Salstrom for sharing their thoughts with me on this subject. My colleagues in the Department of History probably have heard more than they ever wanted to know about this project, and for their good-natured forbearance I thank them.

My wife, Susan E. Lewis, has proofread the entire manuscript, a risk not lightly taken by one who wants to remain happily married. She is good at it, however, and her skills invariably rise to the challenge. My teenaged daughter, Jennifer, has always been patient with a father who spends too much time in his study and has allowed me to indulge my intellectual interests without excessive feelings of guilt. I thank them for their love and support. It is to Susan and Jennifer, the hardwood giants in my personal forest, that I dedicate this book.

TRANSFORMING

THE APPALACHIAN

COUNTRYSIDE

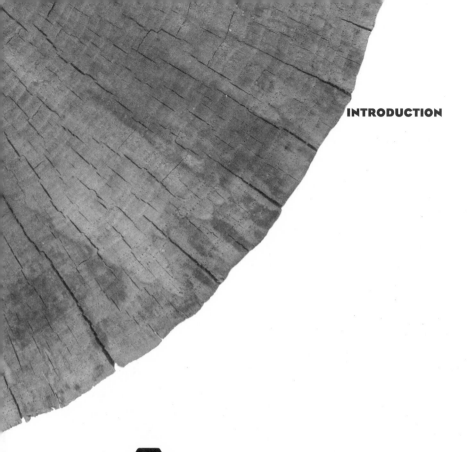

Appalachia is a region without a formal history. Beyond the obvious physical reality of its mountains, "Appalachia" is a socially constructed conceptual place. Born in the fertile minds of late-nineteenth-century local color writers, Appalachia was invented in the caricatures and atmospheric landscapes of the escapist fiction they penned to entertain an emergent urban middle class. Their stories and travelogues generated little or no critical evaluation of the characterizations of either mountain people or the landscape portrayed in their writings. John Fox Jr., undoubtedly the most popular author of the genre, perpetrated, and then helped perpetuate, the myth of Appalachian otherness to facilitate absentee corporate control of the region's natural resources by marginalizing indigenous residents. In short, "Appalachia" was a willful creation and not merely the product of literary imagination.[1]

The publication in 1899 of Berea College President William Goodell Frost's famous article, "Our Contemporary Ancestors in the Southern Mountains," signified the maturity of the concept of Appalachia as a spatially and culturally remote region that could be identified by a set of fixed cultural attributes. His appeals for gifts to finance his missionary work in the mountains contain some of the most widely recognized phrases applied to Appalachian mountain dwellers. They were "our contemporary ancestors," our "eighteenth century neighbors," who had just awakened from a long "Rip Van Winkle sleep," pure Anglo-Saxons "beleaguered by nature" in "Appalachian America," one of "God's grand divisions."[2] Frost the publicist certainly knew how to turn a phrase.

This fictional representation became accepted, and then reified, as "history" by twentieth-century reporters, scholars, and policy makers into what Henry Shapiro has called the "Myth of Appalachia," and Allen Batteau refers to as the "invention" of Appalachia as a physically and culturally homogeneous region economically isolated from mainstream America.[3] In the absence of basic historical knowledge, social theory was substituted to explain past developments. The "culture of poverty" theory found the reasons for economic backwardness in the culture itself. Writers generally perceived culture as a set of immutable traits that shaped daily life and social values, particularly individualism, traditionalism, fatalism, and religious fundamentalism. These core Appalachian traits were culled from early writings fixed into the scholarly literature by sociologist Thomas Ford in the 1950s.[4] In the 1970s, Jack Weller's widely read book, *Yesterday's People*, claimed that these characteristics had produced a degenerate culture that inhibited economic "progress" in the region.

The culture of poverty model was grounded in modernization theory, which claims that societies move through five developmental stages. Most critical is the takeoff stage when a society passes from the subsistence to capitalist mode of production. It is assumed that progress from one stage to the next depends on internal social conditions and cultural characteristics that either facilitate or impede the transition. Social relations that inhibit the penetration of capital investment in Appalachia, such as farmers' resistance to exploiting the natural resources or wage earners' desire to seek protection in unions, was evidence of a lag in those cultural preconditions necessary for the transition to the next stage of economic progress.[5]

Modernization theory ignores the transformations of indigenous social and political institutions and relations imposed on local people by the process itself. Instead, local people are seen merely as passive receivers and, to the extent that they fail to participate in or benefit from a system that provides unequal access to capital and power designed to ensure that capital migrates to those elites who control the process, the victims themselves are at fault.

The problem with models is that they do not detail what actually happened to indigenous social and political institutions as a result of the transition to industrial capitalism—a few exceptional studies, such as John Gaventa's *Power and Powerlessness*, notwithstanding. Beyond Ronald Eller's chapter on the timber industry in *Miners, Millhands, and Mountaineers*, or Michael Frome's *Strangers in High Places*, a book on the establishment of the Great Smoky Mountains National Park, few scholarly studies examine the transformative effects of deforestation on Appalachian society.

This book examines the transformation of Appalachia from a rural-agricultural society dependent on the virgin forest, to a twentieth-century society denuded of the forest and fully enmeshed in capitalism and the markets. I provide a concrete empirical foundation for understanding this transition by examining the social, political, economic, legal, and environmental changes that resulted from cutting the virgin forest.

I have concentrated on deforestation in order to trace the wrenching social changes that accompanied the removal of the forests. The primary focus of my research is the spine of mountain counties that make up West Virginia's southern and eastern border, where coal had the least, and timber the greatest, influence on society.

I have chosen West Virginia as a mirror of this much larger story for a variety of reasons. Two-thirds of West Virginia was still covered by ancient growth hardwood forest on the eve of the transition in 1880, but by the 1920s virtually the entire state had been deforested. Moreover, as the only Appalachian state entirely within the region, West Virginia serves as a microcosm of the region itself. Also, concentrating on a single state avoids confusing the historical processes with evidence from different political and legal systems. A regionwide study would require the selection of specific areas to be examined and, though this approach provides a measure of breadth, it also precludes the depth that might be gained from close contextual analysis of a single place. West Virginia has broad settled valleys where market connections were developed early in the nation's history, and yet on the eve of industrialization more than two-thirds of the state was still backcountry, or "backcounties" as contemporary residents referred to them. Spatially, much of West Virginia, particularly the mountainous interior, was shaped by timbering instead of coal mining. Culturally, it is a southern state subjected to powerful northern economic and political influences. Even though its sectionalism welcomes comparative analysis, West Virginia is a large but definable unit in which the social, economic, political, legal, and environmental changes spurred by deforestation reveal the answers to major questions relating not only to the state's history but to Appalachian and American history as well.

The history of the lumber industry in West Virginia and Appalachia is a local and regional variation of the industry's inexorable westward migration. Along with farming, fur trapping, and fishing, lumber was one of colonial America's first industries. As the population of colonial America grew, water-powered sawmills multiplied along the rivers of the Atlantic seaboard. The completion of the Erie Canal in 1825 connected the incomparable white pine forests of the Great Lakes states with the eastern population centers. Steam-powered circular sawmills developed along with the logging railroad during this period to feed the expanding demand for wood products and accelerated the lumbermen's conquest of the vast north woods.[6]

First Maine, then New York, Pennsylvania, and, after the Civil War, the Great Lakes states led the nation in lumber production. Lumbermen's access to the public lands in the north woods and subsequently to the southern and western forests was facilitated by laws intended to distribute the public domain quickly and cheaply. Through means fair and foul, lumber companies blocked huge timber tracts on a scale that the previous generations of lumbermen could only dream of, and railroads opened up the new forests and transported lumber to markets in a volume that only a few years earlier would have seemed impossible. Taking advantage of such enormous opportunities required complex business organization, and the lumber industry emerged as a big business during the years after the Civil War to meet the challenge. Big business required major capital investment, however, and the heavy debt burden demanded maximum and constant production if lumber companies were to remain solvent. The result was the rapid skinning of American timberland. The normal lifetime of a sawmill was twenty years, and then the company moved on. In this business environment, lumbermen came to think of logging as "timber mining" whereby timber was cut and the land sold or abandoned. This attitude was reinforced by the commonly held idea that removal of the virgin forest would result in agricultural settlement; "the plow will follow the ax" was often a justification for wasteful deforestation.[7]

By the late nineteenth century, the end of the north woods was on the horizon, and talk of a coming "timber famine" sent savvy lumbermen scrambling for new stumpage in the South and West. To those regions they transplanted their ideological commitment to constant economic growth, ever-expanding production, and the largest mills with the latest technology that they could finance. Millions in capital released from the Great Lakes states flowed into public lands in the South and West, where land could still be acquired for next to nothing. Alongside this heavily capitalized segment of the industry stood the smaller, unencumbered mills, the "peckerwoods," "coffeepots," and "fire splitters," which rushed in when economic conditions were favorable and shut down when times were bad. Nearly fifty thousand sawmills were counted in the census of 1909, but three-fourths of them cut less than a million feet of lumber a year; the other one-fourth cut between 100 and 200 million board feet in a year.[8]

The lumber industry reached its peak in the first decade of the twentieth century just as the conservation movement became established. Lumbermen of the migratory era are condemned for the almost unimaginable devastation they left behind. The expansion of the industry into the South and West during this period left it burdened with excess timberlands and sawing capacity just when the development of new building materials challenged the dominance of wood in the construction market. The resulting wave of cutthroat competition and overproduction initiated structural changes intended to bring more predictability and less risk for fewer, larger companies.

It is worth asking why the lumber industry was so migratory, why it was more profitable to move on to new stands than to cultivate trees as a crop. The answer in a word is *competition*. The wealth of the virgin forest invited exploitation, and the American ideology of unrestrained expansion, a federal policy of cheap land, and notions linking civilization with open country legitimized the wasteful methods of nineteenth-century lumbermen. At the same time, improvements in milling technology and the rapid development of railroad transportation enlarged the opportunities available to lumbermen. Lumber financing played a significant role in the cut out and get out philosophy as well. The industry borrowed capital for expansion on a fixed schedule of liquidation, and often it was cheaper for big mills to continue to cut even at a loss than to stop production during market downturns.[9]

In 1920, in a survey of forest resources in the United States, the U.S. Forest Service estimated that of every ten acres of primeval forest about four acres had been converted into farms and pastures; four acres had been cutover where the plow did not follow; and the other two acres were still in uncut woods. About half of the logged-over virgin forest in America had become farms, and half was divided into various classifications of forestland. Of the latter, one-fourth had been burned—81 million acres barren of trees, farms, and people.[10]

The lumber industry in Appalachia and West Virginia followed the same general pattern as the national industry, but with two major differences. First, there was no public land in Appalachia available to lumbermen, and yet to be competitive in the industry they needed ready access to cheap timber. Thus they had to buy on favorable terms from private landowners, which they did by relying on superior knowledge of the law and market value of the resources, by favorable legislation intended to protect their investments, and by producing a constant flow of timber to market. The importance of favorable prices and predictable control was accentuated by the second major difference between the forests of Appalachia and those of the North and South: Appalachia was clothed in hardwoods rather than pine. While hardwood products generally fetched higher prices, hardwoods were more difficult to cut, transport, and mill than softwoods, and therefore production costs were higher. Logging in the mountains also was physically more challenging and dangerous than in the flat pineries of the lowlands; there were many more opportunities for something to go wrong. The rugged terrain and lack of technological capacity and the industry's preference for following the lines of least resistance had preserved large timbersheds in the mountains from exploitation until the turn of the century.

In a rare moment of reflection, Americans paused at the turn of the century to ponder what had happened to the vast wilderness and the meaning behind its disappearance. Although the elimination of the virgin forest was the visible manifestation of changes taking place on the land, it was the railroad that provided the most powerful metaphor of social change in nineteenth-century America. In his deservedly esteemed book *The Machine in the Garden*, Leo Marx points out that the shriek of the locomotive represented an "elemental, irreducible dissonance" in the mid-nineteenth-century rural countryside that was being changed not by human hands themselves but by machines operated by human hands, and this innovation seriously complicated the myth of human triumph over nature. The inevitable social changes sparked by the railroad's arrival were noted early in the century by Ralph Waldo Emerson, who observed in his journal: "I hear the whistle of the locomotive in the woods. Wherever that music comes it has its sequel. It is the voice of the civility of the Nineteenth Century saying, 'Here I am.' It is interrogative: it is prophetic: and this cassandra is believed: 'Whew! Whew! Whew! How is real estate here in the swamp and wilderness? Ho for Boston! Whew! Whew! . . . I will plant a dozen houses on this pasture next moon, and a village anon.' "[11]

A similar acknowledgment of the railroad's power to transform was related in a travelogue written by Philip Pendleton Kennedy, who accompanied a group of Virginians on a journey to the Blackwater Falls in 1853. One man was so taken with the country that he vowed to purchase five thousand acres and more later, as an inheritance for his children. "Why, sir, in twenty years, the whole of it would be worth fifty dollars an acre at the least. The railroad, when finished, will open out the country to market at once: it will make tidewater at your door!" In Kennedy's opinion, the enthusiasm was not misplaced for "the railroad must put this noble country alongside of the sea," the forest would be turned into lumber and cleared away for the plow, and the coal and other mineral treasures dug from the earth. "Therefore the land (such land! that can be bought now for sixty cents to a dollar an acre) must be worth fifty dollars—and that at no very distant day." Kennedy realized, however, that this work required "the hardy enterprise of men in whose souls poetry and imagination are not predominant" but rather "by men with necessity at their elbow, who are resolute upon acquisition, and who have been trained to the rougher realities of life."[12] This was the American myth restated, but now it demanded a railroad, and Kennedy's vision for western Virginia did not materialize until the railroad penetrated the backcounties.

From the beginning backcounty farmers depended on the forest to supply building materials and the logs they floated to downstream mills to sell for cash. As in Appalachia generally, there were at least two preindustrial West Virginias: one in the settled farm and town sections around the periphery and the broad river valleys, the other in the underdeveloped wilderness backcounties that made up about two-thirds of the state on the eve of deforestation. Change came slowly during the first century after permanent settlements were planted in the mountains of West Virginia and then accelerated geometrically to a crescendo between 1880 and 1920. During this period, the state's remote interior was integrated into the national economy as industrial capitalism unlocked the storehouse of natural resources. West Virginia officials promoted the exploitation of these resources as the surest road to economic development and the railroad as the most efficient engine for delivering economic growth. By World War I nearly four thousand miles of track conveyed the heavy equipment necessary to cut and haul the big virgin timber away and connected even the deepest recesses of the mountains to national markets.

The railroads spawned a multitude of small towns and milling centers in the backcounties where previously there had been only a small, scattered farm population. Market outposts and nodes in the production and distribution system that stimulated further internal expansion, these towns acted as commercial magnets for local farmers and workers, who in turn attracted merchants and professionals to service a growing population increasingly dependent on a cash economy. The market revolution transformed the relations of exchange in the backcountry and pulled subsistence farmers into the market economy. The penetration of industrial capitalism into the back-counties also fractured previous political alignments and stimulated the emergence of a new political culture. The old Confederate-Democrat versus Yankee-Republican split was replaced by pro- versus anti-industrialist factions in both parties, and the industrial factions generally prevailed. This trend is amply demonstrated at the state level, but scholars have seldom considered how the struggle for control actually took place at the local level. This book examines how county political machines were reconfigured around issues such as the location of county seats. The railroad changed the spatial conception of centrality from one that was geographic to one that required strategic location on the railroad transportation network. Because the county seat would become a commercial hub as well as the center of political power in the county, more than twenty wars over location of county seats were fought in West Virginia between "Ironheaded Industrialists" and "Bourbon Agrarians" to determine which local elites would control the economic transition and therefore its rewards.

The industrial transition also required a corollary legal revolution to make capital investment secure. Legislators were always ready to assist, but it took the new generation of jurists who came to the state supreme court of appeals in 1888–90 to encourage industrial development by recognizing the principle of "reasonable use" in conflicts between agricultural and industrial users of the land and shift the burden of proof from industry to farmers in cases involving negligence. Similar changes came in riparian law. Although local circuit court juries overwhelmingly sided with farmers in these disputes, the supreme court of appeals generally overturned their decisions on appeal. This was a dramatic reversal of the legal tradition inherited from Virginia, which usually protected agrarian landowners.

The railroad and timber boom accelerated business for land lawyers but precipitated the decline of agriculture. The cutting of the mountainside forests where farmers traditionally ranged their livestock and acquired other staples removed the very foundation of backcountry agriculture, and within a generation the system collapsed. Farmers were forced to shift to a commercial system by acquiring better grades of stock, to rely on machinery, and to use commercial fertilizer. Predictably, mountain farmers could not compete with their counterparts in the Midwest. Between 1880 and 1920 farm families increasingly abandoned or were forced off the land into wage labor, and West Virginia agriculture began its precipitous slide toward marginality.

The squeeze on agriculture was aggravated by the environmental disaster that deforestation inflicted on the land. Contemporary conservationists understood this, but the clamor for industrial growth drowned out their alarms. Forest fires repeatedly swept through the slashing, 710 of them covering 1.7 million acres in 1908 alone. The streams became so polluted that they were devoid of life, while floods ravaged the valleys below, and erosion washed away topsoil into the streams and silted up navigable watercourses. To save the inland waterways, the federal government embarked on a plan to protect the Ohio and Potomac watersheds by establishing the Monongahela National Forest in 1920. By then entire ecological systems had been destroyed, the backcountry had been tied to the market system, independent farmers had become wage hands, and the political system had been transformed into a mechanism for the protection of capital.

Once the mountains had been skinned of their forest, the lumber companies closed their operations and moved on to greener country in the South and West. Without lumber the railroads soon pulled up their track and withdrew from the mountains as well. Again the countryside fell silent, once booming mill towns declined, and propertyless wage earners were left to drift away or become members of the new marginalized rural poor. In this condition, West Virginia confronted the Great Depression and its modern paradox as a state whose robust expansion had saddled it with an anemic economy. As elsewhere in America, government and private efforts at conservation were begun only after the forest wealth had been exploited.

Deforestation followed a common pattern throughout the Appalachian region, and though the internal social and political consequences of that process generally have been ignored, West Virginia's experience can point the way for similar studies in the future. Throughout the region the process was the same. First, pioneer efforts to open the forests made only slight inroads; then a few early lumber companies entered the business, often using the log drive or rafting method to transport timber to a few small mills; then the railroads penetrated the region, introducing steam power and greatly expanding production. Since the capital required for this next level of steam-powered transportation and milling was scarce in the sparsely populated mountains, external capital investment was required, which meant absentee ownership.[13]

"The home and permanent interests of the lumberman are generally in another State or region, and his interest in these mountains begins and ends with the hope of profit," the U.S. Department of Agriculture reported in 1902. External capital first entered West Virginia in the 1880s and 1890s, and when it was clear that the timber supply would soon be exhausted, capital looked southward. A report of the U.S. secretary of agriculture in 1902 observed that 5.4 million acres of the southern Appalachians had been surveyed for the report and that 75 percent of it was still in forest.[14]

The survey was taken none too soon for about this time the great migration of capital followed the hardwoods further down the chain to the southern Appalachians. The William M. Ritter Lumber Company was organized during the 1890s in West Virginia by Pennsylvania lumbermen and became one of the largest in the state. The "dean of the Hardwood Lumbermen of America," William Ritter expanded his timber holdings into the surrounding states of Kentucky, Tennessee, and Virginia. He also acquired at least two hundred thousand acres of timberland in North Carolina. By 1913 Ritter controlled over 2 billion board feet of hardwood timber in the Appalachians. Another large West Virginia company, Parsons Pulp and Lumber Company, which was established by a group of Philadelphia investors, acquired thirty-five thousand acres of timberland in North Carolina. Other corporations from New York, Pennsylvania, Maryland, Ohio, Michigan, and Illinois joined the West Virginia companies in exploiting the great timber of western North Carolina. The largest company entering the southern Appalachians by far was the Champion Fibre Company. Champion was organized in 1905 by Peter G. Thompson to supply pulp for his paper company in Hamilton, Ohio. The company erected its large pulp mill in the Pigeon River country, where it built Canton, a company town named after Canton, Ohio. The company acquired hundreds of thousands of acres of mountain forest to ensure a steady supply for its pulp mill.[15]

On the Tennessee side of the mountains, the largest timber operator was the Little River Lumber Company, a firm composed of Pennsylvania capitalists. Nearby another Pennsylvania firm, the Tellico River Lumber Company, was busily removing the timber from its one-hundred-thousand-acre holdings. Outside capitalists controlled the rest of the lumber industry in eastern Tennessee as well. Among them were several West Virginia investors.[16]

Promoters of the lumber industry, whether local elites or absentee owners, saw the commercial value of the forest and little else. West Virginia learned this lesson first, but its neighbors in southern Appalachia were not ignored for long. A. E. Brown, superintendent of the mountain school department of the Southern Baptist Convention, complained in 1910 that "those who have destroyed the forests reaped the only benefit" and left the mess for residents. Brown observed that the companies were "utterly indifferent to the interest of the natives." In fact, the lumbermen did not seem to realize the forests had "any other value beyond what they could get for them," and though it was true that the industry had given natives employment, it also destroyed their future because the denuded mountainsides of southern Appalachia were now "practically worthless."[17]

Horace Kephart, the outdoors writer who lived and found his inspiration in the Smoky Mountains, joined the chorus of laments when he observed in 1913 that "the curse of our invading civilization is that its vanguard is composed of men who care nothing for the welfare of the people they dispossess." A northern lumberman admitted to Kephart, "with frankness unusual in his class," that "all we want here is to get the most we can out of this country, as quick as we can, and then get out." On the other side of the fence, an "old mountaineer" expressed his disapproval to Kephart: "I don't like these improvements. . . . Some calls them 'progress', and says they put money to circulatin'. So they do; but who gets it?" Kephart's neighbor claimed that in the old days life was hard, and "nowadays we dress better, and live better," but he pronounced, "some other feller allers has his hands in our pockets."[18]

The marriage of business and politics was not unique to the lumber industry, of course, but in few states was politics so dominated by extraction industries as in West Virginia. West Virginia was first in the southern Appalachians to be cutover, and the model of absentee control migrated down the Appalachian Mountain chain with the industry. It is true that "cut out and get out" was the modus operandi of the industry everywhere in America, but historians generally have not explored the political and legal changes implemented in the statehouses and courthouses of the region in support of the industrial transition. These social and political realignments within Appalachian society can reveal new insights into political relations between the mountain and lowland constituencies of other Appalachian states in the promotion of industrial development.

Legislation was passed in West Virginia to accommodate capitalist development, and there is every indication that lumber capitalists and their local boosters received favorable treatment throughout the region. Even the rumor of a pulp mill on the Pigeon River in the western North Carolina mountains resulted in such legislation. In 1901 S. A. Jones of Waynesville secured passage in the North Carolina General Assembly of an act "to encourage the building of pulp mills and paper mills and tanneries" in

Haywood and Swain Counties near the Tennessee border. To protect a company's investment and probably in response to the demands of the Champion Company's preliminary demands, the bill stipulated that any company that invested $100,000 or more to convert wood to pulp "shall not be subject to any criminal prosecution for the pollution of any watercourses" on which the factory was located and restricted the liability of the factory or factories to damage suits brought by people through whose property the river flowed. In the event of such a suit, the company could simply file bond to be relieved of the threat of an injunction or restraining order to halt the pollution. In 1907, Thompson secured amending legislation through D. L. Boyd, a member of the House of Delegates from Haywood County, where Champion Fibre was located, further protecting the company from suits for polluting the Pigeon River. Champion was protected from damage suits for the twenty-six miles of the Pigeon River it polluted in North Carolina, but the river also flowed into Tennessee. Champion retained a prominent attorney from Newport, Tennessee, in 1908 to engineer the defeat of a series of attempts by the legislature to bring suit against the company for damages. The company succeeded at every turn, and eventually Tennessee legislators decided to ignore the polluted Pigeon River.[19] Champion succeeded in using the legislature and the courts to protect its private interests to the public detriment; its methods were replicated in West Virginia and undoubtedly throughout the region.

Few mountain residents understood the social costs that would accompany the railroad and timber boom. Who could have anticipated what happened to the streams? In an interview in 1984 Charles C. Chambers recalled that he was nineteen when the Champion Fibre mill was completed at Canton in 1908. Before the mill, he remembered, the Pigeon River was clear, full of fish, and pure enough to drink, but within a week after the mill started operations, the river "turned as black as molasses," and the fish disappeared. "They never did even say what would happen to the water before they turned the mill on. They didn't say anything about it until it was all over."[20]

Nothing prepared local people to predict the scale of destruction left on the land either. "When I first came into the Smokies," wrote Horace Kephart in 1925, "the whole region was one of superb forest primeval. I lived for several years in the heart of it. . . . The vast trees met overhead like cathedral roofs. I am not a very religious man; but often when standing alone before my Maker in this house not made with hands I bowed my head with reverence." Recently, he wrote, he had returned to this location and found it "wrecked, ruined, desecrated, turned into a thousand rubbish heaps, utterly vile and mean. Did anyone ever thank God for a lumberman's slashing?"[21]

As in West Virginia, the denuded mountains of southern Appalachia produced an environmental disaster from fire, flood, erosion, and the silting and polluting of once pure streams, the utter waste of natural resources, and the destruction of a way of life that struck many as a terrible loss relative to the meager, and temporary, gains.[22] When the lumber boom was over, the companies throughout the mountains followed the common pattern and simply pulled up stakes and left. Few residents anywhere in the region could have imagined that they would be permanently dispossessed from the ancestral lands. When the Little River Lumber Company closed its mill in Tennessee, "the end of an era had come," remembered Dorie Cope, a native who followed her husband from the farm to the lumber industry:

> Once again, the mountains were silent. No trains, no skidders, no portable housing stuck on the hillside. . . . The lumber companies had opened the door to the outside world. We became aware of "things"— things that money could buy, things that made life easier (or harder), things to see, things to do. Our isolation had ended. They had opened a door—a door we were forced to use as an exit from our ancestral homes. Then, after the exit, the door was closed to us. We were given visitors' rights to the land—to come and look, but not to stay.[23]

Throughout Appalachia, and to a lesser extent in all of America, the lumbermen left an unambiguous legacy of environmental destruction. In West Virginia the U.S. Forest Service was charged with acquiring lands for the Monongahela National Forest only after the timber that protected the Potomac and Ohio riversheds was removed, and the same was true in Virginia and Kentucky. Fortunately, the federal government entered the picture soon enough in North Carolina and Tennessee to save much of the Smoky Mountains before they too were completely denuded, but the social and political changes brought to mountain society by the railroads and forest industries transformed institutional life forever. People who moved off the land in the southern Appalachians often migrated to wage-paying jobs in the textile mill villages where an estimated 750,000 mountain people migrated.[24] In West Virginia farm families who either abandoned or were forced off the land generally found their way into the multiplying coal towns of an industry that soon replaced lumber as the dominant employer in the state's extractive economy.

By the 1920s, most lumbermen had abandoned the mountains for lands further west. Eventually, nature reclaimed the mountains and reclothed them in a luxuriant forest. This new forest has matured under the watchful eye of conservation-minded professionals and a sympathetic public determined to prevent a repetition of the first deforestation. I hope this book makes a contribution to this end by outlining some of the complex links that tie human institutions to their natural landscape.

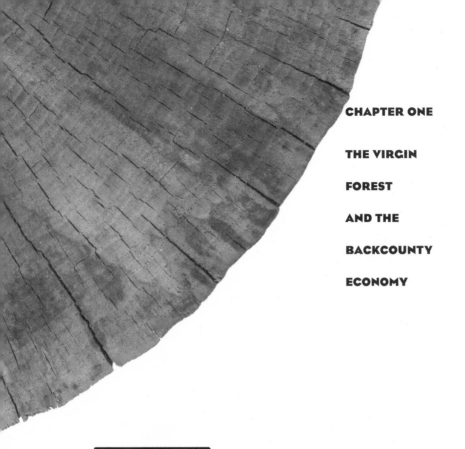

CHAPTER ONE

THE VIRGIN

FOREST

AND THE

BACKCOUNTY

ECONOMY

To the early pioneers, the trackless American wilderness elicited emotions of awe and foreboding which had deep cultural roots. The millennium-long struggle to domesticate nature had spawned a mythology among Europeans that associated the forest with a dark, evil, and forbidding land alien to human habitation, whereas towns and cleared areas came to be regarded as suitable for civilized life. The American wilderness provided ample opportunity for the earliest settlers to expand on this cultural preconditioning. At an immediate physical level, they saw the American wilderness as a direct threat to their survival. The primeval forests harbored wild animals, hostile natives, and a dark immensity in which one might get lost and never be found. To succeed in clearing the land was a triumph of human control over the wild randomness of nature. Failure was awful to contemplate for it meant human beings would become less civilized and even revert to an original state of savagery. For the pioneers, the forest was, as the nineteenth-century frontier historian Francis Parkman observed, "an enemy to be overcome by any means, fair or foul."[1] His assessment was remarkably

15

similar to that of the earliest seventeenth-century settlers, summed up by a Puritan in 1662 who saw the great forest as "a waste & howling wilderness where none inhabited but hellish fiends & brutish men."[2] With such an obstacle to confront on a daily basis, it was little wonder that frontiersmen generally spoke of the wilderness in military metaphors; its conquest and subjugation continues to be a major source of American pride and identity.[3]

Like their forebears, eighteenth-century explorers still viewed the wilderness of western Virginia with a mixture of awe and terror. A party of Virginians, which included Colonel Peter Jefferson, Thomas Jefferson's father, climbed Cabin Mountain in October 1746 and looked out on the Canaan Valley spruce forest in present-day Tucker County. The following day the men descended into the forest. Thomas Lewis, a surveyor, recorded in his journal that from the moment the party entered the forest they "Did not See aplain Big Enough for aman to Lye on nor a horse to Stand" and soon found themselves ensnarled in an understory of rhododendron, or "laurel," eight to ten feet high. "Never was any poor Creaturs in Such a Condition as we were in nor Ever was a Criminal more glad by having made his Escape out of prison as we were to Get Rid of those Accursed Lorals," Lewis wrote afterward. The tone of his description is that of a man who had visited hell and managed to escape the devil's grasp.[4]

The mid-nineteenth-century writer and illustrator David Hunter Strother ("Porte Crayon") helped to perpetuate the notion that the western Virginia mountain wilderness was threatening and "impenetrable." Describing a hunting trip he had made to the Canaan Valley in 1857, more than a century after the exploration recorded in Thomas Lewis's journal, Strother wrote that his comrades and he had been "dodging the laurel-brakes all day," some of which stretched for miles and were so dense that even the deer could not pass through them. Strother noted that "they had heard stories of men who had spent days in them, wandering in circles, and who had finally perished from starvation."[5] Others were not so much terrified as awestruck by the Canaan wilderness. The West Virginia novelist Rebecca Harding Davis wrote in 1880 that the total silence was as "strange and oppressive as noonday," and "human voices were an impertinence in the great and wordless meanings of the woods."[6]

Actually, the ancient Appalachian forest was much more varied and forgiving than the popular vision perpetuated by early descriptions of places like the Canaan wildlands. The forest of West Virginia is divided into three grand sections. The eastern ridge and valley section incorporates the eastern panhandle and a narrow strip extending along the southeastern border. The

Virgin spruce forest at headwaters of Cherry River, Greenbrier County, 1912. (West Virginia and Regional History Collection, West Virginia University Libraries)

westerly winds lose much of their moisture as they pass over the high Alleghenies so that the eastern section of the state receives relatively low rainfall and produces an original forest composed of oak, chestnut, and yellow pine.[7] Much of the land in this section was turned into farm and pasture early in the eighteenth century.

The Allegheny mountain and upland section presented settlers with their first great physical barrier to western migration. It includes the high ridges and plateaus of Preston, Tucker, Randolph, Pocahontas, Webster, Nicholas, Greenbrier, and contiguous counties. The mountains reach their highest point in West Virginia at Spruce Knob, which stands 4,860 feet above sea level; numerous other peaks reach over 4,000 feet in elevation. The forest in this section receives twice as much moisture as does that on the eastern slopes. The most valuable trees of the Allegheny mountain and upland section were in the spruce belt atop the highest elevations. The northern hardwoods were most commonly found between 2,000 and 2,500 feet and contained timber of extraordinary diversity, size, and commercial value. Northern hardwoods such as sugar maple, yellow birch, red maple, beech, basswood, and red spruce dominated the higher elevations. On the northern exposures, hemlock, which the tanning industry prized for its bark, was generally found mixed with the hardwoods. White pine and central hardwoods predominated in the lower elevations.[8]

The western hill section, which extends over the state to the west and south of the Allegheny mountain and upland section, is less rugged and gradually diminishes into a rolling plateau. Explorers and settlers who entered this virgin timbershed found a mixed oak and chestnut forest in which individual trees often grew to enormous size. The white oak was the largest tree to be found in the virgin forest, often exceeding 100 feet in height and 6 feet in diameter. One of the largest of these giants, the "Mingo Oak," was 9 feet 10 inches in diameter and 145 feet high. But the largest known tree ever felled by loggers in West Virginia was cut near Lead Mine, Tucker County, a white oak that was 13 feet in diameter 16 feet from the base. It was too large to be moved, and dynamite was required to split it into quarters so that loggers could skid it to the railroad landing. Another giant of this forest was the yellow poplar, which frequently reached 5 to 7 feet in diameter. One of these trees cut in Tucker County completely filled an entire log train with 12,469 board feet of lumber. Walnut, cherry, white pine, and sycamore also abounded in the central hardwood forest. Early settlers found the forest floor free of underbrush and the trees were evenly spaced, making a particularly inviting land for improvement into farms.[9]

The first settlers on the western Virginia slopes of the Allegheny Mountains naturally took the most fertile and accessible lands located along the major rivers. They confronted an overwhelming task in clearing the bottomlands, but necessity provided the initial, and most compelling, motive to begin forest removal in West Virginia.[10]

Backwoods settlers developed a syncretistic culture cobbled together from the experience and practices of Native American, British, Germanic, and Scandinavian cultures on the middle frontier during the eighteenth century. Historian John Otto has argued that their "generalized stockman-farmer-hunter economy" enabled descending generations to settle and preempt the upcountry hardwood forest as well as the lowland "piney woods" of the southern frontier between 1775 and 1835.[11]

The profile of the backcountry settlers in Appalachia and Virginia is a familiar one. The backcountry was settled by relatively poor farmers primarily of British and Germanic extraction who migrated from Virginia or southeastern Pennsylvania. These small farmers generally lived in dispersed rural neighborhoods, where families often were related by blood or marriage. Scattered gristmills and country stores provided them with the essential services or goods they could not provide for themselves and became the nuclei for crossroads hamlets. Backcountry families built houses and out-buildings of horizontally joined logs, a construction technique of Scandinavian origin, which also evolved in southeastern Pennsylvania and then was dispersed by migrating settlers. Religion was less formal than in the population centers and generally was affiliated with British dissenting sects, primarily Presbyterian, Baptist, or Methodist, who worshiped at crossroads churches and occasional revival meetings. They were residents of counties, local units of government whose officers convened at courthouses located near the center of each county, typically not more than one day's ride on horseback.[12]

This generalized, now highly stylized, silhouette of the Appalachian backcountry has been enlarged into a mythical Appalachia as a land of homogeneous, isolated subsistence farmers with a distinctive oppositional subculture. The earlier American idea of the bountiful wilderness had evolved into the "agrarian myth" by the early nineteenth century, a permutation of Thomas Jefferson's idealized yeoman farmer. An apparently unlimited supply of land stretched out before Americans of the new nation. This abundance of land, they believed, would reproduce a class of self-sufficient farmers, who, because of their independence, would provide an electorate intuitively capable of guiding the young democratic republic. The idea became one of the ideological foundation stones for the development of the continent.[13]

Thanks to the local color writers of the late nineteenth century, southern Appalachia became fixed in the American imagination as the last bastion of the old frontier virtues of independence, egalitarianism, and self-sufficiency. This view essentialized Appalachia as a region where land was equitably distributed, agriculture was based on the self-sufficient family-operated farm, and people relied on neighborhood rather than external trade in the broader commercial markets. Mountain isolation permitted this economy to survive long after it had disappeared elsewhere in America. Consequently, Appalachia was portrayed as an "arrested frontier," bypassed by the sweeping economic forces that propelled America's rise as a leading industrial nation during the late nineteenth century.[14] Thus was Appalachia remolded to fit into the agrarian myth of a tranquil American past.

One of the issues most energetically debated in the scholarship of early Appalachian history stems from the reapplication of a debate over community in colonial America. That debate centered around the question of whether early settlers were truly self-sufficient, precapitalist people who owned the means of production, produced for their own use, and emphasized community harmony over personal self-interest. Or, in fact, did they produce for exchange at market prices and divide profits among producers and a class of capitalists who owned the means of production? The answer leads to the heart of how colonial American, and hence Appalachian, culture is interpreted: were initially communal farmers "modernized" into petty capitalists, or was capitalism part of their culture from the beginning?[15]

It seems clear from several decades of scholarship on this issue that the U.S. economy traversed a historical continuum from a system marginally engaged in production for exchange to a mature capitalist economy whose production, exchange, and social relations are associated with modern society. The timing of this process varied by region, but it transpired first in eighteenth-century New England and did not reach Appalachia until the nineteenth century. In the mountains, capitalism progressed unevenly from the periphery in the early part of the century but did not penetrate the rugged interior of the region until after the Civil War. While precapitalist peoples may engage in commercial markets occasionally, capitalist societies are commercial societies both structurally and culturally. The varying degree to which residents of the Appalachian region were capitalist in the nineteenth century, spatially and temporally, must await further scholarship for a definitive answer, but from the beginning they engaged in market exchange whenever circumstances permitted a realistic opportunity. Few scholars are as emphatic in their assessment as Wilma Dunaway, who declares that "settler Appalachia was *born capitalist*," for the region was not settled by peasants but rather by "the children and grandchildren of eighteenth century colonists . . . [who came] from an agricultural and mercantile capitalist country about to enter the industrial revolution."[16]

West Virginia certainly offers evidence that, whatever else might be said of its residents in the nineteenth century, they were not a uniform population of homogeneous subsistence farmers devoted to a static cashless economy free of the national markets. In fact, many West Virginians displayed a desire for commercial development from the very beginning. Van Beck Hall's study of politics in Appalachian Virginia between 1790 and 1830 documents just how early, vigorous, and universal was the push for economic development. In his analysis of voting patterns on key economic development issues in the Virginia Assembly and at state conventions, Hall found that settlers in Appalachian Virginia were more diversified, less fearful of change, and more inclined to use government to accomplish development than were "the more cosmopolitan, longer-settled residents of Virginia counties east of the Blue Ridge."[17]

A cursory examination of western Virginia reveals the folly of essentializing the region as a land of isolated, precapitalist subsistence farmers even during its early period. By 1830 the number of counties in Appalachian Virginia, those west of the Blue Ridge, had grown to forty, and seventeen counties had sizable towns. This region experienced a rapid population growth and an expanding development of artisanal crafts as well as processing and extractive industries. Because of the rural-urban demography and mountainous topography, however, commercial and economic development was uneven. Few slaves were found in the region, but many Revolutionary War pensioners from other states settled there during the period. This diversified agricultural region also lacked a dominant single cash crop, such as tobacco or cotton, found in the older plantation counties. Livestock raising (cattle, swine, sheep, and horses) was far more extensive in the western counties than in the eastern, far outstripped eastern production of cereal grains, and surpassed or equaled the production of all other agricultural products.[18]

Most rural settlements had their own grain mills, tanneries, and salt and iron manufacture. Numerous small towns and resorts along the Allegheny Front provided not only local markets for farmers throughout the nineteenth century but also an annual influx of tourists from the eastern urban centers. Larger towns also dotted the western landscape. Wheeling, Martinsburg, Harpers Ferry, and Wellsburg in present West Virginia were among the fifteen largest towns in the state, where an urban-commercializing process was evolving that increased the political influence of merchants and professionals and the growth of social institutions associated with urban life.[19]

The growth of these towns created two Appalachias, Hall contends, one composed of counties with growth centers and another made up of interior rural farm counties, the backcounties. Counties with growing towns spearheaded the economic diversification of Appalachian Virginia, while the counties without towns failed to develop much commercialization or diversity. Significant differences existed within the western counties. Although there were a few pockets, such as Greenbrier County, the Kanawha Valley, and the eastern panhandle, where slavery was significant, slavery was a relatively weak institution in the western counties, and the aristocracy of planters that dominated eastern Virginia did not develop west of the mountains. The upper and middle classes tended to be concentrated in the more urbanized areas and depended on commerce, industry, or the professions, although many had some connections with the countryside through the ownership of land and farms. The political influence of the western elite was based on its strategic position in commerce or industry. Politicians of the rural backcounties tended to be more conservative on social and constitutional questions than their colleagues in the more developed counties.[20]

Although they differed somewhat among themselves in philosophical orientation, western Virginians stood as one in demanding economic development measures such an expansion in the number of bank charters and particularly internal improvements. Westerners, both rural and urban, almost unanimously favored improvements in transportation. They supported improving navigation of the Potomac in 1795, constructing a bridge over the Cheat River in 1805, and improvement of the James River and Kanawha Canal from 1816 forward. Likewise, their support for the improvement and construction of existing roads and turnpikes in the West was nearly unanimous, with little difference between rural and urban counties. Both groups were pragmatic about developments that raised taxes but did not affect them directly and therefore expressed little interest in improvements for the eastern part of the state.[21]

According to Hall, historians have failed to recognize that supposedly backward Appalachian residents actually sponsored democratization through a greater involvement of citizens in the political process, the expansion of banks, internal improvements, and free public education, and occasionally even challenging the institution of slavery. Backcounty farmers joined their colleagues from the developed counties in voting for programs that many historians associate with modernization. The voting record of western delegates does not accord with "the usual portrayal of an Appalachia trapped in a sort of late-eighteenth or early-nineteenth-century 'time warp' or of a culture and society that was easily manipulated by powerful outside interests," Hall argues. What popular and scholarly writers alike have failed to appreciate, Hall concludes, is that in western Virginia,

> two Appalachias existed side by side. The one with towns, newspapers, banks, and early industries already differed from the more rural, isolated, farming counties. These counties, much easier to identify with the traditional picture of Appalachia, were less interested in many of the programs backed by their more urbanized colleagues, but even those who lived in the second Appalachia worked much harder for reform and development than did the supposedly more commercial, involved, and aware residents of eastern Virginia. The traditional picture of isolated mountain folk uninterested or uninvolved in outside political questions did not yet exist by 1830.[22]

Nearly half a century after the period examined by Hall, West Virginia was still characterized by a well-settled commercial town and farm section along the rivers and in cleared bottomlands and the thinly settled interior back-counties still covered by virgin forest.

A common misconception that has skewed the interpretation of the region's history is that *subsistence* and *market* are dichotomous, antagonistic forms of economic relations. Subsistence often has been used imprecisely to mean self-sufficient, supplementary, household production, and sometimes to express a nostalgic preference for a time before Americans embraced capitalism and fell from grace. Here *subsistence* refers to the degree to which families produce their own sustenance, are able to reproduce themselves, and includes a range of farmers who span the continuum between rich and poor. Wealthy farmers consume their own produce, too, but are proportionally less dependent on growing their own food than poor farmers. Actually, we should not expect to find both modes of production coexisting in preindustrial Appalachia. Convention would lead us to conclude that the backcounties differed from the developed counties because farming was for subsistence in the former and for commerce in the latter. But it would be incorrect to assume that because subsistence farmers predominated in the backcounties they were therefore devoid of commercial mentality and did not engage in market-related enterprises, for clearly this was not the case. An adequate subsistence should go hand in glove with enterprise. The early American ideals of a "competency" and "self-sufficiency" are not the same as subsistence. Scholars would do well to remember Morton Rothstein's observation that self-sufficient is merely a "delightful euphemism for rural poverty."[23]

One important point must be underscored in examining the economic culture of the uncleared backcounties: the woods were not necessarily a disadvantage to mountain farmers, a point generally lost on residents of the developed counties. In fact, backcounty West Virginia farmers planted not only their crops but also the roots of a highly adaptive agricultural system that depended on the forests.

The culture that evolved among backwoods farmers was a blend of old ways and new adaptations. Land rotation was one of the traditions brought to Appalachia by the Scots-Irish settlers, and it became the basis of the mountain system of farming. There is some controversy over the origins of this system and its associated culture between those who argue that it was transferred from Britain's Celtic Fringe or from the English borderlands and those who believe that it is a more synthetic adaptation from a variety of

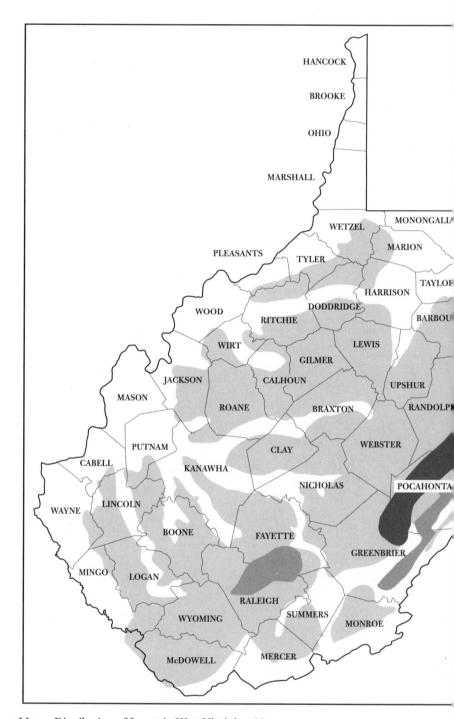

Map 1. Distribution of forests in West Virginia, 1882.
(U.S. Bureau of the Census; adapted by Debra Benson)

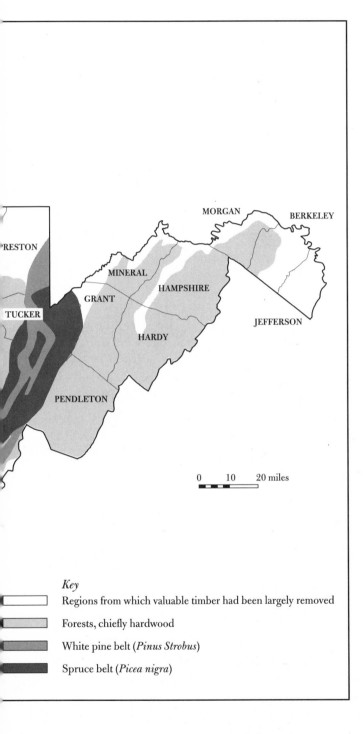

RESTON

MORGAN

BERKELEY

MINERAL

HAMPSHIRE

GRANT

TUCKER

JEFFERSON

HARDY

PENDLETON

0   10   20 miles

Key

Regions from which valuable timber had been largely removed

Forests, chiefly hardwood

White pine belt (*Pinus Strobus*)

Spruce belt (*Picea nigra*)

cultural traditions.[24] Whatever its origins, this basic land rotation scheme in Appalachia has been described as follows:

> After a piece of ground had been cleared of trees it was planted to row crops (corn and perhaps a patch of tobacco) until the topsoil had "washed away," and then it was abandoned to poor-quality pasture. Soon Mother Nature foreclosed her mortgage: the pasture was invaded by saplings, and in a decade the old field was covered with trees once again. After a generation or so under trees the soil had regained enough of its fertility to be worth reclearing, and the cycle of cultivation, pasture, and woodland was repeated.[25]

This rotation extended over several generations so that few individuals ever witnessed the entire cycle.

Forest fallowing, or forest farming, as this system of land rotation is known, was a ubiquitous feature of backcountry agriculture that is still used today in some corners of Appalachia. The continuation of forest fallowing was well documented by local color writers of the late nineteenth century whose descriptions of mountain life fed the urban desire to read about "quaint" American customs. To outsiders, Appalachia was a "retarded frontier," a "strange land and peculiar people," a land of "contemporary ancestors" so isolated from the historical mainstream of American development that pioneer cultural traits still survived. The practice of forest fallowing and the land use patterns that went with it served as yet another example for outsiders of pioneer survivals in an archaic region.[26]

To dismiss these agricultural practices as archaic, however, distorts their historical context and meaning. Whether rural mountain farmers practiced commercial or subsistence farming depended largely on access to adequate transportation and the economic attractiveness of potential markets. Where Appalachian farmers retained the old practices, they did so for very good economic reasons: they confronted serious limitations in the lack of transportation to distant markets, as well as unseasonable frosts, poor soils, and steep slopes. Mountain farmers retained forest fallowing because it was an important thread in their cultural fabric that, in the absence of change, provided them with a blueprint for survival. Because most agricultural products were consumed rather than sold, farming did not generate the cash surplus required to purchase the machinery and commercial fertilizers that, if other requirements such as transportation were met, would have enabled them to practice commercial farming. To avoid the expense, mountain farmers survived by raising corn, which almost never failed even when grown on unimproved woodlands and without fertilizer, and by using the forest floor as commons on which to graze their livestock.[27]

It was the "deadenings," however, that provided outsiders with the evidence that the agricultural practices of small mountain farmers were devoid of scientific method. Forced to clear openings out of the dense forest, pioneers considered trees an encumbrance on the land they wished to farm, and they sought the quickest and easiest way to get rid of them. Girdling trees and leaving them to die and be removed as time permitted had several distinct advantages. The deadenings facilitated the formation of dew and fog that might save the corn crop from untimely frosts. More important, the root networks of the girdled trees and underbrush contained mineral nutrients not found in the soils, and burning the forest underbrush released these minerals to fertilize the soils and killed insects and weeds.[28] If the small farmer moved into a newly settled area, he could make his own clearing by grubbing up the undergrowth, burning the brush, and girdling the trees so that the sap could not reach the branches. The sunlight could then reach the crops, and the dead trees could be removed for firewood in the farmer's own good time, or he might call neighbors in for a "log-rolling" to fell the timber for lumber, fence posts, or simply to burn it.[29] "Slovenly" as it might appear to progressive agriculturists, girdling and using the "bull-tongue," or shovel plow, which was light enough to till the soil around the dead trees or stumps for a corn crop, was a practical, labor-saving adaptation far preferable to grubbing up stumps in a labor-scarce and forest-abundant environment.

Backwoods farmers raised a variety of produce, including native American corn, beans, pumpkins, squash, and tobacco, but primarily they were stockmen. Another labor-saving adaptation in the backcountry was the open-range herding of cattle and hogs, a practice that had obvious British antecedents. Stock farmers in the rural backcounties continued this practice by allowing their branded livestock to forage on the unfenced mountainsides. Open-range livestock required far less care than animals that had to be stabled, fed, and protected, but it did necessitate an extensive open range. Few backwoodsmen could obtain title to the extensive grazing lands required under this system, so they fenced their cultivated fields and treated the remaining lands, whether they were claimed or not, as open range. Hogs thrived in the forests, consuming mast or grubbing for roots and sprouts. Cattle fared less well because the underbrush and forest canopy shaded out grasses. Therefore, farmers set fire to the forest floor in late winter to reduce the underbrush, curb parasites, and "green up" the floor with grasses.[30]

Despite its labor-saving advantages for the small mountain farmer, forest farming placed a ceiling on the productivity of the land. With most of the land in forest, fallow pasture, or fields in some stage of reforestation, less than a third of the actual farm acreage was ever under cultivation at any one time. If newly reforested lands were brought back into cultivation prematurely, before nutrients had been fully restored, the result was declining yields, soil exhaustion, and severe erosion. Ideally, a patch was cropped for several years and then often fallowed for twenty or more years. Reforestation took decades so the natural reclamation of old lands always lagged far behind the fields that had been cleared, and the system required the availability of new forest lands for clearing to provide crops and pasture.[31]

This backwoods farming system was evident in many of West Virginia's rural backcounties on the eve of deforestation, although it came under increasing pressure from population growth and the closing of the open range that accompanied industrial development. William M. Fontaine, a professor of natural history at West Virginia University, authored a state-supported assessment of West Virginia agriculture in 1876 in which he lamented that "almost every condition requisite for the present full development" of the state's abundant resources was lacking. The population was sparse, and much of the land was still covered by primeval forests. A great deficiency of labor and capital also prevailed, and "railways and roads, until of late, have been rare within her borders." Fontaine acknowledged that much progress had been made, but he hoped to see "introduced into our State, that great stimulus to active farming, a ready and cheap transportation to market."[32]

An advocate of "scientific" farming, Fontaine regarded the older system of farming as backward and specialized commercial farming for the market as progressive. In his view, poor transportation was not the major reason for the persistence of backwoods agriculture; rather, the culprit was the culture of the backcountrymen. A way of life had been woven into a culture that was unfavorable to scientific farming, he believed. Remote from markets, the early settlers were primarily "men without means" who cleared small patches of land sufficient for their subsistence. In this clearing the pioneer cultivated corn and vegetables, along with a hog or two, a cow, possibly a horse, and fowls. Abounding in game, the forest readily supplied meat for the table. "Even now, in many parts of the State, this is the mode of life," Fontaine wrote. When the original clearing became exhausted, the pioneer simply girdled the trees of another deadening and in this haphazard fashion "cleared lands gradually grew around the cabins." The problem, according to Fontaine, was that succeeding generations simply continued in the old pattern and failed to establish trade connections with the "outside world." This "independent mode of life impressed upon the people habits of thought and action, which, though calculated to foster industry, frugality, and hardiness, were not most favorable for the promotion of undertakings which require communication with, and dependence upon, other countries." Moreover, backcounty farmers continued to be influenced by this culture: "Until of late West Virginians have paid but small attention to the raising of agricultural products for exportation," he observed. "They are usually content with the production of a sufficiency for home consumption. But rarely is an improved system of farming employed, and the cultivation is of the rudest kind."[33]

In the less populated backcounties of the state's interior, Fontaine observed, the descendants of the pioneers inherited this "almost incurable taste for slovenly agriculture." The tendency of mountain farmers "to travel in well-worn ruts" was Fontaine's explanation, but he offered no instruction as to how backcounty farmers were to develop the transportation system that would allow them to shift to commercial farming.[34]

If traditional methods of subsistence farming held sway in the backcounties, the economy of both rural and urban counties had been modified for decades as the state was gradually, unevenly, incorporated into the national market system during the course of the nineteenth century. This change can be seen in the evolution of stock farming, the most important segment of West Virginia's agricultural sector and dominant industry in the economy before the Civil War. As Joseph H. Diss Debar, the state's first commissioner of immigration, observed in 1870, "Until recently, when the mineral excitement built up mushroom fortunes among us," the greatest portion of private wealth in the state was a direct product of stock farming. In fact, raising livestock was "the pulsating artery of agricultural prosperity in West Virginia, and it is by her natural capacity in this line, and by no other standard, that her future agricultural development may be estimated with any degree of accuracy." In 1860, one-half of all the livestock in the state was owned in the developed counties of Barbour, Harrison, Hampshire, Greenbrier, Monroe, Hardy, Jefferson, Marion, Monongalia, and Preston. Fifteen other counties also produced significant herds of livestock: Brooke, Doddridge, Hancock, Jackson, Lewis, Marshall, Mason, Mercer, Pocahontas, Pendleton, Ohio, Nicholas, Randolph, Taylor, and Upshur.[35]

The number of cattle relative to hogs raised by farmers shows a different picture of West Virginia agriculture from the popular image of corn and hog culture associated with the backcountry. Actually, farmers raised a much larger number of cattle than hogs, and cattle were raised primarily for market whereas hogs were more likely to be consumed at home. The growth in the total number of livestock during the last half of the nineteenth century reflects the gradual evolution of West Virginia agriculture away from subsistence farming toward the first linkages with external markets, a process that originated in the previous century. Even William M. Fontaine, an outspoken critic of the backcounty farmers' methods, noted in 1876 that "the history of stock raising in our State presents an instance of a people gradually forced by natural causes, out of the channels of industry, in which their prejudices and habits of life impelled them, into others totally different." After the land had been opened up from the forest and experience taught farmers the disadvantages of plowing the fields too frequently, they began to seek some means of deriving a quicker return from their grasses. Fontaine claimed that not more than "one-twentieth of our cattle find a home consumption. Our markets are of speedy access, in Maryland, Pennsylvania, and New York, principally in the city sale yards" where most of the cattle went to market. In 1875 West Virginia stockmen exported at least $5 million worth of cattle. Along the Baltimore and Ohio Railroad (B&O) line between Pennsboro and Patterson's Creek, for example, one dealer shipped more than nine thousand cattle valued at over $700,000.[36]

Many forces, both natural and human, shaped stock-raising methods in West Virginia. Topsoil was lost every time the fields were plowed, and the only way to prevent this loss was to leave the land in grass. Removing the timber resulted in the spontaneous growth of bluegrass native to many sections in which the soil had a lime base. Moreover, poor transportation and the bulkiness of hay forbade its export so farmers turned the grass into flesh to attain the greatest concentration of value. The consumption of grains in fattening stock resulted in "a profitable means of consuming, without the cost of transport, a good deal of our surplus corn."[37]

Most of the cattle in the backcounties were the so-called native breeds, or common stock, which had descended from the original stock brought in by the settlers. Generally, they were left in the pasture to graze as long as possible, usually until November or December. During the dead of winter they were fed cornstalks or later some hay. If they had any shelters at all, they were rude coverings. In the southern counties cattle were left in the pasture year-round and not fed in the winter.[38] Whereas Fontaine deplored this practice as management of the "worst manner," Diss Debar wrote of meeting a herd of two-year-old steers, browsing in the wilds of Logan, about the middle of January, "looking but little the worse in flesh." Because of their hardiness and adaptability to the rugged countryside, Diss Debar claimed, the common stock were still preferred in the interior and mountain counties, although in the older settled sections the stock had been greatly improved by breeding. Diss Debar noted in 1870 that "stock cattle of all grades and ages are bought up and grazed in W.Va. until ready for market."[39]

Studies that have assessed whether Appalachian farmers were "precapitalist" and therefore did not seek commercial goals or were driven by "capitalist" goals to acquire the benefits of commerce when the opportunity presented itself have amply documented a commercial orientation in sections of the region suitable to market production. Modern scholars certainly have found a wide variety of economic activities in nineteenth-century preindustrial Appalachia which deflate the popular image of mountain farmers. By far the most significant of these economic enterprises, both economically and historically, was the livestock business. During the antebellum era, Appalachia was the livestock-raising center of the United States. This is an established fact among scholars but has not replaced the popular conception of Appalachian isolation. One reason can be attributed to Frederick Jackson Turner's frontier thesis, first articulated in the 1890s, which claimed that the grazier and drover were characteristic of a transitional phase in the nation's development. They came first but were supplanted by succeeding waves of farmers until the frontier disappeared. This thesis was applied to the South by Frank L. Owsley and his students during the 1940s. According to Owsley, agriculture drove the herdsmen from frontier to frontier and finally into the pine barrens, hills, and mountains. Southern herdsmen became farmers or, if they continued to drive stock, became ever more marginalized in the Appalachian and Ozark Mountains.[40]

The Turner-Owsley thesis was challenged during the 1970s and 1980s, however, by southern historians Forrest McDonald and Grady McWhiney, who claimed that cultural traits interpreted as distinctively southern were in fact Celtic in origin, and herding practices were one clear example of how Celtic folkways permeated southern culture.[41] It is clear that staple crop production dominated agriculture in the lowlands of the South and that livestock raising dominated in the mountains. Before it can be determined whether the concentration on livestock in Appalachia was a remnant of an arrested frontier or a rational economic choice, however, we must first discern whether stock-raising methods derived from ethnic heritage or were an adaptation to environmental and locational conditions. Richard MacMaster's study of the early cattle industry in western Virginia found that these cattlemen do not fit the McDonald and McWhiney Celtic diffusion model, which argues that Scots-Irish frontiersmen continued herding practices carried over from Britain because it required little capital or labor. In fact, MacMaster found that from the colonial era forward backcountry stock raisers were "remarkable" in their receptivity to new methods, improved breeding stock, and scientific agriculture in a way that most planters were not. They introduced corn feeding, were among the first to import pedigreed cattle, and played a major role in the diffusion of the beef cattle industry beyond the Appalachians into Kentucky and Ohio. Stock raising had a broad and significant role in the upper Shenandoah Valley and Potomac highlands of western Virginia. The South Branch area was known for cattle raising as early as the 1750s, and by the 1780s cattle raising and feeding was driven by production for export to eastern markets. These stockmen were not easily identified as Celtic but were instead a mixture of English, Irish, German, and Dutch families living side by side. In the 1850s shipment by train had taken the place of driving for stock farmers of the upper valley, and feeders tracked prices so as to have their stock arrive in the markets at the most advantageous moment.[42]

Even a cursory review of the cattle-feeding, or feedlot, system demonstrates that West Virginia stock farming was a dynamic and competitive, rather than static and traditional, sector of the economy in the developed districts as well as in the backcounties. In fact, the feedlot system was founded in West Virginia, where even before 1800 cattle raising and feeding had evolved into a commercial system for exporting cattle to the eastern cities.[43]

The stock-feeding industry was established in the late eighteenth century primarily in two western Virginia valleys: the South Branch of the Potomac River, which flows northward, and the Big Levels along the Greenbrier River, which flows southward. Separated by the same dividing mountain in Pocahontas County where their headwaters originate, these two valleys traverse nearly the entire length of the Allegheny Mountains, which make up the southern and eastern borders of West Virginia. The South Branch and Greenbrier valleys provided the fertile soil and extensive pasture that made them ideal for growing corn and raising cattle. Here the McNeill and Renick families and other stock farmers raised cattle for market in nearby cities such as Winchester and Staunton or the larger, more distant cities of Richmond, Baltimore, and Philadelphia.[44]

Stock feeders in the region purchased cattle to be fattened for market from other areas of Virginia, Kentucky, and eastern Ohio as early as 1800. John Stealey, who has studied the early cattle business in West Virginia, found that between 1800 and 1860 there was a cattle trade between the Scioto River Valley in Ohio and the South Branch–Greenbrier area. Migrants from the South Branch and Greenbrier carried their knowledge and experience with corn-fed stock with them to neighboring states. According to Stealey, when corn was harvested, it was cut and shocked in the open field. During the winter, the shocks were brought in from the field and fed to the cattle that were being fattened for market in an eight- to ten-acre feedlot. Hogs and stock cattle might be brought into the lot eventually, but all livestock remained unsheltered throughout the winter.[45]

By the first decade of the nineteenth century, members of the Renick family who had migrated to Ohio had become the "undisputed leaders in the cattle business of the Scioto Valley." The Renicks, whose interests were intertwined with those of the McNeill family by marriage and business, maintained close connections with the Daniel McNeill family in the South Branch. The Renicks ran stock farms in Ohio while Daniel McNeill ran feeder operations in the South Branch. McNeill kept the Renicks abreast of market conditions in the eastern cities, particularly Philadelphia and Baltimore, while the latter provided him with information about the departures of cattle from Ohio for eastern markets. Thus McNeill could drive the cattle he had been "finishing," or feeding for market, to those cities before the Ohio stock arrived and the price for beef on the hoof declined.[46]

Farmers in the developed counties of West Virginia followed the practice common throughout the Appalachians of summering their stock in the less improved sections of the interior mountain counties. The best of these so-called mountain farms were found on the tablelands of Randolph, Pocahontas, Webster, and Nicholas Counties, where local farmers rented their high pasture for summer grazing and watched over the herds. Other mountain farms belonged to the owner of the cattle, who engaged local farm laborers to clear and fence them. The clearing of high pastures, called "balds," was accomplished by a process known as "hacking." A worm fence was erected around the area, and the trees were girdled and left to die. In a few years these "hackings" were burned to kill the undergrowth and fallen timber. Blackberry briers were the first thing to grow, but within a year or two, if cattle browsed on the clearing, native bluegrass would take possession. It was widely recognized that these farms produced the finest beef and mutton in the state.[47]

West Virginia cattle, like those in other districts of the Appalachian region, usually were driven to market in the fall. Throughout most of the nineteenth century, West Virginia cattle and other livestock competed well in the eastern markets, especially Baltimore, where they arrived with relatively little weight loss compared with cattle driven from further south and west. The National Pike was choked with livestock being driven to eastern markets during the season, as were many pikes leading from the backcountry to urban centers. The practice of driving animals to market created a subculture and specialization of skills that lasted throughout the nineteenth century and into the twentieth. Local drovers rounded up stock and drove them to strategic locations where they were sold to professional dealers. Professional drovers were middlemen in the consumer chain between the farmers and commercial buyers and therefore possessed a specialized knowledge generally unavailable to local stockmen.[48]

Professional drovers tended to gather their herds from the older settled areas of the region, such as the Ohio River, South Branch, and Greenbrier River valleys, which were the centers of stock-feeding operations. In turn, these centers provided local stock markets where mountain graziers could exchange their livestock for the cash to purchase items they did not produce for themselves. In 1823, John Howe Peyton, a Staunton, Virginia, attorney, trying a case in Huntersville, then the Pocahontas County seat, wrote to his wife describing his surroundings. "Pocahontas is a fine grazing county," he observed, "and the support of the people is mainly derived from their flocks of cattle, horses and sheep, which they drive over the mountains to market." The circuit-riding attorney noted that there was little money among the residents "except after these excursions, but they have little need of it— every want is supplied by the happy country they possess, and of which they are as fond as the Swiss of their mountains."[49]

Towns and even small cities grew around the local and regional cattle-gathering centers where local producers sold their stock to the middlemen. Lewisburg, West Virginia, the Greenbrier County seat, was a local node in the network that pointed livestock toward the regional center of Covington, Virginia, from which stock were shipped by rail to Richmond in the 1850s. Winchester, in the Shenandoah Valley, became the regional center for export for stockmen of the South Branch. Lewisburg became an important local stock-trading center, and traveler Anne Royall of Pennsylvania recorded in the mid-1820s that Lewisburg bustled with commerce, stock driving in particular. Stock towns such as Lewisburg served as local markets where smaller herds were purchased by professional drovers. G. W. Featherstonhaugh, an English aristocrat on an excursion to the slave states in the 1840s, visited nearby White Sulphur Springs, where he observed drovers with herds of twenty to fifty animals arriving from the outlying countryside.

When the Chesapeake and Ohio Railroad (C&O) laid track through Greenbrier County in the early 1870s, livestock exporting became an even larger business.[50]

Rural mountain people showed a willingness to enter commercial arrangements in other resource markets as well, and none so readily as that for timber, a product they could extract and transport to market with little capital investment. The people who occupied the virgin forest for the first century and a half were completely dependent on wood. So vast was the forest that it was inconceivable to Joseph Martin that the forests in the mountains could ever be "conquered." West of the Allegheny Mountains, "a large portion of the country must for ever remain in its primitive forest," he wrote in his famous *Gazetteer of Virginia* printed in 1835.[51] Indeed, wood was an abundant resource and settlers used it for everything. The cabin walls were made of logs, the roof of clapboards or wooden shingles, the puncheon floors, furniture, even eating utensils and some tools were of wood taken from the forest. Walnut trees, which would have made their owners rich if they could have transported them to market, were split and used for fences, and other trees were destroyed to clear the land for planting and pasture. Even with this rapacious consumption, however, by 1880 most of West Virginia still remained under the cover of virgin forest.[52]

In this regard West Virginia's rural backcounties were not exceptional; where backcountry conditions continued to exist in the rural regions of America, whether Appalachia, the Ouachita Mountains of Oklahoma and Arkansas, or the piney woods of Mississippi and east Texas, a wood-dependent culture existed.[53] Diss Debar erroneously claimed in 1870 that West Virginians were "slow to realize the importance and value" of the forests that surrounded them.[54] Actually, from the very beginning West Virginians made every attempt to use the woods to maximum economic advantage. The alternatives available to them, however, were restricted by the lack of capital, technology, and transportation facilities; these were the influences that shaped their economic relationship to the forest around them, not the lack of enterprise or a precapitalist mentality.

The early settlers' technology for cutting timber precluded the wholesale cutting of the virgin forest. The whipsaws they carried over the mountains enabled them to cut rough planks for flooring, doors, roofs, and other uses and helped them produce more refined dwellings than those of the first and poorest pioneers, whose cabins and outbuildings were fashioned by ax. The timber to be sawed was first squared with the broadax, then hoisted onto a frame about seven feet high. Two men then took the saw in hand, one standing on the scaffold and the other beneath it, and commenced sawing up and down. The labor was extraordinarily difficult, and two men per day were considered to have put in a hard day's work if they cut one hundred feet. Even when more advanced saw technology became widespread, the whipsaw continued to be useful where labor was more readily available than cash.[55]

West Virginia's population grew, and as settlements began to emerge, the demand for lumber increased. At this stage of development the water-powered sash saw appeared in the backcountry. The first sash mill, which derived its name from the large wooden sashes (planks) to which the saw was attached, was operated in conjunction with a gristmill. The saw was erected within a framework and moved up and down when the large wooden rod connecting the saw to the waterwheel was activated. The log, mounted on a carriage, was pulled through the saw by a rachet mechanism that was also connected to the waterwheel. When one cut had been completed, the water was diverted until the carriage was repositioned for another cut.[56]

As western settlements expanded, water-powered sawmills were erected to meet the demand for lumber and other basic wood products. The first water-powered sash mill was brought across the Alleghenies in 1776 by John Minear, a pioneer who established Saint George, the first community in Tucker County, which also became the first county seat. As late as 1860, seven-eighths of the lumber produced in West Virginia was manufactured by waterpower, and nearly all of it was consumed locally. These sawmills harnessed cheap waterpower, but they were also at the mercy of nature, particularly during periods of drought. Although the mills were vulnerable, they did not require large investments beyond the labor to construct the dam, race, and mill. Every inch of wood sawed into lumber in these mills was in response to demand, and so in a minimalist way they were very efficient.[57]

The sash mill also had significant limitations. The speed of the early waterpowered mills was so slow that settlers called the saws "up today and down tomorrow." Nevertheless, they were an improvement over the whip-saw and could cut five hundred board feet of lumber in one day with much less labor. Subsequent modifications to the basic design of the sash mill increased its production to over one thousand feet of lumber per day, and further technological improvements such as the gang saw, which positioned two or more saws side by side and permitted several boards to be cut at the same time, greatly increased productivity.[58]

The steam-powered circular saw was the next advance in the development of sawing technology. The circular saw had been invented in England during the 1770s, but the technology was not generally applied in the United States until the nineteenth century. Circular sawmills varied enormously in size, capacity, and complexity, but all were powered by steam engines. Some circular sawmills were small and portable, with the steam engine on wheels so it could be moved easily; other mills were very large for their day, occasionally harnessing multiple saws to boiler-powered steam engines. The first such mill was built by the St. Lawrence Boom and Manufacturing Company at Ronceverte, Greenbrier County, during the 1880s.[59]

Little is known of the earliest steam-powered sawmills in West Virginia, but like their technological predecessors, they were probably such a natural part of their communities that few people felt compelled to comment on them. Martin's *Gazetteer* listed fifteen steam sawmills in 1835, all of which were located in the older settled counties either on rivers or major roads. Their numbers did not multiply as rapidly as might be expected because demand and availability of transportation had to justify the investment. Long-distance wagon haulage was not profitable, and so most steam mills were located along navigable streams. As the railroads penetrated the virgin forests of West Virginia during the late nineteenth century, however, the number of these mills began to multiply rapidly. At least 472 sawmills were in operation in West Virginia in 1880, most of them steam-powered circular saws, which cut over 180,000 board feet of lumber and employed 3,765 workers.[60]

The final evolution of sawing technology was the band saw, which, like the circular saw, was initially powered by steam and later was converted to electric power. It was the band saw that conquered the virgin forest. Its enormous power to transform timber into lumber was the result of endless belts of saw-edged steel traveling at a high velocity around a great pulley driven by steam or electricity. The logs were carried through the saw on a carriage propelled by a steam piston. Although the band saw was first patented in Britain in 1808 and in the United States in the 1830s, problems with securing the endless steel band kept it out of general production until the late nineteenth century. In West Virginia and elsewhere in Appalachia, the band sawmill is associated with the capital-intensive development of the railroad era discussed in Chapter 2.[61]

As the lumber industry expanded, it became necessary to transport logs greater distances, generally to larger mills downstream or located on one of the railroad main lines. Before a railroad network was constructed in the mountains, mill owners could choose either to move their mills further upstream closer to the standing timber or to wait for crews to float the timber downstream to the mill. Usually it was cheaper to choose the latter. This was the most colorful phase of the timber industry's history, a period of log driving and rafting that gave birth to the heroic lumberjack legends of the north woods and marks an early stage in the transition to advanced capitalism in West Virginia before production was fully integrated from the cutting edge of the forest to mill and market.

Loggers who worked the forests along navigable rivers generally constructed log rafts to float their timber downstream to the mills. The average log raft consisted of seventy logs that would produce about twenty-five thousand board feet of lumber at the mill, although smaller rafts were built to navigate smaller streams. The earliest rafts generally were assembled by fastening the logs together with poles running across the timbers and held together with wooden pins. Nails and chain dogs soon replaced this more time-consuming method. Chain dogs, two wedges joined by a chain, made the raft strong and gave it flexibility and yet allowed the raft to be constructed and dismantled quickly. To the rear of the raft were attached oars from twenty to fifty feet long to permit steering the raft away from dangerous rocks and cliffs that could break up the raft before it reached its downriver destination.[62]

Rafting logs to milling centers was common wherever the streams were navigable, but the history of rafting was as varied as the rivers themselves. At Rowlesburg, Preston County, a lumber depot built at the juncture of the Baltimore and Ohio Railroad and Cheat River served as the destination of many rafts steered down the Cheat River during the 1870s and 1880s. Above Rowlesburg, the Cheat and its tributaries, the Black Fork and Shaver's Fork, were good rafting rivers. Several small mills operated along the Cheat in the 1880s and also rafted wood products such as shingles and staves downriver to Rowlesburg. Log drives were not possible on the Cheat before 1880 because as yet no log boom had been constructed to catch them. In the southern part of the state, the Coal River was navigable for barges thirty-six miles above its confluence with the Kanawha River, but little timber had been driven or rafted out of the Coal timbershed before the 1890s. Rafting that did take place on the Coal was soon eclipsed by the railroad that carried most of the timber to the big mill at St. Albans. The Kanawha River was, of course, the drainage stem of several important interior rivers, and large sawmills along its banks were the destination of innumerable rafts down out of the mountains during the nineteenth century. The Kanawha was one of the major rafting rivers of West Virginia. From early days enterprising rafts-

Log raft and ark on the Guyandotte River, Lincoln County, ca. 1900. (West Virginia State Archives)

men steered over 300 million board feet of timber and other products to mills and markets downstream on the Kanawha and the Ohio. The Big Sandy River, which forms the Kentucky–West Virginia border, also carried millions of feet of timber rafted annually to mills along the Ohio River. Rafting began on the Guyandotte River before the Civil War but reached its peak between 1880 and 1920. One of the largest firms, C. Crane and Company, which operated a triple band mill in Cincinnati, reputedly floated 1.25 billion board feet of lumber down the Guyandotte to its mill on the Ohio. The Guyandotte River abounded with log rafts on the eve of industrialization, some of them floated from one hundred miles above the river's confluence with the Ohio River near Huntington, where four or five major mills processed timber into lumber.[63]

Many West Virginia rivers could not be successfully rafted because their descent was either too precipitous, narrow, or filled with obstacles. Other streams, such as Shaver's Fork and the Greenbrier River, were ideally suited for log drives. The Greenbrier River became the most famous of the driving rivers of the period, its reputation mythologized in the popular novels of W. E. Blackhurst.[64] The first company to initiate log driving on the Greenbrier was the St. Lawrence Boom and Manufacturing Company, which needed timber for its large mill at Ronceverte on the Chesapeake and Ohio

Logjam on the Elk River near Sutton, Braxton County, 1898. (West Virginia and Regional History Collection, West Virginia University Libraries)

mainline. The company began purchasing white pine in Pocahontas County during the 1870s and eventually acquired about twenty thousand acres of timberland. Most of the timber was contracted to logging crews made up of men from Pennsylvania who taught their skills to local West Virginians, and natives soon dominated the work crews in the woods and on the river drives.[65]

The rhythms of felling and driving timber down the Greenbrier are typical of the patterns that governed this phase of the process. During the summer and fall seasons, woodsmen labored from daylight until dark six days a week. A cutting crew generally consisted of five men: two sawyers, who felled and "bucked" or cut the tree into sixteen-foot logs; a fitter, who notched the tree, cleared brush away from its base, and "bumped" limbs after the tree was on the ground; and two peelers, who used double-bitted axes ground flat on the side to peel the bark off the tree. Barked logs dried out quicker and were easier for the men to drive. Once cut, the logs were skidded to the slide by teamsters with horses especially trained for the work.[66]

Cutting and skidding continued during the winter until the weather became cold enough that water froze on the slides. Typically, the slide was constructed of similar-sized logs stretching end to end from the stream bank up the mountain to the cutting edge. These logs were split in two with the flat sides open, facing each other, and angled outward at the top to give the appearance of a trough. Then the slide was watered until a thick coat of ice built up on the skidding surface to facilitate the quick passage of the logs down off the mountain to the landing below. All hands turned to skidding for as long as the ice was frozen hard, propelling the logs down the skidway onto a pile on the stream bank. Here they were either stacked neatly or left in a "rough and tumble" pile.[67]

During the summer months, "splash" dams were constructed on the smaller streams, a method common throughout the Appalachians. These dams would catch the spring runoff and back up the water until the logs could be floated, at which time the gates were opened and the rushing water carried the logs downstream. At the confluence with the main stream, the logs were caught and held by booms until the main drive began. "Arks" from seventy to one hundred feet long and eighteen feet wide were constructed in preparation for the drive. A bunkhouse was built on this platform, which covered nearly the entire length and width of the structure. The bunkhouse ark contained double-decked bunks and a large stove to keep the men warm as they rested their cold, weary bodies from the great physical strain required of "river hogs," as river drivers were known. A second ark contained the cook shack and dining room. During the drive the men ate breakfast long before dawn, lunch at 9:00 A.M., another lunch at 3:00 P.M., and supper long after dark. Sometimes a third ark carried the horse teams and equipment.[68]

The main drive down the river began with the first sign of spring when the ice began to break up and move downstream. The logs were then rolled into the swollen stream and carried along by the current. The arks followed the main body of logs, and the men and their teams followed along on the shore to refloat logs that became stranded on the banks. Driving was very demanding work, much of it performed in the icy water from before light until after dark. The most dangerous work during the drives came when logjams occurred, piling logs into chaotic stacks. Only the most skilled rivermen were called on to walk out on the face of the jam to pick loose the key logs that would free the others. When the pressure was released, the jam would suddenly break, and the men would have to scramble for safety, jumping from one to another of the churning mass of logs.[69] Lumberjack legends are replete with the heroic exploits of those jam-breakers who succeeded and eulogizing those who failed. Most of the drives down the Greenbrier were made with white pine, but sometimes hardwood drives were made. On one such occasion it required twelve days to drive the logs

Arks and crew of log drivers tied up along the Greenbrier River near Cass, Pocahontas County, 1898. (West Virginia and Regional History Collection, West Virginia University Libraries)

from what is now Watoga State Park in Pocahontas County to Ronceverte in Greenbrier County, a distance of about fifty-five miles downstream.[70]

Log driving and rafting on the rising spring waters was the common means of transporting timber to the mills in the nineteenth century. Before the railroads penetrated West Virginia's backcounties, lumber companies usually were located at depots where a railroad intersected a floatable river. Those companies contracted for drives with independent woods contractors and captured the floating logs in booms constructed at the mill site. There were several kinds of booms, but they all had the same basic purpose. Most common was the flexible pocket boom, which consisted of heavy timbers chained together in a line of two or three hundred feet and three timbers wide. The lower end of this line was attached to the mill side or mill pond, and the upper end was stretched across the river to trap the logs and then pulled back to the same side as the mill to enclose the timber until it was ready for milling.[71]

At this stage in its development, the timber industry was dependent on the condition of the rivers, and many rivers in the state were not "floatable"

Table 1. Little Kanawha Navigation Company, March 1876–February 1877

Product Value	Quantity and Product
$69,600.00	388 log rafts, 696,000 cu. ft. ($.10 per ft.)
23,258.00	1,162,900 feet sawed lumber ($20 per M)
54,499.20	3,406,200 oil-barrel staves ($16 per M)
34,649.40	57,749 railroad ties ($.60 each)
2,744.00	343,000 hoop-poles ($8 per M)
9,010.00	45,050 cu. ft. ship timber ($.20 per ft.)
$193,760.60	

Source: U.S. House of Representatives, *Index to the Executive Documents of the House of Representatives: Report of the Chief of Engineers*, 45th Cong., 2d sess., 1878, 664. Except for the staves, these products were exported to Ohio, New York, Pennsylvania, and Maryland and ship timber to England.

without improvements. For example, the Gauley River and its tributaries, the Meadow, Cherry, Cranberry, and Williams Rivers, drained much of the higher elevations of south-central West Virginia, but these streams were so full of boulders that they could not be driven unless improvements were made.[72]

The Little Kanawha is a good example of how important even a partial river improvement was to West Virginians who lived in the backcounties. In 1847, the Little Kanawha Navigation Company was formed to improve the river from Parkersburg upstream to Bulltown in Braxton County by channeling and the construction of a series of locks and dams. Not much was accomplished, however, until 1860, when the Burning Springs oil field was brought into production. After considerable delays, fifty miles of the river finally were opened to toll traffic in 1874. Above this point, the river remained unimproved and unnavigable.[73] Little hard data survived to document the variety and quantity of the timber products transported on West Virginia's rivers before the railroad era. One collection does suggest the scale and proportions of the wood products conveyed downriver from the backcountry. It is the records of the Little Kanawha Navigation Company, which reported the data to the Corps of Engineers. The year ending March 1, 1877, was the first successful year of operation for the company when it reported the timber products on which tolls were paid (see Table 1).

The traffic in forest products increased by 1882–83, when the Little Kanawha Navigation Company reported the passage through its locks of 1,322,000 staves, 1,208 rafts, 6,230,000 board feet of cut lumber, and

623,000 cross-ties.[74] The traffic in timber and other forest products from the interior counties drained by the Little Kanawha continued well into the twentieth century. For example, in March 1911, John R. Lynch of Glenville shipped twenty-six rafts of logs down the river. His gross return for these logs was $8,031.02, or $.26 per foot delivered.[75]

Despite the backcountry sentiment that the forest was, in Francis Parkman's phrase, "an enemy to be overcome by any means, fair or foul," settlers and their descendants came to depend on the forest for survival. They developed a system of farming that maximized the forest to fallow their fields and provide forage for their livestock. They also harvested the wood itself, both for home consumption and for limited shipments to downstream markets. Nevertheless, even after 130 years of settlement, the virgin forest of West Virginia still covered two-thirds of the state on the eve of industrial transition.

Throughout the preindustrial period, the West Virginia backwoods was an evolving agricultural economy supplemented by slowly expanding resource extraction industries with links to external markets. Between 1880 and 1920, however, the direction of economic development shifted from agriculture to industry. The rich storehouse of natural resources locked in the deep forests of the state's interior had been preserved from full exploitation by the primitive technologies available to backcountry residents. The railroad network constructed during this period of transition, however, opened those resources for advanced capitalist development and transferred control of the economy from local farmers to local elites and then to distant investors.

CHAPTER TWO

THE TOUCH

OF CAPITAL:

RAILROADS,

TIMBER, AND

ECONOMIC

DEVELOPMENT

OF THE BACK-

COUNTIES

West Virginia's semicentennial was celebrated in 1913 with an array of activities and venues. Most popular were
the speeches of prominent businessmen and politicians such as Henry
Gassaway Davis, who still remembered the day when West Virginia became
the thirty-fifth state. In retrospect, however, few words better crystallize the
spirit, pride, and sense of accomplishment than the poem "West Virginia"
written for the occasion by Herbert Putnam:

> To-day we celebrate
> The ripe achievements of our fifty years:—
>   The mastery
> Of forest, field, and mine, the mill which rears
> Its bulk o'er many a stream, the forge and factory's
>   Incessant hum,
> The railways linking mart to mart and home to home,
> The growth of trade in each emporium,

And other wealth material that has come
  To bless
Our subjugation of a wilderness,
And mien undaunted in a time of stress:—
  All these we proudly sum.[1]

The loggers who had subjugated the "wilderness" and brought West Virginia in line with contemporary conceptions of the meaning of "civilization" were proud of their role in this heroic conquest. Their accomplishments are amply demonstrated in the thousands of photographs of loggers leaning, standing, or sitting on the fallen giants of the forest. They were conscious of the scale of their actions. Early loggers floated timber down the state's streams to be gathered by distant log booms using a technology that made little more than small clearings in the vast virgin forest of West Virginia. They were proud of their physical conquest, for technology played little role in their efforts. It was, after all, an extension of American exceptionalism and the frontier tradition. Deforestation of any magnitude required the technology and heavy equipment that could be brought to the forests only by the railroads. With that technology came a specialization of skills in timbering operations which served to confirm that civilization was indeed on its way.

Railroads, however, called for a level of capital investment that exceeded the financial and technical resources of all but a few of the state's most important industrial capitalists during the mid-nineteenth century. Moreover, development of the interior forests was only a dream until the east-west trunk lines of the Baltimore and Ohio Railroad were laid through northern West Virginia and then the Chesapeake and Ohio Railroad bisected southern West Virginia, on their way to connect the eastern seaboard with the American West.

After these two trunk lines had been laid in the 1850s and 1870s, independent railroad companies and feeder lines were networked to ship out natural resources to national markets. Numerous small independent railroads sprouted out from the main lines. These, and more than six hundred logging railroads, completed an elaborate web of rails that linked the cutting face deep in the forest, the processing mills along the main lines, and the national markets.[2] Even excluding the small logging and tram roads, track mileage in the state doubled in the 1880s, doubled again in the 1890s, and covered 3,705 miles in 1917.[3] The coming of the railroads saw small towns spring up along the lines like wildflowers where previously there had been only a thinly scattered farming population. According to James Morton Callahan, a prominent state historian writing at the peak of the timber boom in 1913, the railroads "carried into the silence of the primeval woods the hum of modern industry," bringing forth "gigantic lumber plants" and bustling new towns.[4] As the lines penetrated ever deeper into the forest, lumber towns were constructed as processing centers and staging areas for the final assault on the timber at the highest summits and most remote mountain recesses. Over the logging lines the heavy steam-powered equipment required to remove the largest timber was hauled to the very cutting edge integrating the state's forest resources into the national economy.

The historical evolution of Appalachia's economy has been the subject of debate for several decades and, much like the larger debate over the development of capitalism in America, depends largely on ideological perspectives and one's conceptualization of economic history. Explanations of the industrial transition fit into several general categories. The traditional view is that from colonial times to the Civil War, American farmers were small subsistence producers who lived in an agrarian society characterized by isolation and the absence of linkages with external markets. Others reject the idea that capitalism and market economics did not affect rural Americans until the Civil War, and they push the transition period back earlier in the nineteenth century. They contend that a "market revolution" occurred during the Jacksonian era which effected the transition of American society from an economy based on local self-sufficiency to one dependent on external markets. A third group of scholars reject the "agrarian myth" that American farmers were ever self-sufficient and either culturally or geographically isolated from larger market relations, arguing instead that capitalism had prevailed since earliest colonial times. American farmers always wanted money, not subsistence, because they were always consumers as well as producers.[5]

A fourth, more recent, perspective emanates from the writings of the French scholar Emmanuel Wallerstein. This view conceptualizes capitalism as an expansionist "world system" evolving over centuries. Those who share this perspective reject as too narrow and parochial the definition of capitalism as a set of relations in which labor is separated from ownership of the means of production and people earn their livelihood from wage labor, and hence implies an urban-industrial society as a precondition. The view that the transition to capitalism is a continuum, rather than reflecting a rural-industrial polarity, accommodates the coexistence in society of both older agrarian practices and newer market structures and acknowledges that internal conditions and agents are instrumental in the transition to capitalism;

Map 2. Major railroads in West Virginia, 1917.
(West Virginia Geological Survey; adapted by Debra Benson)

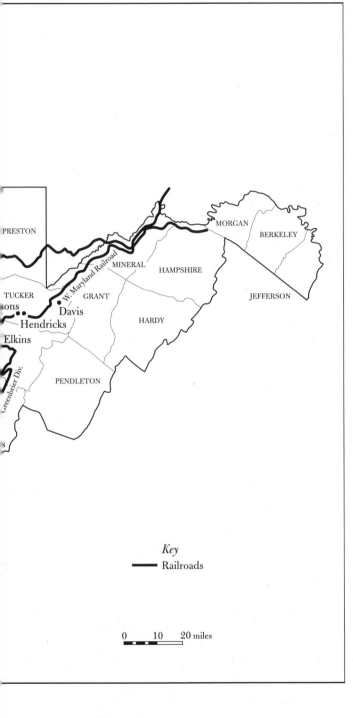

PRESTON

MORGAN

BERKELEY

MINERAL

HAMPSHIRE

TUCKER

W. Maryland Railroad

GRANT

JEFFERSON

ons

Davis

Hendricks

HARDY

Elkins

Greenbrier Div.

PENDLETON

Key

Railroads

0   10   20 miles

change is not simply an external imposition. Capitalism is continuously expansive in its search for markets until the world is organized within its web at various stages of incorporation: the "core" is the major metropoles of investment capital and commerce; "semiperiphery" regions are highly developed commercial "staging areas" for capital and trade; and regions are at the "periphery" of the system, where raw materials are extracted to support the more developed spheres within the system. In this conceptualization, the relations suggested by the world system are replicated on the periphery and fringe frontiers. Thus in preindustrial Appalachia the developed sections provided staging areas for the importation and transshipment of money and goods from the fringe to the semiperipheral urban areas of America. This view promises to provide a new way of understanding the economic history of West Virginia, as well as Appalachia.[6]

Appalachian scholarship has shadowed writing on the broader issue of the transition to capitalism in rural America. From the late nineteenth century until the 1970s, scholars and popular writers described the mountains as a region increasingly isolated from the dynamic economic development that swept the nation after 1800. In being bypassed by the forces of capitalist development, Appalachians were isolated not only physically by the rugged terrain but also culturally. Hence mountaineers retained the folkways of their frontier forebears in a "land where time stood still."[7]

Not until the 1970s did a counterinterpretation find an audience. Influenced by the radical reassessment of American society and its history, the revisionists argued that discontinuity was the central theme of Appalachian history, a history broken into two distinct periods: a preindustrial era dominated by independent, self-sufficient farmers with egalitarian and Jeffersonian values, and an era of rapid upheaval dominated by industry and economic dependency on wage labor. This dependency signaled the loss of the people's ability to control their own lives and their dependency on the hostile outside interests of big capital. In dramatizing the difference between their interpretation and the one they were contesting, revisionists juxtaposed the modern industrial Appalachia of poverty and dependency with the preindustrial countryside where self-sufficient farm families enjoyed a life of relative comfort and egalitarian independence.[8] The result of this dichotomous approach has been merely to reverse the normative value placed on a static preindustrial Appalachia, leaving the conception itself unchallenged.

Many historians would agree with the argument that the Civil War was the decisive historical break between a preindustrial nineteenth-century Appalachia with rising prospects and an industrialized twentieth-century Appalachia confronted by a bleak economic future of poverty. This view supports the revisionist school of discontinuity, which holds that the Civil War and its aftermath caused a sharp break in the region's development, a transitional period between the preindustrial and industrial eras when the old society lay prostrate among the ruins of war. The decline of the region began during this period, they claim, not during the turn-of-the-century industrial transition. Indeed, in this view much of the region had already begun the transition to capitalism before the war, as demonstrated particularly by the Baltimore and Ohio Railroad in northwestern Virginia and the Virginia and Tennessee Railroad of southwestern Virginia, both of which penetrated their respective regions in the 1850s.[9]

Modern scholars of southern Appalachia typically reject the uniform application of this great polarity between preindustrial and industrial Appalachia or the cataclysmic transition of a region previously untouched by capital. Even the most remote sections of the region were involved in the market, and true isolation was rare and momentary in time. Moreover, although the gap was not so great as between the cotton elite and the mudsills of the South, preindustrial Appalachia still was stratified by class. Several scholars have demonstrated the existence of elites, landowning yeoman farmers, landless tenant farmers, laborers, servants, and slaves and have shown that antebellum developments actually helped to shape the industrial transition that began in the 1880s. As Kenneth Noe observes, "Modernization did not strike a primitive culture in the 1880s"; it was already under way in the 1850s.[10] Wilma Dunaway would go further and argue that the region was capitalist from the moment of European intrusion.[11]

West Virginia's uneven development was not caused by a lack of capital investment until the transition to industry; rather, capital invested in industrialization was limited and confined to the older, settled portions of the state. Typically, development occurred at strategic locations in the emerging transportation nexus, first along the major streams, later augmented by roads and increasingly during the last half of the nineteenth century by railroads. At these strategic locations, commercial towns became "bulking centers" at the periphery of the national economy for small towns, farms, and extraction industries in the hinterland, hubs for exporting local raw materials and importing finished goods. Wheeling on the Ohio River, Morgantown on the upper Monongahela River, and Charleston on the Kanawha River became distribution points early in the nineteenth century, with linkages to larger nodes in the emerging national market system such as Cincinnati, Pittsburgh, Philadelphia, Baltimore, and Richmond. As Appalachia was at the periphery of American, not to mention global, capitalism, so, too, the undeveloped interior of West Virginia was at the periphery of those more urbanized areas around its edges where linkages with the market system were first established.[12]

The wealth generated in these developing areas was great enough to distinguish them from the backwoods but insufficient to accumulate the capital necessary for massive industrial investment or for railroad construction. Even those West Virginia capitalists who distinguished themselves as industrialists relied on access to capital from eastern urban financial centers. Whether the industrial transition began during the colonial era, the 1850s, or the 1890s, investment and economic development was uneven in Appalachia, and certainly that pattern was reflected in West Virginia. Moreover, the scale of the industrial transition in West Virginia, which occurred with the development of the railroads and extraction industries, represented a major escalation in the region's economic development that profoundly altered life for most people in the state and certainly had a direct impact on those who lived in the two-thirds of the state still covered by virgin forest on the eve of industrialization.

Truly massive investment in industrial expansion began earlier, however, with the Baltimore and Ohio Railroad, which was incorporated in 1827 by Baltimore businessmen who feared the diversion of trans-Allegheny trade that would result from completion of the National Turnpike and the Erie Canal. After overcoming major engineering and political obstacles, the B&O finally completed construction over the mountains by way of Cumberland, Maryland, and on to Grafton and Wheeling, West Virginia, in 1853. By 1857 the B&O made connections through to St. Louis and in the mid-1870s was opened to Chicago and New York.[13]

Virginia politics had determined that the B&O would lay its rails to Wheeling, but the company's original preference was to establish its Ohio River terminus further downriver at Parkersburg. With the support of a large hinterland, Parkersburg boosters continued to pursue their own line along that original route, which would have taken the B&O from Grafton through Clarksburg to Parkersburg. Irritated but undaunted by the loss to Wheeling, local business interests, with the support of the B&O directors who still preferred the Parkersburg terminus, completed construction of the Northwestern Virginia Railroad along this route in 1857. Shortly thereafter, the B&O assumed control of the branch.[14]

The B&O exerted an immediate economic stimulus in northwestern

Virginia through which it passed, increasing the production and shipment of cattle, timber, coal, and manufacturing, spawning new industrial towns, and invigorating new enterprises in old ones. In Preston County, for example, Tunnelton came into existence at the edge of the virgin forest, growing from an initial house and store to an industrial town with a circular sawmill and large tannery in 1858. Later, mines were opened and began to ship coal over the road. Newburg and Austen opened circular sawmills shortly thereafter, and extensive timber and lumber businesses were established at Summit and Rowlesburg. Extensive coal mining also was undertaken almost immediately at Newburg, and a renewed interest in iron production was kindled by arrival of the B&O at Independence (Irondale). Grafton grew from humble beginnings as a single house along the Tygart Valley River built by an Irish railroad worker to become a B&O division stop with railroad shops and headquarters buildings, as well as the terminus of the Parkersburg branch. Capital was attracted to Grafton because of its location, and the town also became a lumber processing center as well as a commercial hub for the countryside.[15]

Seeing the effect of the B&O on the eastern panhandle and the northern corner of the state, West Virginia politicians, like their counterparts everywhere in America, became devotees of the railroad as the sure way to economic prosperity. During the last half of the nineteenth century, the construction of railroads to bind sectional economies into one national marketplace was regarded as a prerequisite for economic development. Numerous railroads were chartered in West Virginia by the new state government during the 1860s with the presumption that the more railroads that were chartered, the greater the likelihood some of them would succeed.

The "development faith," with the railroad as its icon, became the foundation of a near religious conviction among West Virginia's leaders between the Civil War and World War I. In this conviction West Virginians merely conformed with broader bourgeois American ideas about "progress." In fact, the founding fathers who led the movement for separate statehood, which culminated in 1863 with the assistance of federal troops, can be understood to have led a middle-class revolution. They saw themselves as men of liberal, progressive views struggling to throw off the shackles of Virginia's feudal social system with its rigid class lines dominated by a decadent slaveholding aristocracy.[16]

The revolution was precipitated when Virginia joined the other southern states in seceding from the Union. A special session of the Virginia legislature met in January 1861 to consider whether Virginia's future lay with the

Union or the Confederacy, and after a statewide plebiscite on the issue in favor of secession, the delegates reassembled on April 17, 1861, and voted eighty-eight to fifty-five in favor of secession. Of the thirty-one delegates from northwestern Virginia, twenty-four voted against secession, five voted with the majority, and two abstained. Delegates from the northwestern section of Virginia emerged as the champions of the Union, a position so unpopular in Richmond that the governor had to provide them with safe-conduct passes to return home.[17]

The secession crisis precipitated a movement for a separate state in the northwest, but its roots ran much deeper. The lack of internal improvements and state support for railroads or canals, a tax system that discouraged free enterprise, inadequate political representation based on free population, a land system that retarded settlement, and viva voce voting at the polls all were western grievances stretching back to the early years of the nineteenth century.[18] "The people of West Virginia," wrote Marshall Dent, a Morgantown newspaper editor and a delegate to the secession convention, "have borne the burden just about as long as we can stand it. We have been hewers of wood and drawers of water for Eastern Virginia long enough, and it is time that that section understood it; and it is time that our would-be leaders in our own section understood it."[19]

The 439 delegates of northwestern Virginia who met at the first Wheeling Convention in May 1861 reflected not Virginia's western elite but rather "the frugal farmer, the hard working mechanic, the enterprising merchant and manufacturer, who had all been toiling and suffering for years against the oppression of a government which did not foster their interests, but instead, burdened them with unequal taxes and unequal laws," editorialized a Wheeling newspaper.[20] Actually, northwestern Virginia diverged in important ways not only from eastern Virginia but also from the people who lived in approximately one-half of the territory that became West Virginia. The region was more economically developed and industrial than the interior backcounties, with burgeoning woolen, iron, and flour milling industries. Also, the people who settled there were largely Scots-Irish, Germans, Welsh, Irish, and American-born stock from northern states who settled the region by way of the Ohio and Monongahela River system rather than trekking over the mountains from Virginia. Most had little connection or experience with slavery. A secessionist from Clarksburg wrote to Governor John Letcher in 1861 urging him to send in state troops immediately because Unionism was so strong. "It must be recollected," the governor responded, "that our intercourse is almost entirely with the West and North, we have none with the central and eastern portions of Virginia. We are not slaveholders, many of us are of Northern birth, we read almost exclusively Northern newspapers and books, and listen to Northern preachers."[21]

The completion of the Baltimore and Ohio Railroad to Wheeling in 1853 undoubtedly had much to do with stimulating Unionist resolve in northwestern Virginia, not because of the "modernizing" influences it exerted but because northern influences followed those economic tracks that tied the northwestern counties to the markets of the North. In general, counties in the interior of the state were more identifiably Virginian, agrarian, and secessionist, whereas the more populous and established counties of the northwest were identifiably more northern, bourgeois, and Unionist. A young Union officer and future president, Captain Rutherford B. Hayes, was stationed for a time in the Clarksburg vicinity. In letters to his family he observed that the secessionists were either "the wealthy and well educated" or the "ignorant barbarians of the country." In contrast, he wrote, "The Union men are the middle classes—law and order, well-behaved folks."[22]

A profile of the statehood leaders also reveals the middle-class origins of Unionism in the region. As John Williams observes, the "outs" of Virginia politics, the "frugal farmer," mechanics, merchants, manufacturers, and lawyers who served them, challenged the old regime. Newspapers in the region played a key role by giving voice to western grievances and educating the people about statehood. Indeed, the *Wheeling Intelligencer* became known as "the paper that sired a state" for its leadership role in the movement.[23] Ministers, Methodists in particular, also preached statehood as a moral cause in opposition to slavery and to southern decadence generally.[24]

The link between the market economy, the B&O Railroad, and Unionism in northwestern Virginia also can be seen in the occupational profile of those who assumed leadership roles in the statehood conventions. John Carlisle of Clarksburg was a mill owner and investor in two newspapers; Jesse Sturm of Marion County was a bridge builder; Thomas Hough was a Fairmont tinsmith; Francis Pierpont of Fairmont was an industrialist and businessman; another Fairmont native and partner of Pierpont, James O. Watson, owned a coal mine and brickyard; Harrison Hagans of Preston County owned an iron furnace. Among Harrison County's fourteen delegates to the first Wheeling Convention, five were involved in "mercantile activities," three were merchants, one was a cattle dealer, one was a cheese maker, one a minister, and the others were either farmers or lawyers. It was in the railroad towns, linked as they were to the markets of the North, however, where the statehood movement drew its greatest strength.[25]

Almost immediately after secession, the Union army moved across the Ohio River to occupy northwestern Virginia, and under Union protection the statehood leaders had their opportunity to inaugurate the revolution in economic development which they anticipated would inevitably emerge from a liberal political and economic system.[26] On June 20, 1863, the authority of government was handed over to the officers of the new state of West Virginia at a ceremony in Wheeling. Recalling the occasion in 1901, Granville D. Hall, one of the statemakers, observed that the event was so special because "the dream of generations had 'come true.' . . . At last we were out of the wilderness; not only in the sight but in possession of the promised land." Now, "all faces turned to the future, rosy in the dawn of . . . progress."[27] Now, out from under the "feudal domination" of Virginia slaveholders, progress-minded westerners were free to devote their energies and resources to fostering internal improvements, industrial development, factories, schools, and towns. One recent student of these events suggests that the movement toward statehood was part of what Barrington Moore described as the "last capitalist revolution" of the Civil War, the bourgeois revolution that "removed the political and economic obstacles to industrialization and modernization" presented by slavery and the traditional social order it sustained.[28]

The Unionists were primarily Union Democrats and Whigs, but by 1863–64 they had become Republicans seeking to control the course of their new ship of state and the longevity of their party. Republican statemakers were destined to hold a grip on the helm in West Virginia only briefly, however. They made a major mistake in adopting an expanded geographic West Virginia that incorporated twenty-four counties on its southern perimeter representing about 40 percent of the state's population who were southern sympathizers. In these counties, there were few subscribers to the northern and Republican revolution. Far from middle-class, market-oriented modernizers, they followed the old Virginia style of politics of family, deference, and parochialism.[29]

Neither the B&O itself, however, nor the economic development it spawned originated in Union sympathies in the northern part of the state. The significance of the line and other river and road connections is that they linked the region to the North. Goods were transported in and out of the region over this emerging transportation system, but so were political ideas, cultural baggage, and the self-interest identified with those markets upon which the people depended. The railroad itself was a politically neutral engine of change, not a formulator of progressive "modernizing" ideas.

While the B&O and other transportation linked northwestern Virginia to the North, the Virginia and Tennessee Railroad (V&T) tied the economic fortunes of southwestern Virginia to the South. The V&T stimulated economic development almost immediately upon its opening in the 1850s, but that development was linked with Richmond. Over these lines moved not only the goods of trade but also the culture and ideology of slavery. There, despite the mountain environment, the seeds of southern culture were planted and nurtured by the railroad. When the test came, southwestern Virginia joined the South in secession.[30] The railroad per se did not shape a free market bourgeois ideology so much as provide a means for acting out prevailing ideological ideas about "progress."

Some statemakers recognized that, as the B&O tied the northwest to the northern markets and the Union, the Virginia and Tennessee Railroad linked southwestern Virginia with the South and the Confederacy. At the constitutional convention in 1861–62, John S. Carlisle, a delegate from Clarksburg and a future senator, argued against incorporating the southern tier of counties within the new boundary: "But Sir, look at the lines of improvement in Western Virginia outside the Northwest. Where do they lead? Where is the railroad that penetrates Monroe and Greenbrier and the whole southwest? And the canal that has its commencement there and extends on into Covington? They all lead and connect with the East. It is idle for gentlemen to talk of any other west save the Northwest. All the rest and residue of the State is bound by iron bands and commercial ties to the Eastern part of the State, and can never have any commercial interests or intercourse with us." Later he added that "we never can have business relations with the rest of the State. The southwestern part has its railroads, turnpikes, and canals penetrating through its valleys and mountains and leading to the capital of the State."[31]

Economic development was neither a new concept, nor was it imposed on West Virginians by "outsiders." Indeed, well before the state's founding in 1863, industry-oriented public officials promoted development of West Virginia's natural resource extraction industries.[32] During the ensuing decades, state government was captured by industrial boosters, who turned its machinery to accomplishing that goal. In 1906, nearly a half-century after the "bourgeois revolution," the *Manufacturers' Record* reported that in West Virginia "the entire machinery of State government" was used "to attract capital to the State to develop its railroads, its coal, and its timber interests." Governors, congressmen, and senators were all recognized promoters in eastern financial circles, and in this respect, the business periodical noted,

"West Virginia holds a unique position not duplicated by the governmental machinery of any other State in the South."[33] Reinforcing the booster spirit among industrial developers was the aspiration of most West Virginians for a material improvement in their economic condition. The assumption that the state's abundant timber and coal resources would provide the basis for industrial development grew into a conviction that was seldom successfully challenged, nor was its corollary, that only the railroads to transport those resources to market were required.[34]

Pro-industry newspapers seldom lost an opportunity to beat the development drum. Boosters were captivated by the popular conception of the railroad as the great modernizing agent that would bring civilization to the wilderness. Since the arrival of the first English colonists, Americans had equated the forest with primitivism, the lack of "civilized" society and high culture. Hence its elimination connoted the triumph of civilization over "raw nature," the ascent to a European cultural standard. In this worldview, elimination of the wilderness became a metaphor for the rise of America as a civilized society. West Virginia developers concurred. "What wonder that the heart of West Virginia is set on railroads," proclaimed the *Wheeling Register* in 1881. "They are the life giving currents of modern civilization without which prosperity and progress are solecisms." Several years later, the paper approvingly reprinted the speech supporting industrialist Johnson Newlon Camden's renomination to the Senate: "We do not belong to that class of people who climb the forest trees . . . to their hiding places in order to escape the sight or avoid the sound of a locomotive engine. We believe sir, that if West Virginia has suffered in connection with the subject of railroads, it has been because we have not had enough of them." It was clear that "the woods" presented an affront to the prevailing economic faith of the era in its proper metaphoric context when the paper declared: "We must have railroads. . . . We must help our people out of the woods." The *Register* editorialized: "West Virginia has been in the woods for a long time," but people living in the interior were "longing for the time to come when capital and enterprise shall reach their borders and unlock their doors."[35] Hope had arrived by the turn of the century for, as one booster observed in 1902, "even in the heads of the hollows, the 'moss-backs' are being hustled out of their hibernation" and "jostled" awake by industrial developers with money to buy land and natural resources.[36]

The B&O became enmeshed in the politics and economics of industrial expansion in northern West Virginia from its initial penetration into the region in the 1850s, but not until 1873, twenty years later and a decade after statehood, did the southern part of the state receive its equivalent trunk line. In that year the Chesapeake and Ohio Railroad was opened from Newport News, Virginia, to the Ohio River city of Huntington, West Virginia, which was founded as the terminus of the line. C&O president Collis P. Huntington, like his B&O counterpart, was not primarily interested in developing the natural resources of West Virginia but rather in linking the eastern cities with the Midwest and West Coast. Following a path well-trod by other railroad moguls of his day, Huntington soon overreached his finances, and in 1888 he sold the line. Under its new president, Melville E. Ingalls, the railroad took a new interest in developing the timber and coal industries along its right-of-way. Branch lines were constructed up tributary streams of the New and Kanawha Rivers, which provided the railroad bed, and new towns sprang up throughout the valley system when they were opened up for development.[37]

Development of the southern West Virginia coal fields required the companies to provide housing and other services for wage laborers for the mines because adequate facilities did not exist. Therefore, more than 90 percent of the miners in the southern part of the state lived in company towns.[38] This expansion created a demand for lumber on an unprecedented scale to construct those towns and other mine facilities in addition to exports. The C&O erected a sawmill along the Kanawha River at St. Albans in 1871 to cut lumber for the railroad, and the industrial expansion soon called other mills into existence in the city and along the Coal River, which reached its confluence with the Kanawha at St. Albans. By 1882 numerous forest product mills were in operation along the C&O line in West Virginia.[39] When the C&O directors finally realized that the potential profits from developing the resources in southern West Virginia could be substantial, other capitalists had entered the field as well.[40]

Unlike the C&O, the Norfolk and Western Railway Company (N&W) penetrated southern West Virginia during the 1880s specifically to develop the rich coal reserves in the Flat Top–Pocahontas and Winding Gulf coal fields of Raleigh, McDowell, and Wyoming Counties. Seeking a route to the Ohio River, the N&W followed Elkhorn Creek to the Tug Fork, crossed over the mountain, and followed Twelve Pole Creek north through Wayne County to Kenova on the Ohio River, where the extension was completed in 1892. The practice followed by the N&W of concentrating large holdings of timber and coal lands within captive land companies was a prominent feature of resource ownership and development in southern West Virginia. Here coal operators did not work their own lands but leased them from land companies. For example, E. W. Clark and Company controlled not only the stock of the N&W but also the stock of two companies that owned lands along the N&W right-of-way, the Flat Top Land Association and the Southwest Virginia Improvement Company.[41]

Although coal quickly dominated economic life in southern West Virginia, timbering came first and already had reached peak production levels by 1895. Timber was rafted out of the region to Ohio River markets even during antebellum days, but by the 1890s drifting had supplanted this traditional mode of transporting logs. The people who lived between the Kanawha and Tug Fork Rivers practiced a mixed economy of timbering and farming with some hunting and gathering of herbal roots on the side, but timbering seems to have been the preferred occupation. Even before the railroads, several major commercial companies entered the region, such as the Little Kanawha Lumber Company (from Maine), which owned sawmills at Portsmouth, Ohio, the Yellow Poplar Lumber Company of Ironton, Ohio, and C. Crane and Company of Cincinnati. Rafting days on the Guyandotte River are commemorated in the famous poem of that title written in the 1850s by Thomas Dunn English when he lived in the town that became Logan.[42]

Major lumber concerns set up significant timbering operations in McDowell and Wyoming Counties, too, but they were railroad operations from the start. Most notable was that of the William M. Ritter Lumber Company, which set up two band mills on tributaries of the Dry Fork. Ritter was unique in southern West Virginia in that the company manufactured lumber at the cutting edge, a mode of operation made possible because it owned thirty miles of tram roads and sixty miles of its own railroad, which eventually became the Dry Fork Branch of the N&W.[43]

By the 1880s industrial expansion was in the takeoff phase for those parts of the state that were served by the three major lines. But not everybody in West Virginia was pleased with these changes. Although farmers and other shippers recognized the importance of railroads in delivering their products to market and returning with their seed, commercial fertilizers, industrial supplies, and farm machinery, they soon realized that the railroads discriminated against them by giving rebates to favored customers and charging higher rates for short hauls. Their irritation was aggravated by the railroads' refusal to pay their fair share of taxes and prompted serious political opposition, particularly against the B&O and the C&O.

Certainly the attitude toward railroads changed in the decade following the demise of the founding Republican administration and the ascension of the Bourbon Democrats to power in the early 1870s. The founders viewed railroad developers as public benefactors who would save the state from isolation and link its natural resources with the urban manufacturing centers. Liberal franchises were awarded to large corporations to the detriment of farmers whose land bore the brunt of taxation. Governor William E. Stevenson (1869–71), the last of the two governors who had been state founders, declared in his annual message of 1870 that "if we are to compete successfully with the surrounding states in attracting population and securing additional capital from abroad," West Virginia should develop a plan to attract industrial investors. He cheerfully recommended passage of "the most liberal legislation in favor of capitalists who propose to make actual improvements within the state, and who give satisfactory assurances that they mean to execute what they promise."[44]

The attitude had changed in some quarters when the constitutional convention met in 1872, called by the Democrats to rewrite the 1863 document. Daniel D. T. Farnsworth, a delegate from Upshur County, voiced the concern of many that the Baltimore and Ohio Railroad, the largest corporation operating in West Virginia, would actually assume control of the state. The controversy of the decade, which precipitated the challenge to the "development faith," was with the B&O's refusal to pay either local or state taxes on the grounds that its 1847 Virginia statute of incorporation exempted the corporation from taxation until its earnings exceeded 6 percent annually the amount of capital invested. Between 1869 and 1871 the railroad had paid no taxes at all, and in 1870 it turned over $87,000 of its $100,000 back taxes, but for the next five years it paid only $4,000 annually of the state's approximately $20,000 assessment.[45]

Against this background, the constitution of 1872 was written with language intended to prevent railroad officials from exercising undue influence in government policy. Article VI barred railroad company officials from holding seats in the legislature, while Article XI proclaimed that all railroads were public highways in the eyes of the law. The companies were defined as common carriers and therefore subject to regulation by the legislature. The Railroad Incorporation Act of 1873 built on the constitution's provision empowering the state to enact and enforce legislation regulating corporations, prohibited two different railroad companies from combining in such a way as to abandon their routes through a town without permission, established maximum passenger and freight rates, and prohibited discriminatory practices employed by most railroads of the day.[46]

The official policy of the state Grange, like its counterparts in other rural states, was to support development of railroads, but it attacked the special privileges in railroad franchises and protested the power of railroads (which received land grants) to take private lands without compensation under condemnation proceedings. Moreover, the Grange demanded that the railroads be held strictly liable in all cases involving personal injury or damage to property along their lines. In 1875 two more pieces of important railroad legislation were passed by the legislature reflecting Granger demands. One required that railroads be assessed for all of their property, money, credits, and investment, including rolling stock, that was not specifically exempted from taxation in the company's charter. The second measure required county attorneys to prosecute violators of the law.[47]

The conflict between the Grange, which spearheaded the revolt, and the B&O broke out in full public fury when the Grange requested special rates for its members to attend the annual meeting at Alderson. The C&O readily complied, but the B&O refused because the meeting was not being held at a site along the railroad line. The Grange pointed to the rejection as an example of the B&O's arbitrary and capricious use of the power entrusted to it by the public to discriminate against its critics even as it awarded free passes to influential citizens such as newspaper editors, legislators, and executive and judicial officers of the state. Hostility toward the railroads swept through the Grange convention that year and resulted in the passage of resolutions against unfair taxation and the issuance of free passes. The resolutions were submitted to the legislature in 1877 and prompted a special investigation into the passenger and freight rates charged by the B&O. The evidence gathered by a joint committee of the senate and house demonstrated that the abuses were real, not just the dying cries of the "moldy element" or "those 'yahoos' who stand in the way of all improvements and decency," as J. N. Camden called the agrarian rebels.[48]

The anticorporation sentiment in West Virginia during the 1870s and 1880s was much stronger than might be suggested by reading history backward with the knowledge that the industrial interests prevailed by the end of the century. For example, Johnson N. Camden, one of the state's foremost industrialists and John D. Rockefeller's "right arm," was summoned to appear before the joint investigating committee in 1879 and received a stiff dose of salts. When asked the amount of rebates his company, Camden Consolidated Oil Company, received from the B&O for shipping its oil, Camden responded that "the arrangement between the Baltimore and Ohio Railroad company and ourselves, affects our private interests, and it might be to our disadvantage to answer that question, which at present I decline to answer." In response, the committee chairman introduced in the senate a joint resolution declaring Camden in contempt of the legislature and ordered him to be brought before the senate to answer the charge. The House of Delegates balked, however, and added amendments that gave Camden two days to appear and explain his action. Camden promptly did just that, pacifying the house, but the senate demanded a formal punishment. Unable to reach a compromise, the legislature took no action against Camden. Not only was the matter forgotten, but in 1881 the state legislature elected Camden to the U.S. Senate.[49]

These and related abuses stiffened the resolve of the legislature to force the railroads to comply with state tax regulations. The constitution of 1863 required that all property be taxed and provided no authority to the legislature to exempt railroad property. Nevertheless, the act incorporating the Covington and Ohio Railroad in 1866 provided that the company was exempt from state property taxes until its profits amounted to 10 percent on its capital, an arrangement similar to that made for the B&O. Subsequently, the Covington and Ohio was reorganized into the Chesapeake and Ohio Railroad Company, and the new charter carried the old tax exemption forward to the new company. With the reform movement in full swing, the tax exemption was no longer politically expedient and so the legislature repealed the tax exemption in 1879, at which time the state auditor billed the C&O for taxes past due. The company refused to pay, claiming that the act of 1879 impaired the obligation of a contract and was, therefore, unconstitutional. The state contended that franchises were privileges granted by the state and that immunity from taxation is not a personal privilege of the corporation to be passed on to a purchaser of the property. The company secured an injunction from the circuit court judge in Ohio County, but when the West Virginia Supreme Court of Appeals dissolved the injunction, the company appealed its case to the U.S. Supreme Court. In 1885 the high court upheld the decision of the West Virginia Supreme Court of Appeals, agreeing that "the exemption granted to the Covington and Ohio Railroad Company did not inhere in the property so as to pass by transfer of it, and that immunity from taxation conferred on a corporation by legislation is not a franchise."[50]

The constitution of 1872 also required that taxation be uniform and equal throughout the state, and in 1883 the legislature authorized the Tax Commission to investigate the issue of taxation as it related to "foreign" companies. The commission's report, printed in 1884, remonstrated against the process by which control over the state's resources was rapidly passing into the hands of a relatively few absentee corporations.

The report stands as the first clear official notice of the problems associated with absentee ownership of the state's land and resources. Declaring that "the people have been educated to believe that our immediate development must be obtained at any cost," the commission warned that "the public mind has become saturated with an idea that progress means one railroad where there is no railroad, and two railroads where there is only one," but the result of this mentality was a "worse than reckless" waste of local resources. The Tax Commission went on to redefine "progress": a state prospers only when "those who permanently reside within her limits are increasing in wealth; a state is prospering only when her citizens are accumulating property." Appearances may be deceiving, however. Railroads may be constructed, enterprises and towns may spring up along them, the population may swell, "but if the entire enterprise is owned by non-residents, if all the profits belong to persons who reside abroad, if those who are permanently identified with the locality do not participate in the harvest, the State is going backwards." Citizens may not realize until it is too late that when the resources are exhausted, the companies will leave and the sources of natural wealth will be gone. "Twenty years have passed; the treasures, untouched in 1865, have been considerably exhausted, vast private fortunes have been accumulated, but not by those who are our permanent citizens, and to-day the home population probably does not own one-half the property which it owned when the war ended."[51]

The commission outlined many of the abuses complained of by the agrarians and confirmed the illegal manipulations that many suspected. For example, an 1881 legislative committee investigation of railroad rates uncovered a secret combination of C&O officials and a few coal and lumber company executives called the Coal and Lumber Agency. It was an illegal association in restraint of trade. Agency members enjoyed cheaper rates than any other coal and lumber producers along the line, which forced other producers to sell their goods to the agency at fixed rather than market prices in order to stay in business. The authors of the 1884 Tax Commission report complained that it was revealing that the legislature ignored the problem, and they were confident that the situation on the Baltimore and Ohio was not much better.[52]

The commission also warned that exaggerated expectations of immediate economic development from railroad construction were unwise, for the process was far more insidious than the commissioners had imagined. They outlined "three stages of railroad enterprise." In the first stage, a road is constructed through an area that will "furnish sufficient traffic to yield a profit on the work," and all customers have equal access to the road. In the second stage, a road is built because the promoters expect to be the contractors for the work; if the road costs $1 million, the company expects to receive $3 million in return. Moreover, the countryside served by the road "must pay five times as much for the transportation as it ought to do, because it is taxed to pay interest on three million dollars, when the road only cost one million." In the third and most insidious stage, the promoters construct a railroad because custody of a line will enable them to control the country depending on it. This extraordinary power leads to exorbitant prices that absorb the profits of every enterprise along the line and gives the railroad "the power to appropriate the entire net earnings of the community." This was the stage of "railroad enterprise that we now witness in its worst form in West Virginia and, unless we call a halt, the sacrifice of our property is inevitable and irretrievable."[53]

But the situation in West Virginia was still worse, according to the commissioners. Railroad developers planned to profit not only from selling transportation, developing resources along the line, and gaining a windfall from buying land at wild-land prices and selling at developed prices, but they also hoped to persuade the towns and counties along the line to mortgage their future prosperity by issuing bonds to aid the construction of the enterprise. To ensure that this nefarious system once installed continued in place, the report continued, influential citizens were provided a personal stake sufficient to "outweigh their concern for the common Welfare." Thus, "one man is promised a depot on his farm; another man has property immediately on the road; another is given a contract; another a salary; and presently many persons, stimulated by a personal motive, are all arguing the same way and advocating the same measure. On the other hand, the great body of voters, occupied with private affairs, give the matter no consideration and there is no one to argue against it; the local newspapers publish everything to encourage subscription, and suppress every fact that would enable the people to form an intelligent judgment."[54]

Jefferson County's experience with bonding the Shenandoah Valley Railroad illustrated how development did not necessarily mean progress. In this case, the promoters persuaded the voters to approve a subscription of $250,000 by arguing that building the road would spread wealth throughout the county. This did not happen, however, for workers were brought in from a distance, the contractors operated their own stores, and the company spent only several thousand dollars locally beyond what was paid for the right-of-way. It was claimed that the new railroad would cheapen transportation, too, but rates were not reduced except at points where there was competition. Moreover, property was expected to rise in value, but that did not happen because no buyers would step forward except those who had some relationship with the managers of the railroad and therefore were guaranteed favorable treatment. The county was promised stock for its investment, but the railroad was so heavily indebted that the stock was unsalable. Nor did the railroads improve the county tax base, for while the county paid $15,000 a year in interest on the debt, the railroad paid no more than $500 in taxes to the county in 1882. Even with this great investment of public monies, the county had no representation in management of the corporation. Perhaps worse yet was the bottom line: the county would be paying its debt for no less than twenty-five years, which, including interest on the $250,000, came to a total debt of $450,000. If this money had been invested in locally owned businesses, the commissioners argued, residents would have been vastly better off. They did not claim that no local benefits were realized from the road but that the costs exceeded the benefits by a ratio of three to one.[55]

That the legislature was not moved to action by such illegal combinations as the Coal and Lumber Agency or the exploitative methods used by the railroads provided clear evidence to the Tax Commission that legislators had a vested stake in the system. Therefore, it recommended that a railroad commission be established to gather information on the railroads so that the public could protect itself.[56] This was an anemic recommendation and far too little, far too late, since the commissioners already claimed that absentees owned one-half of the land in West Virginia in 1884.

The commissioners and agrarian protesters were right about the railroads not paying their fair share of taxes. They also were correct in their suspicions that the legislature would do nothing to rectify the situation. In 1897, the State Board of Agriculture surveyed the fifty-five counties on two questions: "What percent of the wealth of your county is actually owned by farmers?" and "What percent of the taxes of your county is paid by the farmers?" In twenty-two counties ownership of wealth and taxation were in balance. For example, in McDowell County farmers owned only 10 percent of the county's wealth, but they also paid only 10 percent of the taxes; on the other extreme, Pendleton County farmers owned 95 percent of the wealth and paid 95 percent of the taxes. In the other thirty-three counties, where ownership of wealth and tax payment were out of balance, the range of disparities was very widespread. For example, in Cabell County farmers owned only 25 percent of the wealth but paid 65 percent of the taxes, and in Kanawha County the spread was the greatest at 35 percent of the wealth versus 80 percent of the taxes. In twenty of these counties the gap between farmer ownership and taxes paid was between 10 and 30 percent; the gap in eight counties was less than 10 percent and in four counties 35 to 45 percent. For the state as a whole, farmers owned 65 percent of the wealth but paid 80 percent of the taxes.[57]

Between the C&O and the B&O lay a vast virgin forest beckoning developers. Since neither of the two railroad corporations originally intended to risk investment in development in the state, other means for financing natural resource development in the vast interior were required. Into the breach stepped West Virginia's leading politicians: industrialists Johnson Newlon Camden, Henry Gassaway Davis, and the latter's son-in-law Stephen B. Elkins. They would be the first to lay the iron rails of progress into the great interior forests, transforming life in the remotest recesses of north-central West Virginia.

The West Virginia and Pittsburgh Railroad (WV&P) was formed from the merger of several smaller lines to connect with the B&O at Clarksburg. The first major branch in the B&O system was completed in 1866 when the Northwestern Division, which ran between Grafton and Parkersburg, was turned over to the B&O. The branch ran through Clarksburg, where local initiatives began immediately to link regional towns and thereby open up the area's timber, coal, and agricultural resources for development.[58] Seeking connections with outside markets, during the 1870s local citizens of Weston, Lewis County, incorporated the Weston and West Fork Railroad to connect Weston with the B&O at Clarksburg in Harrison County. The first of several independent short lines that would evolve through mergers into the West Virginia and Pittsburgh, the Weston and West Fork Railroad generated its capital by selling stock and issuing bonds. The delays stemming from local political struggles to control these initial, and therefore all the more vital, lines of economic development are worth sketching for the process was repeated throughout the state during the late nineteenth century. No sooner had the right-of-way been surveyed between Weston and Clarksburg than the project was delayed by an offer from neighboring Bridgeport, a few miles east of Clarksburg on the B&O, to provide a free right-of-way with the terminus located in that town. The offer spurred the Clarksburg developers into action lest they lose their struggle for strategic economic position. Soon the necessary land was purchased for the right-of-way and terminal, and the new railroad was completed along its original route.[59]

Like the multitude of similar small lines of the period, this short line suffered from lack of capital and expertise but was saved from extinction when Johnson Newlon Camden took over as director in 1878. One of the state's leading industrialists, Camden invested heavily in land, natural resources, and railroads. Like many other industrialists of the period, he served in the U.S. Senate (1881–87). Other short lines between towns in the area were constructed and merged during the 1880s into the expanding WV&P, one from Weston to Buckhannon in Upshur County and one to Pickens in Randolph County. Another line was extended southward to Sutton, Braxton County, which continued on through the seemingly impenetrable forests of Webster County to Camden-on-Gauley and in 1899 reached its terminus at Richwood, Nicholas County. In April 1889 the numerous short lines were formally merged into a single line, the West Virginia and Pittsburgh Railroad, with Camden, whose election to the U.S. Senate in 1880 greatly assisted him in his role as railroad developer, as president. The potential traffic along the line was so great that the B&O leased the new road in January 1890 for a term of 999 years. Those terms were changed to outright purchase, and the B&O assumed total control.[60]

In his Golden Anniversary history of the state in 1913, historian and booster James Morton Callahan observed that each branch of the West Virginia and Pittsburgh Railroad "terminated in a region previously unopened, but quickly responsive to the touch of capital." The "touch of capital" immediately left its mark on the countryside, most visibly in the increased bustle of formerly sleepy towns or in the development of new towns where none had previously existed. Clarksburg, the Harrison County seat, had evolved into a substantial town even before the Civil War, and when intersected north-south by Camden's road and east-west by the B&O branch between Grafton and Parkersburg, the town continued to grow under the stimulus of new industrial activity. Harrison probably was the most improved inland agricultural county in West Virginia; stock farming expanded as did industrial enterprises engaged in the manufacture of lumber. Weston, the Lewis County seat, had been a local trade center before the Civil War and "received a wonderful forward impetus" when the railroad came in 1879, followed by the construction of railroad offices and shops, factories, and the extraction of timber and coal.[61]

Buckhannon, the Upshur County seat, also was a commercial center for the surrounding countryside before the railroad arrived, but its growth and development as a lumber town was further stimulated by improved transportation. A. J. G. Griffith Lumber Company mills drew timber from the surrounding counties, as did the Buckhannon Boom and Lumber Company. Approximately one-half of Upshur County was still covered with virgin forest in 1893, but after the arrival of the railroad the remainder soon disappeared.[62] In 1884, a reporter for the *Wheeling Register* wrote that before the arrival of the connecting line, Buckhannon had been "a quiet, pleasant, but apathetic little country town." Now, he observed, the "noise of pounding hammers" was heard from every direction, drays moved constantly through the streets, and new churches, stores, and schools were being built. A large woolen mill, a handle factory, a large planing mill, two wagon and carriage factories, sawmills, lumber yards, a log boom, and two large flouring mills had also been constructed in the village. Given the economic development stimulated by railroads, the reporter declared, "It is not surprising that the people further on in the interior are longing for the time to come when capital and enterprise shall reach their borders and unlock their doors."[63]

Sutton, the Braxton County seat, also received a new impetus from new blood and industries, particularly the large Pardee-Curtin Lumber Company mill, and the advantages resulting from becoming a commercial center for the rural hinterland.[64] Camden-on-Gauley, Webster County, was opened out of the virgin forest by Johnson N. Camden as the site for his Gauley Lumber Company. Located on the Gauley River and within a few miles of the Williams, Cranberry, and Cherry Rivers, the settlement was served by the WV&P Railroad, which was established to develop a 140,000-acre tract of timberland purchased by Camden in Webster, Pocahontas, and Nicholas Counties. The railroad-timber boom here, as elsewhere in the backcounties where land titles were clouded, produced conflict. A local newspaper reported in 1894 that "there is a great controversy over the title to a certain tract of about 100,000 acres adjoining the lands of the WV&P. Both parties have erected houses and moved families in and are guarding them with Winchesters."[65] The machinery for the first large lumber plant was hauled overland from the Chesapeake and Ohio Railroad, a distance of forty miles, so the plant would be completed and ready for operation when the WV&P extension reached the mill town. Within eighteen months the place became a thriving industrial and commercial town.[66]

Another regional railroad system was developed in northern West Virginia from Cumberland, Maryland, to Parsons and on to Elkins, with the inevitable short, independent feeder lines from forest and mine. This system was established and operated by two members of the state's most prominent troika of industrialist-senators, Henry Gassaway Davis and his son-in-law Stephen B. Elkins.

The policy of the trunk lines, in this case the B&O, to leave to individual entrepreneurs the construction of independent feeder lines to bring the timber and coal of the interior of West Virginia to the main line provided men like Davis and Elkins with enormous opportunities. During the Civil War, H. G. Davis had quit his job as station agent for the B&O at Piedmont, Maryland, and entered business for himself selling cross-ties and other supplies for the war. A loyal Unionist and supporter of separate statehood for West Virginia in 1863, Davis served in the West Virginia legislature and then as U.S. senator from 1871 to 1883.[67]

His superior knowledge of the timberlands, which he acquired during the search for war supplies, prompted Davis to initiate a plan to drive his own railroad into northern West Virginia after the war. Davis began by purchasing options on timber and coal lands in Mineral, Grant, and Tucker Counties, then in 1866 he organized the Potomac and Piedmont Coal and Railroad Company to bring the resources of the Potomac Basin to market. The road was to run from Bloomington, Garrett County, Maryland, to Piedmont, West Virginia. No ordinary businessman, Davis personally explored the northern mountains on horseback, searching out resources and buying lands, always with an eye to the best routes for railroad construction. The wilderness held the potential for unlimited wealth, but building railroads in the mountains also was fraught with the potential for financial disaster.[68]

As his vision of the economic potential of the wilderness expanded, so did the plan for tapping those resources. With his brother Thomas and Stephen B. Elkins, Davis raised the capital for a new enlarged road, the West Virginia Central and Pittsburgh Railroad (WVC&P). Davis and Elkins were well connected politically, and both were well known as experienced businessmen, so they approached other businessmen in politics with the option to invest in company stock. As a result, the list of stockholders in the new company was a "Who's Who among the business-minded politicians." In fact, the line became known as the "Senatorial Railway" because so many senators purchased stock; prominent congressmen, several cabinet members, and other powerful national figures also became stockholders in the company.[69]

Davis and Elkins's political connections linked up and out to Washington and New York but also down and into state politics, which was a great strategic advantage for their entrepreneurial projects. The West Virginia legislature approved the West Virginia Central and Pittsburgh Railroad charter on February 23, 1881. A very liberal document, the charter granted Davis and Elkins a flexible route "from any point on the line of the Baltimore and Ohio Railroad" on the North Branch of the Potomac River to "any lands or mines owned by said company in the counties of Mineral, Grant, Tucker, Randolph, Pocahontas, and Greenbrier." The company also was given the right to condemn land or material necessary for the construction of the railroad should it encounter resistance from reluctant landowners. Davis was named president of the company and Elkins vice-president.[70]

The WVC&P extended work begun under the Piedmont and Potomac in 1880, opened a line beyond the Piedmont junction on the B&O, up the North Branch, and passed over the divide at the headwaters of the Potomac. In November 1884, the rails reached Davis in the heart of the Tucker County hardwood forest. Before pushing on to its projected terminus at Elkins, however, Davis and Elkins had a practical problem to solve. Freight shipped over the WVC&P bound for Cumberland or Baltimore had to be transferred at Piedmont to the B&O, carried to Cumberland, and then transferred again. Because each transfer drove up costs for the company, Davis and Elkins decided to build their own line to cover the twenty-nine miles between Piedmont and Cumberland. The Piedmont and Cumberland Railroad, as it was chartered, was placed under Elkins's supervision.[71]

When the connection to Cumberland was completed in 1887, the WVC&P was pushed beyond Parsons and finally reached Leadsville in the summer of 1889. Leadsville, a hamlet of a few houses in 1888, had its name changed to Elkins as a tribute to Stephen B., and city lots were laid out and land set aside for erecting the necessary railroad shop buildings. By 1895, the population of Elkins had grown to a few thousand, the town had a substantial business district that included the general offices of the WVC&P, and Davis and Elkins had established their permanent residences there.[72]

Before the arrival of the WVC&P in the northern mountain counties, this region remained almost completely undeveloped. Following the penetration of Camden's West Virginia and Pittsburgh Railroad into the Upper Cheat and Tygart Valley country in 1885, however, contemporaries reported that the most dramatic industrial development had occurred in Tucker and Randolph Counties than anywhere else in northern West Virginia since the Civil War. Although settled a century earlier, these counties remained so inaccessible that few people had settled there, with the exception of the Tygart Valley. Other parts of the region, Callahan wrote in 1913, were in a wild and unsettled condition resulting from the difficulty of building mountain roads and the distance from a railroad connection. The streams as a rule were not navigable for boats and were too swift for any use except to float timber. Consequently, this high, rugged region had been "neglected while the tide of investment and immigration passed by to the far west."[73] With the arrival of the WVC&P all of that would change.

According to Callahan, "The new road . . . carried into the silence of the primeval woods the hum of modern industry, and expressed its material usefulness in gigantic lumber plants and rich coal mines, and in newly made and growing towns—living monuments to men such as Windom, Blaine, Gorman, Bayard, Wilson, Fairfax, Davis, Douglas, Hendricks and Elkins. The opening of mineral and timber resources created towns such as Bayard, Thomas, Davis, Douglas, Hendricks, Bretz and Parsons in Tucker; such as Montrose and Elkins in Randolph; and such as Belington in Barbour. . . . The resulting activity attracted a good class of merchants who increasingly attracted trade from the surrounding country."[74]

Completion of the West Virginia Central and Pittsburgh into the higher elevations of the forest in Randolph, Tucker, and northern Pocahontas Counties furnished an outlet for timber that was previously unexploitable. Numerous independent railroads shot out from the main line into the deepest heart of the high forest, followed by sawmills, pulp mills, tanneries, and lumber camps. Steam whistles broke the solitude that had reigned in this wilderness from its botanical birth and sounded the death knell for West Virginia's most awesome primeval forest. As these smaller lines sought junctions with the main line, company logging railroads completed the elaborate web by linking mills on the main lines with the cutting edge of the forest. At least forty of the fifty-five counties in West Virginia had one or more logging railroads, the numbers ranging from one in Taylor to more than sixty in Pocahontas County. One authority on these logging railroads estimates that their number exceeded six hundred, and "with concentrated research" this number would increase substantially.[75]

As did the trunk lines, the West Virginia Central and Pittsburgh relied on coal shipments to generate revenues, but timber played a more significant role than coal in the industrial development of the northern mountain section of the state. Coal and coke operations were physically concentrated in specific locations and spread out underground in nonsocial space. The timber industry, in contrast, spread out aboveground to incorporate the landscape, which was entirely covered with magnificent merchantable timber. Therefore, the timber industry left its indelible stamp on the countryside in this section of West Virginia to a far greater extent than did coal. The railroad stimulated the development of lumber mills, pulp mills, tanneries, and secondary wood product manufacturing. Farmers also quickly turned to the railroad to ship livestock out of the counties through which it passed.[76]

Increasingly under pricing pressures from the railroad trust, Davis and Elkins sold the West Virginia Central and Pittsburgh in 1902 to a syndicate headed by George J. Gould, the railroad magnate who was fashioning a cartel among the nation's largest carriers so he could control rates.[77] Davis used the several million dollars from the sale of the WVC&P to reinvest in still another railroad, the Coal and Coke Railway Company, which was incorporated in May 1902. The proposed route of the Coal and Coke was from Elkins to Charleston, West Virginia, by way of the Elk River, a distance of 175 miles. The railroad would link the C&O and the Kanawha and Michigan Railway in the southern part of the state with the B&O in the north and make the interior accessible to tidewater as well as to Great Lakes markets. First, however, more than 100 miles of track through very difficult terrain had to be constructed before traffic began to move between Elkins and Charleston, a goal achieved in December 1905. An extension of the road from Elkins east to Durbin at the headwaters of the Greenbrier River, the Coal and Iron Railroad, was completed in 1903.[78]

The "touch of capital" gave birth to new communities and stimulated old ones all along the Coal and Coke and the Coal and Iron. Along the forty-three miles of Coal and Coke Railroad between Elkins and Durbin at least forty-nine sawmills ripped their way through the region's timber.[79] This figure excludes those mills along independent feeder lines such as the Dry Fork Railroad, which extended southward from Hendricks in Tucker County up the Dry Fork of Cheat River to Horton in Randolph County, a distance of a little over thirty-one miles. The smaller railroad lines generally suffered from even greater financial instability than the larger roads, and therefore their histories also are very complex. For example, the Dry Fork Railroad became the Central West Virginia and Southern Railroad in 1913. Twenty-nine and one-half miles of the railroad were owned by the railroad company and the remainder by the Spears Lumber Company. Extensions were driven off this short line, such as the Evenwood branch, which extended to the Raine-Andrews double-band sawmill located in that company town. In this fashion, even the most remote hollows and mountains were tied into the national transportation network as lumber, pulpwood, and livestock were shipped out, manufactured products were hauled in, and passenger service enabled people to come and go freely.[80]

Along the southern thrust of the Coal and Coke, the new town of Gassaway was established about midway between Elkins and Charleston to serve as divisional headquarters and to create maintenance shops.[81] As in other interior sections of the state, the railroad created opportunities for other industrial developers. For example, the Coal and Coke bisected Clay County as it meandered along the valley of the Elk River, and that provided Joseph G. Bradley with the opportunity to develop 102,000 acres of virgin timberland which his family had owned for decades. Bradley's grandfather, Simon Cameron, a prominent Pennsylvania politician who served as secretary of war in Abraham Lincoln's cabinet, left him the land when he died in 1880, but it had remained dormant until the Coal and Coke penetrated Clay County.[82]

In 1903 Bradley organized the Elk River Coal and Lumber Company to develop the coal and timber on his extensive properties in the county's southeastern corner. To tap these resources, Bradley organized the Buffalo Creek and Gauley Railroad in 1904. His intention was to run the 104 miles from Dundon on the Coal and Coke east to Huttonsville, Randolph County, but the railroad never made it out of Clay County. After laying 18.6 miles of track, Bradley decided he had gone far enough, and at that point he dug an entry into the nearest coal seam and established the company town of Widen. Bradley also established a farm and thriving dairy at Cressmont and the town of Swandale, where a large band sawmill and supporting tramlines were erected to cut his extensive timber holdings. Bradley's "Appalachian Empire" withstood union assaults and strikes for four decades before the sick and ailing coal and lumber baron sold his coal, timber, and railroad properties to the Clinchfield Coal Company in 1958.[83]

Before the construction of the Coal and Coke, the Charleston, Clendenin and Sutton Railroad (CC&S), which Davis bought out, had reached into the lower end of Clay County and sparked a modest development of timberlands. Earlier loggers along Porter's Creek, just twenty-nine miles up the Elk River from its confluence with the Kanawha, had made up small log rafts or drifted timber downstream from Porter's Creek since the Civil War. Above Porter's Creek the Elk was not navigable and was filled with rocks and shoals that rendered it unnavigable and therefore impractical for large-scale river logging. When the CC&S arrived at this point in Clay County, rafting was supplemented by small logging railroads as a means of transporting timber. The Porter's Creek and Gauley Railroad, for example, was built to feed timber to the Clay Lumber Company, which was built by an entrepreneur from Ohio in 1894.[84]

The CC&S provided a modest stimulus to the agricultural economy of

Clay by providing a market for farm products and spreading some cash in a countryside where cash had been very scarce. The people in the upper end of the county had sold some of their products into the nascent wage economy of the lower end of Clay, and the money they earned was spent with local merchants. But it was not until after the Coal and Coke extended the railroad all the way through the county that lumber operations began on a major scale. Large companies such as the C. L. Ritter Lumber Company entered the county and built a large band mill and stave mill at Ivydale. In addition to Bradley's Swandale operation, other large band mills were constructed by the Leatherwood Lumber Company, the Crescent Lumber Company, and David S. Collins at Elkhurst. Numerous smaller operations also were established in the formerly inaccessible sections of Clay following construction of the Coal and Coke.[85] Davis controlled the Coal and Coke Railroad until his death in 1916 at the age of ninety-three. The following year, his estate sold the railroad to the B&O, which continued service along the line.[86]

Not surprisingly, the last section of West Virginia to fall under the spell of railroad building was the high mountainous region that formed the southeastern mountain border of the state. Both economically and geographically the Greenbrier River valley was long regarded as the natural path for north-south railroad development stemming off from the C&O, which cut through Greenbrier County and the southernmost portion of the valley. Pocahontas County in particular possessed abundant pine and hardwoods. The pine had been harvested early, but the hardwoods could be removed only with heavy equipment and therefore remained nearly untouched until the arrival of the railroad at the turn of the century.

Development-minded residents of the Greenbrier valley were repeatedly elated by rumors of railroads only to see their hopes deflated when each new rumor failed to pan out. Hope and resources were insufficient; it took capital, and a lot of it, and the history of Pocahontas County reveals how resources and capital converged to alter life forever in this formerly remote backcounty. Pocahontas provides an ideal case study of the effects of timber industrial development, for exclusive of stock farming, cutting timber was the only industry in this magnificent mountain retreat.

A projected railroad in Pocahontas County was first mentioned in 1850 when the county court ordered an election on the question of subscribing to the capital stock of the Virginia Central Railroad. Whatever the vote may have been, the railroad failed to materialize, nor did any of the other twenty-three railroads that also made plans to enter Pocahontas ever become a reality for the long-suffering nascent local developers of the county's resources. If wishes were horses, beggars would ride, and all of them lacked the capital.[87]

The large amount of capital required to penetrate the high mountains and heavy forests of Pocahontas came from industrial developers with the necessary political and financial connections. The state's leading political industrialists whose interests seemed to be converging on the upper Greenbrier in the early 1890s were Johnson N. Camden, Henry G. Davis, Stephen B. Elkins, and John T. McGraw.

There were two general plans involving Pocahontas in 1891. Camden was planning to extend the West Virginia and Pittsburgh through the county to a junction with the Chesapeake and Ohio at Covington, Virginia, while a second plan being considered by C&O officials would have extended its Hot Springs branch into the Greenbrier valley; the two railroads agreed to connect in Marlinton. This was more than rumor, for Senator Camden had purchased 84,000 acres of timberland in Nicholas and Webster Counties, with Davis and Elkins as partners. Camden went on to acquire additional acreage in the region along the Gauley, Williams, Cherry, and Cranberry Rivers for a total of 135,000 acres. It was these lands that the West Virginia and Pittsburgh Railroad was established to exploit. The only potential competitors for development of the region in 1889 were Davis and Elkins, whose West Virginia Central and Pittsburgh was within striking distance of the Greenbrier headwaters. The potential for conflict was neutralized in 1889, when Camden reached a gentlemen's agreement with Davis and Elkins establishing "spheres of influence" in the undeveloped interior.[88]

The choice of Marlinton as the junction for the C&O and Camden's projected railroad was well suited to the interests of another West Virginia capitalist, John T. McGraw. A Grafton native and son of one of the Irish laborers who laid the original B&O track, McGraw was a lawyer, businessman, and prominent politician in the state's Democratic Party. McGraw had begun to acquire Pocahontas lands in the 1880s and, according to one expert, between 1883 and 1905 held deeds to over 145,000 acres in the county in addition to large holdings in Webster and Randolph Counties. McGraw's land speculations would remain just that without a railroad, and he did everything in his power to convince Davis, Elkins, and Camden to build that railroad. In 1891 it appeared that the three had agreed to extend their railroads into the Greenbrier, where they would meet at Marlinton from whence they would forge on to the junction with the C&O. With this knowledge, McGraw established the Pocahontas Development Company to build and promote the new town of Marlinton and successfully induced county residents to vote for a proposal that would move the county seat from Huntersville to Marlinton.[89]

Unfortunately for McGraw, the railroads did not materialize. Undoubtedly the depression of 1893 played a major role in dampening the spirit of conquest among the railroad builders, including those of the C&O. McGraw relentlessly pushed on, however, in his search for a railroad builder. Eager to turn a profit from these speculative lands, McGraw cut off negotiations with the West Virginia capitalists in 1897 and turned to a New York syndicate that included Cornelius Vanderbilt, H. McKay Twombly, and W. Seward Webb, to whom he sold tracts totaling three hundred thousand acres of timber and coal lands for $520,000.[90]

McGraw was either strapped for cash or unaware that a Greenbrier railroad plan had emerged that would finally materialize. By the late 1890s the C&O was in a financial position to build a railroad the entire length of the Greenbrier valley following a water-level route. The Greenbrier Railroad Company was chartered in November 1897 after the company conferred with capitalists who owned significant timberland in the Greenbrier country. No doubt McGraw and his New York associates in the Greenbrier River Lumber Company, which owned approximately one hundred thousand acres in Pocahontas and Randolph Counties, were among the interested parties contacted by the C&O subsidiary so he was not left out entirely.[91]

Ultimately, however, the action of capitalists from Maryland convinced the C&O to build the long-awaited railroad into the Greenbrier watershed. The Luke family, headed by William Luke, operated West Virginia Pulp and Paper Company mills in Luke, Maryland; Davis, West Virginia; and Tyrone, Pennsylvania. It was their decision to construct a new paper mill at Covington, Virginia, and to haul their pulpwood from a large tract of timberland eventually totaling about 170,000 acres in the upper Greenbrier valley that convinced the C&O that enough freight could be generated to justify the investment.[92]

Finally, by the fall of 1899 work crews totaling fifteen hundred men began clearing the land and laying track up the valley. The work progressed at what seemed to local residents an unimaginable speed of one mile per day. The West Virginia Pulp and Paper Company did not wait for the arrival of the railroad before beginning the construction of a large sawmill and the new town of Cass in June 1900, ninety-five miles up the Greenbrier valley from the C&O main line junction at Whitcomb. On October 26, 1900, the people of Marlinton celebrated the long-awaited arrival of the first train, and by

Christmas the Greenbrier Railroad had reached Cass. Having reached its major objective, the railroad extended the line on to the new towns of Durbin, Bartow, and, by 1905, Winterburn. Winterburn was 100.9 miles from the C&O main line. Although somewhat miffed that C&O president Melville E. Ingalls had not consulted with him before making final arrangements for the Greenbrier Railroad, Davis nevertheless agreed that it and his own newly chartered Coal and Iron Railroad would connect at Durbin. Davis had been so conservative in building into the headwaters of the Greenbrier River no doubt because of the enormous expense involved in crossing two mountains to get there from Elkins. This line was completed to Durbin in July 1903; along with the WVC&P, the Coal and Coke was sold to the Western Maryland Railroad system in November 1905.[93]

While the Greenbrier country was being opened up by the railroad companies with lumber interests, several lumber companies established separate corporations for their railroads. These roads connected their woods operations with the processing plants and the Greenbrier Railroad.[94] The most extensive of these lumber company railroads was the Greenbrier, Cheat, and Elk Railroad, formed by the West Virginia Pulp and Paper Company. Launched even before the Greenbrier line reached Cass, its purpose was to link the large mill at Cass with the red spruce forest at the top of Back Allegheny Mountain and to transport logs being shipped to Covington for woodpulp. Completion of this 6.8-mile railroad to the top of the mountain was a remarkable accomplishment. From Cass to the lowest gap in the mountain leading to the Cheat River valley was a rise of 1,514 feet, and two switchbacks were required. The grade between the switchbacks was 6.7 percent in places, and above the second switchback the steepest grade reached 11 percent before the logging locomotives mounted the summit at 3,950 feet. In 1904 the company built the town of Spruce near the top of the mountain, consisting of thirty-five houses, a school, a general store and post office, a hotel of forty rooms, and a rossing mill to peel the bark from the spruce before it was shipped to Covington. Spruce was unique. At 3,853 feet above sea level, it was one of the highest towns in the eastern United States, and the only access was by railroad.[95]

As West Virginia Pulp and Paper logged over the upper basin of the Cheat River, the railroad was extended northward down Cheat behind the steadily receding cutting edge of the forest. As the railroad tracks grew longer, the company found coal in 1908 and opened its Hopkins Mine near Hopkins, Randolph County. This and other mines subsequently opened by

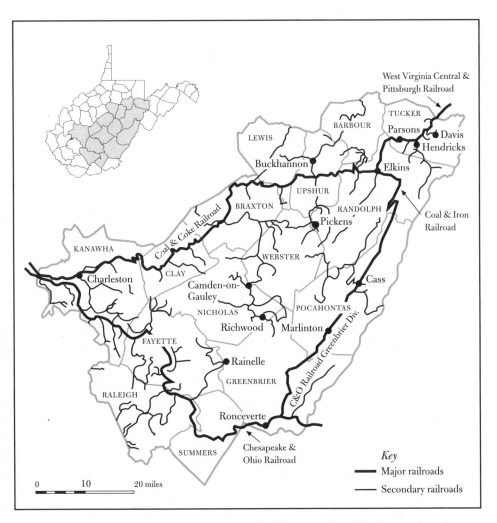

Map 3. Railroads and backcounties in West Virginia, 1917. (West Virginia Geological Survey; adapted by Debra Benson)

the company were used strictly to supply the coal required for the company's locomotives and other steam equipment such as log loaders and skidders. These railroad operations became extensive so the company incorporated the Greenbrier, Cheat and Elk Railroad Company (GC&E) in 1910. The most famous logging railroad in the East, it was chartered to run between Bemis, Randolph County, and Webster Springs in Webster County. The GC&E's Elk River division crossed over an elevation of 4,012 feet and into the Tygart River watershed and followed the Elk River to Bergoo, a distance of seventy-four miles. Since the only reason for its existence was to serve the West Virginia Pulp and Paper Company's timber operations, everywhere the line ran businesses related to the company blossomed.[96]

All along the one hundred miles of the C&O's Greenbrier Railroad, lumber operations and mill towns grew in the wilderness. The economic stimulus given to the mountain economy of the Greenbrier country is illustrated in the observation of a visitor to the valley from Staunton, Virginia, in 1903: "In two years the Greenbrier Valley has become a hive of industry, while the newly opened territory in northern Pocahontas and southern counties along the Coal and Iron road is experiencing the influx of men and capital akin to an Oklahoma rush. . . . Along this indicated line an era of development has set in that astonishes the imagination. The fanciful dreams of a recent past are outstripped in the realization of today."[97]

The construction of the Greenbrier Railroad, which the C&O subsequently named the Greenbrier Division, completed a strategic encirclement of West Virginia's vast interior wilderness that made exploitation possible. Railroad penetration of the mountain backcounties signaled the death knell for the log drives and rafting of timber to downstream processing centers. The level of technology brought to bear on harvesting the timber in West Virginia's wilderness backcounties was escalated from the manual to the mechanical stage by the railroad. Not only did the railroad convey the heavy equipment required to cut the giant timber found there, it also transported the product to market. Hand in glove with the dramatic expansion of the industrial infrastructure was the growth in services provided by towns and the concentration of wood-processing centers closer to the forest's edge. Success is a matter of perspective, but in fewer than three decades railroads had facilitated the complete deforestation of West Virginia.

The infusion of industrial capital from outside the state reinforced the classical core-periphery model of development. When the railroads came, they hauled natural resources from the periphery to the economy's core urban centers, where they were processed into finished products. The large lumber mills built close to the cutting edge of the forest only increased the efficiency of capitalist expansion. Because the railroads carried raw materials to destinations outside the region, economic links were stronger between mill towns and urban destinations than between West Virginia towns. Instead, railroads led to a dispersed "corridor" development along the mountain valleys and stimulated the convergence of technology, heavy transportation facilities, natural resources, and the national markets. Mountain mill towns became processing outposts of the expanding capitalist economy.

A high degree of economic interdependency existed between the railroads and all lumber operations, but this was particularly the case with large mills. Railroads sought the assurance of a high volume of business to justify

Table 2. The Rise of Industry

Year	Number of Establishments	Number of Hands	$Capital Invested	$Value of Products
Pocahontas County				
1870	22	14	20,400	50,482
1880	24	22	24,875	45,544
1900	40	55	82,987	146,750
1920	30	1,693	—	10,937,955
Randolph County				
1870	25	14	32,350	45,881
1880	20	22	27,650	49,487
1900	97	718	1,598,966	1,396,106
1920	53	2,108	—	7,583,106
Tucker County				
1870	7	4	7,950	16,760
1880	5	10	7,000	5,608
1900	59	997	2,614,013	2,376,645
1920	40	1,046	—	4,395,531

Source: U.S. Census of Manufactures.

the heavy financial investment while the mills depended on efficient transportation to the urban markets. An impressive number of band sawmills, the most technologically sophisticated operations, were established in West Virginia between 1890 and 1910. Single, double, and triple band mills operated one to three endless strips of steel saw blades that could cut timber of up to eight feet in diameter. These mills were capable of cutting 100,000 to 140,000 board feet of lumber in an eleven-hour day.[1]

Within two decades a remarkable number of band mills were erected in these backcounties. Towns proliferated wherever the great mills were constructed, flourished for a time, and then declined when the timber was cut out and the mills were closed. In 1909, the peak of the timber boom in West Virginia, 83 band mills and 1,441 smaller lumber mills produced 1.5 billion board feet of lumber. By then many other mills had already cut out their tracts and ceased operations. Over the entire period from 1890 to 1930, an estimated 200 band mills cut through the West Virginia woods.[2] The mountain counties of Tucker, Randolph, Pocahontas, and Nicholas, which contained the state's highest elevations and smallest number of people, led the state in the number of large mills and in the production of lumber. At the

Figure 1. West Virginia Lumber Mills, 1904–1920: Mills Reporting

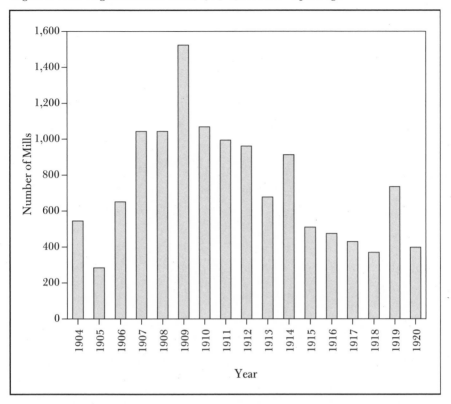

Source: U.S. Bureau of the Census Reports. Graph by Paul Rakes.

peak of production in 1910, twenty-six thousand employees earned direct annual wages of over $16 million in West Virginia's forest industries: fourteen thousand in logging and the band mills, five thousand in smaller mills, five thousand in planing mills and other woodworking enterprises; and two thousand in related forest industry plants such as tanneries and pulp mills. In addition, a large number of carpenters, salesmen, jobbers, and others were indirectly employed by the lumber industry.[3] The pace and scale of the industrial transition ushered into these backcounties by the railroad and timber boom is indicated by the growth in capital investment and value of products recapitulated in Table 2 (see also Figures 1 and 2).

One of the fundamental assumptions in the colonial model of Appalachian development is that advanced capitalism penetrated the region at the turn of the twentieth century. As a precondition to advanced capitalism, the indigenous people were forced off the land they had owned for generations

Figure 2. West Virginia Timber Production: Ten-Year Pattern

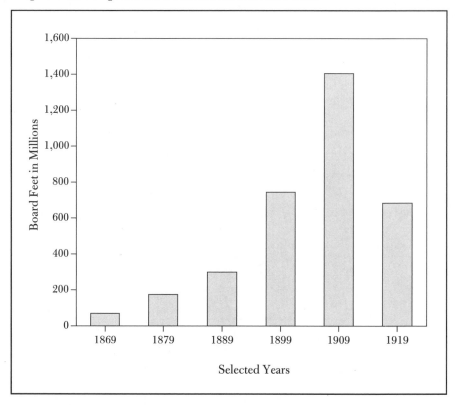

Source: U.S. Bureau of the Census Reports. Graph by Paul Rakes.

by cunning speculators, and, with the assistance of local elites, transferred control of the land to the railroads and natural resource corporations. Separated from the land, indigenous people had no other choice but to join imported native black and foreign laborers in the new industrial towns that grew up around the new mines and mills. In this interpretation, the penetration of capitalism dictated the alienation of labor from the land and the commodification of natural resources so they could be bought and sold. This process was a rapid and wrenching one that demonstrated not only the disparity of power between preindustrial and industrial systems but also the oppressive social conditions stemming from the maldistribution of power that accompanies industrial capitalism in a previously underdeveloped region.[4]

There is considerable explanatory power in this model, particularly as it applies to West Virginia. Corporations did acquire the greatest proportion of land in the state. Modern estimates place two-thirds of all privately owned land in the hands of a few dozen absentee natural resource corporations.[5] Furthermore, indigenous people were indeed squeezed off the land and into industrial wage labor, and for many the complete boom-and-bust cycle evolved within their lifetimes.

This snapshot perspective distorts one very significant fact, however: West Virginia land has been either owned or claimed by a relatively few privileged speculators since colonial times. Most of southern Appalachia fell under the private control of large speculators well before a public domain existed or a federal policy was devised to govern its distribution. In fact, Virginia joined other southern states in refusing to ratify the Articles of Confederation unless their interior lands were excluded from the public domain. By the mid-eighteenth century much of the area west of the Virginia Blue Ridge had been claimed and divided into large estates by the Ohio Company, Greenbrier Company, and the Loyal Company, firms headed by powerful eastern and English merchant-planter-politician land speculators. In present West Virginia, little land was available for ordinary people after 1790. The Virginia Assembly began selling lands at below-market prices in the 1790s, thereby encouraging speculation in Virginia treasury warrants by distant brokerage houses. Of the nearly 5 million acres engrossed in West Virginia by 1810, 93.3 percent were controlled by absentees and managed by local land jobbers and lawyers.[6]

The Virginia frontier lagged in settlement because absentee speculators kept prices too high for ordinary homesteaders, a practice that further concentrated control in the hands of elites who could afford to buy the lands. A relative few resident landowners owned a majority of the land. In West Virginia 62.7 percent of all households were landless in 1810, and only 37.3 percent of all households owned land.[7] Randolph County provides an illustration of the pattern of distribution. Just twenty grants of between 100,000 and 199,999 acres, and one above 200,000, constituted 3.4 percent of all the grants but 49 percent of the aggregate acreage. As late as 1860, 44 percent of the total real estate value reported in the U.S. census for Randolph was owned by only 10 percent of the five hundred people reporting.[8]

The unequal distribution of landowning and speculation continued throughout the nineteenth century. As a result, the land law of West Virginia became tangled by generations of speculation and sporadic attempts at reform and a chaotic system for registering lands that the state inherited from Virginia. Over the course of the nineteenth century land titles gradually were quieted in the developed districts, but in the backcounties confusion continued to reign well into the industrial transition. During the nineteenth century, local elites who managed the vast tracts held by absentees became significant landowners themselves. This rising local elite spearheaded the struggle to prevent recognition of old colonial claims. In 1831 and 1837 they succeeded in convincing the Virginia Assembly to declare all previous grants that had fallen delinquent for taxes as forfeit and liable to entry. Local elites also succeeded in transferring the condemnation and sale of such land from Richmond to the circuit courts in the counties where the land in question was located.[9]

After West Virginia became a state in 1863 and government fell to the local elites, now a ruling landowner class themselves, it became impossible for absentees to defend not only colonial claims but also Virginia grants in the state courts. West Virginia inaugurated the Virginia system for dealing with delinquent and forfeiture laws in its own courts. During the years following statehood, there remained large tracts that had never been entered on the land books for taxation, and these lands were forfeited. Some large tracts, referred to as "waste and unappropriated lands," had never been granted at all. The School Land Law of 1872–73 failed to distinguish between "waste and unappropriated lands" and "forfeited and delinquent lands." Therefore, county commissioners proceeded against all such acres as though they were "waste and unappropriated lands" until 1882, when the legislature transferred authority over forfeited lands from the county commissioners to the circuit courts. Many commissioners either ignored or were ignorant of the law, however, and hundreds of thousands of acres were sold as "waste and unappropriated lands" when they should have been treated as "forfeited and delinquent lands." Their actions attracted little attention until these lands increased in value during the 1890s with the development of railroads, timber, and coal. Then claimants of the old surveys asserted their rights, claiming a violation of the law of 1882, and threatened the homes of settlers.[10]

More significantly, industrial investors also had purchased these lands, and their rights were challenged by these claims. The Henry C. King case was important in setting a precedent because it settled disputes among speculators whose claims were based on old surveys, settlers who purchased their lands in good faith, and industrial developers, in this case the Spruce Coal and Lumber Company. In 1795, Robert Morris of Philadelphia acquired two tracts totaling nearly one million acres of western Virginia land. The land was subsequently sold several times until a five-hundred-thousand-acre tract fell into the hands of Henry C. King in 1893. The lands previously had fallen delinquent and were sold for taxes, and it was the legality of the process which King contested in the state courts and finally was settled by the U.S. Supreme Court in 1909. The high court's ruling validated all previous sales of lands forfeited because of tax delinquency.[11]

Another court case involving the original Morris grant was contested by Max Lansburgh of Baltimore against W. M. Ritter. The suit involved approximately fifty thousand acres of timberland purchased by Ritter in McDowell County which, Lansburgh claimed, belonged to him as part of the 320,000 acres of the original Robert Morris grant he had purchased in Wythe County, Virginia. The West Virginia lands were forfeited, but Lansburgh claimed that he subsequently paid the taxes, and therefore the land belonged to him. Lansburgh sued Ritter for $500,000 he claimed was the value of the timber cut by Ritter on the property, but the state courts rejected his claim.[12]

The loss of cases like the King and Lansburgh suits was pivotal in quieting land claims based on old surveys and determined that the distribution of West Virginia lands would be controlled by the state's new bourgeois industrialist-politicians rather than the old landed aristocratic speculators. Industrialists now had the upper hand, and investment could proceed in the backcounties without threats from those who held old titles.

Land lawyers and land agents stepped forward to assist in the transfer of large speculative tracts into farms and industrial enterprises. Local land lawyers often used their knowledge to become powerful owners themselves. Some quickly abandoned law for the more lucrative business of land development, but others continued to serve in the role of a compradore class. Andrew Price of Marlinton was such a lawyer. Local farmers who could not afford to purchase their own land in the early nineteenth century found the prospects brightened over the course of the century. As the industrial transition reached its critical decades, however, prices climbed again, particularly if the land contained valuable resources. Lawyers such as Price greatly facilitated timbermen and other developers in alienating farmers from the land, and their jobs were made easier by the faith in development at any cost, which found ardent followers among the state's lawmakers. For example, Andrew Price advised one of his client firms to move quickly against the minor heirs of an estate "before there was a chance of them giving you trouble." In another case he advised that land deeded to a woman was invalid because of a technicality that had been overlooked and observed that the timber on the land was "very well worth fighting for."[13]

Andrew Price also used the local Marlinton newspaper to advise readers that selling land to the timber companies was of benefit both to the community and to themselves. For example, he noted that the Greenbrier River Lumber Company paid $1,539.36 taxes in 1898. This timberland, he wrote, now benefited the community by pumping money into the public coffers, whereas previously the taxes had been paid by "smaller landowners who did not realize how much their wild land was costing them."[14] When the C&O branch was extended up the Greenbrier Valley, he chided residents who refused to settle out of court. Price warned them against being too greedy in setting a price for their land and reminded them that if they lost condemnation cases taken before a judge they might incur additional court costs.[15]

The Elk River Coal and Lumber Company, which was controlled by absentee operators Joseph G. Bradley and J. M. Cameron of Harrisburg, Pennsylvania, owned tens of thousands of acres, operated the Buffalo Creek and Gauley Railroad, a coal mine at Dundon, and the Cresant Lumber Company in Clay County. In 1906 James Reed, his brother, and a tenant named Walker, three of the company's one hundred or so tenants scattered throughout its forest lands, were evicted from their homes by George Goad, a farmer, who claimed that he, and not the Elk River Coal and Lumber Company, owned the land. In what was actually a property line dispute, Elk River decided to defend its tenants and took the case to court in 1907. The jury of local residents failed to come to a decision in the first trial, and the company took the case back to circuit court three more times before it won a favorable decision in 1909. The land in question, a one-acre waterfront plot along the Elk River, was valuable to timberman and farmer alike, but the Elk River Company fought with a broader purpose in mind, one articulated by the company's president: "We have made it clear in this case to the community that claims cannot be trumped up to any part of our property without involving the claimant in expensive legal difficulties." This was a tested policy, for the company had used the law as a rod to chasten locals who challenged its claims on several previous occasions and for the same reason.[16]

The scale and complexity of land acquisition by lumber companies spans the spectrum. The organization of timber holdings for the Condon-Lane Boom and Lumber Company illustrates the point. The company was organized out of several smaller lumber companies operating in the Randolph, Pocahontas, and Tucker County district in the 1890s. The land titles stretched back to Philadelphia speculator Levi Hollingsworth, whose holdings reached 137,245 acres of land in Pendleton County alone in 1800. Levi and Emily Condon also sold their extensive holdings in several West Virginia counties to the Condon-Lane Company; the largest contained 28,352 acres straddling Pocahontas and Pendleton Counties in West Virginia and

Highland County, Virginia. There were two exceptions in the deed totaling 3,000 acres, lands belonging to local farmers. In the original deed was a tract of 33,200 acres owned by the widow Maria A. Shaw, who was unsuccessful in her suit to recover the lands from the Randolph West Virginia Boom Company, one of the companies purchased by Condon-Lane. Two smaller exceptions involved two farms of 1,800 and 1,200 acres in Randolph County. Both farms had been purchased in the 1880s by Baltimore land agent L. A. Rheaume, who conveyed the land to the Randolph West Virginia Boom Company, and finally became part of the Condon-Lane holdings. Rheaume also acquired numerous small parcels of land from local farmers in the Cheat-Greenbrier headwaters, which were transferred to the Randolph company and finally to Condon-Lane. Presumably these small parcels were strategically important locations on a river or for "blocking" small parcels into economically significant units. This long, complicated land history demonstrates that absentee owners and land speculators often transferred large portions of land among themselves but also acquired small acreages from farmers when necessary.[17]

Local farmers, who were either forced off their land or sold it willingly to find an easier way of life, saw their lands increasingly concentrated into large holdings acquired by the timber companies. The standard interpretation of industrial development in West Virginia is that absentee capitalists were the villains who alienated settlers from the land and concentrated control in the hands of corporations. There is no lack of evidence for this view, but the distribution of land never was egalitarian, and a disproportionate share has always been controlled by absentees. Despite the emphasis on absentees, measuring their role in the process of land concentration has remained impressionistic. Data collected on timber firms from the West Virginia incorporation records for 1866 through 1909, which was the peak year of the timber boom in the state, provide a count of companies that at least intended to engage in the timber business. The incorporation records distinguished between domestic firms that were "resident," whose principal offices or works were in the state, and "nonresident" firms, those incorporated in West Virginia but whose offices and works were located elsewhere. The latter firms are ignored in this study because they did not operate in the state. "Foreign" firms, however, those that were incorporated and whose principal offices were in other states but had plants in West Virginia were included.[18]

A total of 508 timber firms were incorporated in West Virginia between 1866 and 1909, of which 285 were resident firms. Of this total, only 18 were

Table 3. Incorporators and Timber Firms, 1866–1909

	Firms	Incorporators
Residents of West Virginia	285 (56%)	1,928 (71%)
Foreign	18	
Nonresidents:		786
Firms with majority (3–5) incorporators nonresidents	118	
Firms with minority (1–2) incorporators nonresidents	87	
Absentees (total nonresidents)	223 (44%)	786 (29%)
Total	508	2,714

Source: West Virginia Incorporation Reports, 1866–1909.

"foreign" firms, whereas "resident" firms with a majority of their incorporators (usually three of the required five) were nonresidents totaled 118. If we assume that foreign firms and those in which a majority of the incorporators were nonresidents were controlled by absentees, the number of timber firms in this category is 136, or 26.7 percent of the total. Firms in which some, but not a majority, of the incorporators (usually one or two of the required five) were nonresidents number 87. These firms may have been dominated by the one or two nonresidents if they provided the key financial backing, but this is impossible to determine from the records. Given the broadest interpretation, however, the firms with all three kinds of nonresident incorporators totaled 223, or 43.9 percent of the total.

As a percentage of firms dominated, or at least influenced, by nonresident investors, this represents a disproportionate influence of "outsiders" in the state's timber industry. If we measure influence according to the numbers of individuals engaged in industry, however, a different picture emerges. The records list a total of 2,714 timber company incorporators. Of these, 786, or 29 percent, were nonresidents, and the remaining 1,928, or 71 percent, were residents of West Virginia. In fact, of the 233 West Virginia incorporators for whom biographical information is available, a majority (51 percent) were born in the state (see Table 3).[19]

Even though residents predominated among incorporators, the designation was applied to all incorporators who actually lived in West Virginia. If we are tracing sources of capital and control, the definition does not help much in differentiating between those who were born residents and those born elsewhere who moved their residency to West Virginia to set up a lumber mill. In economic terms the outcome (homegrown capital) is the same in either case. The real difficulty is measuring the relative difference between the scale and value of timber acreage owned by residents and absentees. In all probability, that would be impossible to determine with any accuracy using the records available. Anecdotal evidence, however, tilts decidedly in favor of the absentees.

Natives with small amounts of capital to invest generally organized contracting companies and hired independent woodsmen to deliver timber to lumber mills. In the early stage of the timber boom, contractors were experienced timbermen from Maine and Pennsylvania who brought a core of experienced woodsmen with them to West Virginia. Accustomed to working in the woods, local men soon predominated among the crews and contractors alike. Often contractors were farmer/timbermen who combined their occupations. One such individual, J. W. Kimmell, negotiated numerous contracts to deliver timber to West Virginia mills while continuing to maintain his farm in western Maryland near Oakland. In 1907 Kimmell received a contract to cut timber on Burner Mountain at Braucher, Pocahontas County, five miles north of Durbin. Kimmell and the other members of his family worked in the woods and the sawmill along with the wood hicks and mill men until 1911, when they returned to the family farm.[20] Although contractors like Kimmell occupied an economic rung above the ordinary woodsmen, the social distance between them generally was insignificant.

Many of the operators who migrated to West Virginia from the northern states, disproportionately Pennsylvania, were workingmen looking for new opportunities. Information on conditions in West Virginia was transmitted through informal channels back to family and friends, attracting additional opportunity seekers. William McClellan Ritter, the owner of the William M. Ritter Lumber Company, a large concern in Wyoming County, and the leading spokesman for the industry in West Virginia, grew up on a farm near Hughesville, Pennsylvania. In old age he remembered that as a young man he "had to *work*—there is no doubt about *that*." His father had a sawmill on the farm, and young Ritter decided at an early age to be a lumberman. He asked a "real lumberman" who lived nearby where he could secure a small boundary of timber and was told: "If I were as young as you are, I would go to West Virginia" because it was a "new country being opened up by the railroads" and it was still possible to get in on the ground floor. Connections were arranged with a New York timber developer, and with a minimum of capital Ritter began his economic rise as one-third partner in the Denman and Ritter Lumber Company. During the first two years Ritter boarded with a family who lived in a log cabin near Willeton and the one-thousand-acre tract his fledgling company had acquired. Ritter himself worked on the site and, with the help of some "natives," cut and loaded the first logs on a Norfolk and Western flatcar in 1890.[21]

Other investors with substantially more capital behind them also came from northern states and became residents of West Virginia. John Raine, the president of the Meadow River Lumber Company, was born in Ohio and entered the business in Pennsylvania before coming to West Virginia. William Boa from Canada and Clark Howell of New York were partners who relocated to Alderson in Greenbrier County to establish lumber and wood-processing mills. John Driscoll, James Kinsport, and E. H. Camp were experienced lumbermen from Pennsylvania who moved to Ronceverte, where they established the Saint Lawrence Boom and Manufacturing Company.[22]

West Virginia capitalists made their money from land sales or developing railroads to transport resources out of and products into the region, but the dominant milling centers were established with external capital and by businessmen from other states who had extensive connections with the national markets.

The lumber industry includes the processes of preparing the raw forest material used in secondary wood-using and wood-processing industries. Logging and sawing usually are the basic combination, but planing, shingle, veneer, box, and cooperage production are processes also included in the lumber industry. Other wood-using and wood-processing industries may bear a close association, such as logging pulpwood for paper production and hemlock barking for tanning leather.[23] In key centers of production, all three industries often were concentrated together. Though seemingly alike, their operations and markets differed greatly. From a technical standpoint, the only commonality they shared was that they all used wood.

One of the largest milling centers in the state between the 1880s and 1920s developed in Davis, Tucker County, around the triple band mill operated by the Blackwater Boom and Lumber Company. The town was planned and carved out of the wilderness by Henry G. Davis in 1886, two years after Davis's West Virginia Central and Pittsburgh Railroad reached the site. J. L. Rumbarger of Philadelphia erected the first sawmill in Davis in 1886 to produce hardwood products, primarily flooring. Rumbarger sold his holdings in 1888 to Albert Thompson, a timber operator from Norway, Maine, who reorganized the operation as the Blackwater Boom and Lumber Company. Thompson had purchased thousands of acres of timberland along the Blackwater River in 1887 and built a mill just below Davis. After purchasing the Rumbarger plant, however, he sold the unfinished mill to the smaller Beaver Creek Lumber Company. Two million feet of logs in the Blackwater River also were transferred to Thompson with the sale, and to this supply he supplemented another twelve thousand acres of timber contracted in 1889. These acquisitions gave Thompson effective control of all the timber in the Blackwater basin of the Canaan Valley.[24]

Albert Thompson also built a railroad into the Little Blackwater River timbershed, and extensive improvements were made to the Blackwater River to expedite the transportation of logs to the mill at Davis. In 1893, the mill was sold to W. H. Osterhout of Ridgway, Pennsylvania, although the Thompson family remained stockholders in the firm. After a fire destroyed the mill, Osterhout reorganized the Blackwater Lumber Company in 1894 and installed a large steam gang saw (several circular saws operating at the same time), which lumbermen regarded as one of the best sawmills in the East.[25]

Logging railroads went out from the mill center, even into the precipitous Blackwater Canyon. Albert Thompson regained control of the operation again, reorganizing it as the Thompson Lumber Company, and operated the mill between January 1905 and June 1907, when the Babcock Lumber and Boom Company, a Pennsylvania firm, purchased the company and all of its subsidiary operations. The extent of these operations is suggested by the properties acquired by Babcock: forty miles of standard-gauge railroad, two sawmills, a planing mill, a box factory, 8.5 million feet of lumber stacked in the yards, 8.5 million feet of logs dammed in the Blackwater River, and 46,000 acres of timberland, estimated to contain 450 million feet of lumber. The No. 1 (softwood) mill, located on the north side of the Blackwater River, with two eight-foot and one six-foot band saws, was capable of cutting 100,000 board feet of lumber a day. The No. 2 (hardwood) mill, located on the south side of the Blackwater River, with one eight-foot band saw was capable of cutting 125,000 feet of lumber a day. At peak operation, the Babcock Company employed five hundred men.[26]

This operation was only one of the major forest product plants in Davis, however. The Fairweather and LaDew Tannery, a company based in New York, was established in 1886, the same year Rumbarger built the first sawmill. Hundreds of employees worked in the tannery and in the woods supplying the hemlock bark used in the tanning process. The Marshall Coal and Lumber Company, founded in 1888, operated a coal mine two miles away in Thomas but also supplied timber for the mills of Davis. Between

Clearing the forest to build Davis, Tucker County, 1883. (West Virginia State Archives)

1895 and 1920, the West Virginia Pulp and Paper Company operated a large pulp mill in Davis to supply its Maryland paper mill.[27]

A minimum of twenty-five large band and circular sawmills were operating in Greenbrier County by 1910, including the large band mill of the Saint Lawrence Boom and Manufacturing Company at Ronceverte. At first, lumber production was centered in the white pine district along the Greenbrier River in Pocahontas and Greenbrier Counties, but the white pine soon became scarce and the industry shifted to the vast spruce and hardwood stands in the Meadow River basin of western Pocahontas-Greenbrier district. The Meadow River was too rocky to permit log drives, and with the C&O twenty miles away a branch line was necessary to bring this part of the forest into production. After waiting to no avail for a railroad to be built through its holdings, the Meadow River Lumber Company took matters into its own hands and created the Sewell Valley Railroad Company to haul lumber from the new town of Rainelle to a junction with the C&O main line. Under the guiding hand of its founder, Thomas W. Raine, the Meadow River Lumber Company became the largest hardwood lumber operation in the world. Its voracious triple-band mill consumed three thousand acres of virgin timber a year.[28]

Thomas and John Raine, brothers from Pennsylvania, founded the Meadow River Lumber Company and the "model lumber town" of Rainelle in 1906. The Meadow River Lumber Company operated on the site until it

Panorama of Davis, Tucker County, ca. 1909. (West Virginia and Regional History Collection, West Virginia University Libraries)

was sold in 1970 to Georgia-Pacific. With three band saws under one roof, it was the largest hardwood mill in the world during its first decades. Although it was best known for its hardwood flooring, Meadow River also produced a variety of specialty wood products. In 1932 the company added a shoe heel plant, which continued in operation for over thirty years and produced between four and six million heels for women's shoes. A furniture plant also was in production at Rainelle until World War II, and a planing mill turned out a variety of products such as stair treads and risers, baseboards, window frames, doorjambs, and molding. The company also produced at various times coffins, crates for shipping crystal, frames for automobiles, and ship beams.[29]

Another leading lumber processing center in the state was located in Richwood, Nicholas County, where extensive sawmills, a pulp mill, a tannery, a clothespin factory, a hub factory, and other prosperous wood manufacturing plants were established. Richwood came into existence because of the Cherry River Boom and Lumber Company, which established its original mill on the site and cut its first board on July 25, 1901. Since then over three billion board feet of lumber have been produced in the town. The machinery for the "big mill," as it has been called ever since, was hauled forty miles by wagon from the C&O main line to the mill site, and the construction was finished just in time to take advantage of the completion of the B&O Railroad extension from Flatwoods. No more than eight families

Babcock Lumber Company, Davis, Tucker County, 1909. Closeup of mill in lower right of the previous illustration. (West Virginia and Regional History Collection, West Virginia University Libraries)

lived on the present site of Richwood before the mill was built, but the city grew rapidly thereafter, from a population of 24 in 1900 to 3,061 in 1910, and 5,730 in 1930.[30] The original holdings of the Cherry River Boom and Lumber Company were organized into a block of forty thousand acres by J. W. Oakford, a lumberman from Scranton, Pennsylvania. B. Gilpen Smith, a lumberman from Maryland, who in 1890 also served as president of the Beaver Creek Lumber Company at Davis, became the first superintendent. The Smith family manufactured paper at Conowingo, Cecil County, Maryland. B. Gilpen Smith cruised the timber in the country around the forks of the Cherry River in 1899 and took options on forty thousand acres. Smith found several investors who lived in Scranton, Pennsylvania, led by J. W. Oakford, to purchase the lands, and they established the Cherry River Boom and Lumber Company to cut and manufacture timber from the property. By 1909 the company holdings exceeded two hundred thousand acres lying in five different counties at the headwaters of the Gauley, Williams, and

Cherry River Boom and Lumber Company Mill, Richwood, Nicholas County, 1924. (West Virginia and Regional History Collection, West Virginia University Libraries)

Cranberry Rivers and both forks of the Cherry River. Including company land leases, Cherry River timber covered some three hundred square miles in 1909.[31]

The big mill also maintained an extensive "car shop," a large machine shop with railroad tracks and locomotive turntable, where the railroad equipment and stock were repaired. The shop was fully capable of repairing or rebuilding steam locomotives as well. A coal mine nearby in North Bend supplied the company with fuel for its locomotives, shops, and other local uses.[32]

The Cherry River Company produced lumber, but many other wood manufacturing firms were soon attracted to the town. In 1901 the Dodge Clothespin Company built the largest clothespin factory in the world and subsequently added another plant to manufacture butter trays. One year later, in 1902, the Cherry River Tanning Company came to Richwood and constructed one of the largest tanneries in the world. The Sherwood Manufacturing Company built a factory in 1903 to produce wagon hubs, and in 1904 the Cherry River Paper Company constructed a plant that used waste slabs from other operations. J. D. Westcott and Sons Company built a plant to manufacture broom handles, dowels, and chair rounds in 1913.[33]

Logging contractors, rather than the manufacturing firms themselves, cut and loaded most of the timber used by the Cherry River Boom and Lumber

Company and other Richwood plants. At the peak of the company's operations some ten to fifteen independent contractors with large crews of wood hicks busily felled big timber, estimated at twenty-five to thirty acres of virgin forest each day. The company's operations were extensive enough that three mills were in operation by 1926: the double band mill at Richwood, a single band mill at Gauley Mills, and a smaller circular mill at Holcomb. The company also built its own railroad into the forests, reaching an estimated three hundred miles of tracks in the 1920s. Log trains of 40 to 70 carloads of big timber rolled into Richwood several times a day to feed the city's mills. Cherry River shipped 4,000 carloads of lumber each year out of Richwood, as well as 1,000 carloads of paper, 300 carloads of sole leather from the tannery, 330 carloads of clothespins, 240 carloads of wooden dishes, and 100 carloads of broom handles and chair rounds—a total of 5,970 carloads of lumber and wood products exported from the Richwood depot in a single year.[34]

Neighboring Pocahontas County was home to more of the large band mills than any other county in the state. At least forty-four mills and other timber-related businesses such as kindling wood mills, stave mills, and tanneries were in operation along the Greenbrier Division in 1902. The growth of business along the line is indicated by the tonnage and revenues generated; between 1903 and 1906 freight tonnage increased from 191,677 tons at a value of $220,361 to 378,926 tons valued at $407,531. By far the largest shipper on the line, however, was the West Virginia Pulp and Paper mill at Cass.[35]

Incorporated in 1898 by William Luke and his six sons, the West Virginia Pulp and Paper Company serves as an excellent example of an absentee corporation. The Luke family had considerable experience in the paper business. The patriarch and his two oldest sons had worked in the papermaking business before organizing their own mill in 1888, the Piedmont Pulp and Paper Company, in Maryland across the Potomac River from Piedmont, West Virginia. By 1894 the Lukes operated three mills, one of them at Davis in Tucker County, where the company had acquired fifty thousand acres of virgin spruce timber. That year a sales office was established in New York to maintain a strong link with the markets.

The Lukes reorganized their holdings into the West Virginia Pulp and Paper Company in 1898 because that same year they decided to build another pulp and paper mill closer to the virgin forest. Their original preference for a location was Caldwell, West Virginia, along the Greenbrier River, but when opposition emerged because the mill would pollute the water supply of downstream towns, the Lukes decided to build the mill at Coving-ton, Virginia, instead. This decision was significant because the C&O was laying track up the Greenbrier River to Durbin, and the Lukes decided to purchase a site for their timber operations along the line for easy transport to Covington. The company needed additional capital to finance its expansion and therefore invited longtime associate Joseph K. Cass to merge his own Morrison and Cass Paper Company, located in Tyrone, Pennsylvania, with it in 1899.[36]

The newly formed West Virginia Pulp and Paper Company was char-tered in Delaware and set up a new sales office in Philadelphia under Sam-uel E. Slaymaker, a lumberman with extensive experience in West Virginia and an interest in several lumber companies that operated in the state. Slaymaker, Cass, and the Lukes formed a subsidiary, the West Virginia Boom and Spruce Lumber Company, in 1900 to manage the company's new band mill and company town named after Joseph Cass. The town of Cass, erected at the junction of Leatherbark Run, the Greenbrier River, and the Greenbrier Division of the C&O, was a carefully planned undertaking with electricity and running water in all of the company houses.[37]

The large mill, which began shipping lumber from Cass in February 1902, eventually included a double band sawmill, a planing mill, a dry kiln, and the requisite storage buildings. A "million dollar fire," as a local paper described it, consumed the entire operation in 1922, but the company imme-diately rebuilt the facility and equipped the new mill with two eight-foot band saws, a brick engine house, a boiler house, and dry kilns. In addition, a two-story planing mill 224 feet long was constructed, its machinery operated by forty-five electric motors. The building to store the flooring produced by the planing mill had a capacity of three million feet of flooring, and the lumber docks were 3,250 feet long.[38]

West Virginia Pulp and Paper operations often were conducted in remote sections of the mountains with heavy equipment, and a maintenance shop was established near Cass to keep the machinery in repair. A foundry also was constructed near the shop for casting metal replacement parts for loco-motives and the rolling stock, skidders, loaders, and sawmill machinery. More than fifty men worked in this part of the operation.[39]

West Virginia Pulp and Paper also built a facility on top of Cheat Moun-tain above Cass, exactly eight and one-tenth miles by railroad. For the first several years the pulpwood was shipped to the Covington mill, where the bark was peeled for use in the paper mill. But because a fine ash arose from this process that contaminated the paper, the company decided to erect a peeling mill on top of Cheat Mountain. Originally this was a camp for cutting pulpwood, but as shipments off the mountain increased, the town of Spruce was built to provide permanent quarters for a new rossing (peeling) mill. When the mill began operation in 1906, three hundred people inhabited the town. At 3,853 feet above sea level, Spruce was one of the highest towns in the eastern United States. The company also constructed thirty-five houses, a branch of the company store, and a forty-room hotel. Approximately 480 men were employed in the pulpwood operation, most of them on cutting crews, which shipped between twelve and sixteen carloads to Covington each day. In 1925 the peeling mill at Spruce closed, and the town was eventually abandoned. During World War I the company also operated a tannin-extracting plant near Cass for use in tanning leather and dyeing army uniforms. Two rows of houses were built to house workers at the plant. The plant operated until 1926, when it was closed.[40]

The company also operated two railroad lines. To fire the locomotives and the other boilers and furnaces among its properties, the company owned five coal mines located along its railroad tracks. All told, between twenty-five hundred and three thousand men were employed by the West Virginia Pulp and Paper Company operations.[41]

"Employers, almost without exception, have been rugged individualists," a prominent scholar of the lumber industry observed in 1945. Primarily they were "self-made men who have won out in the difficult competitive struggle because of hard work and superior ability."[42] Like other businessmen, lumbermen were enticed into assuming the risks of the industry by the potential for big profits. Indeed, profits could be substantial from virgin timber. One twenty-two-thousand-acre tract of virgin timber in Pocahontas County contained more than 400 million board feet of hemlock, spruce, cherry, oak, maple, and other valuable species, over 160,000 board feet per acre. The company calculated a "conservative estimate" of profits on this timber operation at over $4 million, an amount that was 230 percent greater than expenses.[43]

Ownership in the lumber industry was primarily by individuals or partnerships throughout the deforestation era. Public corporations were few in the American lumber industry before World War II, and West Virginia was no exception. This lag in organizational development reflected an individualism among employers that rendered it difficult for timber operators to cooperate in solving the multitude of structural problems that beset the industry. Ineffectual organization was the greatest weakness lumbermen confronted in operating their businesses. Successful lumbermen were usually self-made men whose survival depended on their ruthless ambition and dogged determination. Once land deeds were cleared, an intense effort began to liquidate forest stock to generate the revenues that would keep the creditors at bay. This financial pressure stimulated overproduction and instability of individual firms and, ultimately, the markets as well. According to one industry analyst, staying ahead of the bill collectors produced a notable "unbridled individualism" among lumber operators.[44]

Its dispersed spatial distribution also confounded industry efforts to resolve these problems. Several features of the lumber industry were inherently destabilizing. Logging and milling operations, for example, were constantly relocating to new reserves as forests were depleted, and the industry was fragmented by a great diversity among producers. In sawmilling there was great variation of size among the units. Some mills were highly mechanized units with mechanical equipment for handling the lumber from start to finish. Others were medium-sized operations that combined both manual and mechanical processes, and still others constituted hardly more than a circular saw and a carriage to move the log through the saw.[45]

With thousands of producers manufacturing hundreds of different grades, sizes, and products, control was nearly impossible. Economic and cost structures presented the most difficult obstacles to the industry. In medium and large-scale units that had substantial overhead costs, survival depended on controlling those costs. Therefore, the producers required stability and predictability, commodities that were in short supply because thousands of small producers with negligible overhead costs entered or withdrew from production depending on market conditions. Together all these operators glutted the market and drove prices down just as expanding demand should have sent prices up. Market pressures, therefore, perennially pinned prices at their lowest possible levels and forced firms to cut relatively elastic labor costs to the bone. Aggravating these structural difficulties was the long-term decline in demand for wood as stone, brick, and reinforced concrete replaced lumber in building construction, a trend that had already begun by 1906.[46]

The pressures to reduce costs to their lowest possible levels resulted in wasteful logging methods such as clear-cutting, which were frowned on by conservationists. Forced to convert their timber into lumber as soon as possible to stay in business, the lumbermen's methods of extraction and processing often served the moment without regard to the future. They viewed timberland as a resource to be "mined" and abandoned, rather than as a "crop" that was indefinitely renewable if cultivated and harvested wisely.[47]

The large companies operated by men with considerable experience in the industry, established sources of capital, and well positioned in the markets were most likely to survive over the long term. Their size allowed them to benefit from economies of scale, and their access to capital enabled them not only to weather the booms and busts of the business cycle but also eventually to drive the multitude of small to mid-sized competitors from the field. These large absentee firms also acquired a disproportionate influence over West Virginia's backcounty economy, however, and with legislators and jurists eager to secure their investments in the law, they also acquired an inordinate political influence as well.

CHAPTER FOUR

MAKING CAPITAL

SECURE: LAW AND

THE INDUSTRIAL

TRANSFORMATION

OF WEST VIRGINIA

The economic benefits the founders anticipated would spring from the soil of an independent West Virginia eluded them for two
decades after the bourgeois revolution of 1863. While the desire for industrial development was strong among West Virginia's statehood leaders, the
institutional mechanisms necessary to realize that goal simply were not in
place. Before the dream could be fulfilled, another revolution was necessary,
one that would transform the law into a progressive partner in industrial
development rather than a protector of a conservative philosophy and legal
culture carried over from Virginia. The legal revolution would have to start
with the constitution of 1863.

The founders of West Virginia seceded from Virginia in 1863, but they
retained the parent's legal system. The constitution of 1863 provided that
"such parts of the common law and laws of the state of Virginia as are enforced within the boundary of the state of West Virginia when this constitution goes into operation, and are not repugnant thereto, shall be and con-
tinually the law of this state until altered or repealed by the legislature."[1] But

the founders created difficulties for themselves. Although they retained Virginia's constitution, the statemakers "Yankeefied" the organization of government by abandoning the county court, which was the cornerstone of the Virginia system, and replaced it with townships, in which voters exercised their power at meetings reminiscent of New England town meetings.[2]

The Republican Party, which existed in name only before 1860, rose swiftly to power with the statehood movement, secession, and separation from Virginia and declined just as swiftly after the war. Returning Confederate veterans posed a threat to the Republican businessmen, who quickly imposed restrictions to neutralize them politically and block any possibility of their reversing the revolution. Political disabilities only made matters worse among this large segment of the population, and the tide turned against the statemakers. In retrospect, however, it seems inevitable that the party that had Yankeefied government, delivered the vote to Lincoln in 1864, and secured ratification of the Thirteenth, Fourteenth, and Fifteenth Amendments would be doomed to an ignominious death in a state where approximately 40 percent of the population had supported the Confederacy.[3]

The election of 1870 marked the end of Republican rule in West Virginia, swept away by the resurgent tide of a revitalized Democratic Party. The Democratic ascendancy, which lasted from 1870 until a new Republican Party emerged to take control in 1896, marked the reestablishment of governmental control by the older, landed local elites and their lawyers. Their triumphal return was dramatized in the theater of the constitutional convention of 1872. The Democrats swept the elections of 1870, and when the legislature of 1871 promptly submitted a proposal for a constitutional convention, it was approved by the voters. In October that year, of the seventy-eight delegates elected to the convention, only twelve were Republicans. The convention that met in Charleston on January 16, 1872, was presided over by Samuel Price, the former lieutenant governor of Confederate Virginia, a successful land speculator, and a prominent lawyer. Chairing all of the important committees were former Confederates, among them Charles J. Faulkner, a former U.S. minister to France who was arrested by the federal authorities for his secession sympathies and subsequently served at Stonewall Jackson's side; Benjamin Wilson Jr., a future congressman; and Samuel Woods, a future state supreme court justice. In attendance also were Okey Johnson, Alpheus Haymond, and Henry Brannon, who later became justices on the West Virginia Supreme Court of Appeals. Most who can be identified were either former Confederates, Copperheads, or states'-rights

Unionists. Not all of the state's citizens were impressed with the convention's work, however, for when the new document was submitted to the voters they ratified it by a slim majority of only 4,567 votes out of 80,121 cast.[4]

The new constitution cast aside the hated township system adopted in the constitution of 1863 and instituted in its place a revised version of the Virginia Constitution of 1851. The old county court system and the magisterial districts were restored, the number of judges on the supreme court of appeals was increased to four, and the other branches of government were established in conformity with the Virginia Constitution of 1851. Efforts by the more strident reactionaries, particularly the former Confederates, to reproduce in spirit and law the institutional life of Virginia and the Old South were rejected by the comparatively more liberal Union Democrats who feared that the voters would reject a constitution that was too reactionary.[5]

Land lawyers were notably absent at the 1861–62 constitutional convention, but that was not the case in 1872. Delegates at the convention included thirty-four lawyers, twenty farmers, seventeen businessmen, five ministers, and one professor. The land title provisions were written by a select committee of lawyers and were approved without debate. Subsequently, critics would claim that the constitution of 1872 was a "lawyers' constitution," which confused the already complicated land and tax policies and facilitated the transfer of land from smallholders to the coal and lumber companies.[6]

Whereas the Republicans held the liberal view that free markets would produce the desired economic transformation of West Virginia, the Bourbon Democrats who replaced them accepted the views of their antebellum forebears that the elites should control government so they could control the economy. Even though the Democratic Party harbored several major political factions, they all exhibited a faith in the railroad as the engine of that hoped-for economic transformation. All of the factions were dominated by land investors and land lawyers, but they were caught on the horns of a dilemma. On the one hand, they desired modernization; on the other, they clung to outdated legal institutions and philosophies that hindered their ability to achieve the very goal they so ardently desired. The 1870s and 1880s were decades of transition in West Virginia's political economy, and while the industrial capitalists were creating the means that would tie the natural resources of the backcountry to the metropolitan financial capitals, the law remained essentially unchanged from its Virginia antecedent. More important, legal thought and culture were still anchored in the natural rights tradition of Virginia law. Therefore, both statute and common law revealed the ambiguity of an economy in transition with the legislature providing tax favors to railroads, while the courts still referred to precedents inherited from a Virginia tradition that favored agricultural over industrial interests.

West Virginians during this period were deeply engaged in a new political struggle for control of the physical as well as ideological landscape in an expanding capitalist economy. On one side stood the older conservative agrarian world of the nineteenth century, and in opposition stood the emerging industrial world of the twentieth century. The industrial world soon vanquished its predecessor, of course, but the ideological contest was not between the Republican and Democratic Parties for both were converts to the development faith. The struggle was fought along philosophical lines defining the role of government in the economy and the legal system that would adjudicate conflicts between competing worldviews.

Because the Democrats favored the more conservative social traditions at the same time as they supported industrial development, there is a tendency to view this apparent contradiction between ideology and action as an expedient lapse in the pursuit of wealth. Although indeed they, like their Republican opponents, advocated a laissez-faire approach to economic development, our understanding of the philosophical basis for this view often is unclear. The prominent legal scholar James Willard Hurst claimed that the general understanding of laissez-faire actually is a misreading of nineteenth-century attitudes toward business, public policy, and especially the law. According to Hurst, the cornerstone of public policy in the nineteenth century was the assumption that human beings are by nature creative, and therefore society should provide a broad allowance for the exercise of human action. Since a central principle of the American legal order is that the law exists for the benefit of the people, rather than the people for the benefit of the law, citizens should possess the maximum liberty in which to conduct their actions. Therefore, nineteenth-century Americans believed that "the legal order should protect and promote the release of individual creative energy to the greatest extent" possible by ensuring the individual's freedom from arbitrary public or private interference. Given the historical relationship between abundant opportunity and scarcity of capital in early America, Hurst asserted, Americans developed a faith in the productive capacities of a people free to pursue their economic goals. Laissez-faire, or limiting the state's power to intervene, was not the central idea defining the political economy, Hurst asserted, but rather the "release of individual creative energy." In cases in which legal regulation or compulsion might promote the greater release of these creative energies and allow autonomy for private decision making, "we had no hesitancy in making affirmative use of law."[7]

Hurst accepted the idea, expressed by Alexis de Tocqueville and other observers of early America, that Americans were essentially economic creatures. Business wanted the law to legitimize this social philosophy. In part the intention was, of course, to rid business of government-imposed restrictions, but merely to be let alone was not really the central desire of entrepreneurs; they wanted the positive prestige of having the sanction of the state, Hurst observed.[8]

Investment placed a heavy demand on capital, and as production improved, technology became increasingly more expensive. Like their counterparts studied by Hurst in his now classic study of the lumber industry in Wisconsin, West Virginia lumbermen also demanded that the law help them overcome their lack of capital so they could develop the state's resources. Transportation presented perhaps the greatest problem. The improvement of streams and the construction of railroads required the mobilization of capital on a scale that individuals could not accomplish on their own. Therefore, corporations were granted privileges to dam streams or change their flow, which required legal permission, and without the special power of eminent domain railroads were vulnerable to the recalcitrant landowner who refused to sell a right-of-way. State legislators and judges thus were called on to exercise considerable power even though they had little experience in economic regulation and lacked a civil service to provide enforcement.

Their response fits Hurst's model in that both entrepreneurs and legislators saw economic opportunities in abundance but lacked the capital to exploit them. Therefore, government encouraged economic growth by protecting entrepreneurs from some of the perils of doing business because the public generally would benefit. Hence West Virginia regulations and laws provided a generous delegation of power to private decision makers, but the official machinery for enforcing the regulations governing corporate franchises in the public's interest was dramatic in its absence. West Virginia was not exceptional in this regard, for as Hurst has observed about lumbering in Wisconsin, "Implementation was left to the zeal and means of those private individuals affected, and to whom the law offered no support beyond their ability to bear the time and cost of litigation."[9]

Direct public indebtedness to sponsor business projects was unconstitutional in West Virginia, as it was in Virginia and Wisconsin, but that did not stop the state from providing indirect subsidies to major industries such as railroads. Public subsidy to improve water transportation for lumber was never undertaken in West Virginia, especially in comparison with the public assistance provided to railroads. The lumber industry during this period developed no giant corporations that could compare with the railroads, and so its ability to exert political power was comparatively limited. It was through indirect stimulus that the law promoted investment in the lumber industry, which conformed to the principal theme of nineteenth-century policy.[10]

The desire to encourage industrial development in the nineteenth century by releasing individual initiative from state interference and the view that this served rather than exploited the public are amply illustrated by the privileges granted to entrepreneurs by West Virginia legislators. Although mill-dam and timber-boom operators were granted permission to construct dams across streams, for example, they were not permitted to build them in waters navigated by steamboats or to build them in such a way as to block the streams used by other logging companies. Similarly, the legislature granted mill and boom companies the power under eminent domain to condemn land that was needed to operate their businesses. Nevertheless, the thrust of these public franchises, given the government's inability to enforce them, was to bolster the development of business by placing industrial organizations in a much stronger legal position relative to traditional users of the streams. The same laws regarding condemnation under eminent domain pertained to a range of industries in addition to timber, including the railroads, quarries, mills, salt wells, and limekilns.[11]

Similarly, public support for the timber industry is evidenced in the protection granted to companies from financial losses caused by the theft of logs being transported downstream to booms. The state required that each company file a brand with the clerk of the county court, and logs bearing the company's mark were admissible as evidence of ownership. If logs washed up on someone else's land, the company was given sixty days to remove them; to disturb them during this period was a misdemeanor. To steal a branded log worth $10 or more was grand larceny punishable by one to five years in prison.[12]

James Willard Hurst provided a framework for analysis of the law and economic change that has resulted in a discourse among historians and legal scholars critiquing the nineteenth-century view of law and the economy. Modern critics turned the tables, claiming that far from taking a hands-off approach to the economy, government and the law sided with business to exploit the people. This same critique is embedded in the revisionist historians' view that far from the triumphant march of inevitable industrial progress, the history of West Virginia, much like the history of America itself, is marked by its exploitation at the hands of absentee corporations and local elites.[13] Individualism, scarce labor, and even scarcer capital contributed to an economic environment that allowed the market to assume too great a role in social choices, according to Hurst. At the same time, weak government agencies permitted expedient ad hoc choices to flourish. Judges of the period shared the same biases as the legislators regarding economic development and therefore validated laws that stimulated an ethic of short-term private gain at the expense of long-term public interest.[14]

In the 1960s and 1970s reform-minded legal historians, led by Morton J. Horwitz, took Hurst's critique a step further by arguing that nineteenth-century law was deliberately altered to accommodate emerging industrial interests. According to this interpretation, judges abandoned the rule of "strict liability," which had prevailed until then, and replaced it with a lax standard for negligence. Rejecting Hurst's cautious interpretation, reform scholars of the period, Lawrence Friedman in particular, argued that the courts were actually involved in a "conspiracy" not only to provide economic advantages to the industrialists but to immunize the corporations from damages arising out of civil cases. Horwitz also claimed that industry was protected from liabilities for damages generated by its actions, which allowed industry eventually to "overwhelm the weak and relatively powerless segments of the American economy." The larger problem lies in the immorality of providing what Horwitz called a legal subsidy to business by ignoring the rights of individual victims of serious accidents by depriving them of just compensation for their injuries. Therefore, "subsidizing" enterprise is a "ruthless" quality inherent in nineteenth-century negligence law, and the law is seen as an "engine of oppression."[15]

As might be expected, a robust critical scholarship has challenged the subsidy thesis on empirical grounds and for its overemphasis on the New England states.[16] Whatever the case elsewhere in America, this definitely was not the way courts behaved in nineteenth-century Virginia, dominated as it was by conservatives who wanted a common law grounded in custom and tradition rather than science or economics. The roots of this tradition reached deep into the colonial period.[17] Local gentry and justices of the peace maintained their power in Virginia, and the law continued to be a profession practiced in county courthouses before local juries who made decisions based on common law and natural rights philosophy. The system required that government be limited and decentralized and did not sanction using the law as a lever to reform government, society, or the economy.[18]

This preference for the common law and local government, a style characterized as "country over court," evolved in a society dominated by planters who, since the colonial period, confronted periodic debt problems. In this society, the common law practiced by local lawyers before juries made up of their neighbors was considered the "shield of liberty" against strong "foreign" government or debtors suing to take away the farmers' land. Juries of farmers supported their neighbors in such cases because they believed that retention of the land was a more fundamental right than a merchant's right to collect on a debt. Thus in Virginia the county government was ruled by a local gentry elite who served in the state legislature to protect local interests.[19]

Judges of the Virginia Supreme Court of Appeals buttressed this system by rejecting attempts to break down the power of the local courts to foster industrial development, and time and again they interpreted the law in favor of the agrarian landowners in contests with capitalists. In Virginia, the gentry elites dominated government to ensure that political power remained at the county level.[20] West Virginia retained this decentralized, static approach to government and the law when it emerged as a separate state in 1863. One important point of difference between the new state and its eastern relative was that nearly everybody in West Virginia wanted internal improvements, yet they were much more ambivalent than Virginians about how the costs should be allocated. West Virginia subsidized industry through special privileges and tax breaks, but the courts proved resistant because of the legal tradition on which decisions were based. In a transition of personnel and judicial philosophy that has not been duplicated since, the West Virginia Supreme Court of Appeals experienced a "legal revolution" in 1889–90. Resistance to industrial development evaporated on the high court as a generation of judges who adhered to Virginia traditions was replaced by a new generation reflecting a modern, positivist legal philosophy.

The change in approach to industrial development from the Old Court to the New Court was so dramatic as to constitute a watershed event. After 1890 the court abandoned the traditional strict liability principle favoring agrarian over industrial users of the land and adopted an approach that accepted multiple economic uses for the land. The timing of this pivotal redirection is explained in part by the rapid influx of capital into railroad, timber, and coal development. The older system was incapable of withstanding this deluge of capital, which accentuated the inadequacies of the traditional approach and then dissolved it. In the late nineteenth century, lawyers and judges still rode the circuit in West Virginia's rural, isolated countryside, except for the approximately one-third of the state represented by the old settled town and farm areas.

The problems with the legal system were myriad and are exemplified by the conditions of work facing judges on the supreme court of appeals. Composed of four judges, the court frequently deadlocked on decisions. Salaries were totally inadequate, in fact the lowest in the nation, even while the business of the court accelerated dramatically. Nor were there any intermediate courts between the circuits and the supreme court. Law libraries were poor or nonexistent, and judges labored on their own without secretaries, stenographers, or clerks. The supreme court rotated between the state's three grand divisions represented by Charleston, Wheeling, and Charles Town. Judges and lawyers often traveled together between county courthouses, law books in their knapsacks. Because lawsuits had to be heard in the division of origin, plaintiffs had only one opportunity during the year to file a case. Moreover, the system for announcing decisions was so inadequate that lawyers read the newspapers from one of the cities to learn the disposition of their cases. Even though the court decided many contested elections, circuit and supreme court judges themselves were generally active politicians.[21]

These demoralizing conditions made the upgrading and professionalization of the law problematical at best and suggest why the legal system was so ineffectual in controlling the dynamic forces of industrial capitalism at the turn of the century. Nor was there any real hope among "progressive" lawyers, if their lamentations at bar meetings are accurate indicators, that sufficient public will existed to see this weak, decentralized, and grossly underfunded system changed.

The West Virginia Supreme Court of Appeals has gone through several distinct political transitions since statehood. The first court of the 1860s was composed of statehood leaders, men who had been active in the movement and could be depended on to defend the new state from its Virginia enemies. These four judges (Ralph L. Berkshire, William A. Harrison, Edwin Maxwell, and James H. Brown), like those who directed separation from Virginia and the drive for separate statehood, were Republicans who identified with the Union rather than the Confederacy. Three of the four were active at the statehood conventions, and three of them were residents of the more radical northern section of the state. Not surprisingly, the major issues confronting them involved postwar Reconstruction and continuing sectional animosities. The Unionist court lasted a surprisingly short time, however. In 1870 the Democrats were swept into power, and in 1872 they rewrote the

Table 4. Justices of the Supreme Court of Appeals, 1863–1930

Name	Birth–Death	Political Party	Service on Court
Old Court			
Ralph L. Berkshire	1816–1902	Republican	1863–66, 1869–72
William A. Harrison	1795–1870	Republican	1863–68
James H. Brown	1818–1900	Republican	1863–70
Edwin Maxwell	1825–1903	Republican	1867–72
Charles P. T. Moore	1831–1904	Democrat	1871–81
John S. Hoffman	1821–77	Democrat	1873–75
James Paull	1818–75	Democrat	1873–75
Alpheus F. Haymond	1823–93	Democrat	1873–82
Matthew Edmiston	1814–87	Democrat	1876
Thomas H. Green	1820–89	Democrat	1876–89
Okey Johnson	1834–1903	Democrat	1877–88
James F. Patton	1843–82	Democrat	1881–82
Adam C. Snyder	1834–96	Democrat	1882–90
Samuel Woods	1822–97	Democrat	1883–88
New Court			
Henry Brannon	1837–1914	Democrat/Republican	1889–1912
John English	1831–1916	Democrat	1889–1900
Daniel B. Lucas	1836–1909	Democrat	1890–92
Homer A. Holt	1831–98	Democrat	1890–96
Marmaduke H. Dent	1849–1909	Democrat	1893–1904
Henry C. McWhorter	1836–1913	Republican	1897–1908
George Poffenbarger	1861–1951	Republican	1901–22
Warren Miller	1848–1920	Republican	1903–4
Frank Cox	1862–1940	Republican	1905–7
Joseph M. Sanders	1866–1927	Republican	1905–7
William N. Miller	1855–1928	Republican	1907–28
Ira E. Robinson	1869–1951	Republican	1907–15
L. Judson Williams	1856–1921	Republican	1909–20
Charles W. Lynch	1851–1932	Republican	1913–21
John W. Mason	1842–1917	Republican	1915–16
Harold A. Ritz	1873–1948	Republican	1917–22
Frank Lively	1864–1947	Republican	1921–32
James A. Meredith	1875–1982	Republican	1922–24
William H. McGinnis	1855–1930	Democrat	1923–24
M. O. Litz	1874–1955	Republican	1923–36
John H. Hatcher	1875–1950	Republican	1924–40
Homer B. Woods	1869–1941	Republican	1925–36
Haymond Maxwell	1879–1958	Republican	1928–40

Source: Holmes, *West Virginia Blue Book*, 1989, 451–52.

Old Court: Justices of the West Virginia Supreme Court of Appeals, 1863–90.
(West Virginia and Regional History Collection, West Virginia University Libraries)

constitution. The new members who took seats on the court overwhelmingly were men who had supported secession. At least eight of the sixteen judges who served between 1870 and the end of the century had served in the Confederate army (John S. Hoffman, Alpheus F. Haymond, Thomas H. Green, James F. Patton, Adam C. Snyder, Samuel Woods, Daniel B. Lucas, and Homer A. Holt), and three of them were Union conservatives. Five judges (Haymond, Matthew Edmiston, Okey Johnson, Woods, and Holt) had been delegates to the constitutional convention of 1872. With remarkably few exceptions, the judges throughout the period between 1863 and 1930, half of the state's history, were active politicians before ascending the bench. Fifteen of the thirty-seven judges during this period were political appointees who subsequently were elected to the post. Eleven resigned before their terms expired, and another five failed to be reelected. A very high turnover rate of 43 percent can be accounted for by the embarrassingly low pay, demoralizing conditions, and lack of respect shown to judges by the other members of the profession (see Table 4).[22]

The emergence of large corporations in West Virginia produced social and economic problems that forced the old system into bankruptcy. The New Court of 1889–90 finally made a complete break with Virginia legal tradition and reinterpreted the law to favor, rather than hinder, industrial development. A major study of nuisance cases by legal scholar Jeff L. Lewin concludes that, until the Civil War, American courts staunchly supported the legal rule of *sic utere tuo ut alienum non laedas* (so use your own as not to injure that of another) in cases that involved conflicts of property rights emanating from industrial nuisances. Rejecting Horwitz's application of the subsidy thesis to the early decades of the nineteenth century, Lewin argues that American jurists generally viewed property as a "natural right," therefore property owners should enjoy legal protection against any interference with the use of their property. This reasoning, of course, protected a status quo dominated by agricultural interests, which represented the overwhelming majority of Americans in the early nineteenth century. Over the course of the nineteenth century, however, industrial growth forced judges to shift away from natural rights and to adopt a more dynamic approach to nuisances such as smoke, noise, pollution, and other damages created by industry.[23]

Legal history evolved differently in Virginia, however. Throughout the nineteenth century the Virginia Supreme Court adhered to a "static" theory of property rights which focused on maintaining the rights of agricultural plaintiffs in disputes with industrial defendants. Early West Virginia nuisance decisions rendered by the supreme court of appeals generally conformed with Virginia legal tradition by upholding the plaintiffs' right to be free of interference in the enjoyment of their property.[24] In the 1873 case of *Beaty* v. *Baltimore & O. R.R.*, the first important nuisance decision to come before the West Virginia Supreme Court of Appeals, the court upheld the claim against the B&O for damages caused by the flooding of surface water that resulted from the inadequate maintenance of a railroad culvert. The decision was in strict accordance with the principle of *sic utere tuo* and rejected the negligence-based theory of nuisance liability by declaring that "a railroad may be properly constructed for its own purposes, but not so constructed as to prevent injury to the land of a neighboring proprietor."[25]

After 1890, the supreme court of appeals judges abandoned the static view of their Virginia-trained forebears and, to the great relief of business and government leaders, adopted a dynamic theory that recognized the economic use of property for commercial and industrial enterprise as well as for agriculture.[26] The significance of this transformation of nuisance law became readily apparent to farmers, who represented about two-thirds of

New Court: Justices of the West Virginia Supreme Court of Appeals, 1889–1909.
(West Virginia and Regional History Collection, West Virginia University Libraries)

the population in 1890. For them the new approach was revealed in the way
jurists applied the law in fencing cases, in assessing damage liability for
livestock killed by locomotives, and in cases involving fires ignited by sparks
from locomotives or other steam engines. Whether Horwitz's subsidy thesis
applies to American industrialization in the nineteenth century or not, it is
clear that the strategic support provided by the West Virginia Supreme
Court constituted a subsidy for industry in the state.

In Virginia, agriculture continued to enjoy legislative and judicial preference, but in West Virginia the court increasingly gave priority to industrial
developers. The *Virginia Code* required railroads to protect livestock by
fencing in the right-of-way.[27] In 1903, in *Sanger v. Chesapeake & Ohio Ry.
Co.*, the Virginia high court went even further to declare that "a railroad
company is liable to the owner of stock killed or injured on its track by one
of its trains, although he owned no land either at the point where the stock
was killed or injured, or at the point where the stock came upon the track,
though the only negligence alleged was the failure of the company to fence

its track as required."[28] This was a far more sweeping protection of the farmers' property than in West Virginia, where aggrieved farmers were forced to prove that the railroad was negligent in operating its equipment before they could secure damages. Moreover, the West Virginia Supreme Court of Appeals consistently placed the burden of proof squarely on the shoulders of the plaintiff.[29] In 1916, the court ruled that "in order to charge a railway company with damages for killing stock straying upon its tracks, negligence on the part of the company must appear, and the burden of showing it rests upon the plaintiff."[30] Nor was it necessary in West Virginia for the railroads to fence their right-of-way to prevent livestock from straying onto the tracks, unless required to do so by the terms of its charter or by statutory enactment.[31] While the railroads were bound to take "ordinary" precautions to avoid injury to trespassing animals, they were not required to maintain such a "rigid observation" as to "discover" livestock on the track.[32] The logical progression of this reasoning culminated in 1919 when the state enacted legislation "making it unlawful for horses, cattle, etc., to run at large on a railroad right of way, and fixing a penalty on the owner if injury to property results therefrom."[33]

An ironically amusing article published in an 1894 issue of the *West Virginia Law Quarterly* related a story, which undoubtedly struck a resonant cord among its readers, about a cow that wore a bell having been run over and killed on the railroad and the owner having brought suit against the railroad company for damages. It was proven that the driver blew the whistle loudly and tried to frighten the cow off the track. The farmer's lawyer, however, proved that the cow rang her bell and tried to frighten the engine off the track, convincing the jury to decide in the farmer's favor.[34]

Steam-powered locomotives were notorious for showering the country-side with sparks from their boilers, and hot coals often fell out of their cinderboxes, setting fire to field and forest. Ambiguities in the Virginia law were settled in favor of farmers by the Featherstone Act of 1908 and interpreted to mean that a railroad was liable for damages from fires occasioned by sparks or coals beyond the railroad's right-of-way onto the plaintiff's property. The constitutionality of the act was reaffirmed as late as 1932, when the Virginia court ruled that a railroad was liable for damages resulting from "fire caused by sparks from locomotives, regardless of whether it was negligent."[35]

In dramatic contrast, West Virginia law on the question of fire liability evolved in precisely the opposite direction, toward protecting the railroads from suits brought by farmers. The West Virginia Supreme Court ruled in

1911, for example, that "in absence of its negligence, a railroad company is not liable for injury to property contiguous to its line from fire starting from sparks from its locomotive." The railroad was, however, required to take ordinary precautions to prevent property damage, such as equipping locomotives with spark arresters.[36]

West Virginia followed a widespread practice among states in the nineteenth century, particularly in the North and West, in providing various forms of economic assistance to the railroads. But the New Court was so bold in reversing the strict liability standard in nuisance and negligence cases that its decisions can only be interpreted as the judicial subsidization of industry to the disadvantage of other segments of society. Even California, uniformly regarded as a state virtually under the legislative control of the railroads during the late nineteenth century, provided more protection to farmers by requiring railroads to fence off their tracks and to pay for livestock destroyed for lack of a proper fence. The California Supreme Court not only gave effect to this law, but in suits brought by farmers against the railroads for fire damage to their property, the California court ruled in favor of the farmer in nearly all important decisions. Like their Virginia counterparts, California Supreme Court judges ruled that there was no such thing as a steam locomotive that would not produce sparks, and therefore "emission of such sparks afforded 'prima facie proof' of negligence on the railroad's part."[37] Although a comprehensive examination of the propensities of judges to subsidize industry has not been completed for all of the states, the fact that the California Supreme Court recognized a strict liability standard in similar cases of negligence involving railroads and farmers provides some measure of how exceptional the new generation sitting on the supreme court of appeals was in favoring industrial users of property.

In addition to changes in the legal relations to the land, the New Court redefined long-accepted principles regarding the use of streams. The failure of natural rights theories to resolve the tensions created by industrial uses of the land prompted the New Court to adopt a "reasonable use" rule recognizing the rights of both agriculture and industry in nuisance disputes. This approach focused on how property was used on a "scale of reasonableness" defined by the circumstances. If the court determined that plaintiffs contributed to the damage, for example, then their "contributory negligence" shifted some of the absolute liability away from defendants who acted "reasonably." In effect, the court adopted the concept that industry and agriculture represented competing interests, although both had a right to the enjoyment of their property.[38]

This interpretation fit into the broader philosophical boundaries of "legal positivism," which replaced the "natural rights" focus of the court at the turn of the century and substituted a utilitarian criterion quantified by a kind of social cost-benefits analysis to determine what was in the public interest. Thus the intentional invasion of another's right to the use and enjoyment of property was defined as "unreasonable" unless the resultant public good outweighed the gravity of the harm. This was a radical departure from traditional reasoning. Whereas natural rights rested on a foundation of normative, universal principles, legal positivism assumed that costs and benefits were related and should be weighed quantitatively to determine what was in the public's interest.[39]

In addition to the multitude of railroad cases that passed through the supreme court of appeals during the industrial transition, it also heard several cases related to logging and boom companies. These cases demonstrate the dynamic approach taken by the judges in conflicts over industrial activity. The reasonable use rule applied by the New Court was most often associated with cases involving riparian rights and stream flow. Perhaps the most important precedent-setting case heard by the court during the transition was *Gaston* v. *Mace*, which established the legal rights of the lumber interests to use nonnavigable mountain streams. The central issue of this case pivoted around the question of whether the common law interpretation of navigable streams as public highways was applicable to nonnavigable streams in the backcounties where the big timber was located. In *Gaston* v. *Mace* the court simply altered the definition of a public highway as the term applied to watercourses.

The case itself involved the owner of a mill dam on Stone Coal Creek, Lewis County, who sought damages for the destruction of his waterpowered mill and dam by logs driven downstream in November 1884. The defendants claimed that the stream was navigable and that they therefore had a right to float timber on it, but the plaintiff had obstructed the stream with his mill dam by refusing to construct a sluice. The jury rejected the mill owner's claim for damages in July 1885 and sided with the defendants.[40]

Arguing his case before the supreme court of appeals, the mill owner claimed that he had prior rights to the use of his mill and dam because it had been in continuous operation since 1818, on a stream that was not navigable except in the occurrence of floods from rain or melting snow. The plaintiff argued for his common law right to continue using his property without interference and asked that the defendants be held to strict liability for damages to the mill. The circuit judge determined otherwise, however, and emphasized to the jury that the real issue was whether the stream was navigable and whether a dam or "getting the products of the country to market" was more beneficial to society.[41]

The high court affirmed the lower court's verdict but rejected the argument that the stream's navigability was the central issue, declaring that even though the stream was *not* navigable, it was a "floatable" stream. The court held that the rights of the public and riparian property owners in such a stream was governed by "reasonable use." The New Court declared that the true test to be applied in such cases was not whether a stream was navigable but whether it was capable of floating vessels, rafts, or logs for purposes of commerce.[42]

Traditional users of watercourses, who had always relied on a natural rights defense, could take little hope from the court's reasoning that time alone was no determinant of riparian rights. The plaintiff's dam, constructed without a sluice and for most of the nineteenth century regarded as a benefit to society, was now deemed a public nuisance because it did not accommodate the industrial use of the stream.[43] The supreme court affirmed the circuit court's ruling but took the opportunity to move the argument beyond traditional terms by implementing a more dynamic theory of the law's role in shaping society, one that directly benefited industry over agriculture.

The struggle for dominance between the agrarian and industrial worlds played out during the transition is personified in the lives and decisions of two judges on the New Court during the 1890s, Marmaduke H. Dent and Henry Brannon. The legal historian John Phillip Reid has observed that the West Virginia Supreme Court of Appeals was shaped by neither a strong chief nor an outstanding scholar but rather came of age during the industrial transition while Judges Dent and Brannon debated "the important legal questions of their day and, by debating them, defined them." Representing two competing economic and legal philosophies, they made the law "reflect the sociological attitudes of the West Virginia in which they lived." Strong and opinionated judges, Dent defended the natural rights–common law Virginia tradition embedded in the philosophy of the Old Court, while Brannon was one of the principal architects of the legal positivism embraced by the New Court. Their struggle can be read in their opinions, in which one usually dissented from the other, in cases where "competing traditions struggled to control the future direction of West Virginia law."[44]

Marmaduke H. Dent's ancestors were among the first families to settle in Monongalia County. He grew up relatively poor. His father, Marshall Mortimer Dent (born in 1828), was not overly successful in his attempts to make a living at the Monongalia bar, but he was active in politics, and between 1856 and 1862 he edited the *Virginia Weekly Star*, which supported the Douglas Democrats. In 1861 he was elected a delegate to the Richmond convention that considered Virginia's secession from the Union and voted with the antisecessionists. Born April 18, 1849, Marmaduke Dent was only thirteen when West Virginia separated from Virginia and fifteen when the Civil War ended. In 1867 he enrolled in the first class at newly established West Virginia University, receiving the university's first B.A. degree in 1870 and its first M.A. in 1873. Without the funds to attend law school or to pay a law office preceptor, he became a teacher and then Taylor County deputy clerk and notary public to earn a living while he read law. Finally, in 1875 he was admitted to the bar and established an office in Grafton, the Taylor County seat.[45] There is little doubt that Dent's family background and the fact that Grafton was a division headquarters of the B&O Railroad and the home of the lawyer-novelist Melville Davisson Post shaped his view of the law and society. Post dubbed this era in West Virginia's legal history as the "age of the able rogue," a caricature he epitomized in the fictional lawyer Randolph Mason in the 1896 novel *The Strange Schemes of Randolph Mason*. Although his talents as a novelist were limited, Post's modestly popular writing portrayed the West Virginia lawyer of the period as a man with "no sense of moral obligation" although learned in the law, a legal misanthrope who took cases as mere problems requiring a solution without regard for matters of equity or common justice.

Regardless of whether this general characterization of West Virginia lawyers was accurate, it most definitely was not applicable to Marmaduke Dent. Little is known about the first twenty years of his career in the law, but Dent seems to have developed a reputation as a lawyer for the "common man," a role that suited him psychologically. In Republican Taylor County he ran for prosecutor in 1876 on the Democratic ticket and lost, then suffered the same fate in his bid for a seat in the legislature in 1884. He did successfully serve in the city council, as town clerk, and on the county school board but held no major public post until 1893. Although his political career was studded with failures to this point, his time had come in 1892. That year he became a candidate for the supreme court of appeals on the Democratic-People's Party fusion ticket and won handily in a Democratic year. At age forty-five Dent began his term on the court, which lasted from January 1, 1893, to December 31, 1904.[46]

In a day when most lawyers in West Virginia regarded being a lawyer for the railroad as the path to professional security, Marmaduke Dent was intellectually incapable of arguing the case for big business. At the 1888 meeting of the West Virginia Bar Association, Dent offered two resolutions that openly declared war on the railroads. The first resolution called on the association to memorialize Congress to pass a law requiring that "every railroad corporation shall be deemed to be a resident of each State through which it passes, or in which it does business." Dent spoke in favor of the resolution, reminding members that "any railroad corporation can come into the State of West Virginia and take our lands from us under this act of eminent domain, rob us of our property, and when we dare to bring them into our courts of justice they tell us they are non-residents . . . and not subject to the jurisdiction of the courts of West Virginia." The railroads also "insulted" the circuit judges by immediately moving their cases to federal court in Parkersburg, claiming that they could not get a fair hearing in local courts. This was a "great wrong," Dent declared, and the bar association should take a stand against the practice.[47]

The second resolution proposed that the association memorialize the state legislature to write into the statutes that no "foreign corporation" could do business in West Virginia until it agreed in writing to accept the jurisdiction of the state's courts, and any breach of the contract would result in the forfeiture of its rights to operate in the state. To illustrate why he proposed these resolutions, Dent related a story to the assembly that not only reflects his view of railroads and the B&O's attitude toward Dent himself but also explains one important influence in his decision making while on the court:

> I had a case against a railroad company.—They brought some sixty-five great big engines right in front of my house that blew over twelve hundred bushels of cinders right in front of my house. I restrained them from doing that. They certified my case to Parkersburg. . . . When they found they could not blow in front of my house, they went to some poor little Irish woman and blew out those engines within forty feet of her house. They blew into everything she had, every crack of the house. I had them arrested eighteen times; I had them fined eighteen hundred dollars; they appealed in every case—eighteen times. Then they claimed to be non-residents of the State and got an injunction from the court and still blew before this woman's house. She brought a little suit before a justice of the peace, and the railroad company said if necessary they would take that to Parkersburg. . . . The first thing I knew, they got a certiorari and took our little case a hundred miles away, and every time you ride to that place you have to pay a tax to them before you get there to stop them from blowing.

I got her an injunction and stopped them from blowing, and away went that case out of that court.

Apparently the Bar Association was not overly interested in tackling the issue, however, for both resolutions were referred to the Committee on Judicial Administration and Legal Reform, which consigned them to a quiet death.[48]

If Marmaduke Dent was the railroad's nemesis, his chief antagonist on the court, Henry Brannon, was not only a railroad lawyer, he was also a railroad owner. Henry Brannon belonged to one of nine families, intertwined by marriage, that constituted nineteenth-century West Virginia's elite.[49] Henry Brannon was born on November 26, 1837, in Winchester, Virginia, but was raised on a farm in Lewis County under vastly different circumstances than Marmaduke Dent. As a boy he had attended a school in Weston, Lewis County, taught by Homer A. Holt, then recently graduated from the University of Virginia, who subsequently served as a judge on the supreme court of appeals with his former pupil. Brannon attended Winchester Academy, graduated from the University of Virginia, became a member of the Lewis County bar at age twenty-one, and a year later was elected the county's prosecuting attorney. In 1870–71 he served in the West Virginia House of Delegates, in 1880 was elected judge for the eleventh circuit, and in 1889 was elected to the first of three full terms (twenty-four years) on the supreme court of appeals. A biographer of the court observed that among his peers Brannon's reputation as a lawyer was unsurpassed in the state. In politics Judge Brannon was associated with the Democratic Party, but in 1896 he was elected to the court as a Republican.[50] Brannon also engaged in business as president of the Weston and West Fork Railroad Company, was an organizer of the Clarksburg, Weston & Glenville Railroad, and, among other business ventures, was partner in a wholesale supply firm even while sitting on the high court.[51]

Siding with Brannon on the same court was his former teacher and another railroad lawyer, Homer A. Holt. Holt also belonged to one of West Virginia's elite families. Before assuming his seat on the court in 1890, Holt speculated extensively in timber and coal lands, eventually producing a "considerable estate." The same year he was appointed to the court, Holt was engaged in negotiations with the C&O to run a branch line into his Greenbrier County lands. Therefore, Judge Holt also appreciated the economic significance of the railroad, and although it would be unfair to claim that his decisions were motivated by a desire for personal economic gain, it is clear that he had much to gain in making industrial investments secure before the law. Little is known about Judge John W. English, who also served on the New Court between 1888 and 1900, but he usually sided with Brannon and Holt to establish a majority on the four-man court which favored the railroads in cases that came before that body.[52]

In deliberating railroad cases, Judge Dent constituted a minority of one. While he concentrated on the powerlessness of individuals in conflicts with powerful corporations, Judge Brannon and his like-minded colleagues focused on the public benefits generated by railroads in opening West Virginia for economic development. In the face of the awesome responsibilities these corporations confronted, Brannon viewed their enterprise as heroic.[53] Not until 1897 did Judge Dent gain an opportunity to write a majority opinion on a railroad case.

The differences between these two jurists is easily detected in their opinions in cases in which competing traditions struggled for domain in West Virginia law. Judge Dent adhered to the theory that a judge must take "justice" into consideration when deciding a case. Dissenting from an opinion favoring a railroad, Dent argued, "In this case there is a powerful and wealthy corporation on the one hand . . . and a bereaved widow and fatherless children on the other, and my deep sympathies for the appeals of the helpless and needy may cause me to hold the scales of justice unequally between them. . . . An approving conscience can be the only arbiter that a judicial officer can recognize in discharging his individual duties."[54]

Judge Brannon, in complete disagreement with this philosophy, believed that conscience was not a guide to good legal decisions. While Brannon sympathized with the suffering, he regarded hardship as one of the risks that accompanied the opportunity to achieve the benefits provided by industrial society, and abstract notions of justice should never take the place of established precedents. For this reason, Brannon's interpretation of the fellow-servant law seems particularly narrow and harsh in its emphasis on the interests of employers. In effect, Brannon believed that the employer's liability to an injured employee should not depend on rank or authority of the employer over the employee but rather on whether the employer personally ordered the worker to act in such a way as to cause him to be injured. Only under this condition was an employer liable for damages to an injured employee.

Whereas Judge Dent balanced the weakness of the poor victim against the power of the wealthy employer, Brannon concerned himself with the economic effect a decision would have on business. Judge Brannon recognized that his position practically guaranteed employers freedom from liability, but, remarkably, he contended that it benefited workers as well as employers; departure from it would "increase the danger to employees themselves, as it inspires diligence and watchfulness to save themselves and co-laborers, as well as their employers. Abandon the rule, and inducement to care is gone."[55]

Undergirding these decisions and at least partly explaining how two judges could examine the same facts and come to such divergent opinions were their philosophies regarding the role of business and government in a free society. Not unexpectedly, Judge Brannon adhered to a version of the laissez-faire philosophy that embraced Social Darwinism. He considered it "inevitable" that some people would be ruined by free competition. Indeed, the evidence was all around: "The dead are found strewn all along the highways of business and commerce. Has it not always been so?" He presumed it would be so in the future as well, for "the law of survival of the fittest has been inexorable. Human intellect, human laws cannot prevent these disasters. The dead and wounded have no right of action from the working of this imperious law."[56]

Judge Dent quietly accepted mortal combat between corporations, but his blood rose to a quick boil when one of the giants stepped on ordinary people. In these cases, Dent was much more willing than Brannon to impose positive duties or government regulation on corporations. There were two theories for the legal treatment of the corporation in the nineteenth century. The first, the "grant theory," dated back to the early part of the century and treated incorporation as a special privilege conferred by the state for public purposes. Under this theory, the corporation was regarded as an "artificial being" created by the legislature with powers limited by the state. Charters were denounced during the Jacksonian period for encouraging bribery, favoritism, and especially monopoly. As a result, a movement away from this theory of the corporation evolved thereafter that favored "free" incorporation laws. By the end of the century the corporate form of organization was regarded not as a special privilege conferred by the state but as a normal "mode of doing business." The new "entity theory" emerged to replace the older view by the 1890s, and with its triumph the corporation was legally viewed as a "natural entity" entitled to the same rights and privileges as other individuals and groups.[57]

Judge Brannon readily accepted the new theory, but Judge Dent continued to think of the corporation in terms of the grant theory. In Dent's view, the state permitted the creation of corporations, thus it was reasonable to assume that the state not only could but should regulate them in the public interest. In a case involving a pedestrian who was struck by a train while walking on the C&O railroad tracks, the other judges held that the railroad company had a right to assume that a trespasser on railroad property would step aside for an oncoming train. Conversely, Judge Dent's dissent argued that whether the man was a "trespasser" was a mere technicality because the railroad was not private property but rather property belonging to a public franchise. The state had authorized the existence of the railroad for the public good, and "the law, in permitting railroad companies to rush their trains through the country at a great rate of speed, requires them to adopt the necessary means to warn trespassers out of their way in time for them to escape death."[58] This was a constant theme in Judge Dent's decisions—that railroads existed by the grace of the public and should be held to a higher standard of responsibility. In another case involving a little girl who was struck and killed on the C&O Railroad tracks, the engineer testified that at six or seven hundred yards he thought she was a "red rooster" because of her red dress. While Brannon argued that the railroad was not "bound to keep an outlook for trespassers on the track," Judge Dent countered that "it can hardly be maintained, at the present time at least, that a railroad company can negligently kill any one on its tracks, whether passenger, employee, stranger, trespasser, adult or child. It holds its tracks for the public good by sufferance of the people, and, though it cannot be hung, electrocuted, or imprisoned, it cannot take human life with impunity."[59]

In cases involving damage suits against railroads Judge Dent was much more likely to follow the Virginia common law–natural rights tradition by requiring the railroad to prove that it was not negligent and to impose positive duties on railroads, an approach that was in striking contrast to the legalistic precedent approach followed by the New Court. For example, in a case concerning damages for cattle killed by a Norfolk and Western locomotive, Judge English declared for the majority that the paramount duty of the railroad was to its passengers, and in freezing weather it was justified in using salt to keep its switches free of ice even though the salt lured cattle onto the tracks and endangered them. In a sharply worded dissent, Judge Dent stated that salt was not the only means available, merely the cheapest. "To say that the use of salt is the only effective mode of freeing frogs and switches from ice and snow in cold weather is to close our eyes to ordinary human experience. But to say that the use of salt is the only effective mode . . . without an additional expense for manual labor and proper lubricants is, no doubt, true. If the company adopt[s] the cheaper of two modes to accomplish the same purpose, it is no more than justice to require it to provide against the increased danger, occasioned by its choice, to the property of others."[60]

Actually, Dent did not attack the privileges of the railroads, such as their limited liability, so much as he sought to eliminate the advantages granted to them over and above ordinary citizens. He believed railroads should be held to a "special standard of care," a rule considered to be his most important contribution to twentieth-century jurisprudence. In the 1898 case of *Couch v. Chesapeake & Ohio*, Dent argued that "the defendant is in the enjoyment of vast public franchises for private gain," and even though it "bestowed great benefits on the public for privileges granted," its primary purpose was to increase the individual wealth of its stockholders. Therefore, in the exercise of its franchise, "the public permits it to rush its heavy trains with immense speed over its track through all portions of the country, but . . . imposes on it the duty of keeping a lookout for unwary and helpless trespassers upon its right of way."[61]

Dent fully acknowledged the importance of the railroad to West Virginia's economy but contended that economics was not the only important public policy issue. While Dent insisted that justice for the average citizen must be protected, Brannon focused on the disadvantages confronted by the railroads in jury trials because of prejudices of local jurors against railroads. This seems to have been a real problem, acknowledged by Dent and other lawyers at meetings of the West Virginia Bar Association. For example, prominent railroad lawyer Zachary Taylor Vinson of Huntington claimed, at the 1902 meeting, that "it is the experience of every lawyer engaged in . . . damage cases against railway corporations, that in State Courts the juries as a rule are partial to the plaintiff and biased against the corporation." Ordinary citizens believed that the corporation was "enormously rich," Vinson declared, and politicians stirred their hostility by claiming that "large aggregations of wealth" resulted from "ill-gotten gains filched from the poor, the farmer and the laboring man." Therefore, "every time a jury gets the opportunity it is nothing but justice that such corporations should be made to refund or give back some of the plunder wrongfully taken from the poor and the weak." Moreover, railroads are thought to be given special privileges, avoid taxes, and farmers believe they are permitted to "run rough shod through their homes and kill their stock for pastime." A major investor in railroad and coal enterprises, Vinson regarded these ideas to be the product of a "strong and insidious current of socialism flowing through the minds and thoughts of the people, poisoning them to the extent of making them believe that it is wrong for one man to be rich and live in luxury while another is borne down by perpetual labor and poverty."[62] In such a setting, Judge Dent's insistence on "justice" for ordinary citizens must have seemed quaint indeed.

That the New Court initiated a revolution in legal philosophy and approach there can be little doubt. Qualitative evidence from the majority opinions in strategic cases confirms it, but measuring whether the judiciary took a historical redirection by subsidizing industry, as contended by Horwitz, requires a quantitative survey of the judicial opinions. To test the applicability of the Horwitz thesis to West Virginia, a longitudinal study of the supreme court of appeals decisions was undertaken involving the three categories of cases used by Horwitz himself, in which the interests of the railroads, farmers, and other landowners were most likely to collide: fire, injury to animals, and personal injury. Results of the survey support the thesis that the supreme court of appeals did indeed "subsidize" industry as represented by the railroads, not only by abandoning the strict liability standard in favor of "reasonable use" but also by the manner in which the rule was imposed in these nuisance cases.

Between 1876 and 1924, a total of seventy-four cases were appealed to the West Virginia Supreme Court of Appeals in which railroads were defendants: thirty-four injury to animals, nine involving fire, and thirty-one involving personal injury. The court ruled in favor of the railroads in forty-three of these cases, or 58.10 percent. Quantitatively this is not an impressive figure, and it indicates a balanced approach in the decisions for and against the railroads. A closer examination, however, demonstrates that in cases in which the court ruled against the railroads, the defendants failed to adhere to even the most rudimentary precautions required to avoid negligence. In fact, negligence was so flagrant that plaintiffs, as now required by law, were successful in the daunting task of proving it.

The most revealing finding from examining these cases was the extent of the acknowledged hostility toward railroads exhibited by circuit court juries, who voted for the plaintiff and against the railroads so often as to constitute "jury nullification" of the law. In effect, jurors, who were ordinary citizens and neighbors of the plaintiffs, continued to adhere to traditional notions of justice and the old common law standard of strict liability. Jurors saw the system stacked in favor of industry, rather than landowners, and they

Table 5. Jury Nullification versus Judicial Subsidization: Cases Appealed to West Virginia Supreme Court of Appeals

	Total Cases	Circuit Juries against Railroad		Supreme Court for Railroad	
		Cases	%	Cases	%
Injury to animals	34	26	76.47	21	61.76
Fire	9	7	77.77	4	44.44
Personal injury	31	20	64.5	18	58.06
Total	74	53	71.62	43	58.10

Source: Compiled from the *Virginia and West Virginia Digest*, vol. 16; *West Virginia Reports*, vols. 15, 39, 41, 68, 69, 70, 76.

rebelled. The numbers prove the point. Circuit court juries sided with the plaintiffs against the railroads in fifty-three of the seventy-four cases, or 72 percent of the time. The percentage was higher when fire and injury to animals were at issue; jurors voted against the railroads in more than 75 percent of these cases.

The New Court subsidized the railroad in robust defensive actions by reversing circuit court decisions in twenty-eight of the forty-three cases, or 65 percent of the total decisions favoring the railroads. In effect, the bourgeois elite advanced a system that local nonelites refused to ratify. Old republican ideas persisted, and local people resisted what they saw as a breach of trust by the new industrial elites, who seemed to be more intent on looking after themselves than the common good (see Table 5).

Case law built up during the industrial transition, therefore, rendered it increasingly difficult for West Virginia's agrarians to protect themselves against railroad and other industrial abuses. The legal preeminence secured by the railroads in West Virginia gave a green light to large-scale investment in natural resource extraction but flashed a danger signal to the farmers who recognized that they were confronted with a direct assault on their traditional rights and legal privileges.

The obituaries of Judges Dent and Brannon indicate the status of the men and their ideas in West Virginia legal history. Brannon was regarded as the ideal West Virginia judge; he was elected to three terms on the court, wrote books on the law, and was considered one of the greatest jurists the state has produced. Dent, in contrast, was described as an inoffensive man with few enemies who lived a clean life, wrote interesting opinions for style if not substance, and failed in his bid for reelection to the court.[63] In its effort to make capital secure, the New Court abandoned the legal philosophy of the Old Court and adopted the perspective of the twentieth-century industrial world. The New Court and the industrializers whose vision it supported regarded Dent's philosophy as a relic of the past and their own as the harbinger of the future. And so it was.

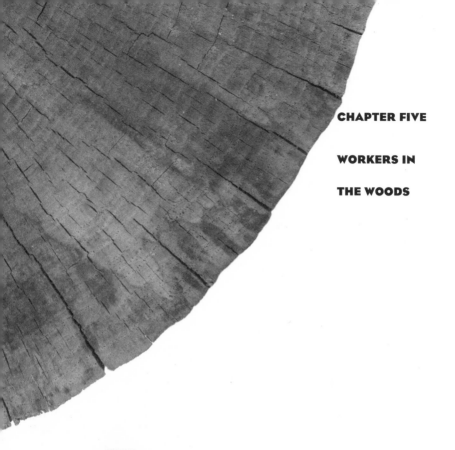

Lumber mill towns were located at strategic nodes in the railroad network that connected the rural lumber supply to the demand in America's growing urban centers. Lumber production in the "machine age" was an integrated process connecting mill and standing timber, and local transportation determined its success. In fact, transportation was the greatest physical obstacle and financial expense confronting timber companies operating in the mountains. Mass production of timber in the mountains awaited the heavy equipment brought in by railroads. Lumbermen had already put this technology to good use in the North and West, and the southern pine industry became completely dependent on railroads and the associated steam equipment.[1] Laying conventional track for standard equipment in the mountains was expensive, labor-intensive, and in the end unsuitable for the terrain. The great demand for timber in the construction of growing population centers of America between 1880 and 1920, however, provided sufficient financial inducement to spawn ingenious adaptations to the needs of mountain logging.

Steam locomotives, reengineered to meet the challenges presented by mountainous terrain, were among the most important of the technological innovations. Three types of steam locomotives were manufactured for use in the mountains. The Shay locomotive was first manufactured by the Lima Machine Company of Lima, Ohio, in 1880. The most widely used engine in West Virginia, the Shay was attractive for its maneuverability and power on steep grades derived from its special gear drive. Two to four wheel "trucks" like those on a freight car, composed of small wheels, were driven by shafts from a cylinder-powered crankshaft on the right side of the locomotive. The shafts were geared to the end of each wheel axle, giving the engine great maneuverability around curves, over bumps, and on rough temporary tracks. Most important, perhaps, was the power of the Shay's direct drive in pulling up steep grades in the mountains. The Climax and Heisler locomotives, two other types of engines used in West Virginia, were rigged with special power trains, but neither was as prevalent in the mountains as the popular Shay engine.[2]

While technological innovation and heavy equipment were prerequisites for logging the big timber of the backcounties, labor was the vital ingredient in the daily operation of the industry. A large work crew had to be assembled for the labor-intensive task of laying tracks in the torturous mountain terrain. Because skill was not as important as it was among the woods crews, a large proportion of the work force was made up of Italian immigrants working ten- and eleven-hour days, six days a week, for a dollar a day. A roadbed had to be laid out by the surveyors who tried to keep the grade at 5 percent, meaning that the grade climbed five feet for every hundred feet of track. Main line railroads consider 2 percent steep, but 5 percent was normal for logging lines, and often they reached 10 percent. The "swampers" cleared the grade of trees and leveled the ground for tracks, adding rock and dirt fill from the nearby mountainside to low spots. The trees along the grade were cut and hewn flat for railroad cross-ties. As the crew progressed, the Shay locomotive, pushing a car of rails, followed behind. Removed and placed by hand, the track was then spiked to the cross-ties, and this process was repeated until the tracks reached the timber to be cut.[3]

When the transportation was laid down, the "improvement" crew built temporary camps for the wood hicks. Logging camps were a distinctive characteristic of the industry's work culture. Buildings in the camp, generally made of temporary rough-hewn lumber or logs cut from the site, were always built near the railroad and a water supply. Great variety existed among logging camps, but the typical camp contained a large bunkhouse with a kitchen, dining room, and lobby downstairs and bunks for the men upstairs. The bunkhouse was designed to sleep and feed between fifty and one hundred woodsmen; sixty-five to seventy men was typical. Other buildings in the camp included the office occupied by the camp boss, another where the cook lived, a blacksmith shop, and a saw filer's shop. A stable sheltered the horses, and there were storage sheds for coal, hay, meat, and other supplies. Another shack might be built for train crews or other special needs. Usually, all of the buildings, and often all the furniture in them, were carved rough hewn from the trees on the site. Supplies for the camp arrived by train once or twice a week.[4]

Logging men demanded the freedom to work when and where they chose, and a very high turnover rate prevailed in the woods camps as men grew tired of one place and left for another. When wood hicks traveled, they walked or rode the log trains from camp to camp. Therefore, a ritual grew among woods workers that was handed down from earlier times in the north woods to new loggers of the Appalachians. "Greenhorns" either quickly adopted these rituals or their tenure as woodsmen was brief. A new man arrived in camp and headed straight for the bunkhouse, where the cook provided him with food. Afterward, he would retire to the lobby, where he waited until the men came in from the woods that evening. Just before the woodsmen came in, he washed his hands in the basin and propped the pan on its side. He kept his hat on his head. He then sat in the corner of the lobby out of the way, and if no one knew him no one spoke. If there was a space available at the table the "cookee," or cook's helper, invited him to sit; if he sat in another fellow's assigned seat, the newcomer was unceremoniously thrown out. No one spoke at the table.

After the meal, the new arrival remained in the lobby until the "lobby hog," whose job was to keep the lobby clean, showed him where to sleep. The woodsmen usually sat talking in small groups, greasing their A. A. Cutter corked boots, or doing other personal chores, until 9:00 P.M., when the cook rang a piece of railroad steel with a hammer for all hands to turn in and douse the lights. Talking after lights out was prohibited, and those who broke the rule risked the ire of co-workers and discharge by the foreman. At 5:00 A.M. the men were rousted from sleep by the cook again applying hammer to steel and to breakfast by another clang at 5:30 A.M. The men returned to the lobby until the foreman called them to the woods, and the cycle of ten- or eleven-hour days, six days a week with Sunday for rest, continued relentlessly, weather and timber permitting. In the 1920s the standard workweek became eight hours a day, five days a week. If the

foreman took notice of the new man who arrived the night before, he was assigned to a crew; if the foreman ignored him, there was no job to offer, and the man set out for the next camp on foot.[5]

Memoirs and oral history accounts confirm this ritual among woodsmen. The reminiscences of a native West Virginian from Upshur County who worked in the woods before World War I, Homer Riggleman, are representative. In his autobiography he wrote that when looking for a job he always planned to show up in a new camp before the men returned from the woods at four or five o'clock for supper. The food served at logging camps was legendary for its quantity and quality; it was part of their payment for work, and the men demanded to be fed well or they left. Riggleman's description of the food supplies brought in twice each week support the stories of the legendary appetites of loggers who worked long and hard in the fresh mountain air. Sugar, flour, and meat were delivered by the barrel twice a week along with stacks of boxes of canned food.[6] Henderson Sharp (born in 1887) recollected in 1983 that in the logging camps "they fed you the best grub. They had everything you wanted: beef twice a day; pork, usually for breakfast; always, biscuits for breakfast, light bread or rolls for dinner and supper."[7] A typical breakfast consisted of hot biscuits, steak, fried eggs, fried potatoes, oatmeal, cake, donuts, prunes or other fruit, and coffee. For dinner the men were served meat, potatoes, vegetables, bread, pie, and cake; supper consisted of more of the same.[8]

It was the foreman's job to ensure good discipline and high morale. All well-run woods camps prohibited the consumption of alcoholic beverages, gambling, fighting, and women. Although women generally were absent from woods camps in West Virginia, there were exceptions. The cook and his wife shared duties at the Meadow River Lumber Company's camp number 2. Both of them were elderly, however.[9] Most oral histories acknowledge that though men gambled, they did so in hiding, that men got drunk off the job site, and that fighting occurred but only infrequently. To break the discipline risked being fired by the foreman. "They kept pretty strict order in the camps back then," remembered Emment Taylor, and Homer Riggleman claimed to have seen only one fight during the eight years he worked in the woods.[10]

Facing page: Moment of relaxation in a woods camp, probably Randolph County, ca. 1900. (West Virginia and Regional History Collection, West Virginia University Libraries)

The old-timers also confirm that the men never took baths; they washed in a basin but took baths only when they went to town or home. Bunks with straw mattresses did not make for healthy conditions either, and the old-timers universally comment on the bedbugs, or "greybacks" as they were called. "I was never in a lumber camp where they didn't have bedbugs but I don't think I ever saw them worse than at this camp. They hibernated in the wintertime, but in the summertime they were out there and ready to work. We'd take gallon cans that applesauce or fruit had come in and would fill them about half full of kerosine. We'd set the bed legs in those buckets of kerosine" to prevent the bedbugs from climbing into the beds. "They were the largest bedbugs I think I ever saw," Riggleman wrote. "I recall one time staying in over Sunday, and out back of the camp the bedbugs sitting up on the end of a log and barking," he claimed in the logger's celebrated hyperbole.[11] Emment Taylor agreed. "Bedbugs! Back in them old camps bedbugs were thick. . . . When you turned the lights off, them suckers would drop off the walls and hit you in the face. . . . We had straw ticks on the beds. I've taken mine off the bed at night and went out and laid under the sugar trees to keep those bedbugs off of me, in the warm summer nights."[12] Bedbugs were joined by lice to torment wood hicks. Rare visits by doctors, crude latrines, drinking water stored in barrels, and a general low standard of sanitation leaves one to wonder why so few woodsmen succumbed to disease.[13]

Most timbermen accepted the rigors of woods life, and instead of grumbling they typically turned the unpleasantries into humorous tall tales to demonstrate the power of their endurance. One native who grew up at Cass reported that "some men claimed they could get to sleep only by turning their underwear inside out and hurrying to fall asleep before the lice got inside again."[14] Old-timers of the Cranberry district, Nicholas County, Pete Hammond, Wilbur Russel, and George Rose, reportedly still got together in 1937 to "spin yarns" about logging in the old days. A sample yarn indicates that West Virginia wood hicks bore a strong resemblance to their lumberjack brethren of the north woods in their penchant for telling tall tales:

The old-timers say that these original Cranberry loggers slept in trees and would eat baled hay if one sprinkled a little whiskey on it. The lumber jacks donned red woolen drawers and double-breasted undershirts when they hit the woods in September and these undergarments were never removed until the snow melted in May and it came time to go down the river on the drive. Bathing in the winter was not only frowned upon but was considered an almost certain way of committing suicide.

These lads had so much freedom and fresh air during the day that they craved companionship at night and slept sixteen to a bunk and one hundred to a room. For this reason it was necessary to bolster the bunk houses with guy wires. Otherwise the roof would have been raised and blown away more than once.

With the exception of a few camp dandies who might on a dull Sunday, run a whetstone over a double-bitted axe, slap a little lye soap into their whiskers and shave in the manner of the great Paul Bunyan, the majority followed the fashion of Samson and groomed beards as thick and lush as a lion's mane. In general shaving was regarded as an effeminate pastime and all those who engaged in it were held as suspicious characters. Some men held shaving in the winter to be pretty nigh as debilitating as the carrying of a handkerchief.

All tobacco in camp, both chewing and smoking, came in one pound plugs and if one weren't man enough to pack 16 ounces around with him, he took his axe and wacked [sic] off a hunk large enough to last until evening. They were mighty chewers of plug, those old shanty boys, and no punk [beginner] considered himself a man until he could spit 15 feet into a head wind and hit a sapling fair in the crotch. The smoking tobacco when inhaled commonly drifted out of the ears in clouds as big as thunderheads.[15]

Braggadocio aside, the potential for serious health problems for men living under these conditions cannot be ignored. In 1900, smallpox broke out in some of the woods camps on Cheat Mountain. The West Virginia Pulp and Paper Company vaccinated its timber workers and prevented strangers from entering the camps to keep the disease under control. Apparently the disease had not been stamped out for in November 1901 smallpox broke out once again. As Thomas Luke, one of the brothers who owned the company, wrote to the general manager, "It must be [a] pretty tough proposition to have smallpox in a camp where men are herded together as they must be in a lumber camp."[16]

Many companies in the southern Appalachians made the camps as portable as possible, either by constructing the buildings so that they could be lifted onto railroad flatcars by the log loader or by converting rolling stock into buildings on wheels. The Parsons Pulp and Lumber Company had both kinds. Camp 22 buildings sat on the ground, but Camp 23 was set on rolling stock except for the barn and blacksmith shop. The bunkhouses, wash car, dining room, kitchen, and storerooms all were mounted on flatcars measuring 10.5 feet by 40 feet. These structures, like their less mobile counterparts, were constructed of the cheapest lumber. The bunk car had walls 9 feet high with a slightly rounded roof covered by tar paper. Each bunk car contained five double bunks sleeping ten men, one wooden table, one wash table with three wash basins, two water pails, and a stove. Nails were driven into the walls to serve as clothes hooks for the occupants, but there was no other furniture. The other cars in this mobile camp, such as the dining car, kitchen car, wash car, and storage car, followed the same general structure with the appropriate adaptations dictated by their functions. Of course, the great advantage of the rolling camps was their mobility, and they saved the time and expense required to break down fixed base units for transport. This was especially true of the kitchen car, which might be combined with the dining car in small camps, where equipment and utensils did not require packing before movement.[17] Their efficiency and mobility prompted lumber companies to begin replacing fixed camps with rolling camps by World War I. For the first time it became possible for the wives and children of woodsmen to join them, although this development came too late in deforestation to put much of a stamp on the industry in West Virginia.

Some of the men worked in the camp itself. The foreman lived and kept an office in the camp. In his domain the foreman was the absolute boss, and no one dared question his authority. He answered only to the company superintendent, and in matters of running the camp, even the superintendent did not challenge the foreman without good cause. Because 80 percent of the cost of production was tied up in labor, the ability of the camp foreman made the difference between profit and loss. The "bull" cook also was an important figure in the camp and the most highly paid member of the woods crew at $3 per day in 1907. The cook earned his wages. He usually rose at 3:30 A.M. to feed the men at 5:30 A.M. and did not quit until after the evening meal. This regimen was followed seven days a week. If the men did not appreciate the cook's food, they might join forces and refuse to leave the lobby for the woods unless the foreman agreed to hire a new one. The cookee had the most difficult job and earned half the cook's salary. As cook's helper, he prepared all of the food, washed dishes, set the tables, kept the kitchen clean, and did anything else required of him in the dining room. The lobby hog also earned his $1.50 a day seven days a week. He awakened the teamsters earlier than the other men, cleaned the stables, and scrubbed the lobby—a difficult job because so many men chewed tobacco. He also carried coal, maintained the fire, and did a host of other jobs. Whereas the cookee was usually a younger man learning his trade, the lobby hog usually was an older man no longer able to work in the woods. The blacksmith made and repaired tools and equipment and kept the horses shod. As a skilled artisan, his pay was second only to the cook's at $2.50 per day, but his life was much less demanding. The woodsmen sharpened their own axes; the saws were sharpened by the saw filer, who earned a wage of $2 per day.[18]

Except for when the rains and snows were heaviest, the woods crews turned out six days a week at 7:00 A.M. The typical work force was divided into several crews. Each crew consisted of a chopper, who cut a notch in the tree to direct its fall, followed by two sawyers, who cut the trees from the opposite side of the notch with a six-foot crosscut saw. Once the tree was on the ground, the chopper marked it in sixteen-foot log lengths. Knot bumpers then cut limbs and knots from the tree trunk with flat axes and threw the slash aside. The tree then was sawed, or bucked, into logs, nosed on one end so it could be skidded over the ground. Then the crew moved on to the next tree. The cutting crew could prepare 225 logs in a good day's work; the sawyers and choppers, being the most skilled, earned $2.00 and the bumpers $1.75. Men who could not cut eight thousand feet a day were soon out of a job.[19] With typical verve, an old wood hick remembered in 1937 that in his day, forty years earlier, "a moderately good axeman could fell a spruce so as to drive a stake in the ground, and a chip from his axe flew out with enough force to fell a yearling bull in his tracks."[20]

The weather provided a variety of problems for workers in the woods. In their oral histories, most of the loggers recalled that they worked in rain, sleet, and snow—and sometimes a lot of it. Emment Taylor observed: "My fingers has got so cold. . . . When you were cutting, you had your ax, your saw, your wedges, and sledge hammer, cant hook, and measuring pole. When you got all of them on your back, you had to use your hands and all of them tools cold. If you had to go a distance to the next tree, your fingers would just go to stinging." In the mountains snow often did not melt until spring, and it accumulated to great depths. On Cheat Mountain the snow was six or seven feet deep some years, and the crews walked on top of the pack to cut the timber. When spring came and the snow melted, tree stumps six or seven feet high emerged as eerie totems to a former grandeur.[21]

In March 1902, all but three of the woodsmen at West Virginia Pulp and Paper's camp 5 left "on account of not wishing to work in the snow." In 1908, the superintendent at Cass, E. P. Shaffer, wrote to Vice-President Samuel Slaymaker that work had been greatly slowed by three feet of snow in the woods, and working conditions were nearly impossible as a result of a "terrible blizzard." Nevertheless, Shaffer wrote, "Our instructions to our men are to get in[to the woods] just as quickly as possible." Shaffer reminded his superior that it was "utterly impossible to chase men into the woods under the present conditions. I regret this . . . but you are familiar enough with the character of business to know that a couple of feet of snow with the crust on makes it impossible."[22]

Snow signaled the approach of Christmas holidays, which also temporarily halted work in the woods. This was particularly significant for local men who went home for the holiday. Usually the crews were paid through Christmas, and the woods foreman had to wait to find out how many men would report to work in the new year. Nonnative workers often changed jobs during this period, but even if they remained in camp, woods operations depended on the return of experienced wood hicks. Only "new men" were on hand, Shaffer reported in January 1901, and so the resumption of work had to wait until the "old men" returned from their Christmas vacations at home.[23]

Cutting timber was dangerous employment. The skilled woodsman could place a felled tree where he wanted it by adjusting the notch cut and placing wedges to improve his aim. Most of the time this practice was successful, but often enough to make men cautious, an otherwise healthy looking tree could be dead or hollow in the center and suddenly begin to split. When this happened with a small tree, choppers could quickly cut and save most of the trunk. If it were large, however, the men ran to a safe distance because it would splinter upward ten feet, break, and kick back off the stump to kill or maim the unwary. Men often were injured by falling limbs and trees, and it was a rare woodsman who did not suffer serious wounds from the saws and axes.[24]

When ten logs had been cut, the grab-driver fastened them together into trails by crotch-grabs, which were short chains with hooks on the ends, and the teamster then skidded them to the railroad or log slide where he released them and returned to the cutting. Teamsters pulled the logs over skid roads prepared by swampers, who chopped out the underbrush to make a downhill lane from the cutting face to the railroad or log skid. Greenhorns generally were assigned to this work until they were experienced enough for another job. Usually these skid roads were no longer than one-half mile, but on some mountain jobs where the incline of the skid road was steep enough, logs might run downhill on their own. In these cases, the teamster attached a j-grab into the log and the horse pulled the log until it began to slide end first down the skid road. The teamster and horse quickly stepped aside into a

Woods crew near Bartow, Pocahontas County, ca. 1910. (West Virginia and Regional History Collection, West Virginia University Libraries)

clearing alongside the road called a jay-hole as the log was propelled down-hill by gravity. This was dangerous work, and both teamster and horse required considerable experience to do it without injury.[25]

The very large timber posed special problems for wood hicks. Emment Taylor remembered felling one giant oak on Cheat Mountain that was larger in diameter than the six-foot saws used by the crew. The handle was taken off one end and the men took turns sawing, pushing, and pulling from one end. The oak was too large for the steam loader tongs to grasp so holes were bored into the log and dynamite was used to blast it apart. Out of this giant of the woods, barrel staves were fashioned.[26]

Sometimes the old technology was still used in the new era. When the distance was too great for horses and the slope toward the railroad in the valley was suitable, a log chute was built by splitting large logs in half and opening them up to make a V-shaped trough. These split logs were placed end on end, water was poured on them until it froze, and then the logs were skidded down off the mountainside to the railroad landing below. This

Snaking logs near Bayard, Grant County, 1903. (West Virginia and Regional History Collection, West Virginia University Libraries)

could be done only during winter, of course, when it was below freezing. During very cold weather the sound of log skidding could be heard in the mountains around the clock for days on end as the men took advantage of icing conditions to slide as much timber as possible. When the incline permitted, some companies, such as Meadow River, cut a trench along the skid road, which was then lined with logs. The teams pulled the logs through the skidway to the landing. This method extended woods operations beyond cold icy weather and was not as environmentally destructive as many other methods. The most common type of landing was the rollway, where logs were rolled from the skid road down a slanted platform onto the flatcar. Logs might also be decked, or stacked, on a landing where they were stored until they were loaded on flatcars and hauled away.[27]

Loading logs onto the railroad cars was a major bottleneck in a logging operation. Loading by hand was not only slow but extremely laborious and

A giant of the forest, Nicholas County, ca. 1920. (West Virginia and Regional History Collection, West Virginia University Libraries)

inefficient. The problem was solved by the steam log loader. The steam log loader was not used in West Virginia for some years after its invention in 1886 but began to appear during the first decade of the twentieth century. A small crane mounted on a railroad car and carried to the landing, the log loader was essentially a hoist with a set of tongs attached to a cable that was lowered and set around the middle of a log by the tong hooker. When the hooker gave the ready signal, the engineer, who operated the loader from the cab, lifted the log aloft and onto the railroad flatcar, where the top-loader guided it into place. This method was, of course, much faster and more efficient than loading by hand, and it greatly boosted productivity. The record on Cheat Mountain was twenty-one cars loaded in a single day.[28]

The steam skidder was another piece of heavy equipment that revolutionized logging in the mountains by making it possible to log not just

Felled white oak, Nicholas County, 1914. (West Virginia and Regional History Collection, West Virginia University Libraries)

downhill but uphill as well. Railroad tracks could not be laid into some canyons, and if they were to be harvested, the timber had to be pulled up and out of the canyon. Such was the case, for example, in Blackwater Canyon, Tucker County, which contained extremely valuable timber but presented technical problems in harvesting. The steam skidder was essential to logging uphill, but it also was useful in swampy stands. Like the steam loader, the skidder entered the West Virginia forest during the first decade of the twentieth century, although it trailed the loader by a few years.

The Lidgerwood aerial skidder probably was the most prevalent in West Virginia because rugged terrain required the kind of technology that earned the Lidgerwood its nickname of the "flying machine." The aerial skidder's engine was set up close to the railroad track near a large main spar tree. Commonly a steel spar was substituted, but either spar required a diameter of twenty-four inches at sixty feet above the ground. Between the main spar and a tail tree the main cable of up to three-quarters of a mile in length was stretched. The tops of both spar and tail tree were secured by cables, or guys, to nearby stumps. On the main cable ran a wheeled carriage, called a

Shay engine and log loader in woods. (West Virginia and Regional History Collection, West Virginia University Libraries)

bicycle, which consisted of block and tackle supplied with tongs for grasp-ing the logs. Steam skidders in West Virginia usually were operated by a seven-man crew. Three bull-chokers, working one-half to three-quarters of a mile away from the skidder, could neither see nor be seen by the leverman who ran the skidder. They choked logs with the thongs about one-third the distance of the log, and the bull-hooker connected it to the cable distended down from the bicycle. Then they hailed the whistle punk to blow the battery-powered whistle twice as a signal that the log was ready. The lever-man answered with his own whistle and started the skidder pulley hauling in the cable. In this way huge logs could be hauled in the air from one side of a mountain to another, sometimes three hundred feet above the valley bottom. One of the skidder's biggest problems was that it destroyed young saplings, inhibiting the growth of a new forest. Moreover, deep gouges were left in the

Steam skidder logging out the Blackwater River Canyon, Tucker County, ca. 1910.
(West Virginia and Regional History Collection, West Virginia University Libraries)

side of the mountain where one end was dragged along the ground and seriously aggravated erosion on the mountainside.[29]

Working on the log trains bringing the timber down the mountains frequently was dangerous and always an adventure. The equipment, with its unshielded gears, belts, shafts, and steel wheels against steel rails, caused the loss of many workers' limbs and lives. Dangerous, too, was the improperly maintained steam engine, which exploded if the pressure became too great for a weak seal. This happened when the locomotive boiler on the Hosterman Lumber Company's log train exploded, killing one man and injuring several others.[30] Members of the train crew often slipped or were jarred and fell under the moving cars. This was a particular hazard for brakemen, who had to jump from car to car to set the brakes on each car when the train descended steep grades. One brakeman on Cheat Mountain fell between the cars, and the wheels "just cut him up in pieces as big as your hand."[31]

The steep grade itself posed a monumental challenge to log train crews. Primitive mechanical brakes, heavy loads, poor track, and foul weather conditions on a steep mountainside made for a potentially lethal combination. Runaway trains were common enough to become part of the legends of mountain logging. Contemporary newspapers are filled with references to

Log train near Dobbin, Grant County, ca. 1910. (West Virginia and Regional History Collection, West Virginia University Libraries)

log train wrecks and injuries. Cheat Mountain was one of the most notoriously dangerous. On one occasion a carload of bark for the West Virginia Pulp and Paper Company tannery began rolling downhill. The track was wet with rain, and the men were unable to stop the car. Two men jumped into a pile of pine limbs and the car continued to gather speed and overshot a curve. One of the men who jumped recalled that "it knocked a big birch tree down and went right on over in the holler. They didn't get nothing out of that car. The wheels was sliding on that wet track. It just slid like a sled. The further it went, the faster it went. . . . There was a lot of boxcars wrecked."[32]

Sometimes the worst seemed miraculously avoided, as when a brakeman "in his cups" forgot to set the hand brakes and the loaded train shot down the mountain out of control. Unable to stop it, the engineer threw the engine into reverse and the crew jumped for their lives. As they walked down the tracks to find the wreckage, they were surprised to see the train appearing around the next curve coming back up the mountain in reverse. Normally a dangerous sequence of events was not miraculously reversed. The worst wreck on the Dry Fork Railroad occurred in 1901. Presumably at the insistence of the superintendent of maintenance, W. A. Booker, the engineer was ordered to go faster and faster until the bridge at Jenningston collapsed

Wreck of the *Lucy Belle* near Lokelia, Pocahontas County. (West Virginia and Regional History Collection, West Virginia University Libraries)

under the strain of the speeding engine and fell into the river. The engineer and fireman died along with Booker in the mishap. Tradition claims that Booker was a slave-driving boss who instructed the engineer to open the throttle, "whistle once for a cow, twice for a man, and three times for God Almighty." As the local historian points out, however, the three men who could have told that story were killed in the wreck.[33]

One of the most legendary train wrecks occurred in the Canaan Valley on February 5, 1924, involving the "hoodoo engine." This engine earned its name from its many previous accidents on the Lehigh Valley Railway Company line in Pennsylvania. The engine was sold to the Laurel River Lumber Company at Jenningston, Tucker County, in 1907 mainly because the trainmen of the Lehigh Valley were superstitious enough to think that it was ill-fated and refused to take it out of the yard. The hoodoo's wrecks in West

Virginia were attributed to weak trestles, poor trackage, or excessive speed. And wreck it did. On April 23, 1910, the hoodoo wrecked near Jenningston, killing its twenty-two-year-old fireman. A few months later, in June, it wrecked again on a bridge over the Laurel River, although fortunately no one was hurt. In 1917 the locomotive wrecked again on the Laurel River section and killed two men. In 1921, the hoodoo engine was purchased by the Babcock Lumber and Boom Company when the Laurel River Lumber Company went out of business and was put into service out of Davis.

On February 5, 1924, the hoodoo wrecked for the last time, killing Frederick W. Viering, the popular and highly respected superintendent of the Babcock operations. That morning, Viering, along with his engineer and fireman, had taken the locomotive over Cabin Mountain on an inspection trip. That evening they picked up two empty flatcars and two men looking for employment in the camps. On the way back, at about 6:15 P.M., Viering called his home in Davis to tell his wife that he would be home in one hour. The fireman, George W. Kline, informed Viering that it was not possible to make Davis in one hour over the crooked and ice-covered rails; Viering responded that it could be done if the engine ran fast enough. When Kline said, "You will go in a corpse if you try that," Viering replied, "I'll eat my supper with the old woman in Davis tonight or I'll eat it with the devil in hell!" This story was provided by Kline and verified by Melvin Heath and Guy George, the two men who caught a ride on the train. All three survived the wreck and subsequently related the story to a local historian. With Viering himself at the controls, the train began picking up speed soon after starting down Cabin Mountain, and Kline noted that Viering had the engine in reverse and the sander valve open to drop sand on the icy rails. As the train picked up momentum, Kline went back on the flatcars with the two riders. When the train entered a sharp curve, the engine left the tracks and turned upside down, pinned Viering in the mud, crushed his chest, scalded him to death with steam, and the sanding valve lever pierced his skull. One of the riders received a broken nose, but the other two survived, although bruised and badly shaken from being thrown from the car. Kline walked a mile to the nearest phone and notified the company at Davis. Many people mourned Viering's loss and took a lesson from the episode that those who ignored the physical dangers of working in the woods did so at their own peril.[34]

"The Cabin Mountain Wreck" was paraphrased in the fashion common to railroad folklore from another old song, "The Wreck of Old Ninety-Seven," by poet Karl Myers:

The Cabin Mountain Wreck

It was February fifth, on a cold winter night,
    And the rails were all covered with snow,
When Old Number four sped down Cabin Mountain
    Like an arrow that was shot from a bow.

Fred Viering said to his coal-blackened fireman,
    "Just shovel in a little more coal,
And when we cross that Cabin Mountain
    You can watch Old Number Four start to roll."

He called his wife from the top of the mountain,
    And said, "The weather is awful mean,
But turn up the fire and get my supper ready,
    And I'll be there at seven-fifteen."

Fireman Kline told him, "You can't make it, Fred,
    It's too far"; and Viering roared, "Well,
I'll eat my supper with the old woman in Davis,
    Or I'll eat it with the devil in hell!"

It's a mighty rough road from Canaan to Davis,
    And a road with many a turn;
It was on this road that he picked up speed,
    And his brakes all began to burn.

He was going down grade at fifty miles an hour
    When his whistle began to scream;
He was found in the wreck with his engine in reverse,
    And was scalded to death by the steam.

Come all you housewives and heed this warning,
    And a lesson from this story learn;
Never speak harsh words to your railroading husband,
    He may leave you and never return.[35]

When the log trains finally wended their way off the mountain to the mill,
logs were rolled off the railroad car down a ramp into the log pond. The
pond served as a place to store the logs, wash off the dirt, and provide easy
movement to the mill itself. The depth of the pond was from four to eight
feet, and through the middle ran a boom that separated sawtimbers from the
pulpwood. A plank runway extended out into the pond so the men could

Unloading logs at Horton, Randolph County. (West Virginia and Regional History Collection, West Virginia University Libraries)

separate and move the logs. "Deadheads," usually hardwood logs that most often sank to the bottom, were raised by a flat raft outfitted with a windless, cable, and tongs. The log was raised and towed to the mill for processing. The log pond generally was kept open in the winter by extending a steam pipe into the water to prevent it from freezing.

Depending on the size of the operation, several pondmen sorted the logs and then worked them toward the jack-slip or jack-ladder, a V-shaped trough extended from the pond up into the mill. The logs were pulled up the trough by log dogs, metal angles that hooked the logs and were fastened to an endless chain running around two sprocket wheels. As the log entered the mill at the top of the ladder, the scaler measured its board feet and kind and credited the camp or contractor that cut the log.

When the log entered the mill it lay parallel to the carriage and was set into place in the log deck by steam-powered mechanical flippers called "kickers." The log deck was inclined and the log rolled toward the carriage, on which a loader placed the log to be sawn. Operated by the sawyer, one of the most skilled and highest paid workers at the mill, the carriage was a steam- or electric-powered machine mounted on a set of steel rails that carried the log back and forth through the saw until it was cut into strips of lumber.

Except for very small mills that used circular saw blades, most lumber

Standard mill pond and jack ladder to the mill. (West Virginia and Regional History Collection, West Virginia University Libraries)

mills worthy of the name operated band mills. The single-cutting band saw was an endless strip of steel with saw teeth that traveled around heavy stationary five- to ten-foot wheels driven by steam power at speeds of seven to nine thousand rim feet per minute. The single band saw had teeth only on one side so the sawyer could cut on one pass but had to return to position to make another pass. A double band mill cut lumber in both directions of the log carriage and consequently was much more efficient. The band ranged from ten to sixteen inches in width and thirty to forty-five feet in length, running around the wheels like a belt.

The saws were maintained by the filer, the most highly skilled mill man, who worked six to ten hours a day and with the foreman was the highest paid worker in the mill. It was his responsibility to keep the saws sharpened, a process that was completed several times a day when the mill was running. For example, at the Parsons Pulp and Lumber Company at Horton in 1922, the foreman and filer earned $8.00 per day, and the sawyer $5.50, while the other workmen averaged between $2.00 and $3.00 a day. Typically, a filer worked under a master filer for at least two years before claiming mastery of the craft.

When the lumber was cut, it passed through edgers, movable circular saws that could be adjusted for different width boards. From there the lumber left the mill through the trimmers, overhead circular drop saws arranged side by side at proper intervals, and were dropped by the trimmer-man to trim the boards into standard lengths. Boards then were rolled out into the "bull pen," where they were sorted and loaded onto trucks and wheeled to the dry kiln or most often to the lumber docks for air-drying. The yards were arranged in alleys between tracks, and there the lumber was stacked to air-dry for sixty to ninety days. Lumber was air-dried because as it lost moisture its shipping weight, and hence shipping cost, was reduced. Moreover, customers usually demanded seasoned wood because there was less shrinkage and depreciation than with green lumber, and it was easier to remanufacture into goods as well. Dry kilns were used only for special grades and orders. At the Parsons Pulp and Lumber Company mill in Horton, an average sized mill, the lumber yard contained one mile of lumber stacked to sixteen feet high.

After the lumber was air-dried it was sent to the planing mill. Located at the same level as the sawmill and next to it, the planing mill was operated by steam equipment that remanufactured, or smoothed, the rough-cut boards to a quality depending on the intended grade and made them easier to handle and ready for use. From the planing mill yardmen loaded the lumber onto boxcars for shipment to urban markets.

Typically, the equipment at the mill was powered by steam generated by a large boiler. For that reason, the water supply was a major consideration, along with railroad access, when locating a large mill. The boiler was fired by sawdust and shavings ground up in a "hog," a machine with multiple steel knife edges that ground pieces of wood to dust and fed it to the boiler by a conveyor. The boiler consumed the sawdust and shavings from the mill to generate steam to operate the mill.[36] Table 6 lists the occupations and daily wages for one company in 1922, but the scale was standard for the industry in West Virginia.

During the early years of the timber boom, lumber companies and woods contractors often found it difficult to find enough local labor to satisfy demand. Even the scattered farm population in the backcounties under-stood that manpower was limited. P. H. Butler, who went to work in the woods of Clay County during the 1890s, recollected in 1936 that before the Great Depression there was "an actual shortage of labor in this section of the country."[37]

As might be expected, laborers with the requisite skills for operating the mills initially were more scarce among the local population than woodsmen. Correspondence in the West Virginia Pulp and Paper Company records

Table 6. Wages at Parsons Pulp and Lumber Company, 1922

Job	Wages per Day
Scaler	$3.60
Filer	8.00
Mill foreman	8.00
Pondman	2.50
Sawyer	5.50
Setter	3.25
Dogger	2.50
Turndownman	2.50
Edgerman	3.75
Trimmerman	3.25
Trimmerman's helper	2.30
Feed hog	2.30
Cutoff	2.30
Mill piler	3.00
Resawyer	3.00
Clean-up	2.30
Oiler	2.50
Engineer	4.00
Millwright	4.00
Pickoff chains	2.30
Sorting table	2.30
Laborer	2.15
Water boy	1.00
Grader	3.50
Tallyman	3.25
Night watchman	2.30

Source: Stickel, "Logging in the Mountains of West Virginia," 54.

during its first decade of operation reveal just how difficult it was to attract and retain skilled craftsmen, particularly sawyers who operated the mills and filers who kept the saws sharpened. These men occupied strategic positions in the production process, which if not performed properly could ruin the product. At Cass the search for a sawyer and filer began in March 1902 because the lumber being milled was unmarketable. The sawyer had not calibrated the mill machinery within the precise limitations required and so most of the lumber it produced was "uneven in thickness." This problem was magnified because the filer also apparently lacked the skill to sharpen the saw teeth properly, and as a result the mill was spitting out shredded lumber. Finding replacements for these critical positions proved no easy matter. E. P. Shaffer, superintendent of the company's operations, offered one sawyer an advance in wages but could not persuade him to leave his job. Shaffer telegraphed another sawyer who worked at the Saint Lawrence Boom and Lumber Company in Ronceverte, but he failed to respond. A company agent was sent to contact a filer working at another mill, but the agent was informed that the man had left for Davis. Unconvinced, Shaffer thought the employer was hiding the filer to prevent other companies from hiring him away. Even though the sawyer and filer at Cass were responsible for the poor quality of lumber and the extraordinary expense incurred, they were not let go until replacements had been found.[38]

The difficulties of mustering a sufficient work force from the local population encouraged timber operators to recruit from the reservoir of experienced timber workers in the northern states where the timber supply was rapidly being depleted. For example, the Thompson family, who migrated from the Maine woods to Tucker County to open lumber operations during the 1890s, relied on laborers from New England, Pennsylvania, and Maryland as well as local West Virginians to staff both their woods and mill operations. The original woodsmen at the Meadow River Lumber Company in Rainelle came from Pennsylvania and other northeastern states when the Raine brothers established their operations in West Virginia.[39]

A larger labor recruitment process pushed farmers out of agriculture and pulled them into the timber industry as seasonal and then full-time workers. Cash was the most tantalizing lure. Young men either followed their fathers into the woods or were expected to find wage labor in the cash-scarce backcounties to assist their families in surviving the adjustment to a market economy. Calvin Price, editor of the *Pocahontas Times*, noted that "many an elderly man with his farm heavily encumbered with debt has had his obligations discharged by his sons who have the enterprise to make them desirable woodsmen." Price saw this as a reflection of character, however, remarking that the homegrown timber worker was "more thrifty than his strolling brother. He has family ties and an inherent tendency to save money." Some "northern men" made good citizens, Price observed, but they were the ones who "married and settled down here." Otherwise, the northern woodsman was "at his worst in store clothes loafing around town, and at his best in his home in the forest."[40]

Issues of character aside, farmers were accustomed to working in the woods. Often cutting and hauling a piece of timber with a team was a farm lad's first opportunity to earn money, and he began at an early age. Markwood Gum was fourteen in 1913 when he started work for the Deer Creek Lumber Company in Pocahontas County; Bob Withers was sixteen when he was hired at a sawmill in Upshur and Randolph Counties before World War I; and P. H. Butler of Clay County began his career in the big timber in 1898 working after school snaking logs to the banks of the Elk River with a team for fifty cents a day.[41] Butler remembered that before the Charleston, Clendenin and Sutton Railroad penetrated the county during the 1890s, "there was nothing to bring money into the county except the sale of livestock, some hoop poles, and a few rafts of logs" that were floated down the Elk River and sold in Charleston. Like many of his neighbors, Butler was pleased to work for cash because as a young man he wanted to buy "store clothes." Up to that point all of his clothing had been homemade.[42]

The work experience of Emmett Heaster, who was eighty-seven when he was interviewed in 1984, reflected the process by which local farmers became timber workers. Heaster began working when he was seven or eight years old. A native of Crawley, Greenbrier County, he lived with his parents and seven siblings on a little "hillside farm" of six or seven acres, "just big enough to make a living." Like many mountaineers living under similar conditions, his family raised their own meat, grew vegetables and fruit on the farm, and purchased only necessities such as sugar and salt. "But it was hard to get hold of any money in those days," he recalled. His father worked for many years at various sawmills for one dollar a day before buying his own portable mill to set it up on the farm. Young Heaster worked as "offbearer" on his father's sawmill stacking the sawn lumber and as a "rachet man" rolling the logs into the carriage that guided the logs through the circular saw. The little farm was covered with virgin timber, which Heaster helped to fell and mill into lumber. His father also took contracts to cut other farmers' woods, and Emmett helped with those jobs as well.[43]

When he took his first job in the logging camps, therefore, Emmett Heaster had been working as a farmer-timberman since his earliest childhood and "could do any job they needed done." Like other youths during this generation of transition, young Heaster did not work steadily in the camps at first. He attended a one-room school for six months of the year and then joined his father and brother working in the camps for six months. In this way, subsistence farming supplemented by timbering was reversed over time to timbering supplemented by farming as the family was drawn into the cash economy. Emmett's first job was with the Cherry River Boom and Lumber Company when he was seventeen, followed by work for the Curtin Lumber Company. Like other farmers who made the transition to woods work, he walked to the logging sites from his home and back.[44] Heaster's career in the woods mirrors the experience of many mountaineers during the transition to capitalism, a process that first drew farmers out of agricultural dependency into the rural-industrial working class. Table 7 indicates the occupational categories for three timber counties and suggests the reciprocity between the two major industries of lumber and farming.

Informal recruitment was an important way of drawing young men from the farm into the woods. Homer F. Riggleman, who grew up on a farm in Upshur County, worked in the woods in the winter of 1909 helping his brother-in-law cut cross-ties for the Croft Lumber Company. Times were hard so his wage of one dollar a tie provided "a little cash to buy a few things. It meant a lot to us then." His first full-time job as a logger in the woods was in 1910 at age nineteen, when Riggleman and his cousin went to work on Rich Mountain in Randolph County. During the fall and winter of 1910 he joined his father and two brothers in cutting pulp wood under contract for two and one-half dollars a cord, and in May 1911 the family crew contracted to peel hemlock bark for the same company. Later, they contracted with the Croft Lumber Company and each day walked the mile and a half from home to the woods. For several years Riggleman followed this cycle, cutting bark and pulpwood under contract and from time to time in the summer returning to the farm to help his father harvest the hay.[45]

Farmers often lived at home and walked to nearby logging sites each day, gradually increasing the radius of their work until they finally left home to stay in the logging camps. Invariably, the new men in the camps were quizzed by veteran woodsmen about home, family, friends, and the outside world. This isolation from kith and kin for months at a time was common for unseasoned locals in the logging camps.[46] Gradually, the woods and mill crews came to be dominated by native mountaineers. A forester's report on the Meadow River Lumber Company of Rainelle noted in 1916 that all of the men employed by the company were Americans, the majority of them natives of the surrounding countryside.[47] Another forester claimed in 1923 that "the labor used in the Parsons Pulp and Lumber Company operations in Horton were Appalachian mountain farmers." He regarded them as "the best type of real Americans, as they have been isolated for long periods of time from contact with the outside world." For the most part, he reported, they were "the descendants of the Scotch, Irish and English that first came to the mountains."[48]

The process observed by the foresters prevailed throughout Appalachia during the transition and is documented in Florence C. Bush's *Dorie:*

Table 7. Occupational Census for Three Timber Counties, 1910

Occupation	Number	Percentage
Pocahontas County		
Government	28	1
Professional	86	2
Artisans	127	3
Service industry	208	5
Railroad	239	5
Forest industries	2,058	45
Farming	1,391	31
Coal	1	0
Laborer	47	0
Own income	20	0
Lodgers[a]	1	8
No occupation	1	0
Total	4,207	100
Randolph County		
Government	8	8
Professional	17	1
Artisans	35	2
Service industry	79	4
Railroad	173	10
Forest industries	672	37
Farming	593	33
Coal	0	0
Laborer	38	2
Own income	1	1
No occupation	24	1
Lodgers[a]	159	9
Total	1,799	100
Tucker County		
Government	23	1
Professional	101	3
Artisans	195	5
Service industry	255	7
Railroad	382	10
Forest industries	1,013	26
Farming	778	20
Coal	562	15
Laborer	109	3
Own Income	42	1
No occupation	147	4
Lodgers[a]	242	6
Total	3,849	100

Source: U.S. Census of Population, 1910.

[a] "Lodgers" represents the individuals who were lodged in the county but could not be linked directly to any occupational category. The census data for Randolph County represent the population of the two timber districts, New Interest, and Dry Fork, which are in the districts connecting Tucker and Pocahontas Counties along the spine of the highest elevations of the mountains. The intent is to measure the impact of the industry in the non-coal-producing backcounties in a spatially contiguous area, rather than the counties as a whole.

Woman of the Mountains, an autobiography of a woman who lived through the timber boom in the Great Smoky Mountains. Like so many Appalachians of the period, Dorie's family wished to stay on the farm, but worn-out land produced ever poorer harvests just as industry demanded ever larger numbers of wage laborers. After migrating between the farm and industrial work, she could no longer hope to restore the farm life she loved so well. The old family farm became a refuge from the instability of industrial capitalism, but it could not provide them with a subsistence.

No autobiographical account of the move from farm to industry in West Virginia compares with *Dorie: Woman of the Mountains*, but the emotional impact of the industrial transition has been captured in the novels of Hubert Skidmore, particularly *I Will Lift up Mine Eyes* (1936) and *Heaven Came So Near* (1938). Skidmore, who was born in 1911 in Webster Springs, recounts in the stark realism of the Depression-scarred 1930s the life of a farm family from the Gauley River country. Like most of his writing, these novels are based on personal knowledge of the place and its people.

The Cutlip family, like Dorie and her family, love their farm on Cherry Knob in the Gauley hills of central West Virginia, but poor harvests force them off the land and into the lumber mill town at Turkey Trot. At first Nat, the father, takes a temporary job in the mill to supplement the short harvest, but soon Maw and the four children join him in the mill town. The story is interpreted from the perspective of Mrs. Cutlip, who attempts to assuage her disappointment in moving by convincing herself that at Turkey Trot they will be able to save the money to purchase the tools required to work the farm once again and that at least the kids can go to school there. But the oldest son soon quits school, takes a job in the mill, marries, and moves out on his own. Nat is killed in an accident at the mill, and Maw picks up the remaining pieces of her life and heads for the refuge of the farm.

Unable to survive there, however, she is forced to return to the mill town. Conditions have changed in the interim. Without a wage earner in the family, she and her school-age son (the daughters have also gone off on their own) are misfits. The epic ends tragically when her youngest son is lynched for a murder he was incapable of committing, and Maw, increasingly marginalized by clinging to the old way of thinking, becomes "crazy Cutlip." The move has resulted in death, both physical and social, for the entire family.

Extended over two novels, the story becomes a family saga, and though it is not historical, the depressing description of the fate of the Cutlips is instructive. Skidmore clearly did not consider the transition from subsistence farming to the industrial marketplace as one willingly undertaken but

Family at a portable camp near Helvetia, Randolph County, 1900. (West Virginia and
Regional History Collection, West Virginia University Libraries)

rather as forced on people who lacked options. Poor harvests and the threat
of hunger drove the family from their farm to the industrial outpost of the
mill town, where they clung to the hope of returning to the farm someday.

At Turkey Trot the family confronts an array of forces that make a return
impossible. A producing unit when on the farm, the family now becomes
segmented into those who produce a wage and those who do not, and social
position is assigned accordingly. Women are no longer producers; they work
hard but do not generate cash and therefore are consigned to a subordinate
role. Moreover, the family becomes primarily a consumer of commodities,
of manufactured store-bought goods; homemade products are disparaged.
They no longer can produce their own goods and must work for the cash to
purchase them. The rhythms of the mill town are governed by the whistle
and paydays, not the seasons, and this life seems artificial, temporary, and
unnatural.

Skidmore recognized that people like the Cutlips were caught between a rock and a hard place. They moved to the mill town to get the cash that would allow them to retain their old ways, but the new cash economy trapped them into a dependency that dragged the family ever deeper into debt in their struggle to survive. Moreover, the fragmentation produced by capitalism broke up the large family, further diminishing the chances of returning to subsistence farming.[49]

Although Skidmore's novels might have exaggerated the emotional impact of the transition from farmer to seasonal and then full-time wage laborer, considerable shifting back and forth between agriculture and the lumber industry had been part of the mountain economy even before the timber boom, and the farming mentality undoubtedly influenced work culture in the woods. Like their lumberjack counterparts in the north woods, lumber industry workers in West Virginia exhibited the same independence of thought and action characteristic of men who had been, and continued to be, part-time farmers. In West Virginia, like the north woods of the Great Lakes states, clear-cutting methods of logging brought an abrupt halt to the industry when the supply of trees was depleted. For workers the choice was to "move on or farm." The industry migrated across the northern part of the nation, and the "homeless, womanless, voteless" lumberjacks carried this subculture with them from Maine to the Great Lakes and on to the Northwest. Over time, and with the development of machine logging, the lumberjack gave way to the ordinary timber worker.[50]

The southern timber industry did not produce a homeless migratory counterpart of the lumberjack. Southern labor remained in family units, and lumbering operations were organized to reflect that pattern by providing housing and stores for family units, not just in the mill towns but in woods operations as well. When the timber was cut out, the families moved with the camps to a new site. Southern operators chose to organize around family units for complex reasons both economic and cultural, but most obviously they saw it as a way to avoid the wild behavior associated with mill towns in the North, including West Virginia. The lack of social control found among northern loggers was avoided in the South, where the overwhelming power of the operators over timber workers, a majority of whom were black, led to grave abuses of justice that sometimes became outright peonage and resulted in some of the worst living conditions in the nation.[51]

Labor in the southern lumber industry was provided largely by impoverished agricultural workers accustomed to living at subsistence levels who were willing to work for marginal wages. Competition born out of dire necessity kept wages low, and the few attempts to address this problem by organizing, such as the efforts of the Brotherhood of Timber Workers among lumber workers in Louisiana and Texas in 1910–13, were brutally suppressed by the companies with full government support. In the Great Lakes states, West, and South the Industrial Workers of the World also attempted to organize the lumber industry, but the effort was crushed and members were subjected to lawless acts of violence and incarceration. For the most part, members were native-born migratory loggers who had no permanent residence or voting power because they were constantly on the move. With little to lose and much to gain, they became militant.[52]

Although unions attempted to organize workers in the lumber industry, their presence in the Appalachians was insignificant before World War II. Workers were, of course, vulnerable to the unscrupulous actions of timber operators, but they were not completely without resources, initiative, or consciousness of the benefits of organizing into a union. Sometimes they even went on strike. In September 1900, for example, the swampers at Cass went on strike for better pay and working conditions, but the stoppage ended in a few days when most of the men left for greener pastures in another state.[53] In September 1901 the tracks at Cass were dynamited, an act that was thought to have been done by a disgruntled employee, and the West Virginia Pulp and Paper Company offered a "good big reward" for the conviction of the perpetrator.[54] On the Greenbrier Division, track laborers also went on strike for a pay increase from $1.25 to $1.50 per ten-hour day, and many of them quit when their demands were ignored.[55]

The Greenbrier, Cheat and Elk Railroad, a subsidiary of the West Virginia Pulp and Paper Company, pushed a spur line into the headwaters of the Williams River in Webster County. When the company refused to reduce the workday from ten to nine hours, half of the fifty-six men working as track layers went on strike, and when the other half attempted to work the next morning they were met with clubs, staves, and revolvers. Wisely they retreated to the stables until the county sheriff arrived and arrested a dozen or so of the more determined strikers.[56] These strikes appear to have been the result of spontaneous combustion rather than a conscious effort to organize into unions to improve conditions through collective bargaining.

The independent nature of the woodsmen, their isolated existence in the forest, and their great mobility rendered them poor candidates for unionization. There is, in fact, no evidence of a single effort to unionize wood hicks. Although there were fraternal orders such as the Woodsmen of America that had members among the wood hicks, any hint of union sympathy in the camp would have resulted in immediate dismissal. The mill workers, in contrast, lived more settled lives, worked in close proximity in well-integrated production centers, and were occasional targets of unionizing. The evidence is meager, however. In the early 1900s the International Woodworkers of the World formed a lodge, but this benevolent society–union was ridiculed by people as "I Won't Work." Among the woods workers, it was said, calling someone an "IWW" was to ask for trouble. The Mechanical Workers of America established thirteen locals in Pocahontas County in 1911, including one at Cass with twenty-eight members, but the organization did not last long nor did it exert any influence.[57]

These early efforts failed to make any significant impact in part because the people were not ready for unions and the companies were adamantly hostile to them. By the early twentieth century, the lumber producers had organized into industry associations, which added to their power the threat of blacklisting and legal influence. Another effort to organize the mill workers of Cass in 1925 turned out three hundred men, but the opposition of the company led to its failure. Not until the 1930s did union organization make any headway in Cass. By 1932 the Junior Order of United American Mechanics was busy among the workers in Cass, and after the retirement of E. P. Shaffer in 1934, a great push to organize led to a strike for recognition that lasted over three months. In October 1936 W. M. Rogers, past president of the West Virginia Federation of Labor, was the main speaker at a well-attended rally in Cass. Nevertheless, unionization played a decidedly minor role in the lives of workers in Cass until after World War II.[58]

Similar patterns are found in other lumber mill towns where the movement for organized labor took several decades to evolve before achieving a level of influence that had to be reckoned with. In Richwood, for example, forty-two hundred mill workers at the Cherry River Boom and Lumber Company went on strike for higher wages and collective bargaining in 1934. The prominent mill operator and current president of the West Virginia Lumberman's Association, John Raine, provided the common response of the lumber operators: "Business conditions did not warrant any increase in wages."[59] It was not until after World War II that lumber mill workers began to organize successfully for collective bargaining, improved pay, and better working conditions. Unfortunately, the industry had succumbed to its own success by then, and few trees remained in West Virginia to sustain the industry on an extensive scale.

Native West Virginians dominated the lumber industry work force after 1910, but during the first decades of the lumber boom most of the woods workers were white Americans from other states and foreign immigrants who had acquired logging skills in the northern woods. Lumberman George Thompson described the first crews of woods and mill workers in his operations near Davis as a "mixed lot." Native West Virginians played a major role, but their numbers were comparatively few. Pennsylvania furnished perhaps the largest number, while New York, Michigan, New England, and Virginia also "contributed liberally." A large number of Swedes came between 1890 and 1893. Most of the Swedes subsequently migrated to the big timber in the Northwest. In 1907 they were replaced by Austrians who took over woods crews and yard work until World War I, when they drifted into other employment. Wood hicks were always on the move, he recalled: "In nearly every camp you could find men that had worked from Maine to the Pacific coast, from Canada to Mexico."[1]

Even though the percentage of foreign immigrants in the West Virginia

Table 8. Population Diversity in Three Timber Counties, 1870–1930

Year	Total Population	Native-born White (%)	African American (%)	Foreign-born (%)
Pocahontas County				
1870	4,069	4,035	259	34
1880	5,591	5,570	334	21
1890	6,814	6,784	353	30
1900	8,572	8,225	625	347
1910	14,740	13,487 (91.5)	445 (3.0)	808 (5.5)
1920	15,002	14,021	638	343
1930	14,555	13,798	558	198
Randolph County				
1870	5,563	5,426	103	137
1880	8,102	7,632	112	470
1890	11,633	11,326	262	307
1900	17,670	16,969	519	701
1910	26,028	23,589 (90.7)	376 (1.4)	2,061 (7.9)
1920	26,804	25,271	431	1,098
1930	25,049	24,350 (97.2)	342 (1.4)	357 (1.4)
Tucker County				
1870	1,907	1,887	27	20
1880	3,151	3,139	26	12
1890	6,459	6,369	183	90
1900	13,433	11,922	353	1,511
1910	18,675	15,321 (82.1)	344 (1.8)	3,010 (16.1)
1920	16,791	15,084 (89.8)	210 (1.3)	1,497 (8.9)
1930	13,374	12,694 (94.9)	77 (0.6)	603 (4.5)

Source: U.S. Census of Population.

timber industry was high in some locations, such as near Davis, their numbers paled when compared with the tens of millions concentrated in American cities during the late nineteenth and early twentieth centuries. Nevertheless, their presence was highly visible in this overwhelmingly native-born, white, Protestant human landscape. Tucker County recorded the largest foreign population in 1910, when 3,010, or 16.1 percent of the total population, were foreigners. Randolph County reported a peak number of foreigners that year as well with 2,061, or 7.9 percent of the population. Some of these foreigners were employed in the coal mines of these two counties, but even Pocahontas County, where industrial activity was almost exclusively forest-related, had a population of 808 foreigners in 1910, or 5.5 percent of the population. Native-born African Americans had made up only a small fraction of the population before the boom, and their numbers increased only marginally with the growth of the timber industry (see Table 8).

Diversity characterized the work crews in railroad construction, as is exemplified by the crews contracted to lay tracks for the Greenbrier Division of the C&O. Julian, Carzza, and Company, a contractor from Baltimore, employed Italian laborers to help lay the tracks for a section of the project. Cutting and grading the Greenbrier right-of-way south of them was another Italian crew, to the north a German crew, and interspersed were black and white native crews. All of the crews were segregated by race and ethnicity. New York contractor J. J. Strang employed separate crews of native blacks and whites. His work camp on Knapp's Creek, near Marlinton, consisted of twenty tents, resembling to curious local residents an "encampment of troops." One local observer described the camp as a square formed by tents around a long rack that sheltered the horses and mules. The dining room was about sixty feet long and contained two large tables, one for whites and the other blacks, he reported. Eleven scraper teams were at work, along with an "immense plow drawn by a magnificent span of horses and equally good span of mules."[2]

Companies generally were forced to hire immigrant work crews through labor agents or some other organized apparatus, particularly for railroad work. In the spring and summer of 1903, the Coal and Coke Railroad Company began an extension of its road from Ivydale, Clay County, to Elkins, a wild and inaccessible region without means to transport goods except by push boat or canoe. In 1937, P. H. Butler of Clay County reminisced about his employment as a timekeeper, payroll clerk, and clerk of the company store for the McAuthor Brothers Company, which had been contracted to build a section of the extension above Ivydale. The large lumber operations along the Elk River below Ivydale, which was already connected to Charleston by rail, and construction of the railroad created a demand for workers that exceeded the local labor supply. Butler's description of railroad building that used only primitive equipment such as steam drills, picks, shovels, mattocks, drills, hammers, dump carts, wheelbarrows, and dump wagons reflects the labor intensiveness of the methods. The large volume of soil and rock moved on such an operation was done by hand, sometimes horse-drawn graders, and was either redistributed over the grade, pushed over the side, or hauled to sections requiring fill. Like the camps described along the Greenbrier, McAuthor Brothers Company employed diverse sets

African American and Italian immigrant track crew near Cass, Pocahontas County.
(West Virginia and Regional History Collection, West Virginia University Libraries)

of work crews, segregated into camps of blacks, foreigners, and native
whites; the latter also ate meals in a tent of their own.[3]

Pressured by deadlines, contractors always needed more workers and
greater production for less money from those already on the job. Labor
scarcity dictated that McAuthor Brothers secure labor through labor agencies. "Of all the crooks I ever dealt with," Butler recalled, "they were the
crookedest." McAuthor Brothers finally abandoned the agencies and sent
company men to the large cities to hire laborers. Butler himself went on several of these recruiting trips. On one trip to Philadelphia in 1904 the recruiters garnered promises from fifty-one prospective immigrants, but when the
train departed the station only three men boarded for West Virginia. Butler
believed that "some labor agency who had been furnishing laborers for us"
had somehow interfered. A few weeks later the McAuthor recruiters traveled
to Pittsburgh and returned with twenty-seven new workers.[4]

Problems transporting workers were numerous even if the men actually arrived at the work site. McAuthor Brothers required new recruits to pay their own transportation if they did not work a full five-day week before paying the labor agency. Often, an agency representative, or padrone, came with the crews to act as interpreter and foreman. During the week the men stocked up on groceries at the company store and worked the five days, but they often slipped off on Friday night, "leaving the company to hold the bag for transportation and other expenses."[5]

Like the Greenbrier Division and the Coal and Coke Railroad, companies building logging lines into the woods also used foreign labor, particularly Italian immigrants. Italian construction crews graded and laid tracks for the West Virginia Pulp and Paper Company's logging line from Cass to the spruce timber at the top of Cheat Mountain. Henderson Sharp, a logging veteran from Frost, Pocahontas County, remembered how hard it was to lay tracks in the spruce country because of the swampy conditions, but "Italians built most all of the train tracks" to haul out this big timber.[6] Most railroad construction crews contained about forty-five men, who lived in temporary shanty camps and worked eleven hours a day six days a week for one dollar a day.[7] Italians often spoke little English and so they were identified by number with metal tags attached to their overalls. For the month of August 1900, Cass superintendent E. P. Shaffer paid the men in checks ranging from a low of $15.64 for Italian number 38 to a high of $46.50 for Italian number 29. Most checks were in the range of $20 to $25. By comparison, Shaffer himself received a check for $300 for the same period.[8] Not all of the Italians were confined to railroad work at Cass. A few, identified on the shop crew roster by number only, were used to a limited extent in the shops as manual laborers at a rate of $1.90 per ten- or eleven-hour day.[9]

West Virginia Pulp and Paper pursued a conscious policy of hiring Italian laborers for the railroad work. Shaffer informed his superior in the Philadelphia office, Vice-President Samuel Slaymaker, that "the Italian camp" was under construction even before a crew had been hired to live in it. Shaffer's correspondence during the period when the line was being built from Cass to the top of Cheat Mountain clearly demonstrated the persistently nagging problem of attracting Italian workers to Cass. Shaffer attempted to lure away some of the Italians working on the Greenbrier Division in the summer of 1900, and his agent reported that forty or fifty men had agreed to come to Cass. The two Italian foremen who promised to deliver the men, however, did not arrive as expected. Shaffer surmised that the contractors had "persuaded them to stay" by telling "the Italians that there was [*sic*] contractors doing the work here and I don't know what else." From the laborers' perspective, being employed by a contractor was worse than working for a company because the contractors "sweated" their workers, driving them harder so as to complete the job within the fixed contract price. The lower their costs, the more money contractors stood to gain from the labor contract. Shaffer was hopeful that another group of forty or fifty Italians who had promised to come when their job was finished would do so, but he urged Slaymaker to "send in 40 or 50 Italians if you can get them" to be safe. When these men also failed to materialize, Shaffer fumed that they probably owed the contractor for transportation and were afraid that he would force them to pay if he found them at Cass. At one point, the superintendent recommended that an Italian padrone be offered the responsibility for the company store in hopes that "the men would stay better."[10]

Companies generally charged the men for their transportation to the work site. Sometimes this was used as an inducement, as when the West Virginia Pulp and Paper Company provided a month's grace period before collecting. The Italian workers soon learned that the demand for their labor could be used as leverage in squeezing concessions from the company. One crew of forty-five Italians agreed to work only after extracting a promise from the company that they would be paid every two weeks rather than once a month. This, of course, gave the men more flexibility to move on if dissatisfied. Shaffer disliked this system, however, because it was too cumbersome and precisely because it afforded the men greater mobility. Turnover continued to be excessive, but by October 1900 enough of the line had been extended up Cheat Mountain that he discharged some of the one hundred men and withdrew the concession because "we will not need all of them and can be more independent." Two years after his initial complaints about too few Italian laborers, however, Shaffer was still pleading for more. "We regret that you are experiencing so much trouble getting Italian laborers," he informed Slaymaker, but Shaffer had news that "a number of Italians at Bradford, Pa." were available and he urged Slaymaker to hire them if possible.[11]

Although Italians were more abundant in the immigrant labor pool, West Virginia Pulp and Paper Company preferred to hire Austrians in the pulpwood operations "for their hearty, cheerful, and contented nature."[12] Approximately 480 men were employed in the company's pulpwood operations during the winter of 1905, most of them engaged in cutting the smaller trees left after the big timber had been removed. A crew of Austrians also was employed laying track on Cheat Mountain.[13] But there never seemed to be enough of the Austrians or Italians to satisfy needs.

The shortage of labor for woods operations created problems for all parties involved. Work in the woods was by its very nature secluded from public scrutiny, and unscrupulous operators were abusive, especially to poor immigrant workers who were not citizens, often did not speak English, and were unfamiliar with their legal rights. On October 28, 1911, a story appeared in the *Cumberland Daily News* relating the experiences of Fred W. Viering, the woods superintendent who died in the wreck of the hoodoo engine, and Andrew Zalor, the boarding boss for the Babcock Lumber and Boom Company, which had bought out the Thompsons' operations in Davis.[14] The paper reported that John W. George, "a well known resident" of Cumberland, Maryland, was placed under arrest at Green Ridge, the site of F. Mertens and Sons' "million dollar orchard." George, the superintendent of security at Mertens and Sons, was charged with assault with intent to murder Viering and Zalor. George was the only man taken at the time, but warrants were issued for several other men who had escaped, including Fred "the German" Ludwig, "Red Irish," and John Iskra, an Austrian. George soon posted $500 bond and swore out a warrant for the arrest of Viering on charges of trespassing on the property of Mertens and Sons and malicious destruction of property. Viering came to Cumberland and also posted $500 bond.[15]

Viering's sworn statement provides a chilling example of the desperate measures some companies resorted to in their efforts to secure a work force and indicates the extralegal means to which they sometimes resorted. It also suggests the risks taken by timber operators when they employed foreign labor. According to Viering, Andrew Zalor, the Austrian-born boarding boss at Camp 45 of the Babcock Lumber and Boom Company at Davis, traveled by train to Cumberland on October 17, 1911, to collect $234 owed by seven Austrian workers to whom he had loaned the money. The men left Babcock's employment and took jobs at Mertens, promising to repay the money their first payday, October 10, 1911, but reneged on their agreement. Therefore, after a night in Cumberland, on the morning of October 18, Zalor went to Green Ridge station on the Western Maryland, outside of Cumberland, which served Mertens's large orchard. A foreman asked one of the Austrians who he was, and on learning that he was a boarding boss for Babcock, a company guard seized Zalor as he walked on a public road and shackled him by the hands to a tree with a mule tied to his left arm. He remained in this position for two hours until the company guard returned. Zalor was then handcuffed, tied to the mule by rope, and forced to walk six or eight miles alongside the mule to the top of the mountain. Along the way the guard cursed Zalor, threatened to kill him if he came back, and then released him in the woods as night descended. After several hours of walking, Zalor finally reached Cumberland, where he boarded the train for Davis.[16]

Upon learning Zalor's story, Viering called a meeting with George B. Thompson, superintendent of Babcock's Davis operations, where the three men agreed that legal steps should be taken to bring the culprits to justice. On the morning of October 21, Zalor and Viering left Davis on the train for Cumberland and proceeded directly to the Mertens orchards. They did not see the man who had tied Zalor to the tree, however, and returned to a hotel in Cumberland for the evening. After supper Zalor and Viering met an Austrian who was working for Mertens, and the man asked if they could use thirty-eight Austrians. The Austrians had quit Mertens because they were supposed to be paid $1.75 a day and Mertens had paid them only $1.60. Viering informed him that the men were needed, provided they were good woodsmen, and agreed to pay their transportation to Davis. The following morning, October 23, Viering and Zalor took the morning train to Green Ridge. After disembarking, they took care to remain on the railroad right-of-way because all of the surrounding land belonged to the Mertens Company. As they walked along the right-of-way, a guard approached them who recognized Zalor from the week before and warned the men to move on. Viering responded: " 'Doesn't the Western Maryland railroad own this property where the station is here—I am waiting on the train.' He [the guard] says: 'They don't own nothin'."[17]

Deciding to walk to the next station, Little Orleans, where they could get dinner and catch a train back to Cumberland, Viering and Zalor were walking in the path between the two Western Maryland tracks when "all at once a man jumped on to us, and he had a revolver, and thrust it into my back." It was a Mertens company guard, who ordered them to halt, cursed them, and struck Viering with the revolver. The guard's name was "Fred the German," and he was soon joined by "John Iskra, an Austrian," who also was armed. After roughing up Zalor, they marched the two Babcock bosses at gunpoint to the Mertens company office. Soon the men were joined by three more guards. Viering asked one of them: "What does this mean?" and he responded: " 'you will find out what this means.' He had a letter from the Babcocks and he said: 'We paid dear for getting these men into the woods and we don't propose to let you people take them away.' "[18]

The two men were taken before the Mertens superintendent, who ordered the guards to put them in the "lock-up." Viering and Zalor were shackled together by the left and right arms and locked in a room without food or drink. That evening, just about dark, "Fred the German" came back and took off the handcuffs and said they were going to the boardinghouse for supper. After they ate, the guards handcuffed the men together again and put them in an automobile and started for the woods at the top of the mountain. There the superintendent handed another pistol to "Reddy, the Irish" and told the guards to shoot to kill if either man tried to escape. Then the guards took all of their personal property, money, and everything else out of their pockets and blindfolded them. The superintendent then said: " 'This is the lesson we teach you all.' 'Now then boys,' he says, 'you can take them either to the river and drown them, or you can hang them in the big tree or you can put them in the old house.' " After a wild ride and rough walk blindfolded and shackled together, the two woodsmen were put in an old abandoned house and locked in the upstairs. On leaving, the guards shot their revolvers a half dozen times and left but soon returned, again firing their pistols. The guards came upstairs and said that they had "decided to take you out of here and hang you," and "Irish" put a rope around Zalor's neck and marched them out into the yard where he tied the other end of the rope around the automobile. " 'We will drag him to death,' " Irish said, as the car started forward. As Zalor stumbled along, Irish drew his revolver and announced that he would cut the rope and commenced shooting at the short length of rope stretched between the automobile and Zalor's neck.[19]

The pathetic episode finally came to a conclusion when the superintendent appeared, saying, " 'I have decided the last two hours to turn you fellows loose on the road and you can go back and tell Babcock that is the way we used you, and if you ever come back again, we will kill you, you will never get out of this place alive.' " The men were driven even farther out into the woods and turned free in the darkness. After walking for at least seven hours, they finally arrived at Cumberland at 5:00 A.M. and sent a telegraph to George B. Thompson. Before returning to Davis, the men retained three Cumberland lawyers, one of them W. C. Capper, a "former Davis boy," who instituted charges against the Mertens guards. With the assistance of the prosecuting attorney for Allegheny County, the guards and superintendent were convicted and fined several thousand dollars. Viering and Zalor brought civil suits for damages in the U.S. Circuit Court as well, but these suits were compromised.[20]

It is clear that the company guards intended to rough up and frighten the two woodsmen but not to kill them. Undoubtedly, the two victims were familiar with company guard tactics because they were commonly used in the Appalachian coal fields, but this was not so obvious at the time. Aside from the willingness of companies to disregard civil and criminal law, not to mention human rights, the episode shows the critical importance of recruiting and retaining laborers in the woods. It suggests how companies "stole" labor from one another during periods of labor shortage. Even under these circumstances, Viering and Zalor could not resist attempting to hire away thirty-eight Austrians from Mertens and Sons, perhaps the very same men the orchard company had stolen from Babcock.

The money Andrew Zalor attempted to collect from the dishonest Austrian workers had been advanced to them for food and supplies at the Babcock Company's commissary and possibly for railroad transportation to Davis. Advancing food, supplies, and transportation as an inducement in the recruitment of labor was common practice in industrializing central Appalachia and West Virginia. But advances also were the source of significant legal and even human rights abuses because workers, usually foreign immigrants, were held against their will until they repaid sums owed to the company. The Babcock Company obviously did not employ this form of "debt peonage" or the Austrians would not have been permitted to leave the woods while still indebted to the company.[21]

The major thrust of the federal government's legal campaign against peonage was directed at the South and primarily involved African Americans. In West Virginia peonage was associated mostly with foreign immigrant workers, but there are suggestive indications that in some cases blacks were involved as well. In an interview in 1940, Strang foreman Robert Earle remembered that the crew working closest to Marlinton was "mainly colored men recruited for the duration of the job in North Carolina and Virginia, who were held in a sort of benevolent subjection until such time as it pleased the management to let them settle with the quartermaster and return whence they came."[22]

That Zalor was attempting to collect a "boarding bill" was significant for often workers were forced to work off company debts under the protection of West Virginia's "Boarding House Law," which permitted the operator of a boardinghouse to obtain a criminal warrant for the arrest of a person who intentionally defrauded the operator of a hotel, restaurant, or boardinghouse of payment. It also applied to cases in which a person obtained credit at any of these facilities under false pretenses, who was fined between $25 and $100, "and at the discretion of the Court of Justice trying the case, be confined in the county jail not less than ten nor more than thirty days."[23] Application of the law to shanty board in a work camp was of dubious legal standing if a squire could be found to issue the warrant. Gino C. Speranza, an Italian American lawyer from New York, who came to West Virginia in 1903 for the Society for the Protection of Italian Immigrants to investigate charges that Italian immigrants were held in labor against their will, observed that there were a variety of factors peculiar to the state that exacerbated the problem. One important one was topography. "Those who have not been to the West Virginian labor camps can hardly understand how lonely and isolated some of them are," he wrote. "Even though geographically near each other, they are completely shut in by the mountains, and the surrounding country is practically uninhabited. . . . The lonesomeness of the camp naturally increased the apprehension of the laborers." This apprehension was justifiably heightened by labor agents for whom Speranza reserved his most vehement denunciation. They "infested" Italian immigrant communities and procured laborers for contractors at a set fee. Preying on those in desperate need of work, agents often misrepresented the opportunities for work, claiming that the immigrants would earn more than contractors had actually agreed to pay and that transportation was eighty cents rather than eight dollars, and the differences between the agreed-upon fee and wage level and the sum arranged with the workers went into the agent's pocket. Moreover, agents often claimed that West Virginia was much farther away than it actually was, and the immigrant laborers were greeted by tough armed guards with nasty dispositions.[24]

Luring laborers to the backwoods work camps was the first problem, and keeping them was the second. Here company power was not seriously challenged by public oversight, and the gravest abuses of civil liberties occurred. Demand for labor far outstripped availability in West Virginia, Speranza observed, and "to supply the feverish demand, laborers of all conditions and classes have been literally dumped into that State by the brokers in human flesh in the cities." When labor was delivered by the agents, he continued, "an even harder task is to keep them there, for the isolation of the camps, the absence of human intercourse, and the hardships of life create a feeling of discontent among the laborers almost from the first day." It was the urgent demand that prompted the financial investment in recruitment, but money constituted the primary motive for contractors to abuse workers. For example, two hundred laborers at $10 each required an investment of $2,000, and if the men became dissatisfied and left, the contractor took a direct loss. However strong the temptation, Speranza observed, "it cannot justify acts of restraint which in practice amount to white slavery." Nevertheless, he concluded, "cases of brutality are frequent and inexcusable."[25]

Although Speranza, reformers, and others seeking simple justice lodged complaints, public officials put forth little effort to correct these abuses for many years. For example, when Speranza sought relief from Governor A. B. White and state attorney general Romeo H. Freer, he was informed that such infractions were outside of their jurisdiction as described in the constitution of West Virginia and in the *Code of West Virginia*. Original jurisdiction for crimes of peonage rested with the justice of the peace and the circuit court. If local officers failed to perform their duties, they could be impeached and removed from office.[26] When state officials did intervene, Speranza wrote, "the Chief Executive of West Virginia admitted to me that it was practically impossible to obtain convictions through the local courts, and, however good his intentions, his powers seem very limited."[27]

The issue of debt peonage resurfaced in 1907, when Secretary of State Elihu Root informed Governor William M. O. Dawson of a report received from the Italian ambassador in Washington, D.C., about Italian laborers forced to work for the Raleigh Lumber Company against their will. Governor Dawson immediately dispatched Kanawha County detective Howard Smith and deputy United States marshal Dan Cunningham along with an interpreter to investigate the charges, secure the release of the men if the charges were true, and file reports on their findings.[28]

According to Smith's report, the twenty-six Italian men and one boy were supplied by the New York labor agency of Sparte, Frank and Company. The men left New York on November 29, 1906, to work on a logging railroad under construction by the Raleigh Lumber Company from its woods operation to the town of Raleigh, which was located on the Piney Branch of the Chesapeake and Ohio Railway. Wages and conditions were at the center of the dispute; the company contract signed by the men before they left New York clearly stated that they would work on the railroad grade for $1.50 to $1.65 per ten-hour day with the company furnishing transportation. The men insisted, however, that they had been promised that their jobs would involve laying steel for the railroad. Moreover, they were charged for their transportation although that was included in the bargain. Smith was quick to put his finger on the problem when he observed that the labor agent probably had misled the men, all of whom were illiterate in English. At any rate, the Italian recruits became dissatisfied and refused to work, Smith reported. That same afternoon, nineteen men and the boy walked off the job and hiked to Prince, a station on the C&O trunk line, where they arrived about daybreak the next morning. There they were arrested by J. C. Lilly, a Raleigh County constable, on a warrant issued by a local justice of the peace charging the laborers with intent to defraud the Raleigh Lumber Company. Upon arrest, five of them paid the $12 transportation and these five and the boy were released.[29]

Before their arrest, the men had paid an Italian living at Prince to send a telegram to New York to get money to pay for their transportation back to that city, but failing to receive the money, they had reluctantly returned to work. Then Smith and Cunningham arrived to make their investigation. Upon learning of the reason for their presence, the Italians threw down their tools and insisted on leaving with the investigators. "They left their camp, leaving their baggage, such as trunks, valises, blankets, etc., and followed us to Raleigh, a distance of six miles, with nothing except the clothing that they wore," Smith reported. Upon instructions from Governor Dawson, Smith brought the remaining Italians to Charleston. There they were boarded until January 7, when an Italian Moses arrived to lead them out of the land of bondage and back to Hoboken, New Jersey.[30]

Smith found that conditions in the Raleigh camps were no different than in similar work camps, but a sworn statement given by a fellow workman who represented the Italians clearly shows that they saw the situation very differently. In addition to the lower than promised pay and grading work rather than laying rails (which the men apparently had been doing in New York for a surface transportation line), Tom Trombo claimed that the men were compelled "to work in rain and snow, and when we refuse to work we get nothing to eat." Food prices were excessive, and although they were assessed fifty cents per month for the doctor, one man who was sick for seventeen days saw the doctor only twice. Also they were assessed fifty cents per month for a shanty thirty by fourteen feet, which slept fifteen men. For the first five days on the job, the men were compelled to sleep in a boxcar without beds and fed bread and water once a day under the watchful eye of an armed guard. Moreover, they had been there since November 30 and had worked steadily but received no pay.[31]

Of course, the company had a different story, denying that the workers had ever been locked in a boxcar, manacled, or held at gunpoint. In a sworn deposition, W. H. Houston, the company's construction superintendent, stated that when the men had arrived at the camp they demanded spring beds and mattresses, that all work together, that they live in a boarding-house, that they be provided with beer and wine, and other conditions the superintendent considered ridiculous. Houston was either unable or re-fused to comply with most of the workers' demands, but he did agree to give them spring beds and mattresses, something he had never done before. He claimed that he had been "handling Italians for twenty-three years," thousands of them, in fact, and employed seventy-two Italian workers on the job for the last six months, but there was no appeasing this group. When the men walked to Prince, Houston talked them into returning to work. Not only had he brought the Italians back in a wagon, he also advanced them blankets, bedding, cooking utensils, "all manner of food which they asked for without any restraint," and mittens and rubber boots, a total of $200 worth of goods, before they had performed a single day's work. Houston claimed that the housing was better than that enjoyed by two-thirds of Americans. These Italians hailed from the provinces of Briutsea and Rome and called for particular foods. "As the labor has been very scarce, we have been very lenient, in fact too much so, allowing the men almost to dictate themselves where they should work, how they should work, and when they should work." According to the bookkeeper, some of the Italians were still in debt to the company.[32]

According to company testimony, the Italians found a gun pointed at them only when they were confronted by Constable Lilly. John H. Hatcher, attorney for the Raleigh Lumber Company, stated that the men had been arrested and detained by Lilly as they were attempting to leave. They refused to pay transportation and were arrested under the Boarding House Law. When the constable attempted to search them for weapons, they refused, whereupon the constable searched them at gunpoint and detained the disgruntled laborers until Houston came for them.[33] It is unlikely that either side held claims to higher morality in this case, but it does demonstrate the perfidious potential in the system. Coal companies in southern West Virginia commonly prevented workers brought in on transportation from leaving until they had paid the charges. Likewise, imported coal miners also ran away, and the Raleigh Lumber Company guards and managers were fully aware of these methods of restraint.

During this same period, a serious charge of peonage was leveled against the Ritter Lumber Company in nearby Wyoming County. On December 1, 1906, Governor Dawson sent Deputy U.S. Marshal Dan Cunningham to Estell (renamed Maben), where Ritter Lumber was constructing a town, a private railroad, and one of the largest lumber mills in the state. According to Cunningham's report, Bureau No. 7 of the Southern Immigration Company, New York, had supplied Ritter with forty-six laborers composed of "mixed races and nationalities." In typical fashion, the railroad transportation charges were paid by the company from New York to West Virginia, and the contractor delivered the men to Estell. Cunningham's investigation revealed that one of these men, an Italian known only as Number 288 on the time book, became dissatisfied and left the company without repaying the transportation charges incurred for his travel to Estell. Italian 288 was overtaken at Prince station in Fayette County, about forty miles from Estell, by Elias Hatfield, a detective for the Virginian Railway. A "scrap" ensued in which the Italian was wounded. According to the sworn affidavit of company guard William Tolliver, to whom Number 288 was turned over, railroad policeman Elias Hatfield "punched him with a pistol, and I saw a ring on his jaw, and he said that was the place where Hatfield had punched him."[34]

Cunningham reported that this was only one of numerous reports of cruelty committed by Ritter guards but the only one he had substantiated. He concluded from the evidence that the men brought in on transportation by the Ritter Lumber Company were "compelled, by force or otherwise, to work" until they had paid off the transportation expenses advanced by the company. "If a man escapes the vigilant guards he is pursued and captured without due process of law, returned and compelled to work again under guard."[35]

Evidence of peonage was not difficult to uncover for the company men themselves provided it in sworn affidavits. The superintendent of the Ritter Lumber Company, S. M. Wolfe, explained that each man brought in on transportation was advanced the transportation expense and required to work it off; it was refunded if the man worked for the company at least six months. Somewhat inconsistently, Wolfe responded to the question of whether Italians had been "detained and not allowed to leave the works by armed men" by claiming that they had not. But when asked if any of the laborers had been detained by "threats, guards or armed men," he admitted that about "ten to twenty" of them had been. Moreover, Wolfe testified that guards were maintained at the Estell operation "for keeping men from leaving without paying us (Wm. Ritter Lumber Company) the amount furnished them for transportation from New York and other places." Ritter company guard William Tolliver also stated in a sworn affidavit that his duties were "to keep peace, and to hold the men on the works until they paid the money due the Wm. Ritter Lumber Co. for transportation and board." He admitted that he had given the workers a choice, "to stand their trial, pay the money, or return to work." Moreover, he had done this "several times," and occasionally used force.[36] Before such compelling testimony, indictments against the Raleigh and Ritter Lumber Companies were quickly issued by the grand jury. A pretrial plea of guilty by both companies was accepted by the prosecuting attorneys of Raleigh and Wyoming Counties as part of a plea bargain for dropping the indictments on peonage charges against employees and Elias Hatfield.[37]

The trials officially began July 12, 1907, in the court of U.S. district judge Alston G. Dayton. In January of that year Ritter had purchased the Raleigh Lumber Company, however, and that focused attention on Ritter. The owner, William Ritter, testified at the trial that the company had agreed to the plea bargain to protect the employees involved. With the company's formal admission of guilt, Judge Dayton abruptly called an end to the trial. Dayton observed that the company ought to be punished to deter others who might commit the same crime but noted that "many times offences are committed, not through improper motives, not with malice and with evil hearts, but through mistaken ideas and conceptions of their rights and of what the law is."[38] To err is human, in other words, and an acknowledgment of ignorance of the law is a mitigating factor if not a legal protection. Because the company had pleaded guilty to the charge, Judge Dayton thus dismissed the charges of a company conspiracy against the defendants. Dayton observed that "looking these men [Ritter and his superintendent] in the face," he concluded that "it is inconceivable to me I say, to believe that these men, for the paltry sums of money involved, went to New York and got these men, paid their transportation and got them into their debt, for the purpose of violating the law." The judge deflated the seriousness of the crime by noting that hardly anyone was actually aware of the law against peonage, although this seemed to ignore the attention devoted to the federal prosecutions for peonage in the South by the national press and even the publicity given to the peonage allegations in West Virginia in 1903. Dayton acknowledged that peonage was a heinous crime, but he heaped most of his opprobrium on the victims. In fact, the judge asserted, he had no "sympathy with these fellows who did not go down there and keep their contracts and live up to their honest debts; but at the same time, this law, tender of the liberty of the people, makes this company technically a violator of the law."[39] Not surprisingly, therefore, Judge Dayton fined the Ritter Lumber Company the minimum penalty of $1,000 for pleading guilty to one charge of peonage. There was no confusing this with a defeat, for even the *Southern Lumberman*, an industry trade journal, reported it as a "victory for the lumber companies."[40]

Much has been made of the close business and family ties between industrialists and public officials in West Virginia, but the Ritter peonage case also demonstrates how local elites were bound together by politics. The presiding trial judge for the U.S. Southern District, Judge Benjamin F. Keller, excused himself from the Ritter case because of his business interests in the Ritter Lumber Company, and Judge Alston G. Dayton of the Northern District of West Virginia replaced him. Dayton owed his judgeship to West Virginia industrialist-senators Stephen B. Elkins and Nathan B. Scott, and the intricate web of business-political associations gave an enormous amount of power to the courts when litigation deemed detrimental to industrial development came before them. This was true not only at the highest level but at the county level as well, where it was difficult to get officials to proceed against companies.[41]

As they did in much of America at the turn of the century, immigrants from southern and eastern Europe encountered discrimination in West Virginia. Expressions of prejudice are abundant in newspaper editorials, court cases, and local responses to general social conflicts, which nativists redefined as ethnic war. Local writers often complained that immigrants were the worst class of people who were recruited from the "slums and dives" of big cities and blamed them for the labor problems experienced by the railroad, lumber, and coal companies in West Virginia. For example, an article in the Raleigh newspaper argued that Welsh, German, or Scottish workers should be substituted for the Italians in the lumber and coal industries because they were more likely to stay in West Virginia and become good citizens, the clear implication being that the Italians would not.[42]

The same attitude was expressed at the highest official level when Governor Dawson devoted most of his special message to the legislature in 1907 to advocating the importation of a "better class" of laborers into the state. Many of the laborers imported on transportation for the lumber and coal industries, he argued, "are of different nationalities; unable to speak our language and unable to protect themselves; many are brutal and vicious; and their manhood and spirit crushed by centuries of oppression in the foreign lands, they confuse liberty with license." Nevertheless, "they are human beings," Dawson observed, and they should be "treated justly." Dawson advised that efforts be made "to induce desirable labor to settle within our borders," a "better class of immigrants" such as those from Poland, Sweden, Norway, and the British Isles. Quoting a letter from an industrialist whose opinions on the subject were in accord with his own, Dawson argued that "unless something is done along this line, we will be swamped by a large influx of immigrants from southern Italy," a large percentage of whom he worried would "remain in the state and become fixed residents." They were clearly an undesirable addition to the population, and Dawson contended that "something should be done towards inducing desirable immigration to this state."[43] The legislature ignored the governor's recommendation, but it did resurrect the Bureau of Immigration, whose director subsequently attempted without much success to recruit labor from England and Wales. The bureau was more successful in recruiting immigrant workers from southern Europe and so added his own contribution to the worries of men like Governor Dawson.[44]

It is clear from the Raleigh and Ritter cases and a considerable body of other evidence that the labor scarcity in the mountains prompted some companies into serious abuses of civil liberties, particularly of those men who did not understand the language and were contracted by a labor agent. An abundance of evidence also shows that racial and ethnic chauvinism was the root cause of the animosity found not just among upper-class modernizers but also local elites and workers. Local newspapers generally referred to blacks and foreigners, especially Italians, in derogatory terms. For example, on August 14, 1905, eight Italians were blown to "Kingdom Come" when dynamite exploded under their cabin at Dunlevie. The local newspaper observed that many believed that the Italians had stolen the dynamite and hidden it under the cabin and accidentally detonated it when they got drunk and fired a bullet through the floor. Most accepted the more plausible explanation that the Italians had been murdered by Americans who resented the Italians taking jobs from natives. This view was reinforced by an occurrence several weeks earlier on Cheat Mountain when an attempt was made to blow up an Italian shack. In neither case were the perpetrators ever identified or brought to justice.[45]

In another of innumerable similar examples, the editor of the *Pocahontas Times* reported the arrest of "a half dozen Dagoes" for fighting with a black worker at the tannery in Marlinton, declaring that "the 'Talys ran a truck over the coon." The same paper reprinted a column from the *Nicholas Republican* about a near "race war" in Tioga, a logging camp near Richwood, with the observation that "the whites have been making trouble for the Bohunks in Nicholas County." The trouble began when a timber contractor fired all of the American workers and replaced them with foreigners. When the authorities learned that approximately one hundred armed "Americans" were marching from Camden-on-Gauley to Tioga "to rid the mills and lumber camps of the foreigners," they at once organized a posse and intercepted them just outside of Tioga, narrowly preventing a bloodbath.[46]

Racial antagonism toward foreigners of southern European extraction extended to other "dark people" as well. Joe Aits, a Syrian storekeeper at the logging camp of Dunlevie, was attacked by local vigilantes who gave him a "terrible beating" and then threw him into the Greenbrier River. The following day he received a notice "to leave town by Jan. 10 [1909] or be tarred and feathered." It was signed "White Caps." Another Syrian, Sain Slyman, a peddler who made his home in Davis, was robbed and murdered on a road in Pocahontas County. Only twenty-six at the time of his death, he left a wife and two children in Syria. Two young men, a farmer from Pendleton County and a logger who worked off-season as his hired hand, were arrested for the murder, and one of them blurted out to authorities that he shot the man and his partner stole $28 from the peddler's pocket. "Peddlers ought all to be killed" was the only justification given.[47]

The oppressive conditions Italian immigrant workers often endured sometimes prompted them to take violent action against the companies that employed them. Approximately four hundred Italians employed on the Roaring Creek and Charleston Railroad in Randolph County reportedly went on strike in 1894 because they had not been paid for three months. The men were said to be near starvation, and there was a fear that they "may become desperate." The strikers had already torn out the switches trapping the only locomotive owned by the logging road.[48]

One of the most violent of such episodes occurred in 1908 when nine Italian laborers who worked for the West Virginia Pulp and Paper Company at Spruce stormed the company office, clubbed a clerk to death, and wounded a company official. Eight of the Italians were immediately captured, tried, and sentenced to eighteen years each in prison. The ninth took to the hills but was captured a few months later in a nearby camp where Italian workers had been feeding him at night with food from the dining hall. The murdered employee was a native, and his death created an avalanche of hostility from local residents against Italians.[49]

Racial and ethnic clashes also occurred among the newcomers themselves. "Beer bottles, stones, axes and butcher knives were the implements of war in a running duel" between three white American "lumbermen," John Mapes, Dan Lary, and James Hawks, and a group of Italians led by "John I and S. Colio" at Glady. The battle culminated in the death of James Hawks; "Lumberman Shot by Dago," read the caption in the news report. The fight had its inception in Italian "hot-headedness," the paper reported. Hawks, Mapes, and Lary were on their way to the depot at Glady and were jesting with one another in "rough language," which the Italians apparently thought was directed at them. Angered, the Italians began following the three lumbermen, "muttering threats." One of the Italians carried an ax, another an "ugly looking butcher knife." Mapes picked up a beer bottle and sharp stones to use on the Italians, but Hawks stopped him and tried to cool the situation. Nevertheless, Mapes got off a few stones at the Italians and the Americans made a "sprint for shelter." Unfortunately, "Hawks being closest to the pursuers received the benefit of one of the three shots fired by I." After firing the shots, the Italian "fled to the bush and has not been definitely located since though believed to have been seen at Beverly and Cass." Hawks died from his wound the following night, and the deputy sheriff immediately launched a search. A local newspaper reported that "feeling against the perpetrators of this crime is of course very strong and there is more or less animosity between the lumbermen and the remaining Italians as a result of the crime."[50]

In another case, a "blood feud" was reportedly the motive behind the stabbing of Summers Mann, an African American youth, by fourteen-year-old Guimm Ross, an Italian immigrant from Naples. The two boys had "fought with each other for some days" before the affray. Both worked at the tannery in Marlinton when the Italian boy called after Mann "the only English words that he knew, which were highly colored and reflected on Summers's ancestry." Summers beat the boy for his impertinence and Ross pulled a knife and stabbed Summers in the lung. Three other boys witnessed the fight and substantiated Ross's claim of self-defense; Summers survived and charges against Ross were dropped.[51]

"Bobo Baskins (Negro)" was murdered by Albert Dawson Alkire in Abraham King's saloon in Hendricks for singing a parody of Amanda Ellen King's song "The West Virginia Hills," the lyrics of which went something like this:

Oh! the West Virginia snakes!
 With their black and yellow bands,
And their fangs as filled with poison
 As Lucretia Borgia's hands;
Oh! the snakes, horrible snakes!
 How I hate those West Virginia snakes;
The devil dooming, slime consuming,
 Writhing, sliding, ugly snakes!

The term "snakes" was intentionally uncomplimentary when "applied to native West Virginians by transient laborers from other states." Alkire, a native worker from Upshur County, ordered the sneering songster to "shut up or be shot," and when he continued, the West Virginian shot him "right between his eyes." Alkire left for parts unknown, and "nobody pursued him because they thought the Negro got what was coming to him."[52]

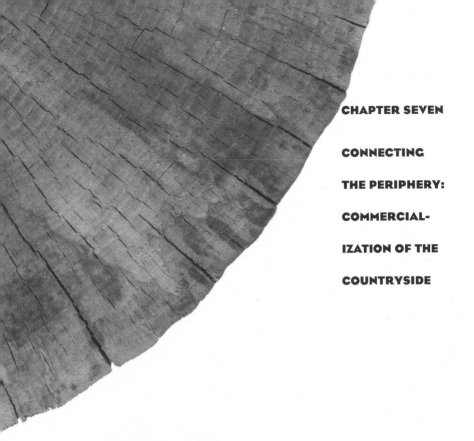

CHAPTER SEVEN

CONNECTING

THE PERIPHERY:

COMMERCIAL-

IZATION OF THE

COUNTRYSIDE

Many lumber towns were commercial centers in addition to being significant industrial sites, depending on their scale of operations. The mills not only brought in workers from outside the region but also attracted job seekers from the countryside. As the population swelled, so too did the need for the social services required of a wage-earning population now dependent on others to produce their subsistence. Many lumber towns were incorporated, and the demand for services attracted independent businesses to augment the services provided by the companies. A middle class of businessmen and professionals emerged in the backcounties to serve residents in the new towns and countryside. The number of stores of all description, hotels, banks, doctors, lawyers, teachers, and clergy increased dramatically throughout the lumber towns and commercial market centers.

The large milling centers such as Davis, Cass, Rainelle, and Richwood attracted a comparatively large population, which in turn sparked a significant expansion in commercial and professional enterprises. Davis was incorporated on December 1, 1889, about five years after the railroad reached the site on November 1, 1884. Henry G. Davis owned all the land, but he divided the town into lots and sold them fee simple. Most owners were responsible for constructing their own dwellings or other buildings.[1] Therefore, while he exerted substantial political and economic influence, Davis was uninterested in running a company-owned town.

In 1889 Davis had a population of 909, which quickly stabilized at 3,000 during the next few years and remained at that level until the late 1920s. In its heyday Davis boasted Tucker County's first high school and first hospital, two national banks served the financial needs of the community, and two hotels provided rooms for travelers from near and far. Fourteen years after the electric light was invented, the Davis Electric Light Company was established to provide electricity for homes and businesses and to light the streets. Two newspapers of different political persuasions served Davis, the *Davis Republican* and the *Davis News*, both founded in the 1890s. During Davis's sensational rise between 1886 and 1890, the town had three lawyers, three doctors, two dentists, two barbershops, two blacksmith shops, three butcher shops, two shoemaker shops, a printing office, a post office, two bakeries, two milliner shops, a harness shop, and numerous clothing, dry goods, and grocery stores. The first church established in Davis was the Presbyterian, organized in 1886, and by 1900 four more churches had opened their doors. In the mid-1890s an opera house was built with a twelve-hundred-seat capacity and private boxes decorated in gold leaf. No lumber town would be complete without saloons; Davis officially listed six of them in 1910, but innumerable illegal saloons, "pigs' ears," existed in the neighborhood.[2]

Tucker County historian Homer Floyd Fansler states that "the Town of Davis struck awe into the rustic bumpkins of Canaan and Dry Fork." Fansler reproduced the following poem by an unknown author in his history, suggesting what proud town dwellers believed was the influence of the changes on isolated rural people in the countryside surrounding Davis:

Jes in frum Caynane

I jes cum in frum the valley of Caynane,
An I heered the folks up thar a sayin
Bout this bein sich a peart like town,
I got on my hoss an thot I'd cum down
An seed for myself if what they said is true,
Bout havin steam injuns an water works tu.

Wall stranger I never wus in har afore;
It sprises me an I tell yer what's more,
If I hadn't cum down I'd never a knowd
How big yer town wus but I'll be blowed!
Jes seed the houses, tu fine fer me I own;
An dash my britches if thar aint one uv stone.

What's em ropes fer hung up on a pole,
An all em glass things, ell bless my soul;
What's that thing bangin up in the street?
It looks right smart, but stranger I'm beat;
Lectricity! An yer say it makes a light?
By gosh I'm gonna seed it if it takes all night.

Is that the thing that pulls out the train?
It must be, fer they say up in Caynane
That it cums to town a puffin an a blowin,
Wus than a hoss when he cums in frum mowin;
Oh! It's an injun, an has a tender behin,
An all em cars a standin in a line!

Do I rub snuff? Wall I reckon I do;
I been a hankerin all day for a chew;
Say, if yer don't keer, I'll take sum home
Fer the gals an my ole woman, Siloam;
She be the best critter an strong as a hoss,
Our kids air all gals an she be the boss.

Now my farm is jes tolable, yer see,
My ole woman says I can't pick a pea,
So her an the gals do the plantin an hoein
An I lay aroun an see the stuff growin;
Course sum days I pick up an go to the brook
An tote home any fish that gits on my hook.

I be bliged tu yer stranger, fer showin me aroun,
An I'll know more next time I cum tu yer town;
The roads up the mountain air powful rough,
Yer reckon yer could spare a little more snuff?
I be bliged agin an I be off fer home
An next time I cum I'll bring Siloam.[3]

D. K. TETER.

FRESH
OYSTERS

Undoubtedly Fansler and his poet exaggerated the awe that boom towns such as Davis inspired in the native population, but their sentiments were more expressions of hope than of confirmation. Actually, the fate of all mill towns depended completely on the lumber business. Throughout the back-counties of West Virginia hundreds of timber towns grew phenomenally and then declined just as dramatically. The town of Hendricks, Tucker County, for example, contained only five buildings in 1887: three houses, a sawmill, and a church. Then H. G. Davis's West Virginia Central and Pittsburgh Railroad passed through in 1889 and Hendricks became a boom town. That the railroad was coming had been known for two years before its arrival, and merchants converged on the site to find strategic locations. Most of the merchants and tradesmen came from elsewhere in West Virginia, but some of these original businessmen came from Indiana, Pennsylvania, New York, and Maryland. The Dry Fork Railway, established in 1893 by Philadelphian Robert F. Whitmer, extended thirty-one miles into the forest to the mill town of Horton, and Hendricks became its headquarters. The railroad shops and wood product industries in Hendricks generated commercial activity far beyond the demand of the town's peak population of fifteen hundred in 1910. In its heyday between 1894 and 1914, probably the typical longevity curve for modest lumber towns, Hendricks had two banks, three hotels, seven restaurants, seven stores, an opera house, a bakery, jewelry store, drugstore, commercial photographer, movie theater, two handle factories, a blacksmith shop, two doctors, two barbers, and four churches. After the lumber was cut out, Hendricks followed the decline typical of many small mill towns, first by losing its industrial base, then its population, and finally the merchants, to settle into a quiet village.[4]

Some of the smaller mill towns experienced an even more dramatic swing of fortune. Hambleton, also in Tucker County, was a only a post office named Black Fork located in a private home before Henry G. Davis's rail-road arrived. Hambleton thrived and died with the lumber industry. The Huling Lumber Company, established by a mill operator from Pennsylvania, began operation in 1889, sold out to investors from New York, and in 1897 was purchased by the Otter Creek Boom and Lumber Company. After a fire in 1899, it was rebuilt into one of the largest and most modern mills in the

Facing page: Railroads regularly delivered goods from the national markets, including fresh oysters served at the Star Restaurant, Whitmer, Randolph County, ca. 1910. (West Virginia and Regional History Collection, West Virginia University Libraries)

state. Families were brought in from New Hampshire, and the largest tannery in the state was operated there for a time. The town's peak years roughly paralleled those of Hendricks, with many commercial businesses supporting a resident population of two thousand. When the lumber industry declined, however, workers moved on and so did the merchants, leaving Hambleton to wither away.[5]

Some towns flourished briefly and then disappeared completely. Evenwood, for example, was founded by the Raine and Andrews Company in 1904. This Randolph County mill town initially was established by about two hundred Pennsylvanians who were brought in to begin lumbering and milling operations. Subsequently, the population grew to over one thousand people. At its peak, the company town had a single-band mill, a planing mill, and a heading mill that employed most of the residents. Noted locally for its community spirit, an unusual quality when most lumber towns had an air of impermanence, Evenwood prohibited saloons, but a community band provided some recreation and was good enough to play throughout the region. A community baseball team was sponsored by the company, and special trains took the fans along when the team played games in other towns. The town was closed in 1922 when the company's owners, Thomas and John Raine, moved their operations and employees to Rainelle.[6]

A multitude of much smaller towns were born, lived briefly, and then disappeared. Mackeyville, for example, named after its mill operator, John Mackey of New York, lasted only from 1890 to 1900. Once the timberlands had been cut over, the reason for the town ceased to exist and so did Mackeyville.[7]

Even though most lumber towns were temporary in that they were either diminished significantly or vanished entirely when the timber was cut out, they influenced the lives of dwellers in both town and countryside by providing employment, binding the country people to the cash economy, and radiating the expanding consumerism of the modern American economy and the professionalization of services.

Large or small, lumber mill towns and the railroads that served them exerted significant commercial influence on the surrounding countryside. A general store was likely to be one of the first buildings erected in new lumber towns. The general store was just that, a store with a general inventory of goods selected to provide basic necessities and perhaps a few small luxuries. Companies often built their own stores to supply services absent in remote areas before logging operations began. Company stores serviced not only company employees but other residents of the countryside. Some of the company stores were very large operations with branches and a form of vertical integration that provided control over delivery of goods, which was so important in the remote backcountry.

When the development of Cass began in 1900, only a small country store was located nearby. Therefore, West Virginia Pulp and Paper decided to build a facility large enough to supply its needs. Incorporated as the Pocahontas Supply Company in 1902, the company store became one of the largest of its kind in the nation and operated successfully until it closed forty-five years later.[8] The store built branches at Spruce, Cheat Bridge, Laurel Bank, and Bemis. The main store at Cass was an impressive operation carrying a wide variety of merchandise for sale to employees and local farmers. Products stocked by the store included fabrics, jewelry, furniture, dishes, household wares, coal, hay, groceries, books, and drugs. Staples such as canned goods, feed, nails, fencing, and loggers' boots were bought by the train carload. As many as four carloads of condensed milk were purchased at one time. It also stocked toys at Christmas and flowers at Easter, and it sent dry cleaning to Baltimore. The store reportedly generated more than $1 million worth of business annually.[9]

Boarding a large number of woodsmen and supplying the mill workers posed a serious strategic problem for the company. For example, the company purchased 11,380 pounds of beef in June 1919 to feed its men in the woods camps. Managers soon recognized that costs would be greatly reduced and supply more reliable if live animals were maintained nearby. Because of the lack of refrigeration, live poultry was kept in a pen nearby, and the company made provisions for the purchase and slaughter of beef cattle from local farmers and also operated two farms and a slaughterhouse to supply its business.[10]

The company store in Cass, as in most lumber (and coal) towns in the mountains, was the social center of town. People of all classes and character intersected at the store: bosses, woodsmen, mill hands and members of their families, passengers waiting for the train to arrive at the depot, or tramps simply following the railroad tracks. The main store was a large building three hundred feet long and sixty feet wide with full basement and second story. Open from 8:00 A.M. to 8:00 P.M., it provided a place for people to pass the time of day and catch up on local gossip. Most business at the store was transacted with employees on a credit basis. Scrip, money redeemable only at the company store, was not used at Cass, although it was in many lumber towns.[11]

Few company stores equaled the Pocahontas Supply Company at Cass in size and influence on the lives of people who lived within its radius, but the numerous general stores established in lumber towns by independent businessmen also were the contact points between country folk and the market system during the transition. Some of these independent stores were sizable operations. The J. E. Poling and Company store in Hendricks, for example, employed thirty-three people and operated a business with gross receipts of $250,000 annually. The building not only supplied local mill town residents but also served as the post office, railway station, and express office.[12]

In the larger commercial and service centers such as Elkins, the general store was eclipsed by the department store and specialized shops, including hardware, clothing, and drugstores. In lumber-dominated towns, however, the general store held its own for the life of the towns even as specialized shops moved in when the logging boom matured. Even though specialized shops came to Davis during its peak years, the number of general stores increased from four in 1891 to eight in 1923. Similarly, Richwood grew quickly to a town of five thousand in 1910, and the number of general stores increased from eight in 1902 to seventeen in 1914. In smaller lumber towns, those without numerous specialized stores, the general store was even more important to the life of the community and farming countryside. Rural residents clearly provided the business that allowed many of the general stores in hamlets like Camden-on-Gauley, Dunmore, and Durbin to survive.[13]

The mill towns attracted people out of all proportion to their size because there were relatively few towns in a vast rural countryside. Whether they came for business or pleasure, people needed a place to sleep, and so hotels were among the first businesses to spring up in lumber towns. Even insignificant logging towns such as Dunmore, population 120, had two hotels, and Durbin, which was only a post office in 1902, had two hotels.[14] As the industry rose toward peak production during the first decade of the century, the number of towns multiplied and so did the number of hotels. An accurate count would be nearly impossible, but it is clear that the multitude of hotels in these small settlements were established not to serve townsfolk but business travelers, railroaders and woodsmen, and rural mountain farmers in town for supplies or recreation.

Banks are another indicator of the economic development that accompanied the industrial transition in the mountains. Before the logging boom, and indeed throughout most of the state's history, the lack of banking facilities was perceived by West Virginians as a serious handicap to the development of the state. Business directories for 1891 indicate no banks in logging towns of the three major logging counties, with the exception of Elkins.

Although only three years old, Elkins had the distinct advantage of being the residence of H. G. Davis and S. B. Elkins, and it served as the headquarters of their railroad. Capital was, therefore, available to start a bank that would handle the industrialists' business transactions. Even though Elkins was destined to become the major commercial center for the surrounding counties, it had only one bank. Over the course of the ensuing decade, the county seats of the focus mountain counties became the financial centers of the county, and only the major lumber towns such as Davis and Richwood had banks of their own. The lack of banks in the small lumber towns is somewhat deceiving, for although the temporary nature of the logging town is highlighted by the lack of banks, financial power along with political power became concentrated in the county seats easily accessed by railroad for those who lived in the lumber towns and camps. From a local contemporary perspective, banks in the nearby large towns and county seats represented a major advance over conditions that prevailed before the transition.

The growth in population and increasing complexity of institutions also required professional services. Not surprisingly, lawyers gravitated to the county seats where court business was transacted or to the large lumber towns such as Richwood. Company towns, even large ones, did not provide an appropriate atmosphere for lawyering. The company employed lawyers, but they too were most likely to reside in the seat of county government. Cass did not have a resident lawyer, but large independent lumber towns might generate sufficient business to attract a few lawyers. Physicians, while increasing in number in the county seats too, were found in almost all the lumber towns. Physicians in the smaller towns were hired by the companies to tend to their employees, and other patients on a paying basis, and hence more physicians than other professionals were found in logging towns. Davis was the exception that proved the rule, with two lawyers and two physicians in 1891 and four lawyers and three physicians in 1906, a number that remained steady for the next decade. By 1923, however, even Davis generally conformed to the pattern that prevailed in logging towns with one lawyer, four physicians, and, out of pattern, one dentist.[15]

The burgeoning business and professional services found in the new towns required utilities previously unknown in the mountains. Most of the significant lumber towns had electricity provided by generators operated by steam from wood waste incinerators. They also generally had telephone service, although at times, as in Horton, which was hooked up through Hendricks, it was not direct. Within a decade, however, all of the major lumber towns had telephone companies to provide connections with the

Table 9. Physicians, Lawyers, and Dentists in Lumber Towns, 1891–1923

Town	1891	1902	1906	1914	1923
Cass					2/0/1
Camden-on-Gauley				1/	1/1/
Davis	2/2/	3/6/	3/4/1	3/4/2	4/1/1
Dobbin		1/		1/	
Dunmore		2/	1/		
Durbin		3/	2/0/1	2/	2/
Hambleton		1/	3/	1/	
Hendricks	2/	1/		1/	
Horton		1/	2/	1/	
Richwood		2/1/	5/2/1	3/2/2	8/7/2

Source: *West Virginia Gazetteer and Business Directory*, respective towns and years. Dentists during this period often traveled a circuit of towns, visiting once or twice a year. They notified local residents of the dates of their visits through the local papers. See, for example, *Pocahontas Times*, January 7, 1892, advertisement page.

outside world. Often, as in Cass, the initial telephone was installed for the company's business purposes but could be used by residents if necessary. Since towns hugged the railroads, Western Union telegraph service also was available, as was railroad express service through the railroad depot.[16]

Photography had become cheap and accessible to ordinary Americans by the turn of the century, and they took great pleasure in posing for individual, group, and thematic photographs of themselves. Wood hicks were no exception. The photographs taken of the downed giants of the woods would seem to be limitless, and their sheer number indicates that Americans generally, like their counterparts among the boosters of West Virginia development, realized that the end of a historic epoch was near; America was finally destined to emerge out of the woods and into the light of "civilization." The conquering heroes of this transformation, the true agents of progress, were the lumberjacks and wood hicks who did battle with the wilderness and laid it low. That they too understood themselves in this role is evidenced by the number of pictures they had made of themselves in their logging outfits by commercial photographers who came to nearly every lumber town in the mountains to document and confirm these ambitions.

Wood hicks came to town for alcohol, poker, prostitutes, and to have their pictures taken. At least one commercial photographer operated in Davis for the first three decades of its existence. Richwood had two photographers in

1914 and three by 1923. One might expect to find professional photographers only in the larger lumber towns, but they also plied their trade in most
of the smaller towns such as Hambleton, Durbin, Horton, and innumerable
others.[17]

For residents and others who lived in the countryside the lumber towns
also provided a social center where recreation and entertainment could be
found. Most often, these were traditionally male activities that appealed to
timber workers in town for a good time. Billiard parlors, or poolrooms,
provided cheap male recreation. Often they were organized as independent
businesses, but saloon keepers found that having a poolroom improved their
business. Bowling was another popular pastime in many lumber towns,
although not usually available in the smallest ones. A bowling alley required
an expert to set up and level the alleys, along with the specialized nature of
the building itself, whereas anyone with a little room and the money could
purchase a pool table or two and be in business.[18]

Some lumber towns worked actively to organize recreational opportunities. Richwood, for example, boasted not only a movie theater, poolroom,
and roller rink but also provided more elevated entertainment through the
Richwood Chautauqua Association, Richwood Lyceum Association, and
Richwood Fair Association. Many towns acquired movie houses early, and
larger towns such as Davis and Richwood boasted opera houses that imported live entertainment, normally musical follies or dramatic troupes.
Music played a much more important role in the lives of lumber towns of all
sizes than might be expected, and not just the rowdy music associated with
saloons and bawdy houses. Amateur bands and orchestras were popular
throughout rural America during this period, and the lumber towns of West
Virginia were no exception. Again the larger towns such as Davis and
Richwood had bands, sometimes more than one. Davis had a cornet band in
1902, and by 1906 Herbert L. Blaker had begun his long career as the leader
of the Mountain City Band. In 1906, the citizens of Richwood enjoyed
music by the Richwood City Band, which shared its audience by 1914 with
the company-sponsored Tannery Band.[19]

Whether a community had a band probably depended on the circumstances and availability of skilled players, a leader, and community or company support. Even the smaller lumber towns supported bands, however.
Tiny Hambleton was home to a cornet band and an orchestra. Perhaps the
most interesting example of a small town band was that found in Hendricks.
In 1910 an all-male twenty-one-piece orchestra was organized in the city, but
a group called the Mountain Beauties Band drew the most attention. Simply

listed as a "ladies band" in the state's business directory, the Mountain Beauties were organized into a twelve-piece band in 1899.[20] Seven of the twelve members were daughters of Joseph and Sophia Craver, who came to Hendricks in 1895 and built the Craver Hotel. According to Tucker County historian Fansler, "As the other girls married and moved away, their places were taken by younger Craver sisters until the band was composed entirely of the nine Craver sisters. They played well and became quite popular, playing at ship launchings in Newport News, Virginia, and on excursion boats plying Chesapeake Bay."[21]

Railroads and wood processing not only generated commercial centers but also refocused services provided by government. As was true in America generally, business and government merged in realigned county seats. Saint George in Tucker County was a typical rustic mountain county seat of the preindustrial era. It had a population of three hundred in 1891 and few outside connections except through Parsons, seven wagon-road miles away on the West Virginia Central and Pittsburgh Railroad, and the nearest bank was twenty-four miles away in Philippi. The town did have two weekly newspapers, the *Pioneer* and the *Democrat*. Serving a farming population, the town had four general stores, a shoemaker, a blacksmith, and a gristmill. As the county seat, it had four hotels, eight lawyers, and one physician. Saint George never was much of a commercial enterprise, but after the county seat was moved to Parsons in 1893, it lost all its previous importance. Although a few artisans continued to serve the farmers and loggers, by 1914 the newspapers had folded, all of the hotels had closed their doors, and not a single lawyer or physician served the community.[22]

The new county seat of Parsons, seven miles upstream on the Cheat River, at the junction of the West Virginia Central and Pittsburgh Railroad was very different. Parsons was developed as a shipping center. Even before the county seat was moved to Parsons, business directories described the town in 1891 as "the distributing point for a large section of country" and as "one of the most prosperous towns on the [WVC&P] road." Mostly lumber and livestock were shipped from Parsons at this time, but "fruit of all kinds and grain [were] produced in abundance," and "vast quantities of timber abound, thousands of acres of which remain untouched."[23] Even before the move, therefore, Parsons was considered an up-and-coming business town in Tucker County. Although it already had four general stores, three hotels, various artisans, and one doctor, not a single lawyer had yet hung out his shingle.

The population of Parsons quadrupled between 1892 and 1902, from three hundred to twelve hundred, mostly because it became the county seat in 1893. Lumber and livestock continued to be the primary commodities shipped by rail from Parsons, which was still described as being surrounded by thousands of acres of "untouched" forests. As might be expected, the town's principal industries in 1902, the Milton Tannery Company and the Parsons Pulp and Paper Company, were forest-related. A large flouring mill processed grains from the countryside both for domestic use and export. Commerce was booming now with eight general stores, two meat markets, three restaurants, a clothing store, one grocer, a druggist, a confectioner, and other artisan-related businesses found in most towns of this period. Perhaps most telling of its new status, however, were the eight lawyers, six physicians, three hotels, one bank, and two weekly newspapers.[24]

By 1914 the population had increased to two thousand residents, and commercial life continued not only to grow but also to become more diverse. To those already in existence were added other businesses such as two dry goods stores, two jewelers, two cigar shops, two hardware stores, a telephone company, a bottler, a motion picture theater, an opera house, a furniture store, an undertaker, a gas company, an electric company, and an insurance company. Again reflecting its new status as Tucker County's political and commercial center were the seven lawyers, five physicians, one dentist, two national banks, and one large hotel.[25]

A similar transformation occurred in Pocahontas County, a mountain-locked retreat that was drawn into the expanding market system after the railroad arrived in 1900. Huntersville, the old county seat located at the geographic center of the county but forty miles from the nearest railroad, possessed a population of one hundred residents in 1891; Marlinton, soon to become the county seat, existed only as a post office at Marlins Bottom.

Like other old county seat towns, Huntersville immediately lost any claim to significance when the county seat was moved to Marlinton. In 1891, Huntersville hosted a weekly newspaper, the *Pocahontas Times*, but it moved to Marlinton immediately when the center of power was transferred in 1893. Huntersville also had two hotels in 1891, but by 1902 the former seat had only one hotel, while Marlinton had three hotels to cater to the needs of transients in town on court or other business. By 1906, Huntersville was listed by the business directories as a post office only. Once again the professions demonstrate most dramatically the shift of influence from the old to the new county seat. Huntersville was home to six lawyers in 1891, but by 1902 the town was without a single law office. Marlinton, however, provided sufficient business for nine attorneys in 1902 and ten by 1906.

Physicians also came to county seats strategically located in growth areas with high customer traffic. In 1902 Marlinton boasted four physicians to none for Huntersville, and by 1914 Marlinton was served by six physicians and two dentists.[26]

Business also boomed. By 1906, Marlinton had diversified considerably, and an increased number of businesses served the population of eight hundred town dwellers and their neighbors in the countryside. In addition to the three general stores, two restaurants, and two meat markets were shops that indicated ready access to the national markets: two hardware stores, an agricultural implements store, a men's clothing store, three real estate agencies, a sewing machine store, three grocers, an undertaker, a photographer, and two contractors. The new county seat of Pocahontas also counted two dressmakers, a harness maker, two livestock dealers, a liveryman, and a shoemaker. Two banks were available to supply capital for further growth. Marlinton also was a busy milling center with various lumber processing mills, and a tannery. By 1914 Marlinton's population of eighteen hundred and outlying country people were served by an even more diversified retinue of commercial enterprises, while Huntersville was a sleepy hamlet of one hundred souls.[27]

The *West Virginia Gazetteer and Business Directory* for 1892 described Beverly, the old county seat of Randolph, as "a prosperous incorporated town" on the Tygart Valley River. Like many old county seats, however, it was far from a financial or commercial center. It was "30 miles from Philippi, the nearest banking point." Beverly's population of 350 people was served by two churches, a public school, a flour mill, sawmill, and the weekly *Randolph Enterprise*. Other businesses were those of artisans such as blacksmith, wagon maker, shoemaker, saddle and harness maker, and an undertaker. All of the stores were general stores. One hotel hosted people in town on court business, and thirteen lawyers were available to manage their legal affairs. Should country people or residents become ill, three physicians were available in Beverly to treat them.[28]

When the county seat moved to the burgeoning industrial and commercial center of Elkins in 1900, businesses in Beverly remained oriented to the farmers just as they always had been. The most notable change was the decline in the number of lawyers, falling from thirteen in 1892 to one in 1924, and in physicians, whose numbers fell from from three in 1891 to one in 1924.[29]

While Beverly remained a typical backcounty town in a prosperous farm valley, it was completely eclipsed by the dynamic growth of the industrial

Table 10. Physicians, Lawyers, and Dentists in Lumber County Seats, 1891–1923

Town	1891	1902	1906	1914	1923
Beverly	3/13/	3/6/	2/8/	2/3/	1/1/
Elkins	2/2/	6/16/	8/18/	10/28/4	15/27/5
Saint George	1/7/	0/1/	1/0/		
Parsons	2/0/	6/8/	5/8/	5/7/1	6/5/3
Huntersville	1/6/			1/1/	1/
Marlinton	1/	4/9/	4/10/1	6/9/2	5/10/2

Source: *West Virginia Gazetteer and Business Directories*, respective towns and years.

city of Elkins, just seven miles away. Elkins was founded in 1889 and named for its founder, the West Virginia senator-industrialist Stephen B. Elkins, as a headquarters for the West Virginia Central and Pittsburgh Railroad owned by Elkins and his father-in-law, Henry G. Davis. Already in 1892 the *Gazetteer and Business Directory* regarded Elkins as "the most accessible point in the State" and opined that the new railroad would open up the "central portions of West Virginia" rapidly.[30] In less than thirteen years the population rose from a small cluster to thirty-five hundred in 1903. The railroad was being extended to other interior towns, and soon the *Gazetteer and Business Directory* predicted that the region's rich timber and mineral resources would find "a direct connection with Pittsburgh and the leading markets of the East and West."[31] By 1915 the city had nearly seven thousand residents, "its growth being largely attributed to natural advantages, coupled with excellent railroad facilities." Important for the new industrial order, Elkins was, stated the business directory, home to "a class of people given to industry and energy, in the very heart of a region whose resources are virtually inexhaustible."[32]

From the beginning Elkins was destined to become the major commercial hub of the upper Tygart Valley. The first sure sign that Elkins was indeed the new seat of political power in Randolph County was the influx of lawyers and physicians. In 1892 Elkins had only two lawyers, but ten years later their numbers had increased to sixteen. Significantly, five of the seven lawyers lost by Beverly during the shift moved their offices to Elkins. The population of Elkins nearly doubled between 1903 and 1915 to seven thousand, and by 1924 twenty-seven lawyers, fifteen physicians, and five dentists had opened offices in Elkins.[33]

A bustling industrial-commercial city with railroad shops, timber- and coal-related enterprises, as well as commerce, the professions, and government services, required hotels. Even in 1892 there were three hotels, and at least the Elkins Hotel had first-class accommodations with "all the modern improvements, including furnace heat, [running] water, gas, electric bells, bath, and all that could be desired" by discriminating customers.[34] By 1915 the city boasted seven hotels, including the Randolph and the Gassaway, which afforded "ample accommodations for hundreds of people."[35] The number of hotels reached eleven by 1924.

Banks were essential to finance this phenomenal growth, and within a decade Elkins had become a banking center for the backcounties. By 1915 the business community of Elkins was supported by three national banks; in 1924 only two banks were recorded by the business directories, but they had a total of more than $5 million in capital.[36]

The railroads provided transportation but also communications by telegraph with manufacturers, shippers, suppliers, and other middlemen in the national marketplace. Newspapers provided communication within the local districts but also linked localities with the national news. Of course, the greatest variety of news on a steady basis came from the county seats, where, in addition to localized columns sent in from smaller towns, lumber camps, or rural neighborhoods, a steady stream of legal and government news was generated and dispensed throughout the county. When the seat of government was moved in Tucker, Pocahontas, and Randolph Counties, newspapers vied with lawyers to be the first to relocate to the new center of business and government. In areas where economic growth was more dynamic, commercial centers often had more than one newspaper. Elkins, for example, had three weeklies, plus a monthly, the *Mystic Tie*, the only Masonic paper in the state, reflective of the new businessmen concentrating in Elkins. By 1915 the three former county seats had faded into obscurity and had no newspapers of their own, while Elkins, Parsons, and Marlinton each boasted three weeklies.[37]

Newspapers also played an important role in creating a demand for new products, a vital ingredient in the new consumerism on which the modern American market system was built. Newspaper advertisements reflect the growing sophistication in marketing, the range of consumer goods available because of the rail connections with the national markets, and the specialized products that signified the arrival of modern readers. The commercial advertisements reflect the impact of modern consumer society and demonstrate, both visually and in content, that the West Virginia backcountry was being called by the sirens of modernity.

Visually, advertisements in the early 1890s were not much different from those earlier in the nineteenth century. Most of them were placed in the advertising section with bold print and relatively crude graphics to set them apart from the rest of the paper. Most of the ads in local mountain papers were for small, low-margin items such as patent medicines that could be ordered by mail, for local products such as shoes, and for services such as those of doctors, lawyers, or hotels. For example, in 1892 the *Pocahontas Times* advertised clothing for men, women, and children that could be purchased from a company in Staunton, Virginia. Readers were promised that they could "reap a harvest of bargains" and assured of a warm welcome if they called "when in our city," the equivalent of "y'all stop by." Patent medicines and cure-alls abounded in the advertisements for products similar to those carried by traveling peddlers, such as Castoria, Carter's Little Liver Pills, Benton's Pile Salve, and Kendall's Spavin Cure (which promised to cure Sweeney shoulder, joint lameness, stiff joints, shoe-bill, and lameness in the fore foot). Some local tradesmen advertised, such as W. L. Douglass, a cobbler in nearby Edray, Pocahontas County, who sold handmade shoes, and G. W. Wagner, who ran the hotel at Huntersville, which boasted an excellent livery stable for the horses.[38]

By 1905 the *Pocahontas Times* had moved to Marlinton, and, because the town was located on the Greenbrier Division of the C&O Railroad, factory-made goods were easily imported and delivered at the depot. With plenty of wage earners and a steady supply of factory goods now available, shops became more specialized. Thus, instead of ordering clothing by mail or having a tailor make a new suit, customers could purchase a wide variety of manufactured clothing from the retailers who moved to town. Large ads depicting a dapper gentleman dressed in fine attire announced a sale at Wallace, King and Company of Marlinton of men's winter clothing that would "command attention" for its quality and style. Gooden's Reliable Shoes offered ten styles of men's shoes of "unquestionable" quality that were "up to the minute in newness." This variety was symptomatic of the expansion of capitalist markets and a new economic phase in a place where but a few years earlier shoes were handmade to order by the local cobbler. Similarly, the Marlinton Furniture Company offered a "large assortment to select from" with "many interesting styles," whereas a few years earlier factory-made furniture was a treasure, shipped in at great expense and considerable difficulty. There is no mistaking that "progress" had arrived, and these were among the most visible signs.[39]

Except that quantities were limited, in 1915 there were few manufactured goods available to urbanites that were not available to residents in back-county West Virginia towns with direct access to the railroad. Where a few years earlier stood a vast wilderness, now the automobile, the symbol of twentieth-century America, was offered for sale to modernized mountain-eers. At least three dealers sold automobiles in Marlinton in 1915. C. A. Yeager sold the Chandler from his showroom and used full-page advertise-ments of the automobile to attract customers. Floyd Dilley also sold the Chandler in Marlinton, and Baxter and Gibson were the agents for Ford automobiles, with a "full line of cars, parts and supplies kept in stock at all times." For those who still lived on farms, a local agent sold the Perfection Automobile Gate, which enabled drivers to open and shut fence gates to their lanes without getting out of the car. Progress indeed had arrived.[40]

Mountaineers who were now wage earners and therefore dependent on the abstract forces of an impersonal national market realized that they were no longer in control of their own financial security. The greater the sense of vulnerability, the more security became a commodity for purchase. The "new" newspapers carried ads for a smorgasbord of insurance companies inveighing people to take out insurance to cover losses from fire, life, illness, accident, loss of livestock, and almost anything else that might happen to anxious, modern people. As the Hunter and Echols Insurance Agency of Marlinton warned, "Better be safe than sorry."[41]

In addition to insurance agencies, the banks played on the people's escalating consciousness of their financial dependency on fickle markets, and both used advertising as a medium to educate readers in the middle-class values compatible with capitalism. The Bank of Marlinton ran a series of ads with the theme of "the prudent man," which graphically demon-strated why men should bank a portion of their wages regularly. "The prudent man banks his money and has no fear," proclaimed one ad against a graphic of an armed burglar sneaking in through the window in the dead of night while the prospective victim smiles from his bed safe in the knowledge that his money is secure in the bank. "Bank your money and be free of fear," for "burglars, thieves and hold-up men make it their business to learn who keeps money in their pockets, or houses, or in holes in the ground."[42] The "prudent man" also was "prepared for sickness. He has a bank account," another ad proclaimed. An illustration depicts a man sick in bed with desperation written in his eyes, against a background of his vulnerable wife and innocent baby; the caption declares: "Don't you see strong, healthy men taken down with sickness every day? Is not this a lesson to teach YOU to have money piled up in our bank so you can tide through your sickness?

Should you DIE would you leave your family helpless? Bank your money; it is your DUTY."[43]

Developers and boosters also promoted the values and moral framework that were compatible with the growth of capitalism. The rapid influx of newcomers into the hitherto geographically isolated and relatively homogeneous interior counties produced social conflict commonly associated with boom towns. Men who worked on timber crews sometimes spent months in the woods before they went to town for "rest and recreation." Wood hicks often spent their money until it was dissipated, and there was no scarcity of townspeople willing to help relieve them of their earnings. Nearly every town had saloons, hotels with prostitutes, and gambling houses, often all under one roof. When their hard-earned money was spent, the hicks wobbled back to camp until the next time they needed to blow off steam. The volume of the liquor business is suggested by the amount of the contraband confiscated by authorities during a raid at Cass in 1906, which included approximately fifteen thousand bottles of beer, several hundred gallons of whiskey, and "gambling tables of almost every description."[44]

In most lumber towns, the prevalence of liquor and related enterprises aggravated the ordinary brawling, shootings, knifings, and other forms of physical violence found in frontier boom towns. The newspapers are replete with stories that, intentionally or not, associated liquor abuse with more serious criminal behavior. For example, one short squib noted that "a gang of Italians liquored up" on tannery row in Marlinton got into a fight and were arrested after being relieved of their knives and pistols. The depot at Cass was robbed one night of thirty-seven quarts of whiskey; nothing else was stolen.[45]

Selling liquor without a license led to the speakeasy, and this caused much consternation among those who demanded more social control over what they regarded as undesirable behavior. Stephen Welch and his wife ran a "speak-easy whiskey joint" in the lumber town of Alexander, Upshur County, along the West Virginia and Pittsburgh Railroad. They were arrested in a raid by the sheriff. During the raid, Welch, who was described as a "desperate character," ran out of the house into the woods dodging a hail of bullets. A crowd of mill and woods workers who were friends of the Welches soon gathered at the site. The thought of losing their liquor supplier angered them, a newspaper reported, and a crowd of fifty lumbermen attempted to liberate Mrs. Welch from the sheriff's custody. Three of the men were wounded, two of whom were expected to die.[46]

Lumber company operators typically considered the speakeasies a menace to the proper management of their investments and participated in efforts to eliminate them. E. P. Shaffer, the superintendent of the West Virginia Pulp and Paper Company in Cass, wrote to the company's general manager, Samuel E. Slaymaker, that there were "two more speakeasies in the course of erection," just below Cass, and opined that "we will soon have to do something to put a stop to it, as the place is today full of drunks." In February 1902, the county sheriff led a raid against the speakeasies and cited the operators. At their court hearing the two men received substantial fines and jail time, but they were soon back in business.[47]

Opponents of the speakeasies were irritated by the seeming impossibility of ridding the county once and for all of those who operated them; no sooner had authorities put them in jail than they were back in business. Some of these operators seemed to be immune to prosecution, and many concluded, correctly in some cases, that the officers of the law had been paid off. One such case involved the brothers Gratz and Charles Slavin, speakeasy operators in Cass and Durbin respectively. Shaffer wrote to Slaymaker in Philadelphia that Gratz Slavin had purchased a lot in Cass "to run a feed store, but you can imagine the kind of feed store." Most irritating, however, was that Gratz Slavin had never been cited or jailed. Worse yet, one of the operators taken into custody by Constable Gum succeeded in getting Gum drunk and then made his escape. Disgusted, Shaffer observed: "Looks as though the only effectual way of breaking up speakeasies is with dynamite."[48] Gratz's brother Charlie Slavin seemed to enjoy even greater immunity from prosecution. Charlie ran a saloon in the nearby lumber town of Durbin for many years and somehow remained open even though he had killed three people. He served two years in prison for killing one man in 1895, but generally he was in and out of trouble with the law throughout the timber boom years. Whether the fact that his cousin C. L. "Bud" Burner was constable for that district had anything to do with it is open to question, but certainly many people must have drawn that conclusion.[49]

Newspaper editors generally identified with the middle class who accepted the need for a stable social order as a prerequisite to progress. In addition to the actual commission of the crime, one editor wrote, "There may be coming a time when the disregard for law and order may be a real menace . . . which we must take seriously." The root of the problem, he argued, was the illegal sale of whiskey. There was something "debasing in the conducting of the 'speak-easy,' both for the seller and the buyer," and while many people were disturbed by their existence, he wrote, "We have lacked men who are willing to take the initiative necessary to enable the officers to close the places." This was unfortunate, for along with carrying concealed weapons he considered the speakeasy "responsible for most of the rowdyism" found in the county. In response to editorials against illegal liquor written by the editor of the *Pocahontas Times*, a resident wrote: "We license a saloon and that makes a man drunk; we pay policemen to remove the drunken men to jail; we pay the officers of the court high fees to try the prisoner; we pay a big salary to a judge to sentence him, and if he commits a crime, we pay the expense of a penitentiary to shut him up in for years. . . . If the law will not stop the accursed speakeasies, neither will it control the saloon." The only solution was to permit neither. The editor published numerous editorials and affirming public opinions of his view that liquor was not only a physical danger to the user but also caused the social degradation of the community as justification for the complete prohibition of liquor.[50]

The rise in crime was directly correlated with liquor and the dramatic increase in a young, drifting population of single men. Convening a Pocahontas County grand jury in 1907, Circuit Judge Andrew Price asked jury members to curb their natural biases against those who were charged with crimes. In a nostalgic ad hominem, Judge Price observed that residents of the county had "paid for the rapid and substantial growth of wealth. We can all remember when this county was an ideal place to live." He, like other citizens of Pocahontas, had "looked forward to and hoped for an industrial development." It finally arrived, "and we would not now go back to the halcyon days, for we would not willingly give up any of our material benefits." But, he continued, "we are now paying for our prosperity," for now "our jail that often had not a single occupant is at this time crowded to overflowing." The grand jury, which had met twice each year, now convened four times and each was "overwhelmed with work." Illegal liquor clearly was to blame, Judge Price declared, not just because people bought and drank liquor from unlicensed "pigs' ears," as locals called the speakeasies, but because the men responsible for this illicit industry had "much shrewdness and capital at their command," and the scale of their illegal operations constituted "the organized defiance of the law."[51]

The docket of the Pocahontas circuit court contained 376 untried criminal cases, the range and scale of which represented a source of great consternation to many citizens. A list of the cases in the local paper included illegal entry to enclosed land (cutting another's timber), illegal hunting (hunting without a license; Italians were charged with shooting songbirds), illegal fishing (using dynamite), and cruelty to animals (beating work horses). But the most common charges were for carrying concealed weapons, violating the revenue laws, and disturbing church services (usually loggers on a spree).[52]

Editorial campaigns for prohibition had scant impact on the boom-town speakeasy operators. Charles Darwin Gillispie, a Virginian who took up residence in Hendricks, Tucker County, offers clear evidence of that fact. Even though he had successfully opened several businesses, Gillispie was unsuccessful in his efforts to open a saloon, and all hopes were dashed on January 3, 1901, when the town of Hendricks voted itself dry. Undaunted, Gillispie purchased land across the Black Fork River from Hendricks, where he set up a distillery, built houses for his employees, constructed a bridge across the Black Fork connecting his new town and Hendricks, and then incorporated the town in June 1902 as Brooklyn Heights. The mayor, recorder, council, and hired policeman all were employees of Gillispie, and they voted the town wet. That same year he secured a liquor license and built the Cream of Kentucky saloon, where he sold his own illegal whiskey along with the legal. A tannery and sawmill paid taxes so the streets were lighted, and the town had its own water system, as well as other public services. The Otter Creek Boom and Lumber Company's logging line ran right past the houses of prostitution on Bedbug Lane and stopped in front of the saloon, thus connecting loggers twenty-five miles back in the woods with the liquor and prostitutes in Brooklyn Heights.[53]

And find them they did. Brooklyn Heights immediately became notorious for sin, gin, murder, and mayhem. During the seventeen years of its existence, which came to an end in 1917, nine people were murdered. But these are only the official numbers; others classified as suicides or accidents were probably murders without the evidence. Innumerable people were stabbed, clubbed, or shot in Brooklyn Heights during this time. When a man got drunk in July 1906 and was killed by the train, no minister would walk across the bridge to conduct the funeral service. An aroused citizenry in Hendricks and nearby communities protested to the county court against renewing Gillispie's liquor license, and the court complied, allowing the license to expire in 1907. The lack of a license meant little in Brooklyn Heights, however, and the town continued on for years openly defying the law; periodic raids netted illegal liquor and fines but yielded little actual change. Finally, in 1913, the legislature abandoned the local option approach to prohibition and passed the Yost Law, which declared West Virginia a dry state. Deciding it was time to find another line of business, Gillispie abandoned Hendricks and purchased the six-story Gassaway Hotel in Elkins.

The town established to taunt the respectable citizens of Hendricks gradually lost its attractions and became a quiet residential settlement.[54]

In this environment social control became a major concern for the lumber companies. Some towns such as Evenwood, Randolph County, successfully prohibited the sale of liquor. During the first decade of the century, the town of five hundred had a school, churches, and other social institutions, but no saloons. These were prohibited by the owner of the Raine-Andrews Lumber Company, T. W. Raine, who also was a resident of the town.[55]

Companies often regarded formal religious institutions as instruments of social control that promoted abstention and, therefore, facilitated their establishment. Rev. Henry W. McLaughlin, a popular local Presbyterian minister, was invited by the West Virginia Pulp and Paper Company to preach the first sermon in the new town of Cass in January 1901. The company dining room was provided for the occasion, and it was proudly announced that "five women and forty or fifty men" attended the service.[56] The church became a permanent institution in Cass, and similar company-sponsored churches were a ubiquitous feature of lumber towns throughout the mountains.

Initially, the company did not purchase the land across the river from Cass, and on that side the settlement of East Cass became a hive of speakeasies, gambling, and prostitution, where drinking, brawling, and gunplay were endemic. East Cass lay outside of company control but was easily accessible to Cass by way of a suspension footbridge, and hundreds of loggers were lured there when they came to town seeking pleasures unavailable in the woods.[57] Whiskey came in regular shipments, prompting the railroad agent at Cass to complain in 1902 that "there has not been a time in the last six months that there has been a consignment of whiskey in the depot for parties whose purpose is to make illegal sale of same."[58]

In 1902, Cass hired Elmer Burner as town sergeant, along with his brothers Allen and Charles as special policemen, to bring some order to the annexed district. Frequent "sin and vice" raids were essentially ineffectual because the laws were so lax that charges were often dismissed when violators were arrested. Certainly the loggers and mill men demonstrated little initiative toward their own conversion. Help was needed, and the three Burners were joined by their sister, temperance reformer Emma Burner. Her role was to go undercover as a man and purchase illegal liquor and then act as a witness when her brothers arrested the culprits.[59]

The logging town of Laneville, Tucker County, reportedly was "a wild and sinful spot" at the turn of the century. Fed up, the wives of the workers and local businessmen decided to organize a reform and temperance committee to clean up the place. An aging former locomotive operator recollected that the church was the center of the reform movement, and the women "wanted to make a Christian out of every good-for-nothing so-in-so in the Red Creek valley." One of their prime projects was the town drunk, "Mose Callahan." On one of his trips to town, a log train engineer gave Mose some whiskey after the women had sworn Mose on the wagon. The next time the engineer chugged back into town, the women physically assaulted him, bound his hands and feet around a pole, rode him out of town on a rail singing "We'll Gather at the River," and then unceremoniously dumped him into the log pond.[60]

Thus a conflict in values and social norms also emerged with industrialization in the mountains, which set law-abiding, sober, middle-class residents against the saloon keepers, both legal and illegal, and those who preferred spending their free time in the bars and brothels rather than the churches. In Whitmer, Randolph County, for example, the contending forces of "good" and "evil" escalated their differences in 1913–14 into a political struggle for town hall in order to control the issuance of liquor licenses. A strong church membership and a growing middle class, often one and the same, condemned drunkenness and the fighting, prostitution, and other behavior that accompanied drinking in boom towns where single young men made up a disproportionate number of the population and the presence of the law made a slight impression.

Such was the case in Whitmer. By 1904 liquor became the leading political issue in Randolph County, and that year Elkins, the largest town and county seat, voted itself dry. One of the most notorious cases to stir the public against saloons in this logging county was the lynching of Joe Brown on March 18, 1909. A resident of Whitmer, Brown was known as a violent man, having served a term in prison for murder. He had been drinking all day when he shot policeman Scott White and ran off into the hills. A posse went after him, wounding him in the arm during the capture. The posse was joined by a drunken mob back in Whitmer, which proceeded to lynch Brown. They made a poor job of it, and Brown remained alive for several hours. A sock was stuffed into his mouth with a poker in a brutal attempt to suffocate him. Brown had terrorized Whitmer on his drinking sprees, and he relished frightening wood hicks by shooting their hats from their heads so that many men considered his death good riddance. Although no one was ever tried for his murder, the episode created a stir in the county, and two months later all liquor license applications from Whitmer were denied.[61]

As in other logging towns, the lack of a license was insufficient to plug the flow of liquor, and an illicit trade continued with bootlegged liquor brought in from Cumberland by train. It was not until January 1913 that the dry faction in Whitmer finally achieved a major victory by electing a new slate of members to the town council from the dry Progressive Party. Another dry, Smith Dugger of the Progressive Party, won election as mayor, and he hired a new chief of police to help close the speakeasies.[62]

During this period the Reverend Harry Robinson led revival meetings at the Methodist Episcopal church, and by February he was said to have converted two hundred men. Conversions may not have been long-lived, but the fervor for reform ignited by the revivals created a strongly supportive social climate that buttressed the town council's campaign to eliminate alcohol. During the summer, a Reverend Bishop organized a town meeting that petitioned the council to close a notorious dance hall where liquor and fighting disturbed the dry citizens of Whitmer. The council responded by closing the establishment.[63]

In 1914 the dry Progressive Party and the Reform Party fought it out again at the polls in a bitter and close election. In the end the election came down to three contested ballots, which the circuit judge awarded to the Reform Party candidate. But facing a council of Progressive drys, the new wet mayor resigned in disgust, and the council quickly appointed the losing dry candidate to the office. The following year a Reform Party candidate won election, but by that time the Reform Party had joined the drys in the struggle to rid the town of alcohol. Moreover, in 1914 the state had passed the prohibition amendment to the West Virginia Constitution making the state completely dry, and prohibition officers joined local law enforcement in drying out the lumber towns along with the rest of the state.[64]

The railroads created an elaborate system for exporting lumber and linking the natural resource periphery with the national markets and a reverse flow of goods and ideas from those same markets. Manufactured goods were imported to fill the demand of wage laborers in the backcounties, and the market revolution took its course, altering the means and mediums of exchange. Towns along the railroad burgeoned with people, and to serve them a middle class of businessmen and professionals also developed who both initiated and reflected the shift to a modern twentieth-century order. The degree of isolation in the backcounties of West Virginia may be debatable, but whatever isolation remained from the preindustrial era was dissolved by the commercialization of the mountain countryside.

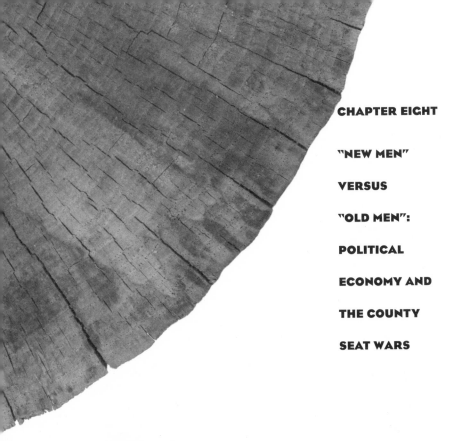

CHAPTER EIGHT

"NEW MEN"

VERSUS

"OLD MEN":

POLITICAL

ECONOMY AND

THE COUNTY

SEAT WARS

I ndustrial development profoundly altered the deter-
minants of the political culture in West Virginia after
the Civil War and Reconstruction. On the eve of
deforestation in the 1880s, political culture had been aligned for a generation along the traditional axes of Democrat-Confederate-agrarian versus
Republican-Unionist-industrial sympathies. With industrialization, however, economic interests marginalized all other concerns in both political
parties. This blend of economics and political organization itself was an
indicator of change in West Virginia, and it mirrored a national process that
dominated American industrial development during the late nineteenth century. The role of railroad expansion and deforestation in West Virginia's
political realignment is clearly revealed in the "county seat wars." The
railroad annihilated spatial relationships previously based on nature, and the
idea that the county seat should be at the physical center of its county was
one of the casualties of the new order in mountainous West Virginia. Struggles among local elites to relocate county seats along the transportation
corridors where economic development would follow reflect the contours of

211

the new political economy that displaced the older, preindustrial political culture of the backcounties.

The new political order fractured traditional party lines and prompted a realignment along economic axes rather than political parties. Charles Ambler, the noted state historian, probably was hinting at this change when he essentialized the contending influences as those between "Bourbon Agrarians" and "Ironheaded Industrialists." Ambler never developed this thought into a thesis, but he alluded to the conflict between those who wanted to maintain the dominance of agrarian life, republican values, and political styles that prevailed in nineteenth-century Virginia against those "progressives" who looked to the industrial, market-oriented world of the twentieth century.[1]

Another state historian, John A. Williams, has expanded Ambler's political divisions within the state during this period by demonstrating that the preindustrial elites owned the land and were drawn from the circuit-riding lawyers who traveled to backcounty courthouses to conduct their business. Therefore, they were well acquainted with the people, and politics evolved into a personalized agrarian style. These networks of personal acquaintances grew into courthouse cliques, which in the backcounties were likely to be traditional Virginia Democrats in politics, and became a major source of resistance to separate statehood and the Union. After statehood, the separatist leaders, most of whom were Republicans, denounced these courthouse cliques as bastions of resistance to the establishment of the new order.[2]

The founders of statehood constituted a new mélange of Whigs, Republicans, and Union Democrats who were more economically utilitarian than they were party faithful or political radicals. The statehood leaders lived in the economically developed industrial and commercial farming counties of northern and western West Virginia. There, according to Williams, the "politics of kinship and deference, isolation and parochialism" had given way to modern communications, bureaucratic organization, and a literate electorate with a partisan press to unify their adherents. In other words, Williams argues, they established the "modern party system" during their relatively short reign between 1863 and 1872.[3]

When the Democrats regained power in the elections of 1870, the grievances stemming from the war and the treatment of former Confederates were quickly resolved by a Democratic-controlled convention in 1872, which approved a new state constitution without the most offensive "Yankee" features of the first document. One of those was the abolition of the township system and restoration of the county court system, which, according to Williams, "reestablished the most important institutional means by which local notables sustained themselves in power and influence" in the backcounties. This also led to the restoration of those courthouse cliques that were so important to traditional Democrats, and future Republican industrialist-politicians learned to control them in the 1890s. As might be expected, the strongest support for the new constitution came from the underdeveloped backcounties, and the greatest opposition came from the older developed railroad and river counties of the northern and western part of the state.[4]

If the Republican developers feared that the Democrats would hinder industrial "progress," they need not have worried. Both main-line Democrats and Republicans in "Redeemed" West Virginia supported development of the state's natural resources and cultivated a religion of economic progress. No better example of this common commitment can be found than the leaders of the two political parties, the Democratic senator Henry G. Davis and his son-in-law, Republican senator Stephen B. Elkins. Two of the state's most powerful industrialists also were state leaders of their respective political parties, and on matters of industrial policy few meaningful distinctions between them were discernible.

Arrival of the railroad was sufficient to stimulate new political alignments in the backcounties as the old courthouse cliques and the location of the county seat came under pressure from those challengers who sought to benefit from commercial and industrial development. The Republicans generally adhered to either the Regular (or Conservative) faction, which controlled the party organization, or the much smaller Liberal reform faction. The Democratic Party, in contrast, housed a complex array of factions, many of which divided even further at the local level. Statewide four major factions struggled for control of the party. The Regulars dominated the official machinery of the party, generally were located in the developed counties, and supported industrialization. The Redeemers generally represented the backcounties and were more southern and traditionalistic in their politics. The Agrarians were reformers, supported particularly by farmers in the older established counties and by citizens near the railroads who harbored grievances against them, particularly the B&O. They favored government regulation of the railroads and resisted the taxation of farmers. Based in Charleston, the Kanawha Ring evolved around the circuit-riding lawyers who developed a political network in the southern counties. They not only favored industrial development, but many of them, such as Governor William A. MacCorkle, were industrialists themselves. They had been circuit-riding lawyers in the backcountry or handled land law in the southern rural counties and had acquired a personal style of politics that ingratiated them to their constituents. Cutting across these factional lines were the "Bitter Enders" who brooded over the past and the "New Departure" Democrats who looked eagerly to the future.[5]

Democrats in the northwestern counties, where the Republican Party was strongest, tended to be Regulars and allied themselves with the Democratic industrialist-senators Johnson Newlon Camden and Henry Gassaway Davis. Redeemers lacked the financial means and organizational abilities enjoyed by the Regulars so they generally were less effective at statewide organization. The same was true for the Agrarians and the Kanawha Ring. Blending their image of old-fashioned statesmen with their roles as political capitalists, the Redeemers "yielded nothing to the industrialists in their anxiety to interest nonresident investors . . . and to avoid 'discouraging' them by legislation of the agrarian type," Williams observes. Although the Redeemers were worthy adversaries, the Regulars "manned the axes of modern communications" and maintained control over party committees that ran the nominating conventions, determined delegates' credentials, wrote platforms, distributed party propaganda, and dispersed party funds.[6]

Williams's analysis is appropriate at the statewide level, but at the county level the struggle for political control and factionalism was much less subtle. In a state that was highly sectionalized and whose rugged terrain determined that politics would be local, the location of the county seat was a leading source of factional conflict from the beginning. Like Kentucky, which also had been part of trans-Allegheny Virginia, there were a variety of reasons for the creation of new counties in West Virginia. Since the county seat usually was the commercial, social, governmental, and geographical center of a county, an inaccessible county seat in the nineteenth century was a significant handicap to residents. Accessibility, therefore, was the most common, and legitimate, rationale for breaking away to form a new county. Most people traveled by horse, and because roads often were little more than bridle paths, travel was always difficult and sometimes impossible.

There were many less legitimate reasons for creating new counties, however. More counties meant additional offices for ambitious office-seekers, and a new county might present the opportunity to gerrymander political jurisdictions to the advantage of the party in power. Land speculation often was at the root of the movement for new counties, and a new county required a new county seat frequently located on land owned by a speculator promoting division of the county. Others might desire to escape indebtedness and the consequent tax burden of an existing county by establishing a new one.[7]

Unlike Kentucky, where counties proliferated until they numbered 119 in 1890, creation of new counties did not become a preoccupation in West Virginia. In 1790 there were 10 counties on the frontier that became West Virginia, and by 1860, 50 of the 55 counties that make up present-day West Virginia were already in existence. The other 5 were created after the Civil War: Mineral (1866), Grant (1866), Lincoln (1867), Summers (1871), and Mingo (1895).[8]

Determining which counties should be included in the boundary of West Virginia guaranteed acrimonious debate in the politics of statehood. At the first constitutional convention (November 26, 1861 to February 12–20, 1862), the Committee on Boundary reported a plan for the inclusion of thirty-two counties beyond the thirty-nine named in the dismemberment ordinance. Opponents objected to the inclusion of Virginia counties with large slave populations and those where secessionist sentiment obviously was strong. In the final vote, the convention decided to include within West Virginia's boundary the original thirty-nine counties and the southernmost counties of Pocahontas, Greenbrier, Monroe, Mercer, and McDowell. Six other counties were included with the voters' approval: Jefferson, Berkeley, Morgan, Hampshire, Hardy, and Pendleton.[9]

Even after voters approved the constitution and the state's boundary, the battle over which counties were Virginian and which were West Virginian flared again when the statehood bill was debated by Congress. In June 1862 Senator John S. Carlile, a new state supporter from West Virginia who had been an advocate of a smaller state and a member of the Committee on Territories, surprised West Virginia separatists by adding fifteen more Virginia counties to the forty-eight included in the constitution, twelve of which the constitutional convention had already rejected. Carlile's Senate colleague from West Virginia, Waitman T. Willey, offered an amendment to the bill which saved the West Virginia boundary in its present form and perhaps saved statehood itself. To this day historians have speculated on the reasons for Carlile's action, but it was an obvious attempt to obstruct, and probably sabotage, the statehood process. From the very beginning, therefore, counties played a defining role in the state's political culture.[10]

The sectional rancor that divided the new state was intensified in counties where the division of loyalties during the war was pronounced. Much was at stake in who controlled the county seat. The courthouse itself was the symbol of dominance in this contested terrain, for the side that ruled the courthouse also controlled official functions such as law enforcement, court proceedings, tax collections, and school administration. In Calhoun County a struggle over the location of the county seat had been waged for a decade before the Civil War. The southern pro-Confederate section of Calhoun County favored Arnoldsburg for the county seat, and the central pro-Union section favored a Little Kanawha River location that became Grantsville. The latter group used the situation to good advantage when the Union army took control of Arnoldsburg in 1862 to hold an election that would approve the Grantsville site. After the war, the conflict resurfaced, now laden with an extra layer of enmity, between the Arnoldsburg former Confederate Democratic Party and the Grantsville Unionist Republicans. The new courthouse in Grantsville was burned before it was occupied in 1869. The unrelenting Arnoldsburg faction saw the seat ordered back to their town by the circuit court only to lose it again to Grantsville in an 1869 election. Arnoldsburg tried once again to win the county seat in 1898 but failed to garner the two-thirds vote required for removal and so the issue slowly died.[11]

In Mercer County the pro-Union citizens of Concord attempted to displace pro-Confederate Princeton as the center of the county's political life. In 1865 Circuit Judge Nathaniel Harrison held court in Concord rather than Princeton because the former was more secure. Unionists used Concord as the county seat, but in 1867 the legislature recognized Princeton as the legitimate county seat. The Republican legislature repealed that act in 1868, however, and accepted a fraudulent election in which voters presumably voted for Concord. Wartime hostilities and intrigue continued in the Mercer contest when county sheriff Benjamin White, a former Confederate and Democrat now presumed to be loyal to the Republican Party, convinced the board of supervisors to move the county's records to Princeton to prevent their destruction by disfranchised former Confederates. This was all subterfuge, however, for once in Princeton White and his former Confederate allies agreed to support the election of Republicans who wanted Princeton to be the county seat. In the end, following much sectional intrigue, Concord lost its effort to retrieve the county seat after another rigged election in which the courts refused to intervene.[12]

More than twenty West Virginia counties experienced such county seat warfare to some degree. Counties torn by divided loyalties during the Civil War accounted for some of them, but economic development played a dominant role in most of these battles during the late nineteenth century. When the railroad ushered in a new age of industrial and commercial development in the backcounties, county seat conflicts were sparks in a combustible atmosphere in which political culture gave great weight to physical control of a friendly local government. The railroad altered the traditional notion that the county seat should be located in the geographic center in order to provide access for all of the county's residents. "Center" now meant strategic location on the transportation network connecting the county to the national markets.

Although physical control translated into material advantages, possession of the courthouse also was symbolically significant for the contesting political cultures. The elections for removal usually involved a long, bitter struggle waged by local elites to win the hearts and minds of the people. In this new contest for the seat of local power, the industrialists and local boosters, such as the shopkeepers, professionals, and land developers, all stood to benefit financially from the economic transition. They were the agents of change in West Virginia whose drive for profits finally pushed aside the "old" agrarian culture and replaced it with the "new" wave of industrial capitalism that would bring the backcounties "out of the woods."

Two clear examples of how the industrial transition precipitated struggles to control the county seat are found in Tucker and Randolph, two timber-rich backcounties. Penetration by the West Virginia Central and Pittsburgh Railroad transformed the social and economic landscape in these previously remote mountain counties and shifted the centers of local political power. The struggle for control of the county seat between the Ironheads and the Agrarians in these counties followed the general contours of a showdown between nineteenth-century agricultural and twentieth-century industrial societies.

The Tucker County historian Homer Floyd Fansler has observed that 1888 was a bad year for the town of Saint George. Fire destroyed three hotels that year, and instead of coming down the Cheat River through Saint George to Rowlesburg, the West Virginia Central and Pittsburgh Railroad bypassed the town on its way to Elkins by following Shavers Fork River. At the confluence of the Shavers Fork and Black Fork Rivers the new town of Parsons began to grow, and it was incorporated in June 1893. Parsons's rapid growth was matched by Saint George's precipitous decline.[13]

The developers of Parsons planned from the beginning, even before the first train arrived, that their town would become the county seat. Parsons boasted a population of fewer than fifty people on February 12, 1889, when a group of town developers headed by Ward Parsons, the primary booster and the town's namesake, filed a petition with the county court requesting

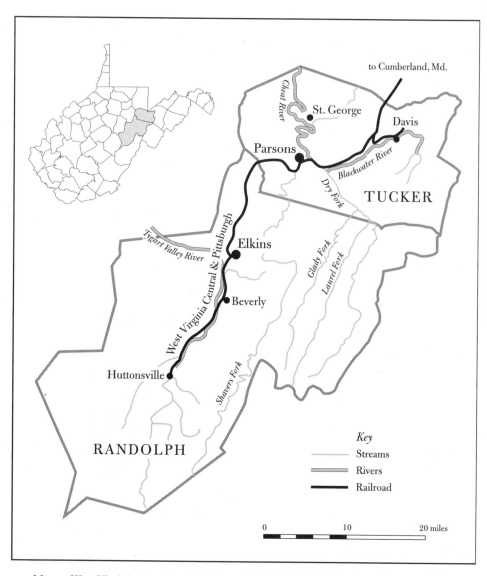

Map 4. West Virginia Central and Pittsburgh Railroad during the county seat wars.
(West Virginia Geological Survey; adapted by Debra Benson)

that the people be canvassed on the issue of relocating the county seat from
Saint George to Parsons. The court determined that the petition was out of
order, however, and it was withdrawn. Ward Parsons and his colleagues
were not deterred so easily, and the following year a sufficient number of
signatures were presented to place the removal question on the ballot for the

general election in November 1890. The final tally lacked by seventy votes the three-fifths majority required to move a county seat.[14]

The petitions may have been dead, but the determination was not. Parsons and his lieutenants immediately regrouped their forces and began the process of collecting petition signatures still again. New petitions were filed with the county court in 1892 requesting yet another vote on removal. In the November 1892 general election, the developers once again failed to carry the question for relocation but missed the three-fifths requirement by only fourteen votes. The Parsons developers did not lose spirit, and yet another petition drive was undertaken in the seven Tucker County electoral districts. In the special election held on April 28, 1893, the voters finally sided with the developers by a vote of 1,110 for and 514 against; Parsons at last would become the new county seat. Bids were opened for moving the records, furniture, and other county property from Saint George to a temporary courthouse in Parsons.[15]

Saint George would not be vanquished so easily, however, and the Saint George men continued to resist the removal. Adam C. Minear, a former sheriff from Saint George's most prominent family, filed a bill of exceptions with the county court protesting election irregularities. When the court overruled this bill, Minear and William M. Cayton, a Saint George resident and the county clerk, secured an injunction from the state supreme court of appeals to prevent the removal.[16]

The Parsons faction received this information with great irritation, realizing that an injunction might delay removal, perhaps for years. Drastic action was called for, and Ward Parsons and his most trusted partners in the removal enterprise decided to take matters into their own hands by physically removing the county property from Saint George by force. Forming an army of about two hundred armed men, with wagon teams and horse-drawn buggies, the men assembled in Parsons on the evening of August 1, 1893, for a march on Saint George to liberate the court records. The train from Davis brought about seventy men enlisted by Robert Ward Eastham, a former Confederate guerrilla with Mosby's Rangers. The people of Saint George heard of the approaching army when Bascom B. Baker, a physician temporarily turned man of action, was seen cutting the telephone wire to Saint George. When a local man walking the road to Saint George inquired why a physician should be perched atop a telephone pole, Baker informed the man of the impending invasion, and the news was swiftly carried to the county seat, where citizens armed themselves in preparation for a defense of the courthouse.[17]

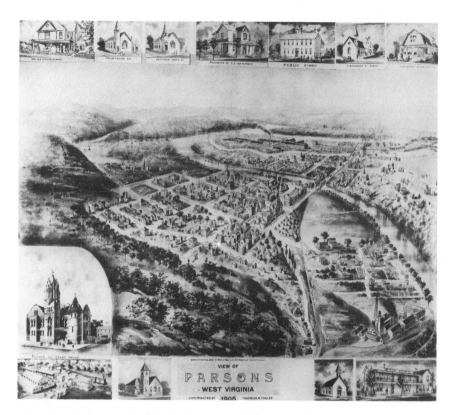

Thaddeus M. Fowler's rendering of Parsons, Tucker County, 1905. (West Virginia and Regional History Collection, West Virginia University Libraries)

The invaders arrived at Saint George at about 9:30 P.M., where they met defenders, who also were armed. The Saint George defenders apparently were intimidated by the much larger force from Parsons, however, and they withdrew—with the notable exception of a woman who assaulted the invaders with a piece of stove wood, which she used to bruise the flesh and egos of several invaders. Sheriff Will E. Cupp ordered the crowd to disperse, but they ignored him. Because the courthouse was locked, entry was gained through a broken window and the doors thrown open from within. All of the county records and furniture were loaded onto the wagons, including the bell that hung in the steeple, and the boisterous procession began its withdrawal to the more friendly confines of Parsons.[18]

The sun came up on the morning of August 2, 1893, to find the Tucker County seat in Parsons, where the courthouse was established temporarily in the same building that housed the Knights of Pythias fraternal lodge.

The "mob" placing the county records in a temporary courthouse in Parsons, Tucker County, 1893. (West Virginia and Regional History Collection, West Virginia University Libraries)

Reports of the episode went out over the wires, and newspapers throughout the state and nation reviled the participants and deplored their action as an insult to law and order by backwoods ruffians.[19] Until 1897 the lease for the temporary courthouse was paid for by eight of the most prominent leaders of the new town, including Ward Parsons. Finally, in 1900 the present Tucker County courthouse was completed and occupied.[20]

If the outcry against the methods employed in moving the court records in Tucker County gave hope to the Saint George men that the supreme court would order the county seat returned, they need not have wasted their time. Minear's appeal for an injunction to prevent the removal failed, but two of the three members of the county court applied to the circuit judge to reverse the order to remove the county records. When the judge refused, the county court convened and issued its own order that the county property be returned to Saint George on grounds that it had been unlawfully removed. Instantly the lawyers for the Parsons developers went to work and presented the circuit judge with a petition to prohibit the county court and the sheriff from executing this order. The petitioners carried their case to the West Virginia Supreme Court of Appeals, and in *Hamilton et al. v. Tucker County*

Court et al. the high court ruled in favor of the Parsons men. Justice Henry Brannon, writing for the court, declared that no matter how the records were removed, the people of Tucker County had voted, and the county court had declared Parsons the new county seat. These proceedings had been lawful, and an earlier, forcible removal did not change that fact.[21]

In a special local dispatch to the *Wheeling Intelligencer*, a reporter claimed that the "best citizens" regarded the forced removal as "a disgrace to Tucker County" and one that was likely to "breed a feud which will be serious in its results."[22] Just who the "best citizens" were is open to interpretation, but the reporter was either ignorant of the facts or did not regard the professionals and businessmen of Parsons and Davis as members of that group for they were the most prominent figures in the removal. Among them were Ward Parsons, the major figure in the struggle to remove the county seat and one of the wealthiest landowners in Tucker County; Solomon W. Kaler, a trustee of the local Presbyterian church, who subsequently served as mayor of Parsons; C. G. Lashley, who served as the mayor of Davis in 1900–1901; Robert Ward Eastham, who was contracted to clear the land on which Davis was laid out and owned a timber supply company and a general store; Cyrus O. Strieby, a prominent lawyer from Davis; Dr. Bascom B. Baker, a graduate of the Baltimore College of Physicians and Surgeons with a medical practice in Tucker County; James P. Scott, a newspaperman who took up the law and became the Tucker County prosecuting attorney; and Samuel O. Billings, a partner in the prosperous Cheat River Milling and Feed Company who served as county clerk and surveyor during this period.[23]

Biographies of the twenty-nine most active individuals involved in the three-year campaign to move the county seat reveal that they cannot be identified by the delineators of the old political system, which pitted northern Unionist-Republican-statehood-industrialists against southern secessionist-Democrat-antistatehood-agrarians.[24] Indeed, as a group the leaders in the movement project a highly diverse collective profile. Some of the removers were either Confederates during the Civil War, or their families took a strong stand for secession. Ward Parsons, the driving force behind the movement, was the most influential local secessionist. Two other members of the Parsons family supported the movement, Ward's son Lemuel and his nephew Job Jr. But Sansome E. Parsons, a half-brother of Ward's father, was a strong Union man. The Union army tried and failed to capture Ward on several occasions; the Confederates did capture Sansome, although he escaped. Arnold H. Bonnifield also was a strong Union man who had gone to California with his family in 1872 after the state was "redeemed" to escape the hostility directed against him for his Union stand. Lorenzo Dow Corrick's father, the first settler on the land where the town of Parsons was constructed and Ward Parson's neighbor, was known as a "rabid Unionist." Robert Ward Eastham of Davis was an unreconstructed Rebel who even in the 1890s fumed against the "damned Yankees." Riley Harper, who served as Tucker County sheriff from 1897 to 1901, also came from a family of Confederates. Most of the men, however, were too young to have identified with either side during the war. A few were not locally born so that little is known of their position on secession, the war, and statehood.

Affiliation with a political party was not a distinguishing feature of this group either. The Parsons family, one of the oldest and largest in the county, was equally divided into Democrats and Republicans, although Ward Parsons was prominent among local Democrats. Samuel O. Billings was a Republican, whereas Robert Ward Eastham and Riley Harper were Democrats. John B. Jenkins, who succeeded Harper as sheriff and held other county offices, was the superintendent of the Cumberland Coal Company in Douglas, Tucker County, and a member of the Republican Party. James P. Scott later was elected prosecuting attorney as a Democrat. Cyrus O. Strieby, a Pennsylvanian who moved to West Virginia and established a prominent legal practice in Tucker County, also was a Democrat. But Arthur Jay Valentine, a corporation lawyer in Parsons who served as local counsel for the West Virginia Central and Pittsburgh Railroad, Mosser and Company, the Otter Creek Boom and Lumber Company, and the Hamilton Leather Company, was a Republican. As with attitudes toward secession and statehood, political affiliation is not a defining element in the profile of the Parsons faction.

Family and bloodlines did not bind these men together either. Unlike the active participants in the Hatfield-McCoy feud studied by Altina Waller, a significant percentage of the active removers were not economically dependent on Ward Parsons. Of those cited, only Lemuel and Job Jr. were tied by blood in a meaningful way. Sansome E. Parsons was Ward's half-uncle, but as the owner of over four thousand acres of timber and the most fertile bottomland in the county and a man known for his independence of mind, it is unlikely he would be swayed by Ward simply on the basis of kinship.

What was it, then, that drew this diverse group of men into a common cause? A general profile of the twenty-nine removers who can be identified from among the approximately two hundred participants in the removal of the county records demonstrates that nearly all of the promoters were native West Virginians, most of them locally born: nine Tucker Countians, six from nearby counties, two Pennsylvanians, one Virginian, and one Englishman by way of Pennsylvania. Their average age was about forty and so they were in the prime of their lives. They were divided by loyalties during the Civil War and split in their preference of political party. Many held public office during their careers, and fifteen of the twenty-nine held numerous local offices. Also, they were leaders in the community: four lawyers, one doctor, eleven businessmen, five in the timber industry, one in the coal industry, and six large farmers. Fourteen of the men whose residences can be determined either lived in or near Parsons or were from Davis, which also was in the Black Fork electoral district. The only common delineators among this very heterogeneous group of removers are economic opportunity and personal gain.

The struggle for removal was initiated by those who expected to gain from the development of commerce and industry near Parsons. One reason that Saint George lost the county seat is that resistance there was not as broad, deep, or well organized as among the determined Parsons faction, who saw themselves creating a new future. The Saint George resisters were not moved by a vision; they were simply protecting the status quo and defending the advantages they had enjoyed in having the courthouse located there. They were farmers for the most part, and along with agriculture they were rudely pushed from the center toward the periphery of economic life in the county.

H. G. Davis's West Virginia Central and Pittsburgh Railroad was completed to Davis in 1888, but throughout the 1880s tens of thousands of acres had been purchased in anticipation of railroad construction. Everybody knew it was coming, and a struggle for control of local politics ensued between the Ironheads and the Agrarians for control of the county Democratic Party. From the moment Davis decided to extend the railroad up the Dry Fork and down the Tygart Valley to Elkins, the industrialists had all the motive required for supporting removal of the county seat to a location on the railroad, and Parsons was located on the most promising commercial real estate in Tucker County. No historical "smoking gun" points directly at Henry G. Davis, but he almost certainly was involved. Several key figures in the removal faction were Davis lieutenants: Valentine and Strieby, for example, handled local legal affairs for H. G. Davis, and Eastham led a large contingent of Davis residents that joined in the forced removal of the court records. Although a direct link cannot be established between Davis and Ward Parsons, the industrialist certainly would have been more confident about doing business with a "heads-up" development booster such as Parsons than the Saint George farmers. Moreover, the commercial ambitions of the removers were in perfect alignment with Davis's understanding of progress.

The movement to transfer the county seat in Tucker County was powered by local men with economic motives, but the directing hand of H. G. Davis was evident in the county seat war in neighboring Randolph County. Explaining the struggle to control the courthouse in Randolph County, a Pittsburgh newspaper reporter observed that "under other circumstances a county seat war might be a mere passing event," but in Randolph County "it stood for everything. It was the meeting of the old and the new civilization," a conflict between "tradition with all of its sentiment and modern industry with all of its disregard for tradition." It was a "collision between the young men who believed in business . . . and the old men who have veneration for their home and the bones of their ancestors." The contest was so spirited because it was "the ruthless assault of nineteenth-century progress upon the posterity of the pioneers" who settled in the mountains "generations ago."[25]

The reporter described the county seat of Beverly as "old, slow, aristocratic, the people coming from some of the best old Virginia stock." Elkins, the aspiring county seat and a rising railroad and lumber-milling center, however, was "lively, Bohemian, its population coming from everywhere." Elkins was composed of young men who were businessmen "from the tops of their heads to their heels." The growing city also was the permanent residence of the industrialist-senators S. B. Elkins and his father-in-law and business partner Henry G. Davis, along with an array of chieftains who worked for them. Founded in 1890, Elkins was a "modern town" in every sense, while Beverly pointed with pride to buildings a century old. Elkins had "many young men from the Northern States," while Beverly was "of the old days when slaves and chivalry gave Virginia an exalted opinion of itself."[26]

The Beverly-Elkins courthouse war is the quintessential illustration of the battle between the Agrarians and the Ironheads, a battle between Beverly Confederates committed to the traditional agrarian-Democrats and the Republicans of Elkins whose politics favored modern industrial development and disparaged tradition; a struggle between those who saw their relative insulation from the national economy as a badge of their independence from the marketplace against those who defined progress as industrial development indelibly integrated into the national markets.

The town of Beverly was nearly as old as Randolph County itself; the histories of Beverly and the county seat were inseparable. Settlers first came into the area in 1753, but permanent settlement waited until 1772 because of

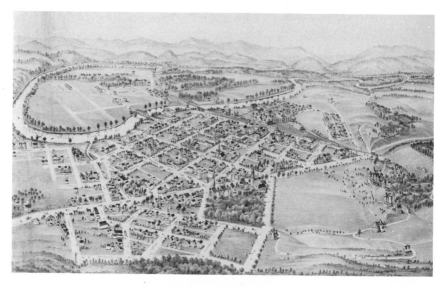

Thaddeus M. Fowler's rendering of Elkins, Randolph County, 1897. (West Virginia and Regional History Collection, West Virginia University Libraries)

the danger from hostile Indian attacks. The first county court met in 1787 in a private home located a few miles from present-day Beverly.[27] The site chosen for the new courthouse was in Edmunton, a hamlet named for Edmund Jennings Randolph, governor of Virginia. When the town was chartered in 1790, it was renamed Beverly in honor of the new governor, Beverly Randolph.[28]

The courthouse completed in 1798 was a log structure that proved totally inadequate for the county's needs, and court sessions were again held in private homes until 1815, when a new two-story brick courthouse was completed, which served Randolph County for nearly eighty years. By 1890, however, the county population had grown to nearly twelve thousand and the facility had outlived its usefulness. Therefore, preliminary plans to construct a new courthouse were approved that year by the court.[29]

Construction of the new courthouse was no longer Beverly's alone to plan, however, for the citizens of Elkins determined that they should have the courthouse instead. Henry G. Davis and Stephen B. Elkins founded Elkins in 1888 as a terminus of the West Virginia Central and Pittsburgh Railroad. Davis and Elkins initially proposed to build the terminus in Beverly because a town was already established there, but they were unable to come to terms with the landowners. Other residents did not want the smoke, dirt, dust, and associated problems the railroad would bring. Therefore, the industrialists chose a site on Leading Creek instead, which at the time was a farm neighborhood with a store and blacksmith shop providing the only commercial services.[30]

The railroad reached Elkins in August 1889, and the town was incorporated in 1890. Under the railroad's stimulus the town prospered. Elkins had a population of only 349 in 1890; twelve years later more than 6,500 people bustled through the streets of what was by then the commercial center of Randolph County.[31] A once tranquil agricultural settlement became an important natural resource processing center for the urban markets and a regional distribution point within the national market matrix. The course was set for conflict between these two profoundly different towns, therefore, when Elkins challenged Beverly's prerogative to build a new courthouse in 1890. The court ordered the issue placed on the November ballot for the people to decide, and Elkins lost in the balloting by a vote of 614 to 1,292.[32]

In 1892 the county commissioners ordered the construction of a new courthouse at Beverly, and two years later the structure was completed. It seemed that the relocation question had been consigned to memory, but three years later, the new courthouse was destroyed by fire. "The janitor, according to custom, was burning the contents of the dry closets in the basement of the building by the aid of kerosene oil," it was reported, and the fire got out of control. The building was a total loss, but fortunately nearly all of the records were saved.[33]

Beverly's dismay was Elkins's revived hope, and the boosters quickly reorganized and circulated petitions for a special election, which was approved for October 5, 1897.[34] After the Elkins petition was presented and the special election set, the political atmosphere took a dramatic turn for the worse with the local newspapers taking the lead in poisoning public opinion. The Elkins newspapers, the *Inter-Mountain* and the *Tygart Valley News*, no longer exist for this period, but Beverly's *Randolph Enterprise* often quoted from its rivals in Elkins to disparage their rendition of developments in the controversy. Therefore, it is possible to reconstruct the deterioration in political relations between the rival towns with a reasonable degree of accuracy.

The *Enterprise* was the arch opponent of the Elkins assault on Beverly's privileged position as county seat, and the paper's inflammatory tone set the tenor for the year-long campaign over the courthouse. Bitter barbs flew fast and thick in the press with the differences between the towns providing the easiest opening to wound the adversary. For example, the *Enterprise* editorialized that "not a single proposition" had been advanced in the Elkins papers "that contains any sound reasoning why the county seat should be removed to Elkins." Nevertheless, "they have made considerable fun of the 'Old Town of Beverly,' but it has usually come from parties, who made all they have, while living in this town." The other boosters came to Elkins "from a distance, some very wise and knowing people who have at all times since they first landed in this county, thought themselves too good to associate with the people of this county." Nevertheless, the *Enterprise* continued, "We are glad to say, that they are few, and are of the kind, that do not sway very many people and will like the locust disappear in a short season and we hope not to return in twice seventeen years."[35]

The editorial war continued with escalating bitterness, but the historically significant issue is that the people of Randolph had a choice in selecting the location of their county seat between old Beverly and new Elkins, and everything that each town represented became a part of the controversy. In the special election of October 6, 1897, Elkins received 1,942 votes for relocation against 1,411 to remain in Beverly but failed to gain the three-fifths majority necessary to win. The *Enterprise* was ecstatic in claiming "a glorious victory all 'round"; Beverly retained the county seat and "the upper end fellows get a railroad." Magnanimous in victory, the editor opined that the conflict had a salutary effect and "actually brought the blue and gray together in the county."[36]

If indeed sectional reconciliation had been achieved, its tenure was brief, for in March 1898 the Elkins men began the petition process all over again, and the war of words marched on in full military plume. In an attempt to close the matter once and for all, the commissioners declared that they had completed a full review of the issue and determined that further elections on removal would be a waste of the taxpayers' money. The outcome of the review probably was foregone since the commissioners accepted plans for a new courthouse building and authorized the county to advertise for sealed bids at the same meeting. In April 1898, the commissioners accepted a bid of $20,000 to rebuild the courthouse in Beverly. Because the voters had not yet approved the funds, however, the contractor was ordered to build as much as he could with the $12,000 the county held in reserve.[37]

The contract was a call to arms for the Elkins men, whose representatives immediately obtained an injunction from the circuit court on the grounds that construction on the new building would be prejudicial to Elkins "in any election they may hereafter have for the removal of the county seat."[38] The county commissioners promptly responded by filing a motion to dismiss the injunction and submitted affidavits to the circuit court charging that the

Elkins petition contained repeated names of noneligible voters and people unknown in the county.[39]

A blizzard of legal documents descended on the circuit court during the first six months of 1898 as both sides jockeyed for position, and the newspapers contributed to the agitation with nearly every issue containing propaganda for one side and libelous allegations against the other. When the county court finally ordered another vote on the issue at the regular 1898 elections in November, the newspaper war whipped public opinion to a frenzy. On the eve of the election, Senators Davis and Elkins publicly endorsed relocating the county seat to Elkins and offered to store the public records in the vaults of Davis's Coal and Coke Railroad office building. The *Enterprise* responded that a vote for relocation to Elkins "is a vote to place the records of the county in the custody of the railroad company." The senators "would bring the jurors of the county under the contaminating influence of an atmosphere of a thousand hirelings as they presume, who will smile or grin to suit their purpose in any controversy between themselves and the people." The Beverly editor charged that the senators had "endorsed and sanctioned a bribe to the voters of the proud old county of Randolph, and that too after promising their political friends in the presence of witnesses that they would take no part in this controversy." Whether the charge was true or not, the election resulted in the necessary three-fifths of the vote to relocate the courthouse in Elkins.[40]

Even though the battle had been waged off and on for a decade, the legal wrangling continued even after the election. Before the Board of Canvassers officially recorded the election results, the Beverly men immediately counterattacked by charging that a critical number of ballots were either marked illegibly or had not been properly certified and that wording on the ballot was confusing to voters.[41] Sympathetic to the Beverly cause, the county court refused to take jurisdiction from the canvassers, and, rather than risk losing to the original balloting, the Elkins men obtained a writ of mandamus from the West Virginia Supreme Court of Appeals commanding the commissioners to determine the final results of the election.[42]

This exasperating struggle became downright unscrupulous when the pro-Beverly commissioners recounted the ballots and, unlike the canvassers, included the 312 illegible ballots as part of the total even though they did not count for either contender. As a result, Elkins no longer had the three-fifths required by law to win the election, and the commissioners overturned the election results, declaring that the county seat would remain in Beverly.[43] As might be expected, Elkins appealed the commissioners' ruling to the circuit court, and on May 6, 1899, Judge John Hoke decided that the commissioners had erred by including the 312 illegal ballots in the total count, thereby restoring Elkins's original three-fifths margin for removal. Judge Hoke granted the Beverly lawyers a forty-day stay to give counsel time to prepare an appeal to the supreme court of appeals.[44]

To this point, the now torturous process had been confined to the courts, and most of the spleen had been vented through the local newspapers. But the forty-day stay seemed to break the patience of the Elkins men, who, on the very same day the stay was issued, threatened to remove the county records from Beverly by force. C. Wood Dailey, chief railroad attorney for Davis and Elkins and the attorney for the city of Elkins in the dispute, was able to persuade the exasperated crowd that a forced removal of the records would be an unwise and illegal action that would redound to the disadvantage of their cause.[45]

Tempers among the Elkins crowd did not cool overnight, however, and the following day several Elkins men formulated a misguided plan to commandeer a train and invade Beverly during the night with six hundred armed men, load the records aboard a freight car, and move them to the railroad offices in Elkins. They believed that they could surprise their counterparts in Beverly, frighten them with guns, and carry away the court records without bloodshed. The would-be commandos made a grave miscalculation, however, for Beverly's "home guard" had received warning of the invasion plan, and the sheriff had deputized and armed fifty men who were then positioned in trenches dug around the courthouse. Patrols were dispatched to watch the roads into town, and measures were taken to dynamite the railroad if a train approached.[46]

Luckily, two Beverly citizens, Jared L. Wamsley, the prosecuting attorney for Randolph County, and Humbolt Yokum, took the initiative to diffuse the impending tragedy by traveling to Elkins through a driving rainstorm on the night of May 6, 1899, and warning the crowd that Beverly was prepared to defend the courthouse with arms if necessary. They convinced the Elkins men to accept a truce. The next day representatives from Elkins and Beverly met, and Elkins agreed to wait until Beverly's appeal had run its course through the supreme court of appeals and Beverly agreed to abide by the decision of the court whatever the outcome.[47] Fortunately, cooler judgment prevailed and the Beverly-Elkins county seat war did not become a shooting war.

The long controversy came to an end when the supreme court of appeals refused to grant a rehearing of the case, a de facto decision that favored Elkins. The "new" men had won, and Elkins would become the undisputed political as well as commercial center of the county. The final act in this drama saw the county records installed in the Coal and Coke Railroad terminal building, which would serve as the surrogate courthouse until the new building was completed in 1907.[48]

H. G. Davis's involvement in the Tucker County courthouse war must be inferred, but in Randolph County the "smoking gun" was found in his hand. Since Stephen B. Elkins was serving in the U.S. Senate at the time, he remained aloof from this local conflict, but he certainly gave his discreet support to both the intention and methods of his father-in-law on the county seat issue. Before the second vote on removal in May 1897, Elkins scrawled across the bottom of a typed letter to Davis: "I telegraphed Wilson at Elkins I favored changing county seat to Elkins. We might as well have it at Elkins as we have to pay ⅔ of the taxes."[49]

Davis threw his considerable resources into the fray. After the newly constructed courthouse burned down, Beverly's newspaper, the *Randolph Enterprise*, cried foul when the Elkins city council passed a resolution pledging to provide quarters for the county court free of charge for five years rather than rebuild in Beverly. Both Davis and Elkins signed the resolution, which the *Enterprise* denounced as "bribery." Upon learning that the court records would be housed in Davis's Coal and Coke Railroad office building, Beverly editor J. Ed Kildow declared that it was difficult for him to believe that the senators would "condescend to take part in the county seat fight, but to them chagrin and shame," he editorialized. "They have endorsed and sanctioned a bribe to the voters. . . . Shame on them!" The county seat would be better off anywhere other than the Coal and Coke headquarters, where the court would fall under their influence, he declared. "What do we owe them? They have a mortgage on every dollar of beef or timber we ship, and no man can ship a dollar's worth of coal, iron, or lime, unless you pay them the difference between hauling by rail and carrying it by a pack mule. They have this valley throttled, and well they know it."[50]

Davis also used a proposed branch of the West Virginia Central and Pittsburgh Railroad from Elkins to Huttonsville as political leverage by implying that Huttonsville would receive the railroad connection as a benefit for its support of Elkins. Huttonsville's support would have isolated Beverly, which stood midway between the two towns, and broken the voting block for Beverly in that district. The company held out the carrot before the election but would not commit to the extension until after the votes had been cast. Beverly proponents naturally denounced this move as a transparent "scheme to railroad the election."[51]

Of course they were right, for Davis used every weapon in his considerable arsenal to ensure a favorable outcome. Privately, Davis expressed his view to Elkins that people had "a right to their political opinions" and objected to the use of coercion to influence their decisions, but he was not above bribing them, as he informed Elkins: "We have given excursion rates for voters to come home to Randolph County, especially in the interest of the county seat."[52]

Through his agents Davis also attempted to influence local officials to side with Elkins in the canvass for removal in 1898. Harry R. Warfield, cashier of the Elkins National Bank, which was owned by Davis, was deeply immersed in the courthouse drama as an operative for the Davis and Elkins interests. Warfield routinely updated his employer on developments in the controversy. One series of letters reveals an attempt to influence the president of the county court, Patrick Crickard, to cast his vote in favor of Elkins. The commissioner must have encountered excruciating pressure from the industrial interests. The Crickards came to America from Ireland in the 1830s after their land was confiscated for political rebellion and settled in western Virginia.[53] To the chagrin of the Elkins men, Patrick Crickard was not so easily controlled. Attorney Cyrus H. Scott, a Davis lieutenant who later became a state senator, visited Crickard one night to "endeavor to get him to also assist." The following day, Warfield wrote Davis that Scott had "arranged matters with Mr. Crickard, and believes that Crickard will treat us fair."[54] Despite their initial confidence, the reliability of Crickard's swing vote soon became the source of great consternation to the Elkins men. WVC&P Railroad attorney C. Wood Dailey now believed that Crickard could not "be relied upon to do what is right, if that should be against the interests of Beverly."[55] The Davis and Elkins interests finally won out, however, for an amazed Dailey informed Davis: "Mr. Crickard performed one feat today in the county seat controversy that I hardly thought him equal to" when he sided with the Elkins faction.[56]

The Elkins leaders co-opted at least one other potential opponent. Davis's attorney William G. Wilson met with Beverly lawyer Jared L. Wamsley, a three-term prosecuting attorney for Randolph County, and "arranged with Wamsley to assist as our attorney in all matters pertaining to the county seat question, which I think was a very good move," Warfield informed Davis.[57]

Davis was not reticent about calling in favors from other industrialists as well. In June 1897, just after the new courthouse had burned down, Martin Lane, an officer in several lumber companies in the Dry Fork district of Randolph County, was enlisted to get out the vote for Elkins in his end of the county. Lane promised Davis that he would use his influence to create sentiment in the Dry Fork district in favor of moving the courthouse to Elkins. "These things can be done quietly and with discretion," Lane suggested, and expressed his "appreciation [for] your many kindnesses. We will cheerfully help you all we can."[58] Unfortunately, Lane's influence did not sway enough people in the special election of 1897, for Dry Fork gave a slim majority to Beverly in the contest. The *Enterprise* chortled that the Elkins men must be depressed for it was in the Republican precincts of Roaring Creek and Dry Fork, both of which were dominated by the lumber industry, that "Beverly found its most loyal friends."[59]

In the fall of 1898, when the third and final election was held on the removal question, Davis solicited the support of R. F. Whitmer, an owner in several major lumber operations in the Dry Fork district, Whitmer Lumber Company and the Condon Lane Boom and Lumber Company being the largest.[60] From company offices in Philadelphia, Whitmer assured Elkins that he intended "to go to West Virginia with a view of working for Elkins Court House, this I am going to take a hand in."[61] As the election drew near, Davis wrote again to Whitmer urging that he assist in getting out the vote in favor of removal, even though Whitmer was a Republican.[62] At the last minute, Davis sent a telegram to Whitmer stating that he had been "informed by a gentleman just in from Dry Fork that your road, stores, and lumber people are talking for and favoring Beverly." Responding for the absent Whitmer, his partner, Samuel E. Slaymaker, assured Davis that he had been misinformed for Slaymaker himself had been to Horton and "instructed our people to do all they possibly could to have the county seat located at Elkins." After Elkins's success in the relocation election, Slaymaker wrote to Davis again stating that he hoped the returns from the Dry Fork district "show to your satisfaction that there was no truth in the reports which came to you, and which you took up with us."[63] An industrialist-politician as powerful as Davis was capable of fielding an army against rebels in the political countryside, and few courted disaster by challenging him. The fact that Whitmer's own lumber cars were dependent on Davis's railroad to reach the market was not lost on the lumberman.

Davis was willing to do whatever was necessary to relocate the county seat to the friendly confines of Elkins, but he consistently warned his local agents against the use of force. "My advice is not to be in a hurry to take records by force. It might become very troublesome in the future," he cautioned Warfield. Davis observed that the Tucker county seat removal occurred several months after the election was declared in favor of removal. The Randolph case was different.[64] Both of Davis's lawyers, Cyrus H. Scott and C. W. Dailey, expressed their concern that a violent removal of the records might jeopardize all the work that had gone into doing things in the proper way.[65] Davis understood that there was a real chance of losing control of the crowd, and he received steady communications from his agents in Elkins to that effect. Dailey realized that removing records by force would be a very serious problem if any death or injury should result. "The boys, however, will be very hard to restrain in case the county commissioners declare the result in favor of this place, and do not at once order the removal of the records," he informed Davis.[66] Warfield echoed Dailey's concern about the crowd: "The men here in Elkins are all determined, and if Beverly don't act fairly and quickly in the matter, I am afraid that it would be a difficult matter to control them."[67] Davis cautioned repeatedly that the crowd must be controlled. "I will direct that no train, nor place for the records, be furnished until the latter can be legally removed."[68]

Party particulars are scarcely noticeable in this conflict. After all, Davis was the "Grand Old Man" of West Virginia's Regular Democratic Party machinery, and yet he was in charge of the campaign to bring the county seat to the Republican stronghold of Elkins. Stark Baker, a prominent businessman and one of the few Republicans in Beverly, was the most visible proponent for retaining the county seat in that old-line Democratic bastion. The real contest was between Ironheads and Agrarians over which world would prevail; this contest gave purpose to the trench warfare in which lieutenants of the industrial moguls completed their capture of local government for the benefit of business.

Commenting on this consolidation of political and economic power, H. G. Davis's biographer notes that since Davis and Elkins controlled the railroads, banks, loan companies, and most of the real estate in Elkins and vicinity, the courthouse would mean more business for utilities, real estate agents, banks, and lawyers associated with their interests.[69] Like so many political capitalists during the Gilded Age, Davis lost little sleep over the ethical conflict inherent in using public office to advance his own business interests. Nor did such men shrink from using the power of business to influence political affairs. The courthouse wars, such as those in Tucker and Randolph, were the result of the same ethical posture played out at the local level where government and business were merged into a modern political economy.

S ome of the most wrenching changes triggered by deforestation were visited on agriculture, and these changes were not always enthusiastically received. Whereas the promoters of development looked forward to the world of the twentieth century and saw economic opportunity and material progress in big business, others continued to view the world from the perspective of nineteenth-century yeoman freeholders. Their values and notions of well-being were shaped by republican ideals of self-sufficiency and independence. Instead of economic opportunity, they often saw moral corruption.

The railroad and timber developers encountered opposition from agrarians whose resistance grew out of Jacksonian attitudes toward monopoly and corporations. This antagonism persisted in the rural countryside throughout the nineteenth century, particularly among the subsistence and semisubsistence farmers who, according to historian J. Mills Thornton III, sought to maintain their freedom and autonomy from both the moral and economic dictates of the marketplace, as well as the speculators and business organizations who manipulated the markets to their own personal advantage. It was a question of "freedom," Thornton argues, to be self-sufficient and independent. Capitalists and their supporters who sought to gain economic advantage over other citizens through government support for railroads and protective tariffs were viewed by these agrarians as a threat to the "autonomy of the individual." Taxing ordinary citizens for the benefit of railroads or any other industry represented the loss of individual freedom.[1]

The coming of the railroad threatened those who saw the iron rails as the leading edge of the market economy and believed that the railroad would dissolve local society and reshuffle the social classes. The "ethic of autonomy" was the heart of the resistance to industrial development, Thornton argues, "whenever the modernizing tendencies of an expanding national economy encountered the more traditional values of those citizens who feared above all else the prospect of being manipulated by powerful institutions and forces beyond their communities, of losing control of their lives and destinies to unseen strangers." When their neighbors were lured away from the land by the siren song of "progress," the competence-seeking farmer saw this as evidence that his world was under attack; "he saw the consequences, but he did not fully understand the cause."[2]

This ambivalence toward modernization is exemplified in the experience of Francis Pierpont, a lawyer who played a prominent role in the movement for West Virginia statehood and served as governor of reorganized Virginia during the Civil War. A young man in 1848, he became the Baltimore and Ohio Company's counsel for Marion and Taylor Counties; his primary duties consisted of securing rights-of-way for the B&O. This was not an easy task, for the business-minded Pierpont found that while some of his neighbors welcomed the railroad's arrival he also encountered stiff resistance from certain segments of the community. Many of those who resisted were either the owners of horses and oxen or innkeepers who benefited from stagecoach traffic on the dirt roads. Others feared the railroad would frighten their livestock and opposed the intrusion of smoke and noise into their lives.[3]

Many West Virginia farmers opposed the railroads, including the logging lines, because they feared economic losses from the destruction of their livestock and property by the locomotives. For example, in the southern part of the state, the *Greenbrier Independent* ran articles in 1872 opposing construction of the Chesapeake and Ohio Railroad because "it carried whiskey, killed chickens and cows, scared the horses, and threw teamsters out of employment." Residents of Tyler County rejected a right-of-way for the

B&O because "the trains would scare the game out of the country." Similarly, farmers held public meetings to oppose the B&O running a line through Monongalia County to Pennsylvania, declaring: "We don't want our hogs and cows run over and killed."[4]

Many farmers believed that the railroads would undermine their personal economic well-being. They were concerned not only that locomotives would set fire to their fields and run over their livestock when the courts were immunizing the railroads from liability for damages, but also feared that the railroads would depress the price of livestock and feed in the local markets. Farmers understood that when the railroads came to haul away timber they would also bring in cheaper products that could undersell their own in the local markets. When the B&O Railroad surveyed a route through Monongalia County, West Virginia, into Greene County, Pennsylvania, for example, many local citizens opposed the route. At public meetings they declared that railroad construction should be halted at Cumberland, "and then all the goods will be wagoned through our country, all the hogs will be fed with our corn, and all the horses with our oats."[5]

Another important reason farmers resisted railroad development was the railroad's practice of shifting the financial burden of construction from themselves to farmers. To capitalize railroad construction, companies often expected counties to tax themselves to purchase company stock. Such was the case in 1885 and 1886 when promoters of the Chicago, Parkersburg, and Norfolk Railway urged the leaders of Pocahontas County to convince the public to bond itself for the purchase of $50,000 of the company's stock to help finance the road's extension through the county. The proposal created considerable controversy over assuming such a debt, and the court decided not to hold a referendum when it became clear that a majority of the citizens were in opposition.[6]

The comments of Wheeling businessman Henry B. Hubbard, who was in the Pocahontas County seat of Huntersville on business at the time, reveal the nature of the opposition to the proposed railroad. Hubbard wrote that a "more hopeless outlook" for the village could hardly be imagined, therefore "it would be natural to suppose that every man, woman and child in the county would be in favor of a railroad." But such was not the case, "as most of the solid men are reported as unfavorable to it, and to be using their influence to prevent it being built." To Hubbard and his associates, such opposition was "almost incredible." A better understanding of the "habits of this class of people, however, did much toward removing our incredulity" and caused Hubbard to wonder if, after all, "they were not wise in their opposition so far as they are individually concerned being as they are a preeminently pastoral people with no desire for the rush, strife and turmoil of trade, but perfectly satisfied with their thousand acres covered with flocks and herds, and the comforts and influences derived from them. A tripling or quadrupling of the value of their lands would not add to their happiness nor change their occupation, but would add to the amount of their taxes without producing an extra blade of grass."[7]

Railroad bonding proposals frequently stirred up violent opposition among West Virginians who opposed schemes of the "soulless corporations," which, in their view, enriched urban investment bankers rather than the local community. This situation was not unique to West Virginia, however. In Pennsylvania most such proposals failed, although the animosity engendered could seriously fragment a community. For example, in 1855 a dispute over the route of a railroad split Union County, Pennsylvania, and resulted in the opponents to railroad bonding separating to create the new county of Snyder.[8]

The grievances of farmers against the railroads sparked organized opposition throughout rural America, including West Virginia, during the late nineteenth century. At its first annual convention, the West Virginia State Grange voiced the strong disapproval of farmers over railroad abuses. Even though the Grange was supportive of railroad development as a stimulus to the state's economy, it expressed concern for the rights of property owners, particularly in light of the special privileges granted to railroads by legislatures to condemn property without compensation.[9]

Their fear of higher taxes was real. H. G. Davis, West Virginia's leading railroad developer, made that very point to demonstrate the advantages that railroads would bring to the state. Comparing two counties without railroads (Hardy and Pendleton) to two counties with railroads (Randolph and Tucker), he demonstrated how property values remained relatively stable in the former case but skyrocketed by over 2,000 percent in the latter between 1880 and 1912. While this news was music to the ears of investors and developers, farmers realized that the increase in property values meant higher taxes, and therefore higher costs, without any corresponding increases in either production or market prices for their commodities. For those farm producers too small to compete in the national markets it could spell financial disaster and loss of the family farm.[10]

These concerns may seem quaint to modern readers, but they nonetheless represented real problems for farmers of the nineteenth century. Because the industrialists ultimately prevailed, opponents of the railroads seem to have been out of touch with the times, their worries backward and archaic. But this view misunderstands the dynamics within which they made their social and economic choices. West Virginia farmers, even prosperous ones, had sound reasons for their resistance. While they had legal tradition on their side, the world that had created that tradition was being reconstructed around them, isolating them, rendering them vulnerable in a way they were powerless to stop. The legal preeminence secured by the railroads in West Virginia gave a green light to large-scale investment in natural resource extraction but flashed a danger signal to the farmers, who recognized that they were confronted with a direct assault on their ability to control their own destiny.

Some farmers grounded their opposition to modernization in a conservative moral and social worldview, and the stridency of the developers' attack against these conservative agrarians confirmed what they regarded as a loss of character resulting from industrial development and closer ties to the national markets. A. B. Brooks, the state's best-known conservationist of his day, voiced the objections of many in 1910 when he wrote of "a great change in the character of the people." Within a comparatively few years nearly "the whole population," which previously had earned its living from the land, was "pushed out from places of seclusion into the whirl of modern industry." The railroads and timber operations attracted "a different class of people whose manners and language were readily adopted by the younger people." Thousands of young men were induced to work on the railroad or in the logging camps and lumber towns, where they were "thrown into intimate association with a rough, drifting, foreign element." Consequently, farmers frequently complained that their sons left the homesteads to take industrial jobs, and so the farms had fallen into neglect and were "grown up in briers." The young men became dissatisfied with farmwork, Brooks lamented, and "a spirit of selfishness and coolheaded business" took the place of the "hospitality that once prevailed."[11]

The developers attacked these conservative agrarians relentlessly in their newspapers. As one promoter observed in the *Wheeling Register*, it was unfortunate for "the development of our rich young state there is a good deal of the musty elements of old fogyism among our people," which had served to retard "progress and prosperity." Those who resisted were a "powerful element" composed of "the old leaders who molded public sentiment in former days when their antiquated ideas were adapted to the conditions which then existed." The paper rejected these "musty elements" because society had "passed into a new era, and stands on another stage where different principles apply and other methods are necessary to carry us forward with the onward tide of progression."[12]

Whether their resistance stemmed from changes in traditional legal protections, higher taxes, potential for direct economic losses, or the threat to their dominance in local markets, West Virginia farmers were responding to the same forces of change that confronted farmers generally in the United States during the late nineteenth century and ignited protests such as the Granger, Greenback, and Populist movements. As in the South and West, the problems confronting West Virginia farmers as a result of the emerging industrial economy produced a long list of grievances. Although they were an ever-declining proportion of the economy during this period, agrarians represented a significant political force in West Virginia until after World War I, when their numbers and political clout dropped precipitously.[13]

Initially, nearly every class of citizens in the state hoped to benefit from railroad development and the consequent exploitation of natural resources. To open the wilderness to development, special concessions were granted to the railroads in the form of tax exemptions and rights-of-way and changes in the law to protect company investments, and many county residents assumed bonded indebtedness to stimulate the infusion of capital. Railroads provided the steel rails that tied the nation together in the nineteenth century, and West Virginia promoters certainly were not unique in viewing the locomotive as the engine of modernization. With the railroad would come jobs and cash wages to satisfy a growing desire for manufactured goods and a means to export raw materials and to import manufactured goods. The railroad would mean that the market revolution had finally surmounted the mountain barriers and would now sweep into the vast wilderness of West Virginia's backcounties.

Many prosperous farmers who lived near the railroads believed that they would be the direct beneficiaries of rapid rail transit to the urban markets. Even before the arrival of railroads, farm products from west of the Ohio River were being transported by road and canal to the eastern markets at such ruinously low prices that local producers were driven from their own local markets. These West Virginia farmers believed that the railroad would help them compete against the flood of surpluses from fertile midwestern farms. In fact, the reverse soon proved to be the case; as a result of the B&O and C&O linkage of eastern urban markets with the agricultural Midwest, cheap farm products soon poured into the soil-depleted Kanawha Valley, and beef from the Midwest was transported through cattle-raising Greenbrier country on its way to eastern markets.[14]

The depression that gripped American agriculture between 1873 and 1897 also affected West Virginia farmers. The depression of 1873 began a long decline from relative prosperity to perennial hard times at precisely the same time that corporations, trusts, and business monopolies were on the ascendancy. Prices for West Virginia produce and livestock reveal the long-term slide. The price for corn, the basic cereal crop in the state, fell from eighty-eight cents per bushel in 1867 to forty-four cents in 1876 and as late as 1880 had not risen above forty-seven cents per bushel. The price for winter wheat also fell precipitously and did not recover. In 1866 West Virginia wheat sold locally at $2.73 per bushel, fell to $1.42 by 1872, and followed a ragged path downward to only ninety-one cents per bushel in 1880. The Civil War took an unspeakable toll on livestock, and the need to replenish the nation's meat supply spurred demand and hence prices. The years from 1867 to 1871, therefore, were profitable for West Virginia livestock producers. Cattle, the principal animal raised throughout the state, rose in price from $20 to $28.20 per head during this period. As was true for other farm products, however, the depression suppressed prices until by 1880 cattle sold for an average of only $19.50 per head.[15]

Other difficulties confronting farmers during this period aggravated the economic impact of the depression. Capital had always been scarce in West Virginia, and the lack of credit continued to plague farmers. The rates on farm mortgages exceeded what many farmers could pay, and even though farm prices declined, interest payments remained constant. Most farms were family owned and operated, and foreclosure loomed as a specter for many farmers. Moreover, farmers endured high and inequitable tax burdens that were placed on farm real estate while business properties were either undervalued or escaped taxation entirely. Farmers thus confronted the problem of meeting tax and interest payments and raising their debts at the same time that farm prices were insufficient to cover the costs of production.[16]

Farm owners were correct in claiming that they bore a disproportionate share of taxation. In 1895–96 the West Virginia Board of Agriculture conducted a statewide study to determine the percentage of wealth and the percentage of taxes borne by farmers. The results showed that on average West Virginia farmers possessed 65 percent of the wealth but paid 80 percent of the taxes. In some counties the wealth and tax gap was significantly greater. Most of the counties where the gap was narrow or nonexistent, such as Boone, Calhoun, Clay, Grant, and Pendleton, were either undeveloped backcounties without railroads or counties where the farm population was very small and taxes were levied disproportionately against industry, such as Ohio County. In counties where railroad development was most extensive and farmers were numerous, the gap between wealth and taxes was widest. In Fayette, for example, farmers owned 40 percent of the wealth but paid 70 percent of the taxes, and in Kanawha the disparity was 35 percent to 80 percent, in Mercer 35 percent to 70 percent, and in Harrison 50 percent to 80 percent.[17]

As in other farm states, the agrarian protest arising out of these economic grievances among farmers in West Virginia manifested itself in the Granger and Populist movements. The first Grange in West Virginia was founded in Jefferson County, and by the peak of its development in 1876 the Patrons of Husbandry had opened 378 subordinate Granges in the state, with 10,752 members, representing approximately 11 percent of the voting population. Originally, only those who were directly involved in "agricultural pursuits" were admitted to the organization. Significantly, the delegates who founded the first Grange in Jefferson County in 1873 were among "the most substantial farmers" in Jefferson and Berkeley. They were galvanized into action because their Shenandoah Valley farms were endangered by western competition and the decline of political influence wielded by the conservative agrarians in both political parties.[18] By 1876, the strongest Grange representation was in the north-central agricultural-railroad counties of Harrison, Lewis, Barbour, Doddridge, Marion, and Upshur, rather than in the eastern panhandle. Only eleven West Virginia counties did not have a Grange, and all of them were in the undeveloped mountainous section or the rugged plateau south of the Kanawha. The Grange found its greatest base of support in the more developed counties, which Paul Salstrom identifies as "Old Appalachia," the eastern panhandle, the north-central section, the counties on the Ohio River, and the southeastern border of the state around Greenbrier County.[19]

Although the Grange was reformist rather than revolutionary and perhaps overly simplistic, the Patrons nevertheless offered a platform around which many farmers could rally. In 1877 the State Grange executive committee issued a declaration of principles that struck at the heart of industrial capitalism: "The great curse of our country is to be found in the gigantic corporations that, holding the thoroughfares of trade, as the robber barons once held the rivers of Europe, deprive labor of all reward." While this sounded like revolution to industrialists, the Grangers preferred to work through the two major political parties, although farmers controlled neither party in West Virginia. Under the leadership of U.S. senator Waitman T.

Willey, between 1863 and 1871 the state Republican Party leadership was drawn primarily from farmers and artisans, and although they welcomed "outside" capital investment, they generally responded to the needs of their farmer constituents. Succeeding Senator Willey as party leader in 1871, however, was Nathan Goff Jr., who allied himself with the business interests of the state. Thereafter, farmers lost their influence in the party to the capitalists and their lawyers. The Democratic Party also was controlled by the business interests in the party whose political alliances were with the rural county courthouse cliques. Industrialists such as Henry G. Davis and Johnson N. Camden dominated the party during the period despite the bitter opposition from the rural "agrarian" wing of the Democratic Party.[20] After 1871, big business appeared to be in control of both parties; therefore the Grange and then the Alliance movement offered farmers their only voice of organized protest.

From the 1870s through the 1890s there was little question that the agrarians regarded the railroads as the major cause of their hardship. They felt betrayed by the railroads, which, even though they had been granted special state tax relief and legislative protection, nonetheless abused their benefactors by discriminating against the very same people who had supported their development. Farmers complained that both freight and passenger rates were excessive and service was both irregular and inadequate. They claimed that the companies charged more for short hauls than for long hauls, pointing, for example, to the fact that West Virginians were charged more to ship their products to Baltimore than competitors were to ship the same products from the Midwest. A West Virginia cattleman complained to Senator Johnson Newlon Camden in 1886 about short-haul discrimination by the railroads, noting that the rate to ship a carload of cattle from Chicago to New York was only $35, but the same carload cost $65 when shipped from Keyser, West Virginia, to New York.[21]

The agrarian reform governor of West Virginia, E. Willis Wilson, complained publicly in his official message to the legislature in 1887, citing numerous instances of rate discrimination against West Virginia farmers. For example, the rate per hundredweight on grain from St. Louis to the Atlantic coast was eight cents while the same shipment from Hinton, West Virginia, cost twenty cents.[22] Short-haul discrimination was made illegal by the Interstate Commerce Act of 1887, but the railroads dodged direct compliance by giving favored shippers rebates until 1906, when rate-setting was vested in the newly established Interstate Commerce Commission. The railroads also offered free passes to individuals who might be influential in protecting the companies' interests, including elected officials, significantly increasing the potential for the widespread abuse of power and political corruption.[23]

As West Virginia industrialized, trusts and railroad pools replaced individual companies as the object of the Grange's ire. Nevertheless, the Grange's powerlessness against the trusts marked a more advanced stage in the transformation of the state's economy. The Grange was simply incapable of countering these forces and began to disintegrate as a political force during the 1880s and early 1890s. Perhaps the greatest shortcoming of the Grange was its restriction on membership, which mirrored a deeper class division within the organization. The West Virginia State Grange restricted membership to substantial farmers and questioned the admission of farmers from the undeveloped interior counties who either practiced a mixed economy of small farming, hunting, and gathering or worked as part-time employees in lumber mills, coal mines, and factories because it feared a possible conflict of economic interest. The Grangers were further separated into camps that supported ties with business and those who were devoted exclusively to the social and educational goals of the organization.[24]

The splintering of the Grange in the 1880s cleared the ground for entry of the Farmers' Alliance into West Virginia. The Alliance was to the Populist movement what the Patrons of Husbandry had been to the Granger movement. The Alliance had already piled up impressive victories in the South and West when it entered West Virginia. The West Virginia Alliance advocated essentially the same platform as its national counterpart: the eradication of trusts and other forms of monopolies; effective government regulation of railroads; alleviating the pressure of taxation on farmers by shifting the burden to industrial and financial corporations; repeal of purely protective tariffs; the creation of agricultural export subsidies; and, most popular, reform of the financial system by abolition of the national banking system, prohibition of usury, the free coinage of silver, and adoption of the subtreasury plan.[25]

The West Virginia Alliance reached the peak of its influence between 1889 and 1892 when contemporaries estimated its membership at between twenty thousand and thirty thousand, although the leading authority on this subject claims that ten thousand probably was a more accurate figure. Forty-one of the fifty-four counties hosted county Alliances at its peak. Most of the Alliancemen exerted political pressure through the Democratic Party, which traditionally had a strong agrarian wing. Democrats who won seats in the legislature with Alliance support, however, often voted the interests of the party rather than of the Alliance, and the farm-labor bloc generally failed to gather sufficient power to force passage of legislation opposed by the industrial-financial interests in the Democratic Party.[26]

Frustrations arising from working within the two-party system led a minority of the West Virginia Alliancemen to create the Populist (or People's) Party. The Populists were unable to win significant offices in state government, but at times their numbers were sufficient to provide a swing vote on pending legislation. Confronted in 1896 with the nomination of the pro-Populist Democratic candidate, William Jennings Bryan, and the adoption of a free silver and low tariff platform by the Democratic national convention, however, a majority of the West Virginia Populists favored fusion with the Democrats. When Bryan was defeated in 1896 and the Republicans succeeded in regaining power in West Virginia, the Farmers' Alliance and the Populist Party disintegrated in the state and with it the last organized farm resistance to railroad and extraction-centered industrialization.[27]

The political atmosphere was already charged with acrimony between farmers and the railroads, therefore, when the railroads penetrated the interior counties to transport the big timber to market. Backcounty farmers were much less likely to belong to organized railroad opposition than were their counterparts in the more developed counties because they were too thinly settled and their economy was still more dependent on household production and local consumption.[28] The railroad and the timber industry quickly changed those basic economic relations and rekindled fears rooted in nineteenth-century moral economy.

Farmers understood that the railroad would connect their farms as well as the forests to the national markets and that competition would be dictated by the national marketplace rather than the local economy. They were essentially correct in their assessment that this was a competition they could not hope to win. The process of deforestation fundamentally altered the agricultural economy in the timbered areas, first by removing the forest where farmers traditionally ranged their livestock and acquired much of the basic supplies for their subsistence agricultural system. Second, deforestation forced farmers to practice commercial agriculture or face ruin as free and independent producers. The commercial orientation of farmers in the older developed counties found outlet to the markets by way of roads and waterways that had evolved gradually as a part of the national market system. The underdeveloped interior counties, conversely, were forced into the new system through swift and wrenching changes in their economy.

Developed town and farm counties were nearly all cleared of virgin forest, except for farmers' woodlots. Thus the eastern panhandle counties of Berkeley and Jefferson were 90 percent cleared in 1894; that same year the northern counties of Hancock, Brooke, Ohio, Monongalia, and Harrison, with their gentler hills and navigable waterways, also were 80 to 90 percent cleared for town and industry or cultivation and grazing. From the percentage of the land improved, it is clear that these were commercial farms rather than self-sufficient farms because the subsistence farm economy required two-thirds of the land to be constantly unimproved.[29]

Conversely, the rural mountain counties remained covered with dense forests at the beginning of the industrial transition. The same State Board of Agriculture data for 1894 show Tucker County to be only 45 percent clear, although already the leading industry in the county was lumbering rather than agriculture or grazing. Hardy County was only 32 percent cleared, Randolph 30 percent, Pocahontas 33 percent, Pendleton 25 percent, Webster only 15 percent. Greenbrier and Monroe were among the earliest settled of those counties that straddled the mountain spine with long-established ties to Virginia. Even here, however, the land was only 50 to 60 percent improved in 1894.[30]

That the agricultural economy of the remote mountain counties was connected to, and influenced by, the markets as the timber and railroad boom progressed is seen in the acreage of cleared lands between 1870 before the boom and at its peak in 1910, as recorded in the U.S. census. Improved acreage in Tucker County grew from 19.8 to 43 percent during those years, in Randolph from 16.6 to 39.7 percent, and in Pocahontas from 12.9 to 35 percent.[31]

Before large-scale timbering occurred in the backcounties, self-sufficient farmers generally raised food for their own household consumption, with the exception of livestock that were driven to market and sold for cash to buy necessities households could not produce for themselves. The local agricultural economy had found an equilibrium between supply and demand for farm production and household consumption, therefore backcounty agricultural producers were unable to provision the railroad and lumber crews with sufficient food. John E. Campbell, editor of the *Pocahontas Times*, of Huntersville and then Marlinton, Pocahontas County, testily reported that the railroad contractors were forced to import nearly all of their supplies, and this led to a "contemptuous remark" by a "stranger" that the county could barely support itself. This Campbell regarded as an undeserved slander, "for while we may not be able to sell the contractors all the farm products they need, still a great many of our people have a surplus in the bank at the end of a year's work." The explanation was simple: "On the farm the market ruled, and for most of the products the only market was the home market, the long haul in wagons precluding any competition with or from the markets of the world." Consequently, farm products "invariably commanded a higher price here than at the depot." Calvin Price, who succeeded Campbell as editor of the *Pocahontas Times*, observed several years later: "We are sorry to have occasioned the resentment of the strangers who were disagreeably surprised to find an isolated county which had a small independent market of its own, but if we have not supported ourselves it would be hard to name who has. We ate what we had and were thankful and what we lacked we did without." One Pocahontas sage summed up the difference between the commercial system found in the lowlands of Virginia and the subsistence farming practiced in the mountains of West Virginia: "There they eat what they can't sell, and here they sell what they can't eat."[32]

Calvin Price claimed that there were two schools of thought among farmers about the effects of the railroad cutting through the county. One was that "the county would be worsted by a railroad as prices would go down on farm products." Some producers also thought they might be better off if they sold their crops for cash at a lower price rather than to charge more and continue the system of barter exchange. These farmers also argued that farm products for which there was no market would command money after the railroad arrived and development resulted in a population of nonfarmers. "They have heard of the thrifty farmers of the Valley of Virginia, where the butter and poultry account keeps the storekeeper in debt to the farmer, and where there is a demand for every product of the farm," Price reported with approval.[33]

Generally, industrialization in Appalachia is interpreted as having destabilized a self-sufficient agricultural society and upset an egalitarian social structure governed by cooperation and the family rather than competition and impersonal market forces.[34] This view portrays preindustrial Appalachia as a society characterized by mountain families who owned their own land, worked their farms on the basis of household self-sufficiency, and, if they were not materially rich, at least were independent from the fluctuations of the market economy. Until industrial capitalism penetrated the region in the late nineteenth century bringing market dependency and class divisions, Ronald D. Eller wrote, "few areas of the United States more closely exemplified Thomas Jefferson's vision of a democratic society."[35]

Recent studies of preindustrial Appalachia's economy call into question this prevailing interpretation by demonstrating that much more diversity

and social stratification existed than is commonly presumed. Robert Mc-
Kenzie has departed from the common interpretation of preindustrial agriculture in Appalachia in his comparative study of three Appalachian Tennessee counties (Granger, Green, and Johnson) with several middle and
western Tennessee counties. Based on a sophisticated analysis of the 1860
manuscript census, McKenzie concluded that Appalachian farmers did not
live in an egalitarian world of landowners without social stratification.[36]

Focusing on the extent to which property ownership was egalitarian, as
well as the prevalence of subsistence-oriented agriculture and the standard
of living offered by such an economy, McKenzie determined that conventional ideas about nineteenth-century Appalachia as the last bastion of Jefferson's agrarian ideal are simply wrong. In fact, the distribution of wealth in
these Appalachian counties was highly *unequal* (as was true throughout
nineteenth-century America) with the top 5 percent of farm households
controlling between 35 and 49 percent of the wealth and the bottom one-half
controlling between 3 and 5 percent.[37]

McKenzie's Appalachian farmers were indeed self-sufficient, but their
position was always precarious. As he points out, the psychological costs of
market involvement were more than offset by the costs of isolation from the
markets, for only those with a commercial orientation saw their standard of
living improve in direct proportion to the degree of their involvement. In
fact, commercial orientation explains the wide variation in per capita wealth
in these counties in 1860.[38]

Because Appalachian farmers in these three eastern Tennessee counties
did not engage in the cotton economy, unlike those studied by Steven Hahn
in up-country Georgia,[39] production for consumption was "entirely consis-
tent" with production for exchange; they were complementary, not competing, goals. If cash were needed, farmers in these northeastern Tennessee
counties followed the same practice Durwood Dunn found in southeastern
Tennessee's Cades Cove; they simply produced for sale more of what they
consumed.[40] With the population growth on a fixed quantity of land, however, farmers at the lower end of the social scale, those with fifty or fewer
acres, could not feasibly subdivide their land among their offspring, therefore two-thirds of the subsistence farmers required supplemental income to
survive. In short, they had to go to work for wages.[41] Thus life in these three
counties already was characterized by an unequal distribution of wealth and
land ownership long before industrialization. This argument is applied to
the entire region by Wilma Dunaway.[42]

There is considerable debate among scholars about the relative importance of subsistence and commercial agriculture in the region. Research on preindustrial eastern Kentucky demonstrates the difficulty of making region-wide generalizations about Appalachia. Mary Beth Pudup argues that land was wealth in preindustrial Appalachia, that land ownership denoted social class membership, and therefore concentration of land (wealth) before, during, and after industrialization is a significant measure of change in the region. She found that in 1850 only 4.7 percent of the farm operators in Harlan County and 3.2 percent in Perry County were tenants.[43] By 1880, the beginning of the industrial transition, the proportion of tenant farm operators rose dramatically in the eastern Kentucky counties to 26 percent in Harlan, 24 percent in Perry, and 33 percent in Floyd. The result was a tightening isolation from America's commercial development and expanding reliance on simple household subsistence.[44] Sociologists Dwight Billings and Kathleen Blee come to similar conclusions in their study of Clay County, Kentucky, between 1850 and 1910, although the number of tenants was higher in the earlier period.[45]

Altina Waller's study of the Tug Fork area of Logan County, West Virginia, and Pike County, Kentucky, led her to conclude similarly that "although based on hierarchical values" the social structure was nonetheless "much more egalitarian in practice than that of tidewater Virginia." Moreover, in 1850 more than two-thirds of Pike and Logan County households owned their own farms. Even the one-third of heads of household who reported no landholdings did not represent a pauper class for "many such households consisted of young families . . . [who were] still part of the parents' domestic economy."[46] Population pressures and declining soil fertility revealed in these studies were responsible for the large number of landless tenants and laborers, but where McKenzie found a highly unequal distribution of land in 1860 Tennessee, Pudup, Billings and Blee, and Waller found a much greater equality in the distribution of land in the preindustrial Kentucky–West Virginia borderland. With the onset of industrialization, however, unequal division of land and wealth forced the landless into employment in the mills and mines.

In still another local variation, Kenneth Noe demonstrates the reverse pattern accompanying industrialization in southwestern Virginia. In 1860, tenants represented about 39 percent of the farmers in Floyd County, 32 percent in Raleigh, and 46 percent in Washington County. He notes that as the Virginia and Tennessee Railroad progressed westward into the mountains between 1850 and 1856, land values escalated 62.6 percent. With rising land values, "profit seeking encouraged landlords to drive away tenants and either sell the land to newcomers from the east or put it into production themselves. Yeomen hard-pressed to pay the higher taxes that went along with rising land values often had no choice but to sell." Herdsmen were especially hard hit as grazing land fell under the plow or was sold and livestock expelled to second-rate land. Many abandoned farming entirely or left for less commercial sections of the mountains. Thus tenancy declined dramatically in southwestern Virginia between 1850 and 1860. Some tenants bought their own land, but former tenants unable to buy land became day laborers.[47]

In what Noe calls a "modernization crisis," developments showed that "while closer market connections had meant profit and expansion for some southwestern Virginians, a deeper immersion in the tobacco and wheat economies, they had been disastrous for others. Deprived of their now over-priced land, driven into tenancy or day labor, many residents of southwestern Virginia retreated deeper into the mountains, away from the intrusive and for them, disastrous commercial way of life the railroad made possible" to such places as Logan County (West Virginia), where "traditional noncapitalist ways survived." Others moved into towns in search of employment.[48] Clearly something was very different in nearby Wise County, Virginia, however, where 85 percent of the farmers owned the land they cultivated in 1880, according to a student of the industrial transition in that county.[49] And Ralph Mann's study of four mountain communities in pre–Civil War Tazewell County, Virginia, which was grazed but not penetrated by the Virginia and Tennessee Railroad, shows that great local variations existed side by side: rural communities dominated by planters, subsistence farmers, tenants and the landless, and one in which all social elements coexisted.[50]

Paul Salstrom's *Appalachia's Path to Dependency*, a reinterpretation of two centuries of economic development in the Appalachian region, reinforces the conclusion that agricultural decline preceded industrialization. Salstrom argues that the development of Appalachian economic dependency was marked by four stages of agricultural decline. The first stage came during the decade before the Civil War, when rapid population expansion reduced the size of farms, forced marginal lands into production, and lowered per capita farm output. The second stage came during the Civil War as the region's economy was further weakened by the destruction of farm capacity, especially livestock. The third stage, between the 1880s and the 1920s, the period bracketing the industrial transition, came about because of the preexisting subsistence crisis that had been accelerating for three decades before the extraction companies entered the region. In this scenario, the resultant poverty prompted farmers who could no longer subsist on the land to supplement their farm incomes with low-wage industrial employment. In the final stage, the Great Depression of the 1930s, Appalachia's economic dependency was finalized by New Deal agencies, which pumped federal subsidies into the region.[51]

By the time of the industrial transition, therefore, agricultural decline in Appalachia was long under way as a result of geometric population growth and resource depletion that undermined the ability of farmers to produce a subsistence. Industrialization only exacerbated a process of decline, a point on which both Salstrom and McKenzie agree.

West Virginia's transition from an agricultural to an industrial economy generally follows Salstrom's stages in the development of Appalachia's economic dependency. This process is reflected in the relative and absolute decline in the number and size of farms. Nearly 90 percent of the state's residents were gainfully employed in agriculture during the 1860s and 1870s, but that percentage began a precipitous decline in the late nineteenth century, reached 50 percent in 1920, and seventy years later in 1994 stood at less than 2 percent. In absolute terms, the number of farms grew from 39,778 in 1870 to a peak in 1910 of 96,685; thereafter the number of farms began to fall each decade until it stabilized at around 20,000 in 1994. The average farm acreage in West Virginia also declined from about 215 acres in 1870 to a low of only 98 acres in 1950 before stabilizing at 185 acres in 1994. The most telling statistic is the aggregate number of acres in farmland. That figure shows the truly dramatic decline of agriculture in West Virginia, a state in which two-thirds of the population still lives in a rural countryside, from 10,193,779 acres in 1880 to 3,700,000 acres in 1994.[52]

Even though deforestation increased the amount of land improved for farming, this advantage was offset by the increase in the number of farms and the decline in average farm size. In Pocahontas County the number of farms grew from 682 in 1880 to 1,198 in 1910, but average farm size fell from 451 acres to 195.7 acres; in Randolph County the total number of farms increased less dramatically from 1,186 to 1,856, but the average size fell from 360 acres to 155.8 acres; and in Tucker County the total number of farms increased from 385 to 828 during this period, but average farm size declined from 223 to 112.7 acres. This pattern mirrored statewide development, where, as the population increased, so too the average farm size declined from 163 acres in 1880 to 103.7 acres in 1910 (see Table 11).[53]

Part of the reason for the growth in the number of farms was the contin-

Table 11. Farm Size and Improved Acreage, 1870–1920

Year	Total County Farms	Average Farm Acreage		Acres	
		County	State	Total	Improved (%)
Pocahontas County					
1870	604	—	—	336,954	43,329 (12.9)
1880	682	451	—	307,283	57,306 (18.7)
1890	908	351	142	319,145	74,260 (23.3)
1900	1,051	241.5	114.7	—	71,667
1910	1,198	195.2	103.7	233,871	83,067 (35.0)
1920	1,283	207.6	109.6	266,346	92,174 (34.6)
Randolph County					
1870	575	—	—	301,885	50,036 (16.6)
1880	1,186	360	—	426,724	84,163 (19.7)
1890	1,358	332	142	450,181	89,220 (19.8)
1900	1,787	202.8	114.7	—	109,891
1910	1,856	155.8	103.7	289,080	114,696 (39.7)
1920	1,774	170.4	109.6	302,327	134,869 (44.6)
Tucker County					
1870	223	—	—	66,095	13,078 (19.8)
1880	385	223	—	85,712	19,632 (22.9)
1890	659	129	142	84,917	26,413 (31.1)
1900	768	122	114.7	—	35,402
1910	828	112.7	103.7	93,314	40,093 (43.0)
1920	724	124.5	109.6	90,166	35,684 (49.3)

Source: U.S. Census of Agriculture for respective years.

uous subdivision of farms under the practice of partible inheritance common in Appalachia. The answer is much more complex, however, than simply being caught in the jaws of a Malthusian trap in which population growth put pressure on a fixed quantity of land. While partible inheritance subdivided the land into smaller plots, large blocks of land also were subdivided into small units for sale by the timber companies. Lumber operators usually purchased their properties for the timber, and once the forest was removed they preferred to sell the denuded land. The State Department of Agriculture actually established a program to assist lumbermen in subdividing their cutover lands for sale as small farms.[54]

Even though lumber companies generally sold their subdivided properties and moved on, in a few notable exceptions the companies farmed their own cutover land. For example, in 1920 the West Virginia commissioner of agriculture reported that the Babcock Lumber Company in Tucker County "produced this year many thousand bushels of fine potatoes, large quantities of ensilage and forage and the purchase, grazing, and feeding of hundreds of cattle, sheep and swine." Other companies consolidated cutover lands into huge holdings, which were removed from agricultural production. The commissioner of agriculture reported in 1920 that several million acres of cutover land were suitable for agriculture, particularly for raising livestock and poultry or gardening. Much of this land, however, was held by timber companies in large tracts ranging from two thousand to sixty thousand acres. The commissioner reported that "no organized or systematic use" was being made of these lands for any purpose except summer ranging of livestock.[55] West Virginia Pulp and Paper Company (now WESTVACO), for example, accumulated, and continues to own, hundreds of thousands of acres to ensure a steady supply of pulpwood for its large paper mill in Covington, Virginia.

The federal government also purchased hundreds of thousands of acres of barren land for the Monongahela National Forest, and the state of West Virginia acquired additional tens of thousands of acres for its extensive system of public parks and forests. These lands too were no longer available for agriculture. Constricting the availability of good farmland even further, especially the all-important bottomland, was that more and more prime acreage was being taken over for use by railroads, mines, factories, and towns as the industrialization of West Virginia progressed.[56]

The population-to-farm squeeze was further aggravated by environmental disaster in the form of fire, floods, erosion, pollution, and silting of navigable downstream waterways inflicted on the land by unrestrained deforestation. This subject is examined in Chapter 10.

Deforestation also prompted an increase in the number of farms in the interior mountain counties when many farmers shifted from traditional forest farming techniques to commercial farming as land was opened up. The shift to commercial agriculture is illustrated in the dramatic increase in the use of commercial fertilizers in the backcounties (see Table 12). The population growth that accompanied the timber boom partially explains the growth in the number of farms during this period. Woodsmen typically had farming backgrounds, and when the boom was over many of those who had saved enough money purchased their own land. Many farmers reduced the acreage they owned by selling their woodlands and then using the money to finance a shift to the fenced-pasture commercial system.[57]

Table 12. Number and Size of Farms and Use of Commercial Fertilizers, 1870–1920

Year	Total County Farms	Average Farm Acreage		$ Commercial Fertilizers
		County	State	
Pocahontas County				
1870	604	—	—	—
1880	682	451	—	679
1890	908	351	142	1,513
1900	1,051	241.5	114.7	5,070
1910	1,198	195.2	103.7	9,507
1920	1,283	207.6	109.6	31,292
Randolph County				
1870	575	—	—	—
1880	1,186	360	—	910
1890	1,358	332	142	3,460
1900	1,787	202.8	114.7	9,670
1910	1,856	155.8	103.7	18,068
1920	1,774	170.4	109.6	51,558
Tucker County				
1870	223	—	—	—
1880	385	223	—	456
1890	659	129	142	393
1900	768	122	114.7	1,130
1910	828	112.7	103.7	3,559
1920	724	124.5	109.6	14,726

Source: U.S. Census of Agriculture for respective years.

Farm trends in three timber counties generally reflected the statewide pattern between 1880 and 1920 with a decline in average farm acreage and a corresponding increase in the number of farms. The percentage of farms under one hundred acres increased from 30.6 to 54.1 percent in Randolph County, from 18.3 to 47.5 percent in Pocahontas County, and from 30.5 to 58.1 percent in Tucker County. But there was a corresponding decrease in the percentage of medium-sized farms from 54 to 39.4 percent in Randolph County, from 57.3 to 45 percent in Pocahontas County, and from 61 to 39.4 percent in Tucker County.

Table 13 shows the percentage of acreage in small, medium, and large farms alongside the percentages of farm operators in each category and illustrates the trend toward fewer people controlling a disproportionate

Table 13. Percentage of Farm Acreage and Farm Owners, by Category, 1880–1920

Year	Small Farms 0–99 Acres (% owners)	Medium Farms 100–499 Acres (% owners)	Large Farms 500+ Acres (% owners)
Pocahontas County			
1880	2.77 (18.3)	31.8 (57.3)	45.7 (24.3)
1890	3.8 (24.4)	41.8 (58.8)	41.6 (16.8)
1900	7.4 (33.7)	57.7 (56)	34.9 (10.2)
1910	10.6 (42.2)	64.77 (50.6)	30 (7.3)
1920	10.7 (47.5)	54.2 (45)	29.48 (7.4)
Randolph County			
1880	4.48 (30.6)	37.6 (54)	36.17 (15.2)
1890	6.49 (38.5)	38.76 (51.4)	25.9 (10)
1900	13.75 (52.6)	52.29 (40)	33.9 (7.6)
1910	17.28 (56)	61.4 (38.2)	32.3 (5.8)
1920	15.78 (54.1)	57.8 (39.4)	32.3 (6.5)
Tucker County			
1880	7.4 (30.5)	68.54 (61)	31.5 (8.5)
1890	21.5 (50.6)	91.5 (47.2)	13.5 (2.1)
1900	20.8 (51.3)	70.2 (46.9)	8.97 (1.82)
1910	13.3 (60)	85.46 (38.5)	10.95 (6.85)
1920	24.4 (58.1)	79 (39.4)	16.63 (10)

Source: U.S. Census of Agriculture for respective years.

percentage of farmland. For example, in Randolph County 15.2 percent of the farm owners controlled 36.17 percent of the total acreage in farms in 1880, and by 1920 that figure was 6.5 percent controlling 32.3 percent of the farmland. Throughout this period there was a significant disparity in the category of small farms of less than one hundred acres whereby a large percentage of farm families relied on a relatively small proportion of farmland for support. In Randolph County, for example, 30.6 percent of the farm operators worked only 4.48 percent of the land in 1880, whereas 54.1 percent worked 15.78 percent of the farmland by 1920.

The pattern revealed in these major timbering counties mirrored that of the state in a general leveling down almost across the entire range of farm size categories. As agriculture became linked into the national markets and fewer and fewer farmers could subsist on their land alone, many went off to work in industry. Probably for the same reason that farm tenancy declined with the railroad-induced industrial development in southwestern Virginia, both the number and the percentage of tenant farmers in West Virginia and the three sample counties declined over the long term. Table 14 demonstrates that tenancy as a sign of landlessness was not high in West Virginia even during the peak transition years with 21.8 percent in 1900 and 20.5 percent in 1910, especially when the usual additional disclaimers for widows and children still within the domestic economy are taken into account. In 1890 West Virginia ranked ahead of all its neighboring states in the percentage of families owning their farms; only Pennsylvania surpassed West Virginia although by less than one percentage point.[58]

In Tucker County tenants made up only 13 percent of the farm population in 1880, but that number fell to 9.4 percent in 1910 and continued to decline thereafter. Pocahontas County farmers, especially in the southern half of the county, displayed ownership patterns that resembled those of their large stock farming neighbors in Greenbrier County and across the line in Virginia, but even here tenancy declined from 10.8 to 8.8 percent during this same period. Curiously, Randolph County saw an increase in the proportion of tenants from 9.3 to 16.1 percent between 1880 and 1910, although the majority of these were cash tenants who rented the land, sometimes from timber companies. By 1920, that number also dropped to 10.5 percent of the total number of farmers, reflecting broader patterns (see Table 14).

There has been a consensus among historians that American farmers have always been motivated by the profit potential in producing for the commercial markets. This interpretation was challenged by revisionist historians during the 1970s and subsequently by their students and followers, who argued that the primary motivation of early farmers was the subsistence of the family and preservation of the farm (a "competence"). These historians viewed the "precapitalist mentality" of farmers as morally superior to that of those who were socialized in the corrupting influence of capitalism, which had overtaken American agriculture by the twentieth century.[59]

Whatever the merits of this now excessively abstract theoretical controversy, it seems clear that stripped of its ideological investments the two paradigms are not mutually exclusive. Recent scholarship on the issue in Appalachia has argued that both commercial and subsistence orientations easily coexisted. The mentality of producers undoubtedly changed as the world around them changed. Nor were subsistence and commercial orientations necessarily competitive; production for household consumption and marketable surplus were complementary facets of the single necessity to

Table 14. Owner- and Tenant-Operated Farms, 1880–1920

Year	Total Farms	Owner-Operated (%)	Tenant-Operated (%)	State: Tenant-Operated (%)
Pocahontas County				
1880	682	608 (87.7)	74 (12.2)	
1890	908	811 (89.3)	97 (10.6)	17.75
1900	1,051	882 (83.9)	142 (13.5)	21.8
1910	1,198	1,059 (88.4)	106 (8.8)	20.5
1920	1,283	1,162 (90.6)	88 (6.9)	16.2
Randolph County				
1880	1,186	1,076 (89.9)	110 (10.2)	
1890	1,358	1,161 (85.5)	197 (14.5)	17.75
1900	1,787	1,425 (79.7)	309 (17.3)	21.8
1910	1,856	1,522 (82)	299 (16.1)	20.5
1920	1,774	1,522 (85.8)	186 (10.5)	16.2
Tucker County				
1880	385	328 (82.6)	57 (17.4)	
1890	659	584 (88.6)	75 (11.4)	17.75
1900	768	633 (82.4)	94 (12.2)	21.8
1910	828	745 (90)	71 (9.4)	20.5
1920	724	659 (91)	55 (7.6)	16.2

Source: U.S. Census of Agriculture for respective years.

Note: Classes of farm tenure were not enumerated by the U.S. Census until 1880. Reconstructing ownership-tenancy rates for earlier periods requires careful use of the manuscript census schedules, a task which lies beyond the scope of this study.

produce a living. Therefore, if farmers needed more cash they simply produced more of what they consumed for the market. The subsistence and commercial orientations of agricultural producers, of course, were directly influenced by a variety of factors, including family size, farm size, soil fertility, transportation connections, and distance to markets.[60]

Scholarly and popular writers alike have accepted the notion that "self-sufficient" farming and a commercial orientation were antithetical, conflicting mentalities, but there are plenty of examples in which these tendencies coexisted harmoniously. The case of Wiley Bower is one of them. Bower was born in a log cabin on a Wyoming County farm in 1867. When he married in 1895, he bought the old home place and an adjoining piece of property for $600. In 1903 the couple sold out to the Pocahontas Land Company for $5,296 and then leased the farm and several hundred adjoining acres. In 1925 they bought back the land, without the mineral rights, plus an additional 100 acres, for $5,000. He and his family farmed the 260 acres for subsistence and cash. At one time the family raised five hundred sheep for mutton and wool for clothing; the rest of the wool they sold to dealers in Cedar Bluff, Virginia. The farm produced more than the family and a steady retinue of guests could consume, and so the surplus was hauled over the mountain by oxcart and sold to railroad, coal mine, and lumber mill employees and their families. The cash earned from their surplus and from goods produced specifically for market paid the taxes and bought seed and fertilizers, necessities the Bower family required, and a few luxuries in addition. When the Ritter Lumber Company established operations at the new mill town of Maben and the new mine town of Itmann was constructed a few miles from the Bower farm, the family prospered even more, and the entire family was employed as subsistence and market-oriented farmers delivering wagon loads of fresh meat, eggs, milk, fruit, and vegetables to the lumber mill families on a regular basis. Neighboring farmers did the same.[61]

The railroad and timber boom provided farmers in the Dry Fork area of Randolph and Tucker Counties with the opportunity to sell their meat and produce, and they periodically loaded their wagons with food for sale in the towns at prices that provided ample incentive to continue serving this market.[62] Similarly, P. H. Butler wrote in 1937 that in preindustrial Clay County, the best store "within reach" was located twenty-two miles away at the foot of Powell's Mountain on the old Gauley Bridge and Weston Turnpike. It was the best because it was on a road, although a rough one, and "we could trade our bacon, lard, eggs, chickens, honey, beeswax, wool, hides, ginseng, etc." for goods that could not be produced on the farm. "We did not pay money for goods because there was no money in circulation." Instead of paying cash, "we bought the supplies for winter we could use and paid for it with our produce."[63] Had there been cash in circulation, it certainly would have been a much appreciated medium of exchange.

Although farm commodities were produced for household consumption or for trade in the local market, raising livestock was the backbone of West Virginia's agricultural economy before, during, and after the transition. The commercial orientation of mountain farmers was usually exhibited primarily in the production of livestock for market. Before the arrival of railroads, mountain farmers drove their stock once or twice a year to regional gathering points where large herds were purchased and driven to distant markets by professional drovers.[64] Railroads changed this regional pattern and precipitated a shift to modern commercial stock farming. Stockmen of Pocahontas County, who formerly had driven their cattle over the mountain to White Sulphur Springs or to Covington, Virginia, began instead to ship their cattle, sheep, and hogs to market by rail from local depots along the Greenbrier Division. In 1910, twelve hundred carloads of sheep and cattle were shipped by rail out of the Greenbrier Valley alone.[65]

Unfortunately, direct connections to urban markets meant competition with cattle shipped from the Midwest to those same markets and dictated that mountain stockmen adopt more efficient methods. The rugged cattle capable of withstanding the rigors of the old open-range system were soon replaced with improved breeds that brought a higher price on the hoof. The investment in better-quality herds and removal of the forest lands where mountain livestock traditionally grazed precipitated the replacement of open-range grazing with the enclosed pasture. Fenced pastures allowed for controlled feeding and, most significantly under the commercial system, enhanced the potential financial return on the farmers' investment.

Throughout the mountains the timber industry first generated an industrial economy, which, once the forests were removed, was succeeded by a shift to the modern commercial stock-raising system. The town of Terra Alta, in Preston County, for example, grew steadily for over sixty years largely because of the railroad and the timber industry. By the 1920s, however, commercial growth had reached a plateau and then declined as the town and its countryside shifted almost completely to stock farming—and for good reason. Bluegrass replaced the trees, permitting extensive sheep and cattle grazing in this altitude above twenty-five hundred feet elevation where few crops prosper other than grass. In the late 1890s, Joshua Whitehair founded the local industry by serving as an agent for the Eden Company of Baltimore, purchasing livestock from the Terra Alta farmers and driving them into the stockyard at the railroad siding for shipment to Baltimore. By the 1920s, Whitehair and his son were transporting their animals by truck to Pittsburgh, where they fetched better prices. Others operated the stockyard at Terra Alta, and at one time it was reputedly one of the largest in the state.[66] The outlines of Terra Alta's evolution were mirrored in small towns throughout the interior counties of West Virginia as the forest was removed.[67]

The ascent of stock raising in the timbered-over West Virginia backcounties is either absent or out of phase in Salstrom's model of agricultural decline. According to Salstrom, during the initial settlement stage, Appalachian farms were large, the soil still fertile, and population growth had not yet reduced farm productivity, which enabled farmers to market their

Table 15. Livestock on Farms in Three Timber Counties, 1870–1920

Year	Cattle	Sheep	Swine	$ Total Valuation of All Domestic Livestock
Pocahontas County				
1870	7,916	10,824	2,789	358,239
1880	9,043	14,707	5,313	294,718
1890	11,894	25,146	4,684	444,860
1900	12,063	33,062	6,324	598,992
1910	13,208	41,517	5,408	859,923
1920	13,272	35,110	8,437	1,474,026
Randolph County				
1870	8,228	8,523	2,834	369,158
1880	14,657	12,403	9,458	474,241
1890	11,894	17,992	2,347	533,310
1900	18,191	23,570	7,023	769,775
1910	17,200	24,662	5,487	984,134
1920	14,684	18,214	5,128	1,502,266
Tucker County				
1870	1,646	2,608	1,045	112,583
1880	2,391	3,545	3,655	102,917
1890	3,549	3,287	2,305	141,870
1900	5,062	6,112	2,983	—
1910	4,144	7,602	2,462	317,427
1920	4,226	5,278	2,248	477,598

Source: West Virginia Department of Agriculture Biennial Reports, respective years.

surplus without risking the family's subsistence. In the second stage, however, population increases, falling farm sizes, and declining fertility diminished the ability of Appalachian farmers to produce a surplus for the market. Finally, according to Salstrom, population pressures on the ability of the land to produce became so severe that farmers were forced to supplement their incomes by entering the industrial work force. This was the situation confronting farmers when the railroad, timber, and coal boom arrived at the turn of the century.[68]

Data from the U.S. Census of Agriculture in Table 15 comparing the pretimber boom year of 1870 with the peak timber boom year of 1910 clearly demonstrate the correlation between the demise of the forest and the ascent of commercial stock raising. In Tucker County the number of cattle raised nearly tripled, while the number of sheep more than tripled and that of swine doubled between 1870 and 1910. Similarly, in Randolph County during these same years, the number of cattle and swine more than doubled, and the number of sheep nearly tripled. Expansion in Pocahontas County livestock during this period was nearly identical, with the number of cattle just about doubling and that of sheep almost quadrupling. Even though agricultural prices declined during the long depression that engulfed American agriculture in the late nineteenth century, the value of all domestic animals (cattle, horses, mules, asses and burros, swine, sheep, goats) raised in these timbered counties also expanded dramatically between 1870 and 1910: more than 200 percent in Tucker, nearly 300 percent in Randolph, and nearly 250 percent in Pocahontas.

Another clear indication of an agricultural economy shifting from subsistence to commercial farming is evidenced by the increasing reliance on commercial fertilizers (see Table 11). Without transportation, remote rural farmers were unable to use bulky commercial fertilizers, even if they could afford them, because there was no practical way to import the product. The railroad provided access, resulting in a dramatic increase in the total value of fertilizers purchased by farmers in the remote mountain counties. Farmers used very little commercial fertilizers of any kind in 1879, but by 1919 the value of fertilizers used in Tucker increased more than thirty-two times, in Randolph more than fifty-six times, and in Pocahontas forty-six times.

Self-sufficient farmers demonstrated a commercial orientation when it was feasible, and many readily shifted to commercial stock raising. The old forest farming agriculture was brushed aside by a modern commercial system that tied the fortunes of the West Virginia backwoods to national markets. Initially this seemed reason for optimism among interior farmers. Like their counterparts in the older settled counties, however, they now competed against midwestern producers who had far fewer geographic disadvantages to overcome than mountain farmers did. They were thrown into a contest they could never win and were forced to accept their own demise, powerless to prevent it, as cheaper products came in by rail and took over local as well as their former markets in the eastern cities. Their lament is expressed in a story told in Pocahontas County in 1909:

A farmer came to town the other day and ate dinner at a local restaurant. He spread butter from Iowa on bread grown in the Valley of Virginia; he put condensed milk from New York in coffee from South America, sweetened with New Orleans sugar. He ate corn bread from Ohio, a bacon from Chicago, and had beans, sweet potatoes, onions, and other vegetables from Michigan while the fruit was grown in California. He sweetened buckwheat cakes from Upshur County with Indiana corn molasses. By chance the potatoes had grown in Pocahontas soil. This, too, in a county where a few short years since every article on many a well laden board from the sugar and substantials to the rye coffee were produced at home. As for the farmer's horse, at a livery stable he was fed on Iowa oats and Michigan hay. Though we send much lumber and many fat cattle, sheep, and fowls to market, what doth it profit when so great an amount for food and fodder is sent to communities not nearly so richly favored by nature.[69]

By the 1920s the question of whether West Virginia farmers could compete in the new national markets had been resolved; the system that was to "help our people out of the woods" would not do so by creating a competitive agricultural system. With the development of alternative employment, farm labor abandoned the countryside for the timber, coal, and manufacturing industries where they could earn wages for their labor. Farmers and farm laborers also increasingly turned to part-time industrial work to supplement their income as the economy became ever more dependent on the national economy. Cash became essential for the purchase of manufactured goods that found their way into the deepest mountain hollows, and self-sufficiency was lost to wage labor. To survive as farmers, many migrated to the western states, while those who remained became part-time farmers and full-time industrial workers. Only a few would survive the shift to a more diversified commercial agriculture conducted more scientifically on fewer acres of land.[70]

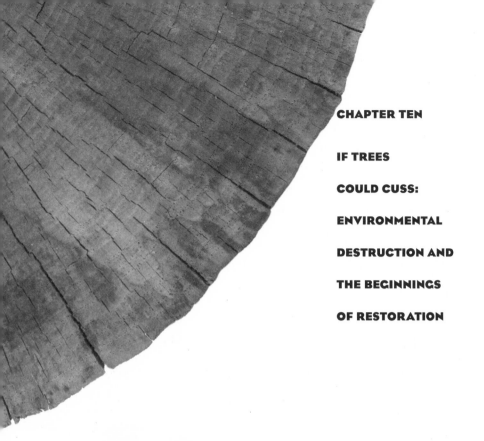

CHAPTER TEN

IF TREES

COULD CUSS:

ENVIRONMENTAL

DESTRUCTION AND

THE BEGINNINGS

OF RESTORATION

Removal of the virgin forest in West Virginia is a story of monumental waste even in a state whose history was forged by a natural resource extraction economy. The degree of wastefulness is well illustrated by an episode at the headwaters of the Cherry River just after the turn of the century. Withrow McClintic, an independent logger who contracted with a company in Richwood to cut a stand of virgin spruce, sent in crews to build splash dams in anticipation of the spring floods that would float the logs down into the Cherry River and on to the mill. The thaw came, but when the dams were opened, the floodwaters stranded the logs on the bottomland instead of carrying them to the river. With no way to rescue the logs, the mill company ordered an immediate halt to cutting so as to limit its losses. McClintic was a stubborn man, however; he ignored the order, and the stately spruces were felled even though there was no way to get them to the mill. The timber cut by McClintic never did make it to market; the logs were simply left to rot on the mountainside where they fell. Episodes such as this prompted Emory N. Wriston, a pioneer conservationist in West Virginia, to remark: "If trees could talk and cuss, West Virginia would be a poor place for a preacher to go on a picnic." McClintic's experience may not have been typical of operations in West Virginia during the logging boom, but then neither was it unique.[1]

The financial benefits derived from the development of the forest industry accrued to a select few over the short term, whereas the costs of the widespread destruction were borne by the taxpayers. This is clearly demonstrated by the environmental disaster the railroad-lumber boom visited upon West Virginia. According to Andrew Price, Pocahontas County lawyer, conservationist, and editor, one of the most common questions recent arrivals asked of natives in the Greenbrier Valley was "how we managed to exist before the railroad came to the county." Price's response was terse: if there were another place like Pocahontas was before the arrival of industry he would move there. Old-timers could not stand to look for long on the desolate slashing and stumps left in the place of the original forest, Price lamented, or to look passively upon the old freight cars, shanties, wires, poles, iron trucks, and other abandoned industrial debris that cluttered the countryside. Indeed, the land was now "as squalid as it could be." Streams once abundant with fish were dead, the game had disappeared, and the grass that once carpeted the floor of the virgin forest had been displaced by brush. There *were* more money and people in the county, Price acknowledged: "The doctors and lawyers make more money, and there is work for every man at high wages." But for this heightened economic vigor, he concluded, "we are paying dearly."[2]

The scale of destruction is suggested by what happened to the spruce forest, which flourished at the higher elevations of three thousand feet and above. The State Board of Agriculture reported in 1900 that the spruce forest that once covered approximately 1.5 million acres had been reduced to no more than 225,000 acres. The near elimination of spruce was the result of greatly improved technologies for cutting, hauling, and manufacturing timber into lumber and pulp, even under the most challenging circumstances. Several companies operated on Spruce Knob, at 4,860 feet the state's highest elevation, removing the timber from thirty to fifty acres each day. The report concluded that the wasteful methods employed by the companies of clear-cutting everything in their path without regard to size turned Spruce Knob into a desolate place.[3] The legendary spruce and hemlock forest of the Canaan Valley, one of the few authentic wilderness areas left in the East, also was obliterated in slightly more than a single generation, leaving behind a vast barren wasteland of stumps and rocks.[4]

Some blamed the "paper trust," the "enemy of the forests," for creating the great demand for pulp. One observer noted that the Sunday edition of an "ordinary city daily" required one dozen acres of woodland to obtain the spruce logs required to make this amount of paper.[5] A professional forester who studied the Horton operations of the Parsons Pulp and Lumber Company in 1922 believed that because West Virginia, like most states, imposed no special taxation on timberlands, it supported a public policy that fostered wasteful methods and a flagrant disregard for the future among lumber companies. As a result, he found silviculture conditions in the spruce belt "very poor indeed, as is the case in all the mountain logging in the Southern Appalachian region." Lumbermen followed a policy of "cut clean and then clear out," he observed, and not a single tree was left on Spruce Knob to witness "one of the best examples of wasteful and destructive logging."[6]

The old-growth forest had a fully developed foliage, and when the tops were cut away and left on the ground to die, they became a virtual tinderbox awaiting the careless spark. With so many steam locomotives, steam skidders, and steam loaders huffing and puffing through the forest, sparks were ever-present to ignite the inevitable conflagration. Fire followed fire until many areas of the state were left fundamentally altered from what nature had created.[7]

The vast majority of forest fires during the logging era originated because of industrial activity. In late 1908 the most extensive body of data yet compiled was gathered by the U.S. Forest Service as part of a national study. According to the *Report of the West Virginia Conservation Commission, 1908*, which cited the data, "the first serious fire occurred on August 28, and from that time there was no cessation for three months." Every county in the state was affected by forest fires. Although some of them were minor, the total reported in 1908 reached 710; 5,821 men were called into service to fight the fires, which burned an area of 1,703,850 acres representing 943,515,000 board feet of lumber worth $2,903,500. More than one-tenth of the entire surface of the state was burned over. Total financial losses from fire in 1908 were estimated at more than $5 million. The origin of these fires is instructive: 71 percent were from locomotives; 20 percent were started by sawmills and campers; 3 percent were set to improve the range for livestock; 2 percent were incendiary; and 4 percent were from other causes. In short, more than 90 percent of the fires in West Virginia in 1908 were caused by locomotives and lumber operations.[8]

With so much to lose, why the industry continued to rely on wasteful and unsafe timbering methods seems puzzling. Since the vast majority of the fires were started by locomotives, it is not surprising that most major fires began along railroad tracks. Firemen cleaning out locomotive ash pans knew that the only safe method was to empty the ashes into a creek or some other wet spot. Despite every precaution, however, a gust of wind might blow a hot coal into the slashing, as happened on Blackwater Lumber Company property near Davis in 1899. The fire ignited by that lone spark was so intense that it "burned a hole in the sky" and forced the woods crews "to work like beavers to cut trails into the green laurel to save themselves and the horses."[9] Other steam equipment such as the skidders required close attention as well. With common lack of foresight, a fireman on a skidder in Tucker County cleaned out the firebox and threw the hot coals out into the brush. The ignition of the brush and slash was so instant that the thoughtless fireman barely escaped with his life.[10]

The Babcock Lumber Company reportedly was a "heavy loser" from a 1908 fire that consumed no less than 10 million feet of hemlock and chestnut timber and three logging camps along the Blackwater River. Babcock completely shut down all of its mills and turned out the entire force to fight the fires, and "several foreigners" lost their lives in the effort.[11] A month later, in the Durbin, Burner, and Willdell district of Pocahontas County, another forest fire burned a seventeen-mile stretch along the Coal and Iron Railroad, consuming everything in its path.[12] On another occasion, fire forced a railroad crew to take refuge in the locomotive's water tank. The heat was so intense that it cracked the glass in the cab, and the tracks were buckled so badly that the line had to be rebuilt.[13]

In July 1930, fire broke out in a big slashing of the Cherry River Lumber Company on the Williams River, and in a week's time it had swept over an area seven miles long and three miles wide. Before the fire was extinguished, it had consumed five hundred acres of green timber, nearly 10 million feet of saw logs, eight thousand cords of tanbark, seven or eight logging camps, along with railroad bridges, tressels, and one steam skidder. In places the loamy soil was burned to the rock. Nearly one thousand men fought the blaze for a week before it was brought under control. Losses to the company were estimated in the millions of dollars, and independent woods contractors lost everything.[14]

The splendor of the giant spruce made such a powerful visual impact that contemporary critics often pointed to their destruction for dramatic illustration. Spruce Knob attracted the most attention as an example of environmental devastation caused by wasteful logging methods. No one understood

Destruction of vegetation and soil by fires in the Canaan Valley, 1912. (West Virginia and Regional History Collection, West Virginia University Libraries)

the problem better than A. B. Brooks, the state's leading conservationist and director of the West Virginia Geological Survey. His firsthand assessment of conditions in the cutover mountain lands in 1911 reveals the scale of destruction that resulted from the fires. The damage was most visible to the eye in the pine forests along the Allegheny summit, which marks the state's southeastern border, where fire had destroyed the humus soil. There, Brooks estimated that the damage could not be reversed in one thousand years. The original spruce forest that grew on the Allegheny summit and surrounding ridges had found an anchorage for roots in the cracks between the broken rocks atop the solid rock base. Over innumerable centuries, pine needles and leaves filled the crevices, and gradually mosses and lichens grew and decomposed until ever so slowly a layer of soil of one to three feet in thickness covered the underlying rocks. Fire reversed the work of centuries in a few brief days, and the process had to begin all over again.[15]

On a camping trip in 1908, Brooks climbed to the windswept summit of Spruce Knob to observe the surrounding countryside. Looking eastward toward Virginia he saw fertile farms and rich forest. In the opposite direction, however, "most of the country was a waste of brake-covered ground from which almost every trace of the original forest had been swept by fires."[16] The State Board of Agriculture confirmed this assessment when it reported as early as 1900 that on Spruce Knob itself there was "not enough soil in a square rod to meet the ordinary requirements of a hill of corn."[17]

One of West Virginia's best-known writers, Louise McNeill, who grew up along Swago Creek in Pocahontas County, has left a riveting description of the forest fire of 1930, which raged from the headwaters of the Gauley almost to the Elk River. "All week down at the village, a smoke pall hung over the schoolyard, and our cow spring up the hollow tasted of smoke," she wrote. "In the wind that fed it, the black, charred leaf-scraps sifted down over our fields and pastures." After the rains came, her brothers spent the day walking the land, sifting through the black ashes, and "saw the roots of the great stumps sticking up three feet above the burned out topsoil as though they still tried to clutch the earth."[18]

Deforestation whether by logging or fire eradicated the habitat for many species of wildlife. After the mountains were cutover, hunters stalked through the woods for weeks without sighting either deer or wild turkey, and the once abundant fish all but disappeared from the streams.[19] U.S. forest ranger Scott White, who grew up in Whitmer, Randolph County, and retired as warden of the Monongahela National Forest, recounted in 1947 that hunting was good in that area before it was logged out in the 1920s. Flocks of seventy-five turkeys and grouse in coveys of fifteen to thirty birds were a common sight. In one hour's time he regularly caught a dozen trout for the next day's meal. White regarded forest fires as the greatest cause of the disappearance of game in the cutover lands. Logging and then fires either removed or destroyed the plant life that created mast, depriving animals of a source of food. Consequently, even the small game such as rabbits and squirrels became scarce in West Virginia's woods.[20]

Human encroachment on the natural habitat of wildlife also had a dramatic effect on the animal population. Farmers had been waging a continuous battle with predators such as wolves and panthers since the earliest settlements, and they were systematically eliminated by stock farmers as the land was cleared for pasture. One of the last wolves in the state was hunted down by a dozen hounds and killed by "a large number" of hunters in Randolph County in 1900 for "committing depredations to the great loss of farmers" in Webster and Randolph Counties. The Randolph County court had posted a reward of $50 and Webster County $100 on the lone wolf's head; his mate had been killed a year or two earlier. The predator was thought to be "the only wolf left in this part of the country." Sheep farmers were greatly relieved, but its passing signaled the end of the wilderness epoch.[21] Sensing the historical significance of the moment, the hunters and their tracking hounds were photographed surrounding the wolf with guns pointed at the dead animal; the lifeless wolf was propped up on wood stilts, a confirmation that the citizens of Randolph County were at long last "out of the woods."[22]

Even after the forests were removed, ill-advised programs intended to increase the numbers of game fish and animals only accelerated the destruction of the state's wildlife. Perhaps the most obnoxious of these programs was the varmint-killing contest popular during the 1930s. Counties cooperated with sportsmen's clubs in holding these contests to rid the land of animals that were predators of more desirable game. The contests assigned points for each designated "varmint" that was killed. Among the animals designated as varmints were red or gray fox, wildcats, weasels, mink, eagles, owls, hawks, crows, red squirrels, turtles, kingfishers, carp, chipmunks, and coyotes. The panther (cougar) was singled out by a particularly high reward. According to contest rules, the heads of offending varmints were delivered to the judge for point credits; the "sportsmen" were permitted to keep the animal hides. The number of animals killed is astonishing: in 1933–34 almost two hundred thousand animals in twenty-six participating counties; in 1934–35 nearly three hundred thousand in forty participating counties.[23]

Americans traditionally thought of the soil as they had the forests—as inexhaustible. Since earliest times Americans had worn out the land and moved on to more fertile soil. By the early twentieth century there were no new lands to open, and it was time to reap the consequences of centuries of abuse. For the first time Americans became aware of the need to conserve the soil because of massive publicity focused on places like the Dust Bowl in the 1930s. Erosion became a national tragedy because the loss of topsoil was largely preventable, and yet the problem had gone unchecked. Hugh H. Bennett, chief of the Soil Conservation Service, stated the case directly before a congressional committee in 1939: "It takes nature from 300 to 1,000 years or more to bring back a single inch of topsoil; and we sometimes lose that much topsoil as a result of a single rain." From a practical standpoint, therefore, "we may properly look upon our soil resource as something that cannot be restored."[24]

When the higher elevations of the backcounties were denuded, erosion further disfigured the land, particularly after forest fires. Rain washed away the already thin layer of topsoil, gullies formed in sandy soils, clay surfaces washed away in sheets, and the fertility was leached out of the soil.[25] Skid trails and trenches gouged into the mountainside by logs hauled in by steam

Deforested rim of Blackwater Canyon, Tucker County, ca. 1910. (West Virginia and Regional History Collection, West Virginia University Libraries)

skidders greatly accelerated this destructive process. No comprehensive effort was made to evaluate, much less solve, the soil erosion problem in West Virginia until 1937, when Congress approved a plan for state participation in demonstration projects with the Soil Conservation Service, although there had been some cooperation earlier with the Soil Erosion Service. The scale of the problem was massive. One survey completed in the 1930s concluded that accelerated soil erosion affected 90 percent of the state's 15.5 million acres of land surface; nearly 10 million acres had lost between 25 and 75 percent of their topsoil, and 4 million acres had lost more than 75 percent.[26]

A document prepared for the U.S. Bureau of Agricultural Economics claimed that the chief sources of erosion in West Virginia were the destruction of the original forest, fire that prevented the forest from reestablishing itself, farming slopes that were too steep for cultivation, and inadequate protection from overgrazing. In the Big Sandy River basin, raging floods washed away the fertile topsoil in the valley bottoms only to deposit large amounts of infertile subsoil in its place. The report listed problems that were "typical" of many thousands of acres in the state: low fertility; erosion, both sheet and gullying; no topsoil; weeds and nonvaluable vegetation; "balds"; topography steeper than 40 percent; unsuitable land being used for agriculture; extensive clearing and intensive farming, or "taking all and returning little to the land"; farms too small; low average crop yields; and poor-quality

Deforestation and logging roads in Blackwater Canyon accelerated erosion, ca. 1910. (West Virginia and Regional History Collection, West Virginia University Libraries)

Log skidding caused trenches that accelerated erosion. This trench was on Meadow River Lumber Company lands, probably Greenbrier County. (West Virginia and Regional History Collection, West Virginia University Libraries)

pasture land. The economic problems generated by the depleted quality of farmland in denuded areas created social problems as well. The bureau surmised that many of the more "enterprising" families had moved on in search of improved opportunities and left behind those who were less capable of reversing these conditions. Further exacerbating the land problem were the "squatters or industrial people temporarily out of work who have little interest in conservation and improvement, deplete the land, and leave as soon as employment opportunities arise in the industrial world."[27]

Soil that washed off the hillsides went into the streams, and farmers' organizations repeatedly called public attention to the serious pollution of the state's streams.[28] The trouble began at the tops of the mountains, where the cutting of the timber exposed the ground to the elements, caused springs to dry up, and substituted surface drainage over the hard-packed soil where springwater once trickled pure and perennial. Lower down, the water picked up drainage from tanneries, pulp mills, sawmills, factories, coal mines, and towns, "all emptying their waste and sewerage into the water-courses with no attempt at purification." In 1911, Brooks declared that many of these streams were open "sewers."[29]

H. E. Williams, state superintendent of farmers' institutes, brought the serious pollution of the state's streams to the attention of the West Virginia State Board of Agriculture in 1907. West Virginia had "an abundant supply of the purest water on earth, but it was fast becoming polluted with refuse from factories, mills and tanneries," he warned. "No man has the moral right, and ought not to have the legal right, to thus trespass upon the rights of another." But more than legal rights were involved for pollution meant "destruction to all life within the stream and danger to the public health and welfare."[30]

Expressions of concern also were common among informed citizens who pressured the West Virginia Natural Resource Commission, established in 1908, to investigate the conditions in the state. The commission learned that cattle had died from drinking the waters of the Cheat River, a stream once synonymous with purity. The waters of the Cheat River reportedly "put locomotives out of commission." Moreover, it took the hair off the legs of cattle that waded in it and was fatal if they drank it. According to Brooks, "Scarcely a living fish remained in the Cheat River between its forks at Parsons and its confluence with the Monongahela River, a distance of seventy-five miles.[31] Nearby Decker's Creek provided another "example of what deforestation and pollution have done," a popular magazine reported. Fish had abounded in this stream, but now it was dead; "even the lizards are giving up the ghost."[32]

Conditions on the West Fork of the Monongahela River were even worse. Turtles died in its waters, and yet the towns of Weston, Clarksburg, and others took their drinking water from this river. "These are not isolated cases," reported the editor of the *Monthly West Virginian*, for similar conditions prevailed throughout the state. "If the instances cited are worse than others, it is because deforestation has gone farther," the editor declared. "Let the destruction of the woods go on, and let factories, tanneries, mills, and towns continue to empty their offal into the streams, and a state-wide condition will prevail which will be worse than war—and 'war is hell.'"[33] Even the Williams River, the trout fishers' paradise high in the mountains of Webster and Pocahontas Counties, was nearly devoid of fish. They had suffocated from the lack of oxygen resulting from decomposing sawdust that lumber mills illegally dumped into the stream.[34]

People in the rural, underdeveloped backcounties were ambivalent about the pollution from wood industry plants. On the one hand, they had become dependent on the wage labor that mills provided, but on the other, the streams still provided them with their water supply, recreation, food, and for many was a vital part of their personal identities. Therefore, new mills often sparked a flurry of worried public discussion among residents who lived along the rivers where the plants were located. As might be expected, the reaction of the people depended on whether their town was located upstream or downstream from the offending site. For example, in late 1898 and early 1899 citizens along the Greenbrier waited for the resolution of a suit brought by the city of Cumberland, Maryland, against the West Virginia Pulp and Paper Company, in Piedmont, West Virginia, which had been indicted for polluting the waters of the Potomac River from whence Cumberland drew its water supply. In the end, the jurors were unable to decide the case and charges were dropped. Residents along the Greenbrier River, nevertheless, continued their nervous vigil for the company was planning to establish a paper mill along the Greenbrier River at Caldwell, not far from Lewisburg, at the junction of the Greenbrier River and the Chesapeake and Ohio Railroad. Daniel O'Conner, a large logging contractor and a noted local booster from Pocahontas County, was instrumental in arranging for the selection of Caldwell for the new plant. The mill would be the largest of its kind in the world, constructed on sixty acres at a cost of approximately $2 million, and projected to employ twelve hundred workers.[35]

Paper mills of this type used the sulfite process, which required large quantities of spruce wood, and discharged the unused material from manufacturing into the water. Sulfuric acid is used in the process to prepare the wood for paper, and when the acid and other toxic chemicals were released into the water, they made a dark, resinous, sticky, slimy substance, which foamed at the top of the water and was carried downstream. The chemicals discolored the bottom of the river and generally killed all life in the stream. City water intake pipes were clogged with this sticky substance, and the water was rendered unfit for human use. These conditions had prompted the Cumberland suit and hence the concern among residents along the Greenbrier River.

Understandably, towns downriver from such plants were opposed to the pollution of their water supply. In this case, the city of Hinton, which was located on the New River just below the confluence of the Greenbrier and well below Caldwell, refused to submit to any pollution of its water and threatened to take any legal action deemed necessary to prevent this from occurring. Hinton's uncompromising stance drew hostile reactions from other towns in the Greenbrier Valley, including Caldwell's neighbors Lewisburg and Ronceverte, where developers anticipated the day when the three towns would be consolidated into one large city in which "electric railways, banks, improvement companies, and other enterprises were projected."[36]

Towns upstream also stood to benefit by supplying the timber for this new plant. Andrew Price, a partner in the Marlinton law firm of Price, Osenton, and McPeak, who served as counsel for West Virginia Pulp and Paper and defended the company in the suit by Cumberland, used his position as editor of the *Pocahontas Times* to proclaim pollution "a sacrifice we must make to progress." Greenbrier residents could not afford "to keep back the development of our country for the sake of a stream of water, and the day is coming when we will have to go back in the woods to find pure streams. You cannot change a forest to farmland without polluting to a considerable extent the streams which drain it. It is the price we have to pay for the benefits of civilization." Hinton's opposition represented a lack of civic consciousness, Price charged, which failed to rise above purely local interests. It was true that Marlinton was upstream from the pulp mill, "but we are quite sure if we were below it we would submit as gracefully as we could."[37]

During the public venting over these conflicting interests, Covington, Virginia, came forward with financial inducements, and the West Virginia Pulp and Paper Company apparently decided to avoid the conflict by locating its new mill across the state line instead.[38] Price chastened the Hinton obstructionists afterward, charging that they should have educated themselves about the limited pollution caused by such mills "before they drove the industry out of the state."[39]

Six years later, the Lewisburg *Greenbrier Valley Democrat* reported: "The ooze has arrived." Pollution raised its ugly head again, this time in Price's own backyard. The black water that arrived at Ronceverte in September 1905 originated at the tannery in Price's hometown of Marlinton. "In due season," the Lewisburg editor wrote, the "ooze" would "render the water totally unfit for drinking or other family uses." He urged the county attorney and Ronceverte officials to make an effort to remedy the evil for "no man, company or set of men should be allowed to destroy the water supply for hundreds of people."[40]

Price's response to the charge that a Marlinton factory was polluting the river was cautiously defensive, for even though he was an industrial booster,

Price was concerned about the environment. Caught on the horns of his own ambivalence, Price was inclined to assume a philosophical posture: "No matter what industries are situated on a stream, the stream is polluted to a certain extent. A farm pollutes a stream as compared to the virgin forest, and the lovers of the beautiful deplore any pollution of the streams of the State. . . . We cannot have the benefits of the woods and town life at the same time." To demand that the tannery put in settling ponds might be even worse, so Price decided to wait and see before making a decision even though the evidence was all around him.[41]

Floods were another inevitable consequence of deforestation. The woodlands at the headwaters of most West Virginia rivers were unsuitable for agriculture, but the forests performed the vital function of serving as a natural sponge, retaining moisture, controlling runoff from rain and snow, and keeping the soil in place. With the forests removed, so too were the natural controls on water flow. Consequently, streambeds dried up during periods of low precipitation, causing problems for the farms, towns, and industries downstream that depended on the streams for their water supply. A U.S. Geological Survey report published in 1911 noted that the construction of the Morgantown and Kingwood Railroad built up Deckers Creek from the Monongahela River to Kingwood and on to Rowlesburg had quickly resulted in the removal of the dense forest and a multitude of cold springs. Once stripped of timber, the land no longer operated as a natural system absorbing and releasing water, particularly after the fires that followed in the wake of the lumbermen. "The summer sun now beats down on a bare and parched land," it was reported, and "forest, stream, cool shade, and cold spring are all gone, and the land is desolate."[42]

Pollutants became more concentrated in the reduced volume of water and stagnant pools during the dry months. When it did rain or the winter snows melted, dry beds were transformed into torrents that overwhelmed their banks in dangerous "tides." For example, in July 1909, the Tygart River rose twenty-one feet in seven hours at Elkins, and Elkins was only forty miles from the Tygart's source. The people living further downstream along the Monongahela River experienced even greater fluctuations.[43]

The inability to control stream flow posed serious economic disadvantages to businesses dependent on an adequate water supply. Along Deckers Creek, it was reported in 1911, eight once profitable mills had been abandoned because the water was so low for several months of the year that they could not continue operations. The only surviving mill was forced to remain idle "a good part of the time" for the same reason. Similar effects on local

Deforestation caused streams to run dry as in 1930, when Morgantown residents walked across the Monongahela River bed. (West Virginia and Regional History Collection, West Virginia University Libraries)

manufacturing had occurred along "other streams that have been denuded of their timber to the same extent," a geologist observed.[44]

Quick rises and droughts also had a ruinous effect on the state's economy by disrupting shipping on navigable waterways. "The road to market is the path to prosperity," wrote A. B. Brooks, "and the easier and better the road the greater the prosperity. Wealth locked up is no better than poverty. Free exchange of commodities is the life and blood of business growth and national development." Some of the main arteries of commerce in West Virginia were its navigable watercourses, which in 1911 totaled 748.5 miles.[45]

The federal government spent large sums improving West Virginia rivers, a total of $38,147,466 between 1790 and 1907. By far the greatest amounts were spent on the Ohio ($24.5 million), Monongahela ($6.8 million), Great Kanawha ($4.7 million), and the Big Sandy and its tributaries ($1.5 million). This amounted to approximately one-twelfth of the total amount expended by the federal government for the improvement of rivers and harbors from the founding of the republic to 1907.[46]

Deforestation seriously jeopardized federal investment in the state's navigable waterways. Without the forest, destructive floods, dried-up stream-beds, and silt-clogged navigational channels all threatened commerce on rivers that carried great amounts of tonnage. The Big Sandy, Great Kanawha, Little Kanawha, Monongahela, and Ohio Rivers carried more than one-fifth of the total river commerce of the United States in 1911. A greater tonnage originated on the banks of the Monongahela and was then transported over that river than on any other stream in the Western Hemisphere.[47] Further improvements would be of questionable value without the forests in the headwaters to control runoff. Because inaction threatened the existing system, the federal government determined that the cutover lands in the higher elevations of the Appalachians must be reforested to protect the river systems of the East. In West Virginia, this decision led to the establishment of the Monongahela National Forest in 1915. Although the process would take decades, it began during this period as the full consequences of deforestation were being realized. In the meantime, the state of West Virginia did little to check, much less reverse, the destruction of its own environment.

The despoilers of West Virginia's wilderness bear the responsibility for the devastation they caused, but their destructive "cut out and get out" methods went unchecked because the state not only abrogated its responsibility but actively encouraged untrammeled exploitation of the state's natural resources. There were, of course, West Virginians whose sensibilities were shocked by the scale of destructiveness that accompanied deforestation. Even within state government a few voices were heard above the clamor urging the conservation of natural resources. The extinction of certain species in western Virginia, such as the elk (1820) and the buffalo (1825), prompted Virginia to enact laws intended to provide the simplest form of game protection. Most of these laws were virtually ignored, however, and in any event no means of enforcement was provided by the legislature. These same laws were reenacted when West Virginia gained its independence in 1863, but, like Virginia, the legislature failed to provide for their enforcement for another thirty-four years.[48]

Environmental protection in West Virginia during the years before the Great Depression is a story of the heroic dedication of individuals whose commitment to public service was met with a profound lack of appreciation and even outright scorn. The first significant steps toward a meaningful conservation policy came about because game fish in West Virginia streams began to disappear, particularly in the developed counties. The legislature established the West Virginia Fish Commission in 1877, a three-member board charged with restocking the state's streams. Signaling a profound lack of commitment, the state established a precedent that would last for the next three decades when it appointed the commissioners to serve without salary and reimbursed them only for approved expenses.[49]

One of the first fish commissioners, C. S. White, purchased three and one-half acres of land on which he built a fish hatchery at his own expense; he then offered the facility to the state at cost. The fish commissioners were dedicated to their cause, but few public officials understood the importance of their work, and even these modest efforts were opposed by hostile obstructionists.[50]

More than a decade later, two of the first three commissioners, C. S. White and F. J. Baxter, were still serving on the Fish Commission without pay. In spite of their pleas, the legislature still provided a mere $500 annually toward restocking the state's streams, and the fish populations continued to decline in the face of this parsimony. The commissioners had become experienced with niggardliness by then, but they were losing patience: "We have been willing to give as we have done, our services in the matter without compensation, and at a very considerable loss of time and resulting pecuniary loss." Nevertheless, they could no longer refrain from expressing their chagrin at seeing the work drag along, "comparatively unsuccessfully, for lack of the pittance from the State which would constitute an adequate support." By way of comparison, the commissioners pointed to the liberal funding provided by other states for promoting fish culture. Pennsylvania, for example, earmarked $600,000, New York over $1 million, and even Maine, with a population not as large as that of West Virginia, provided approximately $500,000 in public funds. In no state or territory was funding for fish conservation so "utterly inadequate" as in West Virginia. Not even the argument that small amounts of investment generated large revenues from sportsmen and tourists persuaded the legislature to increase funding for the Fish Commission.[51] Apparently annoyed with their carping, the legislature abolished the commission in 1895. Such were the rewards for championing conservation in West Virginia—even when it was at one's own expense. Why legislators would be so adamant in their opposition to fish stocking remains a matter of conjecture, but the government's long-standing support of natural resource development undoubtedly prompted lawmakers to support policies favoring industry over subsistence users of the streams.

Laws pertaining to fish and game protection were readily passed by the West Virginia legislature; such measures were found in sixteen sections of the code by 1887. Even though penalties for convictions were stipulated as well, actual enforcement of these laws was left in the hands of local law officers.[52] Of course, it was perfectly understood that reliance on local law enforcement to protect fish and game posed serious obstacles to success. Counties were even more frugal than the state, and county and local law enforcement officers were few in number and generally served large jurisdictions with limited authority. Local magistrates and prosecutors also were too busy with the standard workload to assert themselves aggressively in fish and game enforcement even if they were so inclined. The preference for low taxes and weak government ensured that counties, like the state, operated on a shoestring so they were not in the financial position to enforce the law in the backwoods where major violations were most likely to occur. Moreover, the fish and game laws challenged the backcounty custom of including wildlife in the domestic food supply to be taken when needed rather than when a distant state agency deemed it appropriate. Custom ensured that people would ignore the law unless it was rigorously enforced and that local elected officials would ignore those violations.

There was a definite class bias in the conservation laws, which many mountain residents recognized and resented. Backcounty citizens demonstrated little respect for laws that imposed heavy penalties on individuals for comparatively minor violations when industrialists polluted the streams and set fire to the woods with little fear of reprisal.[53] A speaker at the annual meeting of the West Virginia Bar Association in 1905 acknowledged this inequity in the law when he remarked that until 1903, "the poor wretch who took a stick of dynamite and killed a few fish committed a felony," whereas "the corporation that polluted the waters of a stream for fifty miles and rendered them totally unfit for fishing or any other purpose, escaped all punishment."[54] There were always a few renegade lawyers in West Virginia even during the industrial transition.

In response to these diverse ideological and structural impediments, Governor William MacCorkle initiated what would become a long and often disappointing campaign to bring enforcement power to conservation. In 1895 he urged the creation of a new Fish and Game Commission to be headed by a warden at an annual salary of $1,000 to enforce the laws.[55] The governor's plan was incorporated in an exhaustive bill, which effectively rewrote most of the current fish and game laws, but the measure went down to defeat by a clear majority (twenty-three for, thirty-six against) in the legislature. Legislators must have been in a particularly foul temper for, as mentioned above, on the very same day they voted to abolish the Fish Commission by an overwhelming fifty-four for and six against.[56]

Governor MacCorkle and his progressive supporters persisted despite the setbacks. The governor's 1897 message to the legislature reemphasized the need for conservation and called for a game and fish warden to enforce the law because "our game and fish are being wantonly and recklessly destroyed." Legislators were more responsive during this term, perhaps because the governor was speaking the truth when he informed them that his office was "in daily receipt of communications protesting against these outrages."[57]

Delegate Lloyd Hansford, of Tucker and Randolph Counties, launched the legislative initiative when he introduced House Bill 10. The measure incorporated most of the governor's recommendations but did not provide an annual salary. Instead, the legislation that finally emerged provided that the warden would receive the fines accruing from prosecutions up to $1,200 and expenses of three cents a mile for travel. The legislature did assign important enforcement functions to the new warden, including the power to initiate criminal proceedings, extensive search and seizure powers, and the provision that any attempt to hinder such a search was deemed prima facie evidence of guilt.[58]

Although this was an important advance toward ameliorating the perilous condition of the state's wildlife, the fish and game warden bill contained two fundamental flaws. First, it relied on fines from convictions to pay the warden's salary. Consequently, the most qualified people would be discouraged from seeking the position. On the one hand, the pay was too low, and on the other, inadequate salaries encouraged the overzealous prosecution of offenders so as to assure a reasonable income. Second, the warden had no power to appoint deputies. He was, therefore, the sole authority for the entire state, with responsibility for such a vast territory that a realistic assessment yielded little hope that he would ultimately succeed. Such fundamental shortcomings emanated directly from a legislature bound by parsimony, and philosophically wedded to the idea of a limited government with minimal power that gave single-minded support to resource companies. Thus the burden was shifted to backcounty communities resistant to the encroachments on timeworn customs in the use of natural resources and local politicians who did not want to alienate their constituents.

Over the next six years, during three legislative sessions, Governor George Atkinson continued his predecessor's campaign to bring enforceable game and fish laws to West Virginia. They were years filled with tribulations. Annual reform bills either went down to ignominious defeat or died in committee. The secretary of state, to whom the fish and game warden reported, provided the legislature with expense and revenue data for 1897 that clearly reveal the financial inadequacies that hobbled the warden system. The warden traveled 3,052 miles in 1897 to make ten arrests, which resulted in only three convictions in the local courts. Of the $261.80 in fines imposed on those convicted, the warden received $51.80, of which $13 was spent on expenses. The total salary of the warden for 1897, therefore, amounted to a mere $38.80 for traversing a very rugged distance equaling the breadth of the United States.[59] Figures for the three previous years reveal the same pattern. Sometimes the legislature was unconscionably slow in reimbursing wardens even for their meager expenses. When Governor Atkinson submitted his reform bill in 1899, the previous warden, Captain E. F. Smith, who had rendered "valuable services . . . practically without compensation," still had not been reimbursed for his expenses.[60] Governor Atkinson was still prodding the legislature in 1901 to pay E. F. Smith for his expenses, and it is not clear if the former warden ever received payment.[61]

What prompted the shift is unclear, but at long last the legislature's very high threshold of embarrassment was successfully challenged in 1901, when it finally provided the fish and game warden with a $1,000 annual salary, travel expenses at three cents per mile, and the power to deputize. For their services, deputies were to receive the fines collected from successful prosecutions. The measure became law without serious opposition, and for the first time in its existence West Virginia granted the power to enforce its fish and game laws to a salaried officer of the state.[62] This was a giant step forward for the struggling conservation movement but one that was long delayed and grudgingly given.

The West Virginia legislature has never kept a history of floor debates, so the reasons why legislators supported or opposed conservation laws may forever remain unknown. A roll-call analysis of the votes on key pieces of wildlife protection legislation between 1895 and 1903 reveals no conclusive answers but does suggest that legislators from the underdeveloped backcounties were more inclined to oppose the impingement of central power into their customary uses of fish and game, while legislators from the older, developed counties supported stronger controls. If legislators were representative of their constituents at all, we must conclude that most of them favored environmental protection in principle, but they neither wanted to pay for such a system nor were willing to grant enforcement power to a distant authority.[63]

One environmental abuse that all branches of government acknowledged as destructive was the common practice among sawmill operators of disposing of sawdust, slabs, and other refuse in the streams. Responding to Governor MacCorkle's query about the effect of sawdust on fish, an official with the Saint Lawrence Boom and Manufacturing Company of Ronceverte, Greenbrier County, informed the governor in 1895: "When sawdust is thrown into mountain streams the trout are killed," and it was nearly "impossible to get rid of it as it settles into pools."[64] The fish and game warden reported in 1901 that "more fish are destroyed and driven from the streams from this than from any other cause." The greatest danger to wildlife emanated not from industrialization, the warden observed, but rather from "the onslaughts of more people."[65]

Population growth translated into an increase in the demand for game and therefore a market for willing suppliers. The market aspect of hunting and fishing in the backcounties was an important, now forgotten, economic activity, particularly for those who still lived in the forest. At the turn of the century, before the virgin forest had been removed entirely, traditional customs retained their power in varying degrees over mountain residents. Hunting and gathering practices had evolved out of the necessity of putting food on the table, and the necessity was turned into sport and recreation. But with the passing of the wilderness, the economic transition, and the rising public consciousness of the need to conserve the forests and wildlife, the destructive traditional methods of bagging fish and game met with mounting opposition. A partial list of the convictions reported by the fish and game warden for 1901–2 provides a glimpse into those folk customs which conservationists regarded as detrimental to improving the environment (see Table 16).

These methods reflect practices of an earlier culture dependent on an abundant nature for basic sustenance, and traditionalists now living at the periphery of the wage economy who sold game in the marketplace continued to do so. It was legal for sportsmen to sell their catch or kill, provided they remained within the bag limits and observed the seasons, but it was against the law to transport game, dead or alive, out of state. Steady demand and good prices, however, continued to make this trade attractive to a declining number of forest dwellers. The warden reported in 1901 that the law was making an impact, as evidenced by the "large amount of game in our local markets during the game season." Before shipping game out of the state was prohibited, it was "almost impossible for the people of our State to purchase, in any of our markets, game which had been killed within our State." The reason was that commission merchants of Baltimore, Maryland, most notably S. A. Rice and Company, had been "actively engaged in trying

Table 16. Violations of the Fish and Game Laws, 1901–1902

Violation	Number
Nonresidents hunting without a license	5
Dynamiting fish	4
Killing quail out of season	7
Killing pheasants out of season	2
Killing deer out of season	5
Chasing deer with dogs	1
Seining	28
Killing songbirds	4
Catching fish out of season	3
Shipping game out of state	7
Killing turkeys out of season	1
Failing to put fishways in dams	9
Total violations	79

Source: Game and Fish Warden, *Report*, 1901–1902, 4. This is only a partial list; some of the records were destroyed by fire.

to secure game contrary to the laws" of West Virginia. Other firms were involved as well, and "illegal shippers have tried in almost every conceivable way to smuggle game out of the State."[66]

As the wilderness disappeared, some of these traditional suppliers of game crossed over into the realm of folklore. One of these intrepid woodsmen was Jesse Hammonds, "a patriarchal hunter and trapper," who lived in the Williams River wilderness of Webster County, where he had taken refuge from encroaching civilization. When the Pocahontas attorney-editor-conservationist Andrew Price visited the Hammonds in 1906, he found them to be the "best of hunters and fishers," but he disapproved of their methods for they "kill to sell." When one hundred thousand government trout were stocked in the headwaters of the Williams River the previous year, the Hammonds "spent the summer fishing for these small trout to sell to the lumber camps."[67]

Violations of the state's fish and game laws were not confined to the predators; there also had to be consumers and middlemen. John Luke, the absentee owner of West Virginia Pulp and Paper, wrote to his business partner at Cass, Samuel E. Slaymaker, thanking him for wild turkeys but declined the deer offered by Slaymaker because he was "well stocked at the moment." Luke was not concerned about breaking the law, however: "With reference to the violation of the game laws, the writer is not likely to lose any sleep about it."[68]

These traditional practices and habits of thought, like the great forest that sustained them, were making their last stand during the first decade of the twentieth century. The growing culture of enforcement generated under the fish and game warden system was beginning to produce dramatic changes in 1908 when conservationists were shocked by the ruling of the supreme court of appeals in *State* v. *Parkins*. The ruling in this case undermined the very foundation of the warden system by declaring that the method of paying deputies out of fines collected from violators was unconstitutional. The circuit court held that "a part of the fines could be paid to the deputy, but not all," under the West Virginia Constitution, section 5, article 12. The supreme court of appeals affirmed the lower court's decision and declared that the fines generated from fish and game convictions did not actually "accrue to the state," but rather to the county where the violation occurred and the case was prosecuted, and, therefore, the deputy could not be paid from this source.[69] With the courts reinforcing local prerogatives and the county still the primary unit of power, West Virginia conservation reverted to the unpaid warden system.

The circuit courts also emasculated the operation of the fish and game laws by declaring that out-of-state shipments of game "constitute one offense and is punishable by one fine only, no matter how many pieces of game a shipment consists [of]." Whether the shipment contained one quail or one hundred, if there was one shipment there was only one offense and only one fine. A reasonable man, the warden had assumed that each piece of game represented one offense, but circuit court juries, who not only were closer to the violators and might have committed similar acts themselves, chose to interpret the law in a way that favored local custom over a distant, altruistic law. As if these impediments were not enough, still another disappointment was handed to the reformers when the circuit courts also ruled that the burden of proving that foreign matter disposed of in the streams was deleterious to the fish population rested on the state. The one exception to this standard was sawdust, the ruinous effects of which even the obstructionists could not ignore.[70] With the fish and game enforcement laws declared unconstitutional and void in *State* v. *Parkins* and the circuit courts imposing rigid standards upon enforcement, a disillusioned Governor Dawson declared in his 1909 message that within a short time "the game will disappear and the fish in our streams [will] be exterminated."[71]

Environmental desolation and weak conservation laws were not problems unique to West Virginia but reflected a context for the national catastrophe that emanated from the extraordinary wastefulness accompanying the extraction of natural resources which fed the maturation of industrial capitalism in America between the Civil War and World War I. Unlike the Old Northwest and other eastern regions that also had been deforested, the consequences of clear-cutting the Appalachian Mountains were far more momentous because the rivers that flowed down into the heavily populated and industrialized regions of the eastern United States found their headwaters there. The environmental disaster was interstate and interregional, therefore the voices of reform did not speak with a coherent, unified political voice. What the conservationists needed was direction and leadership.

President Theodore Roosevelt provided both when he convened a Conference of Governors at the White House in May 1908 to "consider the question of the conservation and use of the great fundamental sources of wealth on this Nation," the first such conference ever held in the United States.[72] Governor William M. O. Dawson; I. C. White, an eminent geologist; Hu Maxwell, a conservation reformer; and James W. Paul, the chief of the state's Department of Mines made up the West Virginia delegation. Soon after his return from the White House conference, Governor Dawson, whose credentials on forest and wildlife protection were unwavering, appointed a Conservation Commission in 1908 to complete a study of conservation in West Virginia and to make policy recommendations. Anticipating that funding would be the primary concern of legislators, the commissioners proposed that the state's natural scenery might be "worth money" from recreational tourism. "West Virginia may never rival Switzerland," the commissioners declared, "but it can equal Maine." Maine had been cutover in the nineteenth century, but by the early twentieth century the reforested state had become a popular vacation destination for sportsmen and tourists. Before initiating a tourist development plan, however, West Virginia would have to clean up the polluted streams, stock them with fish, pass "civilized laws" that prevent the "senseless slaughter" of birds and game, and protect the forests.[73] After a single report, however, the commission ceased to exist as a result of legislative apathy.

Appeals by the Conservation Commission and constant prodding from Governor Dawson had less to do with resurrecting the warden system in 1909 than did the devastating fires and floods of 1907 and 1908. The West Virginia Reform Law of 1909 funded a respectable annual salary of $1,800 for the chief warden, permitted him to appoint two chief deputies at $900 annually, and granted him the authority to appoint as many county wardens as required. The deputies were to serve without salary, but they were permitted to keep one-half the fines received from convictions as compensation. Also, all sheriffs, deputy sheriffs, constables, and other law enforcement officials were appointed ex officio wardens. Among the wildlife provisions included in the legislation were many standard prohibitions from the earlier laws: the sale and shipment of game out of state, bag limits, seasons, chasing deer with dogs, killing doe any time, and the use of bird plumage.[74]

A key feature of the act charged the warden with protecting the forest as well as the fish and game. This was a new responsibility, one that finally recognized the forest as a natural resource upon which fish, game, and a host of related vital economic interests were inextricably linked and, therefore, in need of public protection. The law required private citizens to fight forest fires when called upon, established fines and imprisonment for those who set forest fires, and stipulated that railroads, sawmills, and other industrial establishments fell under the same general provisions regulating forest fires as did individuals.[75]

While the public supported forest protection, sportsmen predictably were hostile to the restrictions such as the provision making it illegal for hunters and fishers to camp or build fires on enclosed lands without permission in writing and requiring them to pay a license fee of seventy-five cents to the county clerk and a twenty-five-cent filing fee. A storm of protest arose over this infringement on the traditional uses of the woods.[76] Actually, this legislation was a conservation measure rather than a property owners' law designed to extend the protection of private property at the expense of poor or landless people who depended on the traditional open range for grazing their stock. But legislators were too far ahead of an important segment of public opinion with this bill, and they beat a hasty retreat in 1911, repealing the license fee provision. Unfortunately, the retreat left the warden without the revenues to conduct his work. The very first year of its implementation the license fees had raised $21,500, and revenues from fines reached $5,000. All of this money had gone toward forest, fish, and game protection, and now once again that protection was sacrificed at the aging altar of custom and weak, parsimonious government.[77]

Progressive conservationists never resolved the problem of how to overcome this perennial obstacle to conservation in West Virginia; instead, it was finally dissolved by a massive infusion of federal funds for reforesting the mountain headwaters. West Virginia reformers had advocated the state purchase of cutover lands for reforestation for at least a decade, but support was slow in coming. Governor Albert B. White's message to the legislature in

1905, for example, declared that areas of no value except for growing forests, particularly at the mountain headwaters, should be purchased by the state for reforestation. "The time has gone by when the man who deforests lands is a public benefactor," the governor declared.[78] Although the state of West Virginia had made significant strides toward environmental protection, there can be little question that real progress began only with the active intervention of the federal government.

As early as 1909, West Virginia lawmakers approved legislation empowering the U.S. government to acquire and control cutover lands "by condemnation or otherwise for a national forest reserve."[79] If there was a beginning to environmental restoration in West Virginia, it would have to be 1911, when the Weeks Act was passed by Congress and signed into law by President William Howard Taft on March 1, 1911. The Weeks Act authorized the U.S. Forest Service to purchase denuded lands at the headwaters of navigable streams. Land acquisition under the act concentrated on the Appalachians during the early years, including land that would become part of the 1.6 million acres in the Monongahela National Forest in West Virginia. The authority to purchase lands was further expanded in 1924 by the Clarke-McNary Act to include timberlands unrelated to the flow of navigable streams.[80]

The state was at least minimally responsive to the federal initiative at first. In 1913, West Virginia entered a formal agreement with the U.S. government to match federal funds dollar for dollar for the construction of forest fire lookout stations. Moreover, private agencies such as the West Virginia Fish and Game Protective Association, the West Virginia Audubon Society, the Central West Virginia Fire Protection Association, and the Southern West Virginia Fire Protection Association all began a vigorous campaign to inform the public of the importance of environmental protection.[81] Increasing interest by the federal government and a rising public consciousness in West Virginia gave legislators confidence to reinstate the license fees in 1915 for statewide hunting, although they were careful to avoid applying the fees to residents hunting or fishing in their own counties.[82]

During subsequent years, West Virginia lawmakers continued to chart a meandering conservation program. While financial considerations continued to be paramount, their indecisiveness stemmed at least in part from the political tug-of-war between forest conservationists on the one hand and the fishers and hunters on the other. Sportsmen argued that because they provided most of the funds through license fees, spending priorities should be in protecting game and fish, while forestry advocates remonstrated that without the forests there would be neither game nor fish. This tension was apparent in 1921 in the attempts to establish priorities in the new Game and Fish Commission. Governor John J. Cornwell had recommended the creation of a forestry department to determine which cutover and forfeited lands should be retained by the state for development of forest preserves,[83] but instead the legislature created the new Game and Fish Commission. The commission's name indicates that the sportsmen won this political battle. In fact, only one of the act's thirty-nine sections contained provisions relating to forest protection.[84]

The diminution of forest protection was clearly intentional for Chief Deputy Game Protector George W. Sharp declared in 1925 that "the forest fire protection that is carried on by the commission is for the primary purpose of providing homes for the game." Indeed, he continued, "the main reason the commission is interested in prevention of pollution of streams is to protect the fish."[85]

The Game and Fish Commission made excellent progress toward improving the state's conservation program, but again the reason for this success was related to an outstanding individual, Chief Protector A. B. Brooks, rather than to institutional commitment. Even Brooks, the state's most influential conservationist, was forced to grovel for funds to address the enormous task of rescuing the state's environment.[86] For example, in 1928 the Game and Fish Commission received $176,000 in revenues, all from nonstate sources such as license fees, federal allotments for fire protection, and fire protection assessments on private forest owners. By comparison, Pennsylvania spent more than $1 million on game conservation alone, and New York spent more than $3 million on its conservation programs. The lack of an adequately funded, integrated program of conservation and fire prevention resulted in the state actually working against itself. The chief game protector commented in 1929 that "much of our natural restocking of fish is destroyed . . . by pollution." The commission had asked many of the industrial polluters to cooperate in cleaning up the streams but received no firm commitments, and the law books are practically devoid of suits brought against businesses for polluting the streams during this period.[87]

Despite the lack of institutional investment in conservation in West Virginia, some notable advances in forest protection were realized. Chief Game Protector A. B. Brooks reported in 1927 that the entire state was organized into fire-fighting districts, and a "small army of men" were ready to serve in emergencies. At least some of the state's forests were protected by lookouts who stood duty in the thirty fire towers that had been erected on the highest mountaintops. To ensure a prompt reaction to fires, three hundred miles of telephone lines connected these towers to phone boxes at tool and equipment depots strategically located in the countryside. Moreover, twenty-four game refuges had been established; a game farm at French Creek, Upshur County, raised animals for release into the wild; a trout hatchery was operated in White Sulphur Springs; and two state-owned forests in Pocahontas County, Seneca and Watoga, contained sixteen thousand acres. These important advances offered some measure of progress in the state's recent conversion to conservation even though the investment paled by comparison to that of other deforested states.[88]

Unfortunately, the constant friction between the wildlife and forest constituencies was instrumental in persuading A. B. Brooks to resign as chief protector in 1926. His departure did have the salutary effect of focusing public attention on the issue, however, and in 1927 the legislature responded by creating the West Virginia Forest and Park Commission. The very next year, 1928, the worst forest fire season since 1908 dramatically underscored the need for a centralized and coherent conservation policy. Once again, however, the legislature responded by restructuring, this time creating the West Virginia Game, Fish, and Forestry Commission, which at least reincorporated forests into the same agency and reemphasized the need for forest protection.[89]

Ironically, the Great Depression of the 1930s proved to be a blessing in disguise for the environment in West Virginia. As the Depression settled over the nation like a dense fog, it became necessary to find a way to stimulate the economy and put people back to work. As a result, the federal role in conservation throughout the nation increased exponentially. West Virginia became a major beneficiary of this increased federal role in conservation when reforestation, fire prevention, and stream revitalization were added to the federal government's responsibility for restoring the Ohio and Potomac River watersheds. The conservation projects undertaken by the Civilian Conservation Corps, the Works Projects Administration, and countless other federal agencies went a long way toward revitalizing West Virginia's environment. But all of this came after the countryside had been denuded of its ancient forest, the woodland culture had been uprooted and the people "saved from the woods," and the lumbermen had moved on to more lucrative timberlands in the South and West.

Ultimately, measuring the significance of the passing of the wilderness lies in a realm beyond historical documentation, in a people's deeper consciousness that life would never be the same. No writer has probed this sense of loss among mountaineers at the emotional level with more perception and sensitivity than Louise McNeill. Born in 1911 on a Pocahontas County farm, where her ancestors had lived since 1769, McNeill came into the world at the very peak of the timber boom and the new public awareness of the detrimental consequences of deforestation. McNeill was both scholar and poet. Her beloved home state was the subject of her doctoral dissertation in history as well as all of her creative writing. Critical praise for her poetry eventually brought McNeill popular recognition as West Virginia's poet laureate.

Much of the subject matter in her writing plumbs her own deep feelings about the mountains. The underlying theme of *The Milkweed Ladies*, an autobiographical account of her youth in Pocahontas County, is the relationship of people to the land. Their feelings toward nature are revealed in the trips the "menfolks" of her family had made "Over the Mountain" for more than one hundred years to fish in the Cranberry, Williams, and Gauley Rivers. "Over the Mountain" was the folk measure of a vast wilderness that ran for "sixty unbroken miles beyond our Pinnacle Mountain." Logging had been under way for two decades in the pine along the Greenbrier to the east, but over the mountain to the west a hardwood wilderness awaited the railroad's arrival before falling to the woodsman's axe. "When it all changed, it was not suddenly," McNeill reminisced. "There was no sudden summer or sudden fall; but gradually, as the years moved by, the song turned sour as the north fork of Cranberry River turned muddy." Nevertheless, for most of her childhood her father, G. D., Uncle Dock, Cousin Rush, and brother Ward went "Over the Mountain" and brought home sacks of salted brook trout. "Slowly a deep lament began to run through their stories: for the muddy, silted streams; the forest fires; the skid roads bleeding down the eroded hills; and the terrible waste of it all." And then the "jackleg" lumber companies went bankrupt, and "the lumber shanties were abandoned, and the rusting, twisted rails. The trout began to die with sawdust in their gills, and the great ravaged trees were left rotting along the ridges' slopes."[90]

Louise McNeill acquired her affinity for the land from her father, G. Douglas McNeill, a Pocahontas County educator. G. D. was an excellent storyteller and in 1940 published a book of short stories entitled *The Last Forest: Tales of the Allegheny Woods*. Most of the stories were about the forest in what is now the Cranberry wilderness area as G. D. remembered it before, during, and after it was logged over. The stories portray a rural people who find it difficult to absorb the profound changes that accompanied industrial development and to reconcile the great disparity between the pristine wilderness of their memories with the wasteland all about them. Appropriately, the final story ("The Last Campfire") is about three old men, one of whom had pulled up stakes for a farm in Kansas twenty-five years earlier and returned to see the wilderness of his youth one more time before he died. He and two comrades who had remained in Pocahontas climbed to the top of a high hill to look out for the last time on the Cranberry wilderness where as boys they had hunted and fished:

Where, in other days, the boys had seen blue waves of spruce and hemlock, stretching away mile upon mile, the men now beheld desolation—bare hills, ribbed with shale, from which fire and erosion had swept every vestige of soil: long mountain ranges without a tree, save here and there a gnarled trunk with its few yellowed leaves; a monotonous panorama of destruction, as far as the eye could run.

"Well, fellers," said Zeke, "I knowed it was bad; but if I'd dreamed it was like this, I'd never a asked ye tu come up here. I'm sorry I seen it."

"Me, too," said Dock. "I'd like jist to hev remembered it th' way it uset tu be."[91]

NOTES

Introduction

1. Wilson, "Felicitous Convergence of Mythmaking," 6–8.
2. Frost, "Our Contemporary Ancestors," 311–19, quotes on 311.
3. Shapiro, *Appalachia on Our Mind*; Batteau, *Invention of Appalachia*.
4. Ford, ed., *Southern Appalachian Region*, 9–34.
5. Rostow, *Stages of Economic Growth*.
6. Greeley, *Forests and Men*, 39–40.
7. Ibid., 40–41.
8. Ibid., 43–44.
9. Ibid., 45–48.
10. Ibid., 50–51.
11. Marx, *Machine in the Garden*, 17.
12. Kennedy, *Blackwater Chronicle*, 212, 213.
13. Verhoeff, *Kentucky River Navigation*; Thomas, *Dawn Comes to the Mountains*.
14. U.S. Department of Agriculture, *Message from the President*, 24, 45.
15. Eller, *Miners, Millhands, and Mountaineers*, 104–9; Frome, *Strangers in High Places*, 166–68; Bartlett, *Troubled Waters*, 14–15.
16. Eller, *Miners, Millhands, and Mountaineers*, 106–7; Frome, *Strangers in High Places*, 166–67.
17. Eller, *Miners, Millhands, and Mountaineers*, 11.
18. Kephart, *Our Southern Highlanders*, 456–58.
19. Bartlett, *Troubled Waters*, 32, 38–39.
20. Ibid., 42.
21. Frome, *Strangers in High Places*, 158–59.
22. Ibid., 169–70.
23. Bush, *Dorie*, 220–21.
24. Eller, *Miners, Millhands, and Mountaineers*, 126.

Chapter One

1. Williams, *Americans and Their Forests*, 10–12, quote on 12.
2. Cox, Maxwell, Thomas, and Malone, *This Well-Wooded Land*, 7–8, quote on 8.
3. Nash, *Wilderness and the American Mind*, chaps. 1–2; Slotkin, *Regeneration through Violence*, 3–56. For a romantic interpretation of an earlier generation of nationalistic historians who portrayed the wilderness as "eden newly sprung," see Lillard, *Great Forest*, 3–9.
4. Waugh, "Lumbering before Pinchot," 93–94.
5. Strother, *Virginia Illustrated*, 30.
6. Quoted in Waugh, "Lumbering before Pinchot," 93.

7. Stephenson, *Upland Forests of West Virginia*, 1–8; Clarkson, *Tumult on the Mountains*, 2–3; Core, *Plant Life of West Virginia*, 17.

8. Clarkson, *Tumult on the Mountains*, 3–4; Core, *Plant Life of West Virginia*, 17, 23; Maury and Fontaine, *Resources of West Virginia*, 121, 126; Stephenson, *Upland Forests of West Virginia*, 16–25.

9. Clarkson, *Tumult on the Mountains*, 7–9; Stephenson, *Upland Forests of West Virginia*, 25–31.

10. Otto, *Southern Frontiers*, 58–59; Clarkson, *Tumult on the Mountains*, 13–14; Maury and Fontaine, *Resources of West Virginia*, 142–43. Maury wrote on mineral resources and Fontaine wrote on agriculture and renewable resources.

11. Rehder, "Scotch-Irish and English in Appalachia," 95–100; Otto, "Migration of Southern Plain Folk," 187–88; Williams, *Americans and Their Forests*, 53–81.

12. Williams, *Americans and Their Forests*, 111–45; Fischer, *Albion's Seed*, 755–65; Otto, "Migration of Southern Plain Folk," 185–86; Rehder, "Scotch-Irish and English in Appalachia," 102–18.

13. Hofstadter, *Age of Reform*, 23–25, 30; Hofstadter, "Myth of the Happy Yeoman," 43.

14. Dunaway, *First American Frontier*, 3–4.

15. The essay that touched off this debate is Henretta, "Families and Farms," 3–32. For an important initial counterargument, see Lemon, "Early Americans and Their Social Environment," 115–31. See also Clark, *Roots of Rural Capitalism*; Kulikoff, *Agrarian Origins of American Capitalism*; Rothenberg, *From Market-Places to a Market Economy*. For an attempt at a synthesis, see Kulikoff, "Households and Markets," 342–55.

16. Kulikoff, "Transition to Capitalism," 140–43; Dunaway, *First American Frontier*, 16, quoting Walls and Billings, "Sociology of Southern Appalachia," 131–44. The mentalité debate regarding colonial American farmers has been joined by Appalachian scholars. See, for example, Billings, Blee, and Swanson, "Culture, Family, and Community in Preindustrial Appalachia," 154–70; Mitchell, *Commercialism and the Frontier*; Mitchell, ed., *Appalachian Frontiers*; Pudup, Billings, and Waller, eds., *Appalachia in the Making*; McKenzie, *One South or Many?*; Salstrom, *Appalachia's Path to Dependency*.

17. Hall, "Politics of Appalachian Virginia," 166.

18. Ibid., 166–67.

19. Ibid., 169.

20. Ibid., 169, 172–73, 180–81.

21. Ibid., 180–82; Ambler, *Sectionalism in Virginia*, passim.

22. Quoted in Hall, "Politics of Appalachian Virginia," 186.

23. Rothstein, "Antebellum South," 375.

24. Fischer, *Albion's Seed*, 605–702, for example, accepts the Celtic and English borderlands origins of Appalachian culture. A critique of this thesis is found in McKinney, Cowan, Cunningham, and Waller, "Culture Wars," 161–200. This discussion evolved out of a larger debate over the cultural origins of the South. Forrest McDonald and Grady McWhiney have argued for Celtic origins of southern culture in "The Antebellum Southern Herdsman," 147–66, and "Celtic Origins of Southern Herding," 165–82. McWhiney's *Cracker Culture* is a book-length elaboration of this theme. The Celtic thesis has been challenged by Edward Pessen in "How Different from Each Other Were the Antebellum North and South?," 1119–49, and in an "AHR Forum" discussion in the same issue, 1150–66. See also Berthoff, "Celtic Mist over the South," 523–46, with response and rejoinder on 546–50.

25. Hart, "Land Rotation in Appalachia," 151.

26. See, for example, Batteau, *Invention of Appalachia*, and Shapiro, *Appalachia on Our Mind*.

27. Otto, "Decline of Forest Farming," 22.

28. Clendening, "Early Days," 102; Otto, "Decline of Forest Farming," 23.

29. Cox, Maxwell, Thomas, and Malone, *This Well-Wooded Land*, 10; Otto and Anderson, "Slash-and-Burn Cultivation," 133.

30. Eller, *Miners, Millhands, and Mountaineers*, 16–22; Pyne, *Fire in America*, 146–49; Otto, *Southern Frontiers*, 567; Otto and Anderson, "Slash-and-Burn Cultivation," 137; Otto, "Decline of Forest Farming," 20–21, 23.

31. Otto, "Decline of Forest Farming," 24; Otto and Anderson, "Slash-and-Burn Cultivation," 136.

32. Maury and Fontaine, *Resources of West Virginia*, 62.

33. Ibid., 63–64.

34. Ibid., 68–69.

35. Diss Debar, *West Virginia Hand-Book*, 79–80.

36. Maury and Fontaine, *Resources of West Virginia*, 90, 95–96.

37. Ibid., 91–92.

38. Ibid., 92–93.

39. Diss Debar, *West Virginia Hand-Book*, 82.

40. Turner, "Significance of the Frontier," 199–227; Owsley, *Plain Folk of the Old South*, 23–36.

41. McDonald and McWhiney, "Antebellum Southern Herdsmen," 147–66, and "Celtic Origins of Southern Herding," 165–82; McWhiney, *Cracker Culture*, 51–79.

42. MacMaster, "Cattle Trade in Western Virginia," 130, 132–49.

43. Henlein, *Cattle Kingdom*, 2–3; Stealey, "Notes on the Ante-Bellum Cattle Industry," 39.

44. Henlein, *Cattle Kingdom*, 2–3; Stealey, "Notes on the Ante-Bellum Cattle Industry," 39.

45. Stealey, "Notes on the Ante-Bellum Cattle Industry," 40.

46. Ibid., 41, quote on 43.

47. Diss Debar, *West Virginia Hand-Book*, 94.

48. Inscoe, *Mountain Masters*, 45–52; Wilhelm, "Animal Drives," 327–34. For a contemporary novel about cattle drives in West Virginia, see Post, *Dwellers in the Hills*.

49. Peyton, *Memoir of John Howe Peyton*, 49–50.

50. MacMaster, "Cattle Trade in Western Virginia," 127–49; Stealey, "Notes on the Ante-Bellum Cattle Industry," 38–47, 70–72; Noe, "Appalachia's Civil War Genesis," 91–108; Royall, *Sketches of History*, 30–38; Featherstonhaugh, *Excursions through the Slave States*, 26; Rice, *History of Greenbrier County*, chap. 15.

51. Martin, *New and Comprehensive Gazetteer of Virginia*, 22.

52. Sargent, *Report on the Forests of North America*, map facing p. 121.

53. Lillard, *Great Forest*, 34–42, 65–94. For the Quachita Mountains of Arkansas and Oklahoma, see Smith, *Sawmill*. For east Texas, see Allen, *East Texas Lumber Workers*; Maxwell and Baker, *Sawdust Empire*; and Sitton, *Backwoodsmen*. For north Florida, see Drobney, *Lumbermen and Log Sawyers*. For the Mississippi piney woods, see Claiborne, "A Trip through the Piney Woods," 487–538; Hickman, *Mississippi Harvest*; Polk, ed., *Mississippi's Piney Woods*.

54. Diss Debar, *West Virginia Hand-Book*, 103.

55. Clarkson, *Tumult on the Mountains*, 14–15; Brooks, *Forestry and Wood Industries*, 57.

56. Clarkson, *Tumult on the Mountains*, 15–16; Leitch, "Steps Taken to Preserve Old Up-and-Down Sawmills," 18–19.

57. Maxwell, "Minear's Mill," 220; Clendening, "Early Days in the Southern Appalachians," 102; Diss Debar, *West Virginia Hand-Book*, 112; Brooks, *Forestry and Wood Industries*, 60.

58. Clarkson, *Tumult on the Mountains*, 16–17; Notebook 2, Brown Notebooks.

59. Clarkson, *Tumult on the Mountains*, 19–20; *Greenbrier Independent*, May 24, 1883.

60. Brooks, *Forestry and Wood Industries*, 60; Clarkson, *Tumult on the Mountains*, 21; Sargent, *Report on the Forests of North America*, 121.

61. Clarkson, *Tumult on the Mountains*, 23–24.

62. Ibid., 48–49; Jackson, "Lumbering on Coal River," 15; Byrne, *Tale of the Elk*, 422–25.

63. Sargent, *Report on the Forests of North America*, 513–14; Clendening, "Early Days in the Southern Appalachians," 102–3; Clarkson, *Tumult on the Mountains*, 49; Jackson, "Lumbering on Coal River," 34.

64. Blackhurst, *Riders of the Flood*, is regarded as an authoritative, only thinly fictionalized description of river driving. For a novel that describes log driving on the Gauley River, see Skidmore, *River Rising!*

65. Clarkson, *Tumult on the Mountains*, 50; "Lumbering in the Upper Greenbrier," 97.

66. Clarkson, *Tumult on the Mountains*, 50.

67. Verhoeff, *Kentucky River Navigation*, 190–93; Clarkson, *Tumult on the Mountains*, 50–51; Blackhurst, *Riders of the Flood*.

68. Coy, Fuller, Meadows, and Fig, "Splash Dam Construction," 179–84. For other sources mentioning splash dams in the Appalachians, see Thomas, *Dawn Comes to the Mountains*, 108; Verhoeff, *Kentucky River Navigation*, 191–92; Hawkins, "Logging for Pulp Wood," 689–94; and Kephart, "Pulpwood Drive," 203–9.

69. Clarkson, *Tumult on the Mountains*, 51–52; Byrne, *Tale of the Elk*, 185–87; Verhoeff, *Kentucky River Navigation*, 198–200. See also Hanlon, *Ball-Hooters*.

70. Clarkson, *Tumult on the Mountains*, 52; "Lumbering in the Upper Greenbrier," 97; *Pocahontas Times*, April 26, 1956.

71. Clarkson, *Tumult on the Mountains*, 53; Jackson, "Lumbering on Coal River," 24.

72. Sargent, *Report on the Forests of North America*, 514; "Forests of West Virginia," 79–80; "Logging on Gauley River, West Virginia," 23.

73. Cuthbert, "Riverboat Days on the Little Kanawha," 2–4; Thoenen, *History of the Oil and Gas Industry in West Virginia*, 46–70.

74. *Report of the Secretary of War*, 1574.

75. "Tally Book for Lumbermen, 1911," Lynch Papers.

Chapter Two

1. Pepper, *Life and Times of Henry Gassaway Davis*, 208.

2. Kline, "Nature of the Logging Railroads of West Virginia," 12. For examples, see Dunn, "Beech Mountain Railroad," 79–85, and Lincoln, "Porter's Creek & Gauley Railroad," 5, 9, 15.

3. Williams, *West Virginia and the Captains of Industry*, 168; Callahan, *Semi-Centennial History*, 306–7; Map of West Virginia Showing Railroads, MC 1, DWR 5. This map is

oversized and relatively inaccessible, but a readily available adaptation may be found in Clarkson, *Tumult on the Mountains*, insert.

4. Callahan, *Semi-Centennial History*, 212–13. For the 1860s, see ibid., 188–89, and for the 1870s see Maury and Fontaine, *Resources of West Virginia*.

5. Dunaway, *First American Frontier*, 6–7.

6. Ibid., 8–10. Dunaway's book is an example of the "world system" approach applied to Appalachia.

7. Noe, " 'Appalachia's' Civil War Genesis," 91; Pudup, "Boundaries of Class," 139.

8. Noe, " 'Appalachia's' Civil War Genesis," 91–92; Pudup, "Boundaries of Class," 140.

9. Noe, " 'Appalachia's' Civil War Genesis," 105; Noe, *Southwest Virginia's Railroad*, 3–4.

10. Noe, *Southwest Virginia's Railroad*, 6. For examples of works that argue for a dramatic transformation in West Virginia at the turn of the century, see Simon, "Uneven Development and the Case of West Virginia," 165–86; Eller, *Miners, Millhands, and Mountaineers*. For examples of other works that argue more or less for an earlier transition to capitalism, see Dunn, *Cades Cove*; Dunaway, *First American Frontier*; Mitchell, ed., *Appalachian Frontiers*; Salstrom, *Appalachia's Path to Dependency*; Inscoe, *Mountain Masters*; Mann, "Mountains, Land, and Kin Networks," 411–34; Pudup, Billings, and Waller, eds., *Appalachia in the Making*; McKinney, *Southern Mountain Republicans*; and Waller, *Feud*.

11. Dunaway, *First American Frontier*, 10.

12. Ibid., 198–99, 204–11.

13. Stover, *History of the Baltimore and Ohio*, 47–152. See also Dilts, *Great Road*.

14. Callahan, *Semi-Centennial History*, 123–24; Barnes, "Avenues to a Market Economy," 96–98.

15. Callahan, *Semi-Centennial History*, 117–20.

16. Ambler, *Sectionalism in Virginia*; Ambler, "Cleavage between Eastern and Western Virginia," 762–80; Workman, "Political Culture and the Coal Economy," 125–27.

17. Curry, *House Divided*, 34–35.

18. Hall, *Rending of Virginia*, 70–71. See Ambler, *Sectionalism in Virginia*, for a full treatment.

19. *Virginia Weekly Star*, January 4, 1861, quoted in Hall, *Rending of Virginia*, 126.

20. *Wheeling Intelligencer*, July 3, 1861, quoted in Ambler, *Francis Pierpont*, 409.

21. Quoted in Curry, *House Divided*, 25.

22. R. B. Hayes quoted in Lewis and Hennen, eds., *West Virginia*, 122.

23. Williams, "New Dominion and the Old," 354–55.

24. Ambler, "Cleavage between Eastern and Western Virginia," 771.

25. Workman, "Political Culture and Coal Economy," 120–21.

26. Curry, *House Divided*, 117–18, 56–57.

27. Hall, *Rending of Virginia*, 513–14.

28. Workman, "Political Culture and Coal Economy," 125–27; Moore, *Social Origins of Dictatorship and Democracy*, 111–15, 413.

29. Williams, "New Dominion and the Old," 352.

30. Noe, *Southwest Virginia's Railroad*, 67–84.

31. Lewis, *How West Virginia Was Made*, quote on 304.

32. The literature on this subject is extensive. A classic is Ambler, *Sectionalism in Virginia*. For a recent chapter-length study, see Hall, "Politics of Appalachian Virginia,"

166–86. For the views of a statemaker, see Willey, *An Inside View of the Formation of West Virginia*. See also Maury and Fontaine, *Resources of West Virginia*, 336–37.

33. *Manufacturer's Record* 50 (October 1906): 338; Eller, *Miners, Millhands, and Mountaineers*, 47.

34. Williams, *West Virginia and the Captains of Industry*, 168, 170.

35. Quotations are from the *Wheeling Register*, November 10, 1881, February 15, 1887, August 26, 1884, and August 17, 1884. For the development faith and "gospel of progress," see Williams, *West Virginia and the Captains of Industry*, 166–93.

36. Hall, *Rending of Virginia*, 617.

37. Eller, *Miners, Millhands, and Mountaineers*, 66–67; Callahan, *Semi-Centennial History*, 191–95. See also Evans, *Collis Potter Huntington*, 533–34; Turner, *Chessie's Road*, 95.

38. Corbin, *Life, Work, and Rebellion in the Coal Fields*, 8.

39. "Lumber and Lumbering on the Chesapeake and Ohio."

40. Callahan, *Semi-Centennial History*, 196–97.

41. Eller, *Miners, Millhands, and Mountaineers*, 72–74; Lambie, *From Mine to Market*, 8–9, 33–39, 124; Callahan, *Semi-Centennial History*, 216–17.

42. Spence, *Land of the Guyandot*, 161–202; Cubby, "Timbering Operations in the Tug and Guyandot," 110–14.

43. Cubby, "Timber Operations in the Tug and Guyandot," 116, n. 26.

44. Governor, *Message of Governor William E. Stevenson, 1870*, 18.

45. Barns, "Grange and Populist Movements," 242–43; Callahan, *History of West Virginia*, 1:417, 612.

46. Barns, "Grange and Populist Movements," 244–45; *Acts of the West Virginia Legislature*, 1872–73, 710–24; West Virginia Constitution adopted April 9, 1872, ibid., 37.

47. Barns, "Grange and Populist Movements," 246–48; *Spirit of Jefferson*, February 17, 1874; *Acts of the West Virginia Legislature*, 1875, chap. 54, pp. 102–4, and chap. 102, p. 187.

48. Barns, "Grange and Populist Movements," 248–52; *Acts of the West Virginia Legislature*, 1877, Joint Res. 10, p. 195, and Joint Res. 15, p. 197; "Testimony before Joint Committee of Legislature of West Virginia appointed to enquire into the Charges of Freight and Travel of the Baltimore and Ohio Railroad," bound with *Journal of the Senate*, 1879, 19–69; J. N. Camden to J. A. Fickinger, October 2, 1895, Letterbook 13, Camden Papers. See also Williams, *Captains of Industry*, 198.

49. Summers, *Johnson Newlon Camden*, 168, 204–7, 211; "Testimony," *Journal of the Senate*, 1879, 34.

50. *Journal of the Senate*, 1879, 20–21; Callahan, *History of West Virginia*, 1:612n.

51. Tax Commission, *Second Report*, 1–3.

52. Ibid., 11–12.

53. Ibid., 4–5.

54. Ibid., 5.

55. Ibid., 6.

56. Ibid., 16–20; Rasmussen, *Absentee Landowning and Exploitation*, 118–24.

57. Board of Agriculture, *Biennial Report, 1895 and 1896*, 52.

58. Callahan, *Semi-Centennial History*, 197–98.

59. Fizer, "West Virginia and Pittsburgh Railroad," 3; Rice, *Life of Jonathan M. Bennett*, 214–20.

60. Rice, *Life of Jonathan M. Bennett*, 220–23; Fizer, "West Virginia and Pittsburgh Railroad," 4–7.

61. Callahan, *Semi-Centennial History*, 199–200.

62. Ibid.; Dunn, "Beech Mountain Railroad," 80–81.

63. *Wheeling Register*, August 17, 1884.

64. Callahan, *Semi-Centennial History*, 199n.

65. *Pocahontas Times*, May 31, 1894.

66. Callahan, *Semi-Centennial History*, 199n.

67. Marquess, "West Virginia Venture," 7–8; Ross, *Henry Gassaway Davis*, 34–138 passim.

68. Marquess, "West Virginia Venture," 8–11; Pepper, *Life and Times of Henry Gassaway Davis*, 30–32; Ross, *Henry Gassaway Davis*, 141–43.

69. Pepper, *Life and Times of Henry Gassaway Davis*, 97–98; "W.Va. Central and Pittsburgh R.R.," 85. Stockholders included Secretary of State James G. Blaine and Secretary of the Treasury William Windom, as well as Senators Thomas F. Bayard, H. G. Davis, Arthur P. Gorman, Johnson N. Camden, former senator and Maryland governor William P. Whyte, and U. S. Grant Jr., son of the former president (Ross, *Henry Gassaway Davis*, 142).

70. Marquess, "West Virginia Venture," 12.

71. Hicks, "West Virginia Central & Pittsburgh Railway," 6–8; Marquess, "West Virginia Venture," 16–17.

72. Hicks, "West Virginia Central & Pittsburgh Railway," 10–18; Marquess, "West Virginia Venture," 18–19.

73. Callahan, *Semi-Centennial History*, 210–11.

74. Ibid., 212.

75. Kline, "Nature of the Logging Railroads," 12.

76. Marquess, "West Virginia Venture," 20.

77. Williams, *West Virginia and the Captains of Industry*, 154–57; Marquess, "West Virginia Venture," 25; Pepper, *Life and Times of Henry Gassaway Davis*, 186; Hicks, "West Virginia Central & Pittsburgh Railway," 14–15; Ross, *Henry Gassaway Davis*, 264–65.

78. Marquess, "West Virginia Venture," 26; Pepper, *Life and Times of Henry Gassaway Davis*, 188–91; Ross, *Henry Gassaway Davis*, 265–78.

79. Callahan, *Semi-Centennial History*, 213.

80. Rice, *Bicentennial History of Randolph County*, 71–72; Teter, *Goin' Up Gandy*, 30–47, 101–2.

81. Pepper, *Life and Times of Henry Gassaway Davis*, 192–93.

82. Warden, "Engine Smoke in the Mountains," 74.

83. Ibid., 74–80.

84. Lincoln, "Porter's Creek & Gauley Railroad," 15.

85. "Widen," 67–78.

86. Stover, *History of the Baltimore and Ohio*, 228.

87. McNeel, "Railroads in Pocahontas County," 169; McNeel, *Durbin Route*, 2–3. Numerous prospectuses of the paper railroads of this period have survived. See, for example, *West Virginia Central Railway*.

88. McNeel, *Durbin Route*, 6–7; McNeel, "Railroads in Pocahontas County," 169.

89. McNeel, *Durbin Route*, 7.

90. Ibid., 8–10; Turner, "From Bourbon to Liberal," 105.

91. McNeel, *Durbin Route*, 13.

92. Ibid., 13–14.

93. Hicks, "West Virginia Central & Pittsburgh Railway," 28–29; McNeel, "Railroads in Pocahontas County," 170–71.

94. McNeel, "Railroads in Pocahontas County," 175.

95. Clarkson, *On Beyond Leatherbark*, 36–37, 122.

96. Ibid., 63–65, 77–78.

97. McNeel, "Lumber Industry in Pocahontas County," quote on 179.

Chapter Three

1. McNeel, *Durbin Route*, 13–14; Clarkson, *On Beyond Leatherbark*, 18–29; Clarkson, *Tumult on the Mountains*, 31.

2. Clarkson, *Tumult on the Mountains*, 31.

3. Brooks, *Forestry and Wood Industries*, 20.

4. The most convenient single source is Lewis, Johnson, and Askins, eds., *Colonialism in Modern America*.

5. Miller et al., "Who Owns West Virginia?," 1–28.

6. Dunaway, *First American Frontier*, 53, 56–57; Soltow, "Land Speculation in West Virginia," 111–34.

7. Dunaway, *First American Frontier*, 69–70.

8. Soltow, "Land Speculation in West Virginia," 120, 132.

9. Williams, "Class, Section, and Culture in Nineteenth-Century West Virginia Politics," 215–17.

10. Cubby, "Transformation of the Tug and Guyandot Valleys," 183–86.

11. Ibid., 180–87. See also *King* v. *State of West Virginia and Spruce Coal and Lumber Company*, 216 U.S. 92–101.

12. "Five Millions Involved," 24.

13. Andrew Price to Gilfillan-Neill and Company, July 26, 1907; Price to Osenton and McPeak, May 14, 1907, Box 3, Price Family Papers. See also Hennen, "Benign Betrayal," 56.

14. *Pocahontas Times*, April 27, 1899; Hennen, "Benign Betrayal," 57.

15. *Pocahontas Times*, March 30, 1899.

16. Quoted in Financial Statement for 1908. See also statements for 1904–11, Box 1, Elk River Coal and Lumber Company Collection.

17. Rasmussen, *Absentee Landowning and Exploitation in West Virginia*, 122–24.

18. For the definition of classifications see Auditor, *Biennial Report*, 16–17, which refers to *West Virginia Statutes*, chap. 10, sec. 2, General Corporation Laws.

19. Data drawn from West Virginia Secretary of State, Incorporation Reports. A few names may have been double counted because they incorporated more than one firm.

20. Gilbert, ed., *Mountain Trace*, 44–45; Starkey, "Over the Mountain," 34, 39.

21. Ritter, "Early Days in West Virginia," 167.

22. "Largest Hardwood Lumber Plant," 238; Gove, "Meadow River Lumber Company," 10–11; Dixon, "Lumber Industry at Alderson," 3–4; *Virginias* 2 (September 1881): 133.

23. Jensen, *Lumber and Labor*, 7–8.

24. "Davis," typescript, Notebook 1, Folder 1, Brown Notebooks.

25. Fansler, *History of Tucker County*, 538; Thompson, *History of the Lumber Business at Davis*, 5–6.

26. Inventory taken from Fansler, *History of Tucker County*, 541–42; "Davis," typescript, Notebook 1, Folder 1, Brown Notebooks.

27. Clarkson, *Tumult on the Mountains*, 84–85. "Davis," typescript, Notebook 1, Folder 1, Brown Notebooks.

28. Gove, "Meadow River Lumber Company," 11, 26; Rice, *History of Greenbrier County*, 351–55.

29. Gove, "Meadow River Lumber Company," 10–13, 26–29; Collins, "Built to Carry On," 10–11; Crookshanks, "Nothing but Hardwood," 10.

30. Callahan, *Semi-Centennial History*, 199n.; Nelson, "Big Mill Story," Part 1, 14–15.

31. Nelson, "Big Mill Story," Part 1, 14–15; "Richwood," typescript, Notebook 7, Brown Notebooks.

32. Nelson, "Big Mill Story," Part 3, 8–9.

33. Ibid., Part 1, 14–15.

34. Ibid., Part 4, 14, 23; Clarkson, *Tumult on the Mountains*, 94. Neither source states a precise date, but implies one given year between the mill's peak period of 1910 and 1929.

35. Clarkson, *Tumult on the Mountains*, 34–35; McNeil, *Durbin Route*, 36–37; McNeel, "Lumber Industry in Pocahontas County," 178; Palaszynski and McNeil, "Greenbrier Tannery," 8–9.

36. Clarkson, *On Beyond Leatherbark*, 22–28.

37. Ibid., 31–33, 178–79.

38. Ibid., 128–29, 136–40, and n. 79.

39. Ibid., 152–56.

40. Ibid., 122–26, 139–40, 160–62.

41. Clarkson, *Tumult on the Mountains*, 90.

42. Jensen, *Lumber and Labor*, 4.

43. "Estimate of Revenues and Expenses," 1907, Box 3, Price Family Papers.

44. Jensen, *Lumber and Labor*, 18, 24.

45. Ibid., 13.

46. Ibid., 24–26; Silver, "Hardwood Producers Come of Age," 427–29.

47. Pinkett, *Gifford Pinchot*, 56.

Chapter Four

1. Callahan, *Semi-Centennial History*, 148, quote on 496–97.

2. Ambler and Summers, *West Virginia*, 234.

3. Curry, *House Divided*, 137; Gooden, "Completion of a Revolution," chap. 2; Williams, "New Dominion and the Old," 355.

4. Williams, "New Dominion and the Old," 366; Cometti and Summers, *Thirty-Fifth State*, 462–63; Ambler and Summers, *West Virginia*, 272–75, 291–92; Atkinson, *Bench and Bar of West Virginia*, passim; Atkinson and Gibbens, *Prominent Men of West Virginia*, passim.

5. Callahan, *Semi-Centennial History*, 174–75.

6. Rodd, "Tracing West Virginia's Constitution," 19; Callahan, *Evolution of the Constitution of West Virginia*, 33–39; Williams, "New Dominion and the Old," 367.

7. Hurst, *Law and the Conditions of Freedom*, 5–7.

8. Ibid., 17.

9. Hurst, *Law and Economic Growth*, 262.

10. Ibid., 231.

11. *Acts of the West Virginia Legislature*, 1877, chap. 121, pp. 178–89; 1881, 296–301; 1885, chap. 12, pp. 14–19.

12. Ibid., 1882, chap. 118, pp. 338–40.

13. See, for example, Williams, "New Dominion and the Old," 375–76, and his *West Virginia*.

14. Hurst, *Law and Social Process*, passim.

15. Horwitz, *Transformation of American Law, 1780–1860*, 67–108; Friedman, *History of American Law*, 417, 410.

16. See, for example, Schwartz, "Tort Law and the Economy in Nineteenth-Century America."

17. Roeber, *Faithful Magistrates and Republican Lawyers*, traces this Virginia tradition from 1680 to 1810.

18. Miller, *Juries and Judges versus the Law*, traces this Virginia tradition from 1783 to 1828.

19. Ibid., 3–7, 25.

20. Ibid., 14–15, 103–4.

21. Reid, *American Judge*, 35–37; Atkinson, *Bench and Bar of West Virginia*; Atkinson and Gibbens, *Prominent Men of West Virginia*.

22. Drawn from various biographical directories, including Atkinson, *Bench and Bar in West Virginia*; Atkinson and Gibbens, *Prominent Men of West Virginia*; Callahan, *History of West Virginia*, vol. 3; and Conley, *West Virginia Encyclopedia*.

23. Horwitz, *Transformation of American Law, 1780–1860*, 74–80, 98–99; Lewin, "Silent Revolution in West Virginia's Law," 244–46, 251.

24. Lewin, "Silent Revolution in West Virginia's Law," 252–53, 270.

25. *Beaty* v. *Baltimore & O. R.R.*, 6 W.Va. 388.

26. Lewin, "Silent Revolution in West Virginia's Law," 253–54, 270–72.

27. *Virginia Code*, 1887, p. 1259, as amended by *Acts*, 1897–1898, chaps. 250, 283.

28. *Sanger* v. *Chesapeake & Ohio Ry. Co.*, 45 S.E. 750, 102 Va. 86, quoted in *Virginia and West Virginia Digest*, 16:358.

29. *Johnson* v. *Baltimore & O. Ry. Co.*, 25 W.Va. 570; *Maynard* v. *Norfolk & W. Ry. Co.*, 21 S.E. 733, 40 W.Va. 331; *Talbott* v. *West Virginia, C. & P. Ry. Co.*, 26 S.E. 311, 42 W.Va. 560. *Christian* v. *Chesapeake & O. Ry. Co.*, 89 S.E. 17, 78 W.Va. 378; W.Va. 1923. *Daniels* v. *Chesapeake & O. Ry. Co.*, 117 S.E. 695, 94 W.Va. 56, in *Virginia and West Virginia Digest*, 16:363.

30. *Christian* v. *Chesapeake & O. Ry. Co.*, 89 S.E. 17, 78 W.Va. 378.

31. *Blaine* v. *Chesapeake & O. Ry. Co.*, 9 W.Va. 252, and *Baylor* v. *Baltimore & O. Ry. Co.*, 9 W.Va. 270; *Starks* v. *Baltimore & O. Ry. Co.*, 87 S.E. 88, 77 W.Va. 93.

32. *Ellison* v. *Norfolk & W. Ry. Co.*, 98 S.E. 257, 83 W.Va. 316.

33. *Acts of the West Virginia Legislature*, 1919, sec. 3, chap. 59; *Warden* v. *Hines*, 106 S.E. 130, 87 W.Va. 756, in *Virginia and West Virginia Digest*, 16:360.

34. Item, *West Virginia Bar*, 88.

35. *Acts of the West Virginia Legislature*, 1908, 388; *Chesapeake & O. Ry. Co.* v. *May*, 92 S.E. 801, 120, Va. 790; *Norfolk & W. Ry. Co.* v. *Spates*, 94 S.E. 195, 122; *Virginia Code* 1910, 3992; *Southern Ry.* v. *American Peanut Corporation*, 164 S.E. 261, 158 Va. 359, in *Virginia and West Virginia Digest*, 16:369.

36. *West Virginia Code*, 1913, chaps. 62, 54, sec. 3518; *Jacobs* v. *Baltimore & O. Ry. Co.*,

70 S.E. 369, 68 W.Va. 618, quoted in *Virginia and West Virginia Digest*, 16:369–70; *McLaughlin v. Baltimore & O. Ry. Co.*, 83 S.E. 999, 75 W.Va. 287.

37. Schwartz, "Tort Law and the Economy in Nineteenth-Century America," 1755–56, 1745–46.

38. Lewin, "Silent Revolution in West Virginia's Law," 245–46.

39. Ibid., 263–64.

40. *Gaston v. Mace*, 33 W.Va. 15–16 (1889).

41. Ibid., 18.

42. Ibid., 29.

43. Ibid., 23.

44. Reid, *American Judge*, 47–48.

45. Ibid., 7–12.

46. Reid, *American Judge*, 13–14. See also Atkinson, *Bench and Bar in West Virginia*; and Atkinson and Gibbens, *Prominent Men of West Virginia*; Callahan, *History of West Virginia*, vol. 3; Conley, *West Virginia Encyclopedia*.

47. West Virginia Bar Association, Minutes, 71.

48. Ibid., 72–73.

49. Williams, "New Dominion and the Old," 333–37; Williams, "Class, Section, and Culture in Nineteenth-Century West Virginia Politics," 220.

50. Vandervort, "Supreme Court of West Virginia," 298–99; Callahan, *History of West Virginia*, 3:412; Atkinson, *Bench and Bar of West Virginia*, 62–64.

51. Rice, *Life of Jonathan M. Bennett*, 217–20; Henry Brannon to Gov. [Aretus B.] Fleming, June 28, 1907, Fleming Papers. In this letter, written on supreme court of appeals stationery, Brannon asked then governor Fleming to purchase paper for his coal company stores in the Fairmont field from the Hanlon-Sharpe Paper Company of Wheeling in which Brannon was a major stockholder.

52. Vandervort, "Supreme Court of West Virginia," 292–97, 300–301; Atkinson and Gibbens, *Prominent Men of West Virginia*, 753.

53. Reid, *American Judge*, 140.

54. *Raines v. Chesapeake & O. R'y Co.*, 39 W.Va. 50, 66.

55. *Jackson v. Norfolk & W. R. Co.*, 43 W.Va. 395–96.

56. *Transportation Company v. Standard Oil Company*, 46 W.Va. 621.

57. Horwitz, *Transformation of American Law, 1870–1960*, 73–74.

58. *Raines v. Chesapeake & O. R'y Co.*, 39 W.Va. 50, 65–66.

59. *Bias v. Chesapeake and Ohio Railway Company*, 46 W.Va. 349, 359, 354.

60. *Kirk v. Norfolk & W. R. Co.*, 41 W.Va. 722, 732 (1896); 24 S.E. 639, quote at 643.

61. *Couch v. Chesapeake & Ohio Ry. Co.*, 45 W.Va. 57, 30 S.E., quote at 150.

62. Vinson, "Railway Corporations and the Juries," 42–43.

63. Reid, *American Judge*, 72.

Chapter Five

1. For east Texas, see Allen, *East Texas Lumber Workers*, and Maxwell and Baker, *Sawdust Empire*. For the Mississippi piney woods, see Hickman, *Mississippi Harvest*, and Polk, ed., *Mississippi's Piney Woods*. For northern Florida, see Drobney, *Lumbermen and Log Sawyers*.

2. Deike, *Logging South Cheat*, 3–4, illustration on 5; Gove, "Meadow River Lumber Company," 26.

3. Deike, *Logging South Cheat*, 4–8; Larson, "Report on Meadow River Lumber Company," 18.

4. Deike, *Logging South Cheat*, 10; Clarkson, *Tumult on the Mountains*, 62.

5. Clarkson, *Tumult on the Mountains*, 63–65; Riggleman, *A West Virginia Mountaineer Remembers*, 115–16.

6. Riggleman, *A West Virginia Mountaineer Remembers*, 119.

7. Gilbert, ed., *Mountain Trace*, 12.

8. Clarkson, *Tumult on the Mountains*, 65; Deike, *Logging South Cheat*, 12.

9. Larson, "Report on Meadow River Lumber Company," 12.

10. Gilbert, ed., *Mountain Trace*, 19; Riggleman, *A West Virginia Mountaineer Remembers*, 120.

11. Riggleman, *A West Virginia Mountaineer Remembers*, 122.

12. Gilbert, ed., *Mountain Trace*, 21.

13. Clarkson, *Tumult on the Mountains*, 64; Falkenau, "Report on Southern Field Trip," 11.

14. Clarkson, *Tumult on the Mountains*, 64.

15. "Ye Mighty Men," 2.

16. David Luke to S. E. Slaymaker, December 13, 1900, November 6, 1901; E. P. Shaffer to S. E. Slaymaker, December 23, 1900; quote from Thomas Luke to S. E. Slaymaker, November 5, 1901, Box 1, West Virginia Pulp and Paper Company Papers.

17. Stickel, "Logging in the Mountains of West Virginia," 21–26. For portable camps at Meadow River, see Larson, "Report on Meadow River Lumber Company," 16.

18. Fansler, *History of Tucker County*, 547; Clarkson, *Tumult on the Mountains*, 68–69.

19. Deike, *Logging on South Cheat*, 12; Clarkson, *Tumult on the Mountains*, 71; Gilbert, ed., *Mountain Trace*, 15.

20. "Ye Mighty Men," 2.

21. Gilbert, ed., *Mountain Trace*, 18.

22. E. P. Shaffer to John Innes, January 29, 1908, Box 2, West Virginia Pulp and Paper Company Papers.

23. E. P. Shaffer to S. E. Slaymaker, November 3, December 12, 1900, January 8, 1901, Box 1, West Virginia Pulp and Paper Company Papers.

24. Gilbert, ed., *Mountain Trace*, 25–27.

25. Deike, *Logging South Cheat*, 12; Clarkson, *Tumult on the Mountains*, 71.

26. Gilbert, ed., *Mountain Trace*, 17.

27. Ibid., 4; Deike, *Logging South Cheat*, 15; Larson, "Report on Meadow River Lumber Company," 25.

28. Deike, *Logging South Cheat*, 20; Larson, "Report on Meadow River Lumber Company," 23; Clarkson, *Tumult on the Mountains*, 74.

29. Clarkson, *Tumult on the Mountains*, 74; Deike, *Logging South Cheat*, 29, and skidder illustration on 32; Gove, "Meadow River Lumber Company," 12–13, 26; Larson, "Report on Meadow River Lumber Company," 19–20.

30. *Pocahontas Times*, August 2, 1906.

31. Gilbert, ed., *Mountain Trace*, 28–29.

32. Ibid., 29.

33. Deike, *Logging South Cheat*, 26; Teter, *Goin' Up Gandy*, 39, quote on 44.

34. Fansler, *History of Tucker County*, 552–54; *Davis News*, February 7, 1924; Fansler, "Echoes of the Past: Logging Railways and Wrecks."

35. Fansler, *History of Tucker County*, 553–54.

36. The above description of the mill work process is derived from Stickel, "Logging in the Mountains of West Virginia," 51–54. For similar reports by foresters that reinforce this general description, see Larson, "Report on Meadow River Lumber Company," 28–47, and Falkenau, "Report on Southern Field Trip," 18–30.

37. Butler, "Reminiscences," 39.

38. E. P. Shaffer to S. E. Slaymaker, February 12, 1902, Box 2, and March 4, March 6, March 7, 1902, Box 3, West Virginia Pulp and Paper Company Papers.

39. Interview with George B. Thompson; Larson, "Report on Meadow River Lumber Company," 12; Falkenau, "Report on Southern Field Trip," 9.

40. *Pocahontas Times*, June 1, 1899.

41. Gilbert, ed., *Mountain Trace*, 44–45; Johnson, "Bob Withers," 35; Butler, "Reminiscences," 31–32.

42. Butler, "Reminiscences," 38–39.

43. Julian, " 'We Liked Big Wood,' " 30–31.

44. Ibid., 32.

45. Riggleman, *A West Virginia Mountaineer Remembers*, 111, 114–15.

46. Ibid., 116.

47. Larson, "Report on Meadow River Lumber Company," 12.

48. Stickel, "Logging in the Mountains of West Virginia," 17.

49. Einstein, "Things Fall Apart in Appalachia Too," 32–42.

50. Jensen, *Lumber and Labor*, 3–4, 21.

51. For African American labor in the southern lumber industry, see Allen, *East Texas Lumber Workers*; Drobney, "Lumbermen and Log Sawyers"; Green, "Brotherhood of Timber Workers"; Daniel, *Shadow of Slavery*; Hickman, *Mississippi Harvest*; and Jensen, *Lumber and Labor*.

52. Jensen, *Lumber and Labor*, 5–7; Green, "Brotherhood of Timber Workers," 161–200.

53. E. P. Shaffer to S. E. Slaymaker, September 18, 1900, Box 1, West Virginia Pulp and Paper Company Papers.

54. David Luke to S. E. Slaymaker, October 2, 1901, Box 1, West Virginia Pulp and Paper Company Papers.

55. McNeel, *Durbin Route*, 19.

56. Clarkson, *On Beyond Leatherbark*, 80.

57. *Pocahontas Times*, April 11, 1911; Clarkson, *On Beyond Leatherbark*, 145–46. See also Larson, "Report on Meadow River Lumber Company," 13.

58. *Pocahontas Times*, March 5, 1925, November 15, 1934, October 22, 1936; Clarkson, *On Beyond Leatherbark*, 146.

59. *Nicholas Republican*, August 6, 1934.

Chapter Six

1. Thompson, *History of the Lumber Business at Davis*, 46.

2. McNeel, *Durbin Route*, 19–20.

3. Butler, "Reminiscences," 44–45.

4. Ibid., 45–46.

5. Ibid., 45.

6. Gilbert, ed., *Mountain Trace*, 13.

7. Deike, *Logging South Cheat*, 7.

8. E. P. Shaffer, "Wages," September 5, 1900, Box 1, West Virginia Pulp and Paper Company Papers.

9. Clarkson, *On Beyond Leatherbark*, 154–57.

10. E. P. Shaffer to Samuel Slaymaker, July 3, 1900, telegram dated July 6, 1900, August (n.d.), August 2, 8, 1900, Box 1, West Virginia Pulp and Paper Company Papers.

11. Ibid., August 8, 10, September 6, 1900, May 2, 1901.

12. Clarkson, *On Beyond Leatherbark*, 123.

13. E. P. Shaffer to Samuel Slaymaker, September 25, 1900, January 8, 1901, Box 1, West Virginia Pulp and Paper Company Papers.

14. *Cumberland Daily News*, October 28, 1911, reproduced in Thompson, *History of the Lumber Business at Davis*, 20–35. Several other documents are reproduced therein.

15. Thompson, *History of the Lumber Business at Davis*, 20–21.

16. Ibid., 23.

17. Ibid., 26.

18. Ibid., 27–28.

19. Ibid., 30–31, 33.

20. Ibid., 34–36.

21. The working legal definition for peonage at the time was "a status or condition of compulsory service, based upon indebtedness of the peon to the master. The basal face is indebtedness." To indict anyone of the charge it had to be demonstrated that force was used either to enter or to retain an individual in that condition. See Bailey, "Temptation to Lawlessness," 26. This was a period when the federal government prosecuted peonage vigorously in the South. See Daniels, *Shadow of Slavery*.

22. McNeel, *Durbin Route*, 20.

23. *Code of West Virginia* (1899), chap. 145, sec. 32.

24. Speranza, "Forced Labor," 407.

25. Ibid., 408.

26. *Constitution of West Virginia*, Art. 9, sec. 4; *Code of West Virginia*, Art. 4, sec. 6, chap. 7, and sec. 7; Bailey, "Peonage in West Virginia," 31.

27. Speranza, "Forced Labor," 409.

28. Governor, *Message of Governor William M. O. Dawson, 1907*, 3–5.

29. Ibid., 6.

30. Ibid., 7.

31. Smith's report, ibid., 8.

32. Ibid., 9, 15–19.

33. Ibid., 10–11.

34. Cunningham's report, ibid., 20, 21, quote on 24.

35. Ibid., 22.

36. Ibid., 22–23.

37. Bailey, "Temptation to Lawlessness," 37; *Charleston Gazette*, November 23, 1907.

38. Bailey, "Temptation to Lawlessness," 38.

39. Quoted in *Southern Lumberman* 52 (July 20, 1907): 28; Bailey, "Temptation to Lawlessness," 38–39.

40. Bailey, "Temptation to Lawlessness," 39; *Southern Lumberman* 52 (November 30, 1907): 49.

41. Bailey, "Temptation to Lawlessness," 36–37, 40; *Labor Argus*, June 13, 1907; Williams, *West Virginia and the Captains of Industry*, 144–47.

42. *Raleigh Herald*, August 1, 1907.

43. Governor, *Message of Governor William M. O. Dawson, 1907*, 32.

44. Bailey, "Judicious Mixture," 148–50.

45. *Pocahontas Times*, August 14, 1905; Clarkson, *On Beyond Leatherbark*, 190.

46. *Pocahontas Times*, September 13, July 5, 1906; *Nicholas Republican*, June 28, 1906.

47. *Pocahontas Times*, January 7, 1909, November 9, 1905.

48. Item reprinted from the *Tygart Valley News* in the *Pocahontas Times*, May 31, 1894.

49. *Pocahontas Times*, June, 4, 11, July 23, 1908.

50. *Randolph Enterprise* quoted in the *Pocahontas Times*, May 3, 1906.

51. *Pocahontas Times*, October 26, 1905.

52. Quoted in Fansler, *History of Tucker County*, 607.

Chapter Seven

1. For the sale of Davis town lots see the Tucker County Land Books and Deed Books, 1884–94.

2. Fansler, *History of Tucker County*, 279–86; *West Virginia Central and Pittsburgh Railway Company* (promotional pamphlet); *Davis Industrial Edition*, August 9, 1895.

3. Reproduced in Fansler, *History of Tucker County*, 288–89.

4. Ibid., 353–71; Fansler, "Echoes of the Past: Hendricks."

5. Fansler, "Echoes of the Past: Hambleton"; Fansler, *History of Tucker County*, 291–303.

6. Rice, *Bicentennial History of Randolph County*, 84–85.

7. Fansler, "Echoes of the Past: Vanishing Villages."

8. Clarkson, *On Beyond Leatherbark*, 163; E. P. Shaffer to S. E. Slaymaker, September 22, 1900, West Virginia Pulp and Paper Company Papers.

9. Clarkson, *On Beyond Leatherbark*, 164; Clarkson and Carvell, "West Virginia's Logging Railroad," 63.

10. Clarkson, *On Beyond Leatherbark*, 164–65, 170–74; *Pocahontas Times*, March 21, 1918.

11. Clarkson, *On Beyond Leatherbark*, 165–66.

12. Fansler, "Echoes of the Past: Hendricks."

13. *West Virginia State Gazetteer and Business Directory, 1902–03*. These volumes are a compendium of businesses organized and listed by town. Much of the material on businesses and the professions in this chapter is distilled from them. Page numbers are of much less value than name of town for finding this information, therefore page numbers are used only for direct quotations. For comparative purposes, volumes for 1891–92, 1902–3, 1906–7, 1914–15, and 1923 were used in this study.

14. Ibid.

15. Ibid., by respective years and towns.

16. Ibid.

17. Ibid.

18. Ibid.

19. Ibid.

20. Ibid.

21. Fansler, *History of Tucker County*, 366.

22. *West Virginia Gazetteer and Business Directory*, respective years and towns.

23. Ibid., 1891–92, quotes on 295.

24. Ibid., 1902–3, quote on 592.

25. Ibid., 1914.

26. Ibid., respective years and towns.

27. Ibid.

28. Ibid., 1891–92, 78.

29. Ibid., respective years.

30. Ibid., 1891–92, 157.

31. Ibid., 1902–3, 256.

32. Ibid., 1914–45, 248.

33. Ibid., respective years.

34. Ibid., 1891–92, 157.

35. Ibid., 1914–15, 248.

36. Ibid., 1902–3, 255; 1914–15; 1923, 408.

37. Ibid., 1914–15. The Elkins newspapers were the *Randolph Enterprise*, the *Randolph Review*, and the *Elkins Inter-Mountain*; the Parsons newspapers were the *Tucker Democrat*, the *Mountain State Patriot*, and the *Parsons Advocate*; the Marlinton newspapers were the *Pocahontas Independent*, the *Pocahontas Times*, and the *Republican News*.

38. *Pocahontas Times*, January 7, 1892.

39. Ibid., January 10, 1905.

40. Ibid., January 28, 1915.

41. Ibid., February 11, 1915.

42. Ibid.

43. Ibid., February 18, 1915.

44. Ibid., August 30, 1906. This and other local newspapers are filled with such references.

45. *Pocahontas Times*, November 14, 1907, February 11, 1915.

46. *Wheeling Register*, August 5, 1893.

47. E. P. Shaffer to S. E. Slaymaker, February 21, 24, April 28, 1902, Box 1, West Virginia Pulp and Paper Company Papers.

48. Ibid., February 25, April 28, 1902.

49. Hodges, "Death in Durbin," 20–27.

50. *Pocahontas Times*, May 17, August 2, 1900; see also ibid., November 23, 1905, November 3, 1911.

51. "Charge to Grand Jury," in *Pocahontas Times*, January 17, 1907.

52. "Proceedings of the Circuit Court," ibid.

53. Fansler, *History of Tucker County*, 470–72; Fansler, "Echoes of the Past: Vanishing Villages."

54. Fansler, *History of Tucker County*, 477–78; Fansler, "Echoes of the Past: Vanishing Villages"; *Acts of the West Virginia Legislature*, 1913, 96–107.

55. Teter, *Goin' Up Gandy*, 102.

56. *Pocahontas Times*, January 13, 1901.

57. Ibid., March 7, 13, 1901. See also Clarkson, *On Beyond Leatherbark*, 180–82, 186.

58. *Pocahontas Times*, August 21, 1902.

59. Clarkson, *On Beyond Leatherbark*, 88; Hodges, "Death in Durbin," 27.

60. Fansler, "Echoes of the Past."

61. *Randolph Enterprise*, March 25, 1909; *Weekly Inter-Mountain*, November 11, 18, 1909; Teter, *Goin' Up Gandy*, 3, 8.

62. *Randolph Enterprise*, January 3, 1913, February 13, 26, 1914; Bosworth, *History of Randolph County*, 309.

63. *Randolph Enterprise*, February 13, July 3, 24, 31, 1913; Teter, *Goin' Up Gandy*, 4.

64. Teter, *Goin' Up Gandy*, 2–14. See the regular columns on Whitmer and Horton in the *Randolph Enterprise* during this period, particularly January 15, 22, February 26, 1914, January 14, March 25, 1915.

Chapter Eight

1. "Ironheads" originally referred to the Regular Democrats of the northern and western counties who represented the iron interests, and "Agrarians" referred to Bourbon Democrats of the eastern and southern counties. See Ambler and Summers, *West Virginia*, 400–401; Ambler, *History of Education in West Virginia*, 195; Williams, "New Dominion and the Old," 322.

2. Williams, "Class, Section, and Culture in Nineteenth-Century West Virginia Politics," 224.

3. Williams, "New Dominion and the Old," 349, quotes on 352.

4. Ibid., 368.

5. Ibid., 363–65.

6. Ibid., 375–76.

7. Ireland, *Little Kingdoms*, 1–2.

8. Ibid.; Thorndale and Dollarhide, eds., *Map Guide to the U.S. Federal Censuses*, 367, 374.

9. Ambler and Summers, *West Virginia*, 231–33; Curry, *House Divided*, 86–89, 100–104; Rice and Brown, *West Virginia*, 141–43.

10. Rice and Brown, *West Virginia*, 146–51; Curry, *House Divided*, 102–19; Ambler and Summers, *West Virginia*, 139–41.

11. Gooden, *History of Calhoun County*, 35–36; Carnes, "Courthouse Wars," Part I, 30–31.

12. Johnston, *History of Middle New River Settlements*, 331–43; Carnes, "Courthouse Wars," Part II, 22–23.

13. Fansler, *History of Tucker County*, 248–49.

14. Ibid.; Tucker County Order Book No. 4, 34–35, 75.

15. Fansler, *History of Tucker County*, 249–52; Tucker County Order Book No. 4, 122–23, 189–90; Tucker County Election Record Book No. 1, 1–2, 9–11.

16. Fansler, *History of Tucker County*, 252; Tucker County Election Record Book No. 1, 9–11.

17. Fansler, *History of Tucker County*, 253–54; Fansler, "Tucker County Seat War."

18. Fansler, *History of Tucker County*, 253–54; Fansler, "Tucker County Seat War."

19. *Wheeling Intelligencer*, August 4, 1893.

20. Fansler, *History of Tucker County*, 255; Fansler, "Tucker County Seat War."

21. *Hamilton et al. v. Tucker County Court et al.*, 38 W.Va. 71–79.

22. *Wheeling Intelligencer*, August 4, 1893.

23. Fansler, *History of Tucker County*, 255, identifies these as the removal leaders. Collec-

tive biographies of these men were developed primarily from several sources: Fansler, *History of Tucker County*, Maxwell, *History of Tucker County*, and *Men of West Virginia*.

24. Fansler, *History of Tucker County*, 249–51, 255–56, identifies these men as active in the movement. Their names were drawn from a list of petition captains who led the electoral districts in 1892–93; men who guaranteed to cover the cost of the special election in 1893; men who offered the use of their building in Parsons as a temporary courthouse; men who offered to provide land in Parsons for the site of a new courthouse; and others who served in various capacities as lawyers and organizers. A collective biography of this group was pieced together from diverse sources but primarily from Fansler, *History of Tucker County*, Maxwell, *History of Tucker County*, and biographical directories, particularly *Men of West Virginia*. Biographical information that follows is from these sources.

25. Rice, *Bicentennial History of Randolph County*, 39, reprints the article from the *Pittsburgh Leader*, May 15, 1899. My own search for the original article was unsuccessful.

26. Ibid., 40.

27. Maxwell, *History of Randolph County*, 181–82, 188–89.

28. Repess, *Beverly, West Virginia*, 3; Auld, ed., *Randolph County*, 7.

29. Teter, "Past"; Randolph County Order Book D, 171–73; Hulett, "Beverly-Elkins Courthouse Feud," 4–6.

30. Teter, "Elkins."

31. Ibid.; Rice, *Elkins Centennial Album*, 22.

32. Randolph County Order Book D, 179, 236; Hulett, "Beverly-Randolph Courthouse Feud," 7–8.

33. Randolph County Order Book D, 402, 428, 433–44; *Randolph Enterprise*, May 26, 1897.

34. *Randolph Enterprise*, May 26, 1897; Randolph County Circuit Court, File No. 45-4188.

35. *Randolph Enterprise*, October 6, 1897.

36. Ibid.

37. Randolph County Order Book F, 128–29.

38. *Randolph Enterprise*, May 18, 1898.

39. Randolph Court Order Book F, 141–42.

40. *Randolph Enterprise*, July 20, November 2, 9, 1898.

41. H. R. Warfield to H. G. Davis, November 14, 1898, Box 95, Series 6, Davis Papers.

42. Randolph County Order Book F, 235–36, 262–64; Teter, "Moving the County Seat from Beverly to Elkins."

43. Randolph County Order Book F, 273; *Randolph Enterprise*, April 12, 1899.

44. Randolph Circuit Court Law Order Book D, 403–4; *Randolph Enterprise*, May 10, 1899.

45. *Randolph Enterprise*, May 10, 1899.

46. Rice, *Bicentennial History of Randolph County*, 41–42, quoting a reporter for the *Pittsburgh Leader*.

47. *Randolph Enterprise*, May 10, 1899; Rice, *Bicentennial History of Randolph County*, 44.

48. *Randolph Enterprise*, February 7, 1900.

49. S. B. Elkins to H. G. Davis, May 23, 1897, Box 90, Series 6, Davis Papers.

50. *Randolph Enterprise*, September 8, November 2, 1897.

51. Ibid., September 22, 1897.

52. H. G. Davis to S. B. Elkins, November 4, 1898, Box 10, Series 1, Davis Papers.

53. Patrick's son, born in 1860, also had a radical streak for in 1910 he was elected justice of the peace of Mingo district on the Socialist ticket (Bosworth, *History of Randolph County*, 321–22).

54. H. R. Warfield to H. G. Davis, November 12, 15, 16, 1898, Box 95, Series 6, Davis Papers.

55. C. W. Dailey to H. G. Davis, November 21, 22, 25, 1898, and H. G. Davis to H. R. Warfield, November 24, 1898, Box 94, Series 6, Davis Papers.

56. C. W. Dailey to H. G. Davis, November 29, 1898, Box 94, Series 6, Davis Papers.

57. H. R. Warfield to H. G. Davis, November 12, 1898, Box 95, Series 6, Davis Papers.

58. Martin Lane to H. G. Davis, June 2, 1897, Box 90, Series 6, Davis Papers.

59. *Randolph Enterprise*, October 6, 13, 1897.

60. H. G. Davis to R. F. Whitmer, September 24, 1898, Box 10, Series 1, Davis Papers.

61. R. F. Whitmer to S. B. Elkins, October 14, 1898, Folder 3, Box 5, Elkins Papers.

62. H. G. Davis to R. F. Whitmer, October 24, 1898, Box 10, Series 1, Davis Papers.

63. S. E. Slaymaker to H. G. Davis, November 3, 11, 1898, Box 94, Series 6, Davis Papers.

64. H. G. Davis to H. R. Warfield, November 16, 1898, Box 10, Series 1, Davis Papers.

65. C. H. Scott to H. G. Davis, November 17, 1898, Letterbook, Box 10, Series 1, Davis Papers.

66. C. W. Dailey to H. G. Davis, November 17, 1898, Box 94, Series 6, Davis Papers.

67. H. R. Warfield to H. G. Davis, November 18, 1898, Box 95, Series 6, Davis Papers.

68. H. G. Davis to C. W. Dailey, May 9, 1899, Letterbook, Box 11, Series 1, Davis Papers.

69. Ross, *Henry Gassaway Davis*, 243–44.

Chapter Nine

1. Thornton, "Ethic of Subsistence," 72–73.

2. Ibid., 78, 80.

3. Ambler, *Francis Pierpont*, 28–29.

4. Callahan, *Semi-Centennial History*, 192, 121n, and 111n.

5. Ibid., 111n.

6. McNeel, *Durbin Route*, 2–3.

7. Ibid.

8. Huston, "Economic Change and Political Realignment in Antebellum Pennsylvania," 365; Saylor, *Railroads of Pennsylvania*, 14–16, 192, 269.

9. Barns, "Grange and Populist Movements," 246.

10. Davis, "Railroads in the Development of West Virginia," 307–8.

11. Brooks, *Forestry and Wood Industries*, 44–46.

12. *Wheeling Register*, August 17, 1884. There were many newspaper editors in West Virginia in addition to the Wheeling newspapers cited in this study who followed a "booster" editorial policy toward industry. For example, the role of the *Logan Banner* is assessed in Waller, *Feud*, 144–46, and the position of the *Pocahontas Times* is discussed in Hennen, "Benign Betrayal," 54–60.

13. Among the most influential studies of the agricultural reform movements of the period are Hicks, *Populist Revolt*; Hofstadter, *Age of Reform*; Goodwyn, *Democratic Promise*; and McMath, *American Populism*.

14. Barns, *West Virginia State Grange*, 19–20.

15. Ibid., 22–23.

16. Ibid., 23–24; Barns, "Grange and Populist Movements," 509–12.

17. Board of Agriculture, *Biennial Report, 1895 and 1896*, 52.

18. Barns, *West Virginia State Grange*, 31, 35.

19. Ibid., 35; Rice, *History of Greenbrier County*, 383–89; Salstrom, *Appalachia's Path to Dependency*, xvi–xvii.

20. Barns, *West Virginia State Grange*, 36, 41.

21. Summer, *Johnson Newlon Camden*, 277; Joseph Van Meter to J. N. Camden, April 24, 1886, and Charles Williams to J. N. Camden, March 4, 1886, Letterbook 3, Johnson Newlon Camden Papers.

22. Governor, *Message of the Governor E. Willis Wilson, 1887*, 6–7.

23. Barns, *West Virginia State Grange*, 25; Barns, "Status and Sectionalism in West Virginia," 377.

24. Barns, *West Virginia State Grange*, 67–68, 70–71.

25. Ibid., 73–74. For a standard work on the National Grange, see Nordin, *Rich Harvest*.

26. Ibid.; Barns, *West Virginia State Grange*, 73, 76.

27. Ibid., 77–78.

28. Ibid., 36; Barns, "Grange and Populist Movements," 922.

29. Board of Agriculture, *Biennial Report, 1893 and 1894*, 45.

30. Ibid.

31. U.S. Census of Agriculture, 1870, 276–77, and 1910, 26–27.

32. *Pocahontas Times*, August 19, 1899, September 28, 1894.

33. Ibid., August 19, 1899.

34. This view is most commonly attributed to Ronald D. Eller, who essentialized the traditional interpretation in his popular study, *Miners, Millhands, and Mountaineers*.

35. Ibid., 3–22, quote on 3. See also Eller, "Land and Family," 83–109.

36. See McKenzie, *One South or Many?*, and "Wealth and Income."

37. McKenzie, "Wealth and Income," 264.

38. Ibid., 271–72.

39. See Hahn, *Roots of Southern Populism*.

40. See Dunn, *Cades Cove*, 88–89.

41. McKenzie, "Wealth and Income," 273–74.

42. See Dunaway, *First American Frontier*.

43. Pudup, "Limits of Subsistence," 66.

44. Pudup, "Boundaries of Class in Preindustrial Appalchia," 150; Pudup, "Social Class and Economic Development in Southeast Kentucky," 248.

45. Billings and Blee, "Agriculture and Poverty in the Kentucky Mountains," 233–69.

46. Waller, *Feud*, 22.

47. Noe, *Southwest Virginia's Railroad*, 50, 52.

48. Ibid., 52.

49. Weise, "Big Stone Gap," 175.

50. Mann, "Diversity in Antebellum Appalachia," 132–62.

51. See Salstrom, *Appalachia's Path to Dependency*.

52. U.S. Census of Agriculture, 1880, 1990. A farm is defined as "any establishment of which $1,000 or more of agricultural products were sold or would normally be sold during the year." See West Virginia Department of Agriculture, *West Virginia Agricultural Statistics*, 1. In counties whose economies were dominated by the coal industry, farming almost

ceased to be anything more than raising a few chickens, a cow, and a garden. For example, by the 1920s less than 15 percent of Mingo County and about 7 percent of McDowell County land was devoted to agriculture (Corbin, *Life, Work, and Rebellion in the Coal Fields*, 7). In these counties particularly, Salstrom's description of redundant farmers heading for the mines is particularly poignant.

53. U.S. Census of Agriculture, respective years.

54. West Virginia Department of Agriculture, *Fourth Biennial Report*, 11–12.

55. Ibid.

56. Kahn, "Government's Private Forests," 132–44. WESTVACO, formerly West Virginia Pulp and Paper Company, owns more than 400,000 acres of land in West Virginia. Total acreage of public park and forest lands in the state are divided as follows: federally administered land totals 1,161,642 acres; state-administered land totals 407,247 acres; locally administered land totals 21,327 acres. This amounts to 1,590,216 acres, approximately 10 percent of the landmass in West Virginia (Governor's Office of Community and Industrial Development, *West Virginia State Comprehensive Outdoor Recreation Plan*, 1–2).

57. Hart, "Land Rotation in Appalachia," 150–54; Otto, "Migration of Southern Plain Folk," 183–200; Otto and Anderson, "Slash-and-Burn Cultivation," 131–47; Otto, "Decline of Forest Farming," 18–27.

58. Barns, "Grange and Populist Movements," 505; U.S. Census Office, *Compendium of the Eleventh Census*, 246, 284, 286, 322–23, 429, 464.

59. See, for example, the pioneering essays on this topic by Merrill, "Cash Is Good to Eat," Henretta, "Families and Farms," and Lemon, "Early Americans and Their Social Environment."

60. For examples of scholarship addressing this issue in Appalachia, see Billings, Blee, and Swanson, "Culture, Family, and Community in Preindustrial Appalachia"; Dunaway, *First American Frontier*; Dunn, *Cades Cove*; McKenzie, *One South or Many?*; Mann, "Diversity in the Appalachian South"; and Salstrom, "Appalachia's Informal Economy."

61. Ramella, "On Bower's Ridge," 36–45.

62. Teter, *Goin' Up Gandy*, 51.

63. Butler, "Reminiscences," 51–52.

64. Henlein, *Cattle Kingdom*, 1–20; Stealey, "Notes on the Ante-Bellum Cattle Industry," 38–47, 70–72.

65. McNeel, *Durbin Route*, 35–37; Rice, *History of Greenbrier County*, 348.

66. Teets, *From This Green Glade*, 69–70.

67. Rice, *History of Greenbrier County*, 389.

68. Salstrom, *Appalachia's Path to Dependency*, 60–82.

69. *Pocahontas Times*, December 9, 1909.

70. Barns, *West Virginia State Grange*, 80.

Chapter Ten

1. Widner, "West Virginia," 313.

2. *Pocahontas Times*, June 15, 1911.

3. Board of Agriculture, *Biennial Report, 1899 and 1900*, 257–59, quotes on 258.

4. Waugh, "Lumbering before Pinchot," 96.

5. Dawkins, "Enemies of the Forest," 40–41.

6. Stickel, "Logging in the Mountains of West Virginia," 5–7.

7. Clarkson, *Tumult on the Mountains*, 43.

8. West Virginia, *Report of the West Virginia Conservation Commission, 1908*, 23. The report noted that 1908 was an unusually dry year.

9. Thompson, *History of the Lumber Business at Davis*, 49.

10. Fansler, *History of Tucker County*, 544.

11. "Disastrous Forest Fires," 4.

12. "Our Greatest Forest Fire," 37.

13. Thompson, *History of the Lumber Business at Davis*, 19–20; Fansler, *History of Tucker County*, 544.

14. *Pocahontas Times*, July 17, 1930.

15. Brooks, *Forestry and Wood Industries*, 52–53.

16. Brooks, "Top of West Virginia," 11.

17. Board of Agriculture, *Biennial Report, 1899 and 1900*, 257–59, quote on 251.

18. McNeill, *Milkweed Ladies*, 99–100.

19. Crockett, "The Man Who Fed the Animals," 50.

20. *Pocahontas Times*, January 17, 1907; Butler, "Reminiscences," 30, 50; clipping dated March 1947 in Brown Notebook, Folder 1, Box 1, Brown Notebooks.

21. *Randolph Enterprise*, January 17, 1900.

22. Nelson, Nelson, and Smith, *Haven in the Hardwood*, facing 40.

23. Clarkson, *On Beyond Leatherbark*, 244; *Pocahontas Times*, January 9, February 13, 1936.

24. Statement of Hugh H. Bennett before House Committee on Labor, in U.S. House of Representatives, *To Make the Civilian Conservation Corps a Permanent Agency*, 72.

25. Brooks, *Forestry and Wood Industries*, 35; Conservation Commission, *Report of the West Virginia Conservation Commission, 1908*, 42.

26. Oliverio, *Footprints in the Soil*, 5–13, 21–22; Conservation Commission, *West Virginia*, 27.

27. U.S. Department of Agriculture, Bureau of Agricultural Economics, "Appalachian Land Use Conference Tour," 12–14, quote on 14.

28. Board of Agriculture, *Report of the Farmers' Institutes, 1907*, 8.

29. Brooks, *Forestry and Wood Industries*, 32.

30. Board of Agriculture, *Report of the Farmers' Institutes, 1907*, 8.

31. Brooks, *Forestry and Wood Industries*, 34; Carpenter and Herndon, *Report on Pollution Survey of Cheat River Basin*, 9–10.

32. Item, *Illustrated Monthly West Virginian*, 1908, 42–44, quotes on 43.

33. Ibid.

34. *Fayette Journal*, March 1, 1906.

35. *Pocahontas Times*, November 9, 1898, March 16, 30, 1899.

36. Ibid., May 4, 1899.

37. Ibid., April 27, 1899; Hennen, "Benign Betrayal," 55.

38. *Pocahontas Times*, May 4, 1899.

39. Ibid., November 8, 1900; Hennen, "Benign Betrayal," 56.

40. *Pocahontas Times*, September 17, 1905.

41. Ibid., September 28, 1905. See also ibid., September 17, 1905.

42. Glenn, "Denudation and Erosion," 125.

43. *Randolph Enterprise* quoted in *Pocahontas Times*, November 7, 1909.

44. Glenn, "Denudation and Erosion," 126.

45. Brooks, *Forestry and Wood Industries*, 26. West Virginia's navigable rivers in 1911 were as follows: Monongahela, 33 miles; Ohio, 285 miles; Great Kanawha, 90 miles; Little Kanawha, 120 miles; Guyandotte, 50 miles; Big Sandy and its tributaries, 170.5 miles. The mileage was calculated on the ability of streams to carry rafts or boats in time of medium flood stages (ibid.).

46. Ibid., 27.

47. Ibid., 28.

48. Ambler and Summers, *West Virginia*, 467; Conservation Commission, *West Virginia*, 25.

49. *Acts of the West Virginia Legislature* (1877), chap. 28, sec. 2.

50. Fish Commission, *Report of the Fish Commissioners, 1877–78*, 3–5.

51. Ibid., *1889–1890*, 5–7. For a similar complaint, see ibid., *1881–82*, 4.

52. *Code of West Virginia* (1887), chap. 62, sec. 16.

53. Cometti and Summers, eds., *Thirty-Fifth State*, 561.

54. Ambler, "Plea for the Preservation of Our Forests," 10–11. In 1903 dynamiting fish became a misdemeanor.

55. Governor, *Message of Governor William A. MacCorkle, 1895*, 34–35.

56. House of Delegates, *Journal of the House*, 1895, H.B. 37, sec. 21, H.B. 98, H.B. 117.

57. Governor, *Message of Governor William A. MacCorkle, 1897*, 51.

58. House of Delegates, *Journal of the House* (1897), H.B. 10, sec. 3.

59. Senate, *Journal of the Senate* (1901), 163.

60. Governor, *Message of Governor George W. Atkinson, 1899*, quote on 40.

61. Ibid., *1901*, 56.

62. Senate, *Journal of the Senate* (1901), 47, S.B. 10, sec. 1.

63. These calculations are based on data gathered from roll-call votes by delegates and senators between 1895 and 1903.

64. G. H. Clark to W. A. MacCorkle, August 28, 1895, No. 108, Box 89, MacCorkle Collection.

65. Game and Fish Warden, *Report, 1901–1902*, 5–6.

66. Ibid., 5.

67. Andrew Price also noted that this was the family of Edn Hammonds, a celebrated folk musician in the West Virginia tradition. See Price's story in the *Fayette Journal*, June 28, 1906. A recording of his fiddle tunes has been produced by the West Virginia and Regional History Collection, West Virginia University.

68. John G. Luke to Samuel E. Slaymaker, December 13, 1900, and David Luke to Samuel E. Slaymaker, December 13, 1900, Box 1, West Virginia Pulp and Paper Company Records.

69. Governor, *Message of Governor William M. O. Dawson, 1907*, 66; *State* v. *Parkins* 53 W.Va., 385–88.

70. Governor, *Message of Governor William M. O. Dawson, 1907*, 66.

71. Ibid., *1909*, 32.

72. U.S. House of Representatives, *Proceedings of a Conference of Governors*, 3.

73. Conservation Commission, *Report, 1908*, 39. This did not happen without a struggle in Maine either. See Judd, "Reshaping Maine's Landscape."

74. *Acts of the West Virginia Legislature* (1909), chap. 60, sec. 1-51, pp. 470–92.

75. Ibid., chap. 60, sec. 54-56, pp. 493–94.

76. Ibid. (1911), chap. 47, pp. 133–36.

77. Ambler and Summers, *West Virginia*, 469.

78. Governor, *Message of Governor Albert B. White, 1905*, 75.

79. *Acts of the West Virginia Legislature* (1909), chap. 61, sec. 1-3, pp. 494–95.

80. Clark, *Greening of the South*, 59–65.

81. For the West Virginia Fish and Game Protective Association and the West Virginia Audubon Society, see Folders 2 and 3, Box 4, Price Family Papers; Governor, *Message of Governor Henry D. Hatfield, 1917*, 56–57.

82. Ambler and Summers, *West Virginia*, 469.

83. Governor, *Message of Governor John J. Cornwell, 1921*, 34–35.

84. *Acts of the West Virginia Legislature* (1921), chap. 116, pp. 420–50. For more on the divisions between sportsmen and foresters in the national conservation movement, see Reiger, *American Sportsmen and the Origins of Conservation*, chap. 2.

85. Sharp, "Work of the West Virginia Game and Fish Commission," 170, 184.

86. Brooks, "A Constructive Conservation Program," 229–31.

87. Angelo, "Activities of the West Virginia Game and Fish Commission," 164–66, 258, quote on 166.

88. Brooks, "A Constructive Conservation Program," 229–30.

89. Game and Fish Commission, *Eighth Annual Report*, 16; Ambler and Summers, *West Virginia*, 471.

90. McNeill, *Milkweed Ladies*, 93, 96, 98.

91. G. D. McNeill, *Last Forest*, 153–54.

BIBLIOGRAPHY

Manuscripts

Charleston, West Virginia
West Virginia State Archives
Elk River Coal and Lumber Company Collection
William A. MacCorkle Collection
Meadow River Lumber Company Collection
Falkenau, Gordon E. "Report on Southern Field Trip," May 28, 1935, typescript, Box 4.
Larson, Andrew H. "Report on the Meadow River Lumber Company of Rainelle,
W.Va., May 2, 1916," Typescript, Box 4.

Elkins, West Virginia
Randolph County Courthouse
Randolph Circuit Court File No. 45-4188
Randolph Circuit Court Law Order Book D
Randolph County Clerk Order Book D
Randolph County Clerk Order Book F

Morgantown, West Virginia
West Virginia and Regional History Collection, West Virginia University
D. D. Brown Notebooks
Johnson Newlon Camden Papers
Henry Gassaway Davis Papers
Stephen B. Elkins Papers
Aretus Brooks Fleming Papers
Lumber Corporations. Tucker County Minutes, 1884–1910
John R. Lynch Papers
Map of West Virginia Showing Railroads, MC 1, Drawer 5
J. C. Myers Lumber Company, Journal 1906–7.
Price Family Papers
Randolph County Records
Stickel, Paul W. "Logging in the Mountains of West Virginia. A Report of the Study of
the Lumber Operations of the Horton, West Virginia, Sawmill of Parsons Pulp &
Paper Company." Report submitted for completion of Forest Utilization 5, New York
State College of Forestry, 1923.
Thompson, George Benjamin of Canaan Valley, Tucker County, West Virginia.
Interviewed by O. D. Lambert, Robert F. Munn, and Verl Z. Garster, April 13, 1956.
Oral History Collection 6.
Tucker County Records, 1909–22
West Virginia Pulp and Paper Company Papers

Parsons, West Virginia
Tucker County Courthouse
  Tucker Circuit Court Law Book
  Tucker County Election Record Book No. 1
  Tucker County Land Books and Deed Books
  Tucker County Order Book No. 4

Author's Possession
Hulett, Elizabeth M. "The Beverly-Elkins Courthouse Feud." Unpublished paper.
Morgan, Minerva. Morgantown (former resident of Cass), West Virginia. Interviewed by
  Susan Lewis, September 15, 1992. Audiotape.

United States Documents

Berman, Gillian Mace, Melissa Conley-Spencer, and Barbara J. Howe. "The Monongahela
  National Forest, 1915–1990." Report prepared for U.S. Department of Agriculture,
  Forest Service, Monongahela National Forest, 1992.
Congress. House of Representatives. *Index to the Executive Documents of the House of*
  Representatives: Report of the Chief of Engineers. Vol. 3, pt. 1. 45th Cong., 2d sess., 1878.
———. *Proceedings of a Conference of Governors in the White House, Washington, D.C., May*
  13–15, 1908. 60th Cong., 2d sess. H. Doc. 1425.
———. *Report of the Secretary of War: Messages and Documents.* Vol. 2, pt. 2. 48th Cong., 1st
  sess, 1883.
———. *To Make the Civilian Conservation Corps a Permanent Agency: Hearings before the*
  Committee on Labor. 76th Cong., 1st sess.
Department of Agriculture. Bureau of Agricultural Economics. "Appalachian Land Use
  Conference Tour." November 1939. Appalachian Regional Office, 1934– 45. Folder
  W.Va. 030, Box 5B, Regional Group 83. National Archives.
———. *Message from the President of the United States Transmitting a Report of the Secretary*
  of Agriculture in Relation to the Forests, Rivers, and Mountains of the Southern
  Appalachian Region. Washington, D.C.: U.S. Government Printing Office, 1902.
———. Bureau of Agricultural Economics, Bureau of Home Economics, and the Forest
  Service. *Economic and Social Problems and Conditions of the Southern Appalachians.*
  Misc. Pub. 205. Washington, D.C.: U.S. Government Printing Office, 1935.
———. Forest Service. *Speech of Hon. George C. Sturgiss of West Virginia in the House of*
  Representatives, February 3, 1909. Washington, D.C.: U.S. Government Printing Office,
  1909.
Department of Commerce. Bureau of the Census. *Agriculture.* Vol. 6, pt. 2. Fourteenth
  Census. Washington, D.C.: U.S. Government Printing Office, 1922.
———. *Agriculture.* Vol. 7. Thirteenth Census. Washington, D.C.: U.S. Government
  Printing Office, 1913.
———. *Agriculture: West Virginia. Statistics for the State and Its Counties.* Fourteenth
  Census. Washington, D.C.: U.S. Government Printing Office, 1920.
———. *Manufactures, 1919.* Vol. 9. Fourteenth Census. Washington, D.C.: U.S. Government
  Printing Office, 1922.
———. *Population.* Vol. 1. Fourteenth Census. Washington, D.C.: U.S. Government Printing
  Office, 1922.

———. *Population*. Vol. 3. Thirteenth Census. Washington, D.C.: U.S. Government Printing Office, 1913.

———. *Population Schedules: West Virginia*. Thirteenth Census. Ann Arbor, Mich.: University Microfilms, 1984.

Department of Interior. Census Office. *Agriculture Part I: Farms, Live Stock, and Animal Products*. Eleventh Census. Washington, D.C.: U.S. Census Office, 1902.

———. *Agriculture Part II: Crops and Irrigation*. Eleventh Census. Washington, D.C.: U.S. Census Office, 1902.

———. *Compendium of the Eleventh Census*. Vol. 3. Washington, D.C.: U.S. Government Printing Office, 1897.

———. *Compendium of the Tenth Census of the United States*. Washington, D.C.: U.S. Government Printing Office, 1880.

———. *Population*. Eleventh Census. Washington, D.C.: U.S. Census Office, 1902.

———. *Report of the Manufactures of the United States*. Tenth Census. Washington, D.C.: U.S. Government Printing Office, 1883.

———. *Report of the Productions of Agriculture*. Ninth Census. Washington, D.C.: U.S. Government Printing Office, 1872.

———. *Report of the Productions of Agriculture*. Tenth Census. Washington, D.C.: U.S. Government Printing Office, 1883.

———. *Report of the Statistics of Agriculture in the United States*. Eleventh Census. Washington, D.C.: U.S. Government Printing Office, 1895.

———. *Report on Population of the United States*. Eleventh Census. Washington, D.C.: U.S. Government Printing Office, 1895.

———. *Statistics of the Population of the United States*. Ninth Census. Washington, D.C.: U.S. Government Printing Office, 1872.

———. *Statistics of the Population of the United States*. Tenth Census. Washington, D.C.: U.S. Government Printing Office, 1880.

———. *The Statistics of the Wealth and Industry of the United States*. Ninth Census. Washington, D.C.: U.S. Government Printing Office, 1872.

———. Bureau of Corporations. *The Lumber Industry*. Part 4. Washington, D.C.: U.S. Government Printing Office, 1914.

Glenn, Leonidas Chalmers. *Denudation and Erosion in the Southern Appalachian Region and the Monongahela Basin*. U.S. Geological Survey Professional Paper 72. Washington, D.C.: U.S. Government Printing Office, 1911.

Mastran, Shelley Smith, and Nan Lowerre. *Mountaineers and Rangers: A History of Federal Forest Management in the Southern Appalachians, 1900–81*. U.S. Department of Agriculture, Forest Service, FS-380. Washington, D.C., 1983.

Sargent, Charles S. *Report on the Forests of North America*. Washington, D.C.: U.S. Government Printing Office, 1884.

West Virginia Documents

Acts of the West Virginia Legislature. Wheeling and Charleston, 1877–1917, 1921, 1925.

Auditor. *Biennial Report of the Auditor of State to the Governor, the Legislature and the Taxpayers of West Virginia, 1913–1914*. Charleston: Tribune Printing Company, 1914.

Board of Agriculture. *Biennial Report of the West Virginia State Board of Agriculture, 1893 and 1894*. Charleston: Moses W. Donnally, 1894.

——. *Biennial Report of the West Virginia State Board of Agriculture, 1895 and 1896.* Charleston: Moses W. Donnally, 1896.

——. *Biennial Report of the West Virginia State Board of Agriculture, 1897 and 1898.* Charleston: Will E. Forsyth, 1898.

——. *Biennial Report of the West Virginia State Board of Agriculture, 1899 and 1900.* Charleston: Butler Printing Company, 1900.

——. *Biennial Report of the West Virginia State Board of Agriculture, 1901 and 1902.* Charleston: Tribune Printing Company, 1902.

——. *Biennial Report of the West Virginia State Board of Agriculture, 1903 and 1904.* Charleston: Tribune Printing Company, 1904.

——. *Biennial Report of the State Board of Agriculture of West Virginia, 1905 and 1906.* Charleston: Tribune Printing Company, 1906.

——. *Biennial Report of the State Board of Agriculture of West Virginia, 1907 and 1908.* Charleston: Tribune Printing Company, 1908.

——. *Biennial Report of the State Board of Agriculture of West Virginia, 1909 and 1910.* Charleston: News-Mail Company, 1911.

——. *Biennial Report of the State Board of Agriculture of West Virginia, 1911 and 1912.* Charleston: Union Publishing Company, 1912.

——. *Report of Farmers' Institutes Held under the Auspices of the West Virginia State Board of Agriculture, 1907,* No. 5. Charleston: Tribune Printing Company, 1907.

Carpenter, Lewis V., and L. Kermit Herndon. *Report on Pollution Survey of Cheat River Basin.* Charleston: State Water Commission, 1929.

Code of West Virginia. Charleston: Mail-Tribune, 1887–99.

Conservation Commission. *Report of the West Virginia Conservation Commission, 1908.* Charleston: Tribune Printing Company, 1909.

——. *West Virginia: A Guide to the Mountain State.* New York: Oxford University Press, 1941.

Fish Commission. *Report of the Fish Commissioners of the State of West Virginia, 1877–78.* Wheeling: W. J. Johnston, 1878.

——. *Report of the Fish Commissioners of the State of West Virginia, 1881–82.* Wheeling: W. J. Johnston, 1882.

——. *Report of the Fish Commissioners of the State of West Virginia, 1889–1890.* Charleston: Moses W. Donnally, 1891.

Game and Fish Commission. *Eighth Annual Report.* Charleston: State Printer, 1928.

Game and Fish Warden. *Report of the Game and Fish Warden of West Virginia, 1901–1902.* Charleston: Tribune Printing Company, 1902.

Governor. *Message of Governor Albert B. White, 1905.* Charleston: Tribune Company, 1905.

——. *Message of Governor E. Willis Wilson, 1887.* Charleston: James B. Taney, 1887.

——. *Message of Governor George W. Atkinson, 1899.* Charleston: N.p., 1899.

——. *Message of Governor George W. Atkinson, 1901.* Charleston: N.p., 1901.

——. *Message of Governor Henry D. Hatfield, 1917.* Charleston: Tribune Printing Company, 1917.

——. *Message of Governor John J. Cornwell, 1921.* Charleston: Tribune Printing Co., 1921.

——. *Message of Governor William A. MacCorkle, 1895.* Charleston: Moses W. Donnally, 1895.

——. *Message of Governor William A. MacCorkle, 1897.* Charleston: Moses W. Donnally, 1897.

——. *Message of Governor William E. Stevenson, 1870.* Wheeling: John Frew, 1870.

——. *Message of Governor William M. O. Dawson, 1907.* Charleston: Tribune Printing Company, 1907.

——. *Message of Governor William M. O. Dawson, 1909.* Charleston: News-Mail Company, 1909.

——. *Message of Governor William M. O. Dawson Concerning Cases of Peonage and Labor Conditions to the Legislature of 1907.* Charleston: Tribune Printing Company, 1907.

Governor's Office of Community and Industrial Development. *West Virginia Comprehensive Outdoor Recreation Plan Calendar, 1988–1992.* Charleston: Community Development Division, 1989.

Holmes, Darrel E., ed. *West Virginia Blue Book.* Charleston: Jarrett Printing Company, 1989.

House of Delegates. *Journal of the House of Delegates of the State of West Virginia.* Charleston: State Printer, 1895–1903.

"Incorporation Reports." Compiled from *The Acts of the West Virginia Legislature*, 1866–1901.

Secretary of State. Incorporaton Reports. Compiled from *Secretary of State Corporation Reports*, 1903–9.

Senate. *Journal of the Senate of the State of West Virginia.* Wheeling and Charleston: State Printer, 1865–1901.

——. *Journal of the Senate of the State of West Virginia.* Charleston: Press-Butler, 1901.

Tax Commission. *Second Report*, 1884. Wheeling: Charles H. Taney, 1884.

West Virginia Department of Agriculture. *Fourth Biennial Report of the West Virginia Department of Agriculture, 1919 and 1920.* Charleston: West Virginia Department of Agriculture, 1920.

——. *Second Biennial Report of the West Virginia Department of Agriculture, 1915 and 1916.* Charleston: West Virginia Department of Agriculture, 1916.

——. *West Virginia Agricultural Statistics.* Bulletin 25. Charleston: West Virginia Department of Agriculture, 1994.

——. *West Virginia Forests and Forest Products.* Bulletin 74. June 1928.

West Virginia Historical Records Survey. *Randolph County.* Vol. 42 of *Inventory of the County Archives of West Virginia.* Charleston: West Virginia Historical Records Survey, 1933.

West Virginia Newspapers

Daily Inter-Mountain, Elkins, 1907–13

Davis Industrial Edition, Davis, 1895

Davis News, Davis, 1910, 1913–19

Elkins Weekly Inter-Mountain, Elkins, 1909

Fayette Journal, Fayetteville, 1906

Greenbrier Independent, Lewisburg, 1870–89

Labor Argus, Charleston, 1907

Nicholas Republican, Richwood, 1906, 1911–19, 1933–34

Parsons Advocate, Parsons, 1911–20, 1956, 1958, 1960

Pocahontas Times, Huntersville and Marlinton, 1898–1936

Randolph Enterprise, Beverly, 1897–1915

Spirit of Jefferson, Charles Town, 1872–82

Tucker County Democrat, Saint George and Parsons, 1883–92
Tucker County Pioneer, Saint George, 1884–85, 1892
Tygart Valley News, Elkins, 1901–2
Tygart Valley Press, Elkins, 1978
Virginia Weekly Star, Morgantown, 1861
West Virginia State Weekly, Fairmont, 1911
Wheeling Intelligencer, Wheeling, 1861, 1873–78, 1882–86, 1893
Wheeling Register, Wheeling, 1884–93

Books, Articles, and Theses

Allen, Ruth A. *East Texas Lumber Workers: An Economic and Social Picture, 1870–1950*.
  Austin: University of Texas Press, 1961.
Ambler, Charles Henry. "The Cleavage between Eastern and Western Virginia." *American
  Historical Review* 15 (1909–10): 762–80.
——. *Francis Pierpont: Union War Governor of Virginia and Father of West Virginia*.
  Chapel Hill: University of North Carolina Press, 1937.
——. *A History of Education in West Virginia from Early Colonial Times to 1940*.
  Huntington, W.Va.: Standard Printing and Publishing Company, 1951.
——. *Sectionalism in Virginia from 1776 to 1861*. Chicago: University of Chicago Press, 1910.
Ambler, Charles H., and Festus P. Summers. *West Virginia: The Mountain State*. 2d ed.
  New York: Prentice-Hall, 1958.
Ambler, Mason G. "A Plea for the Preservation of Our Forests, Streams and Fuels."
  *Proceedings of the 21st Annual Meeting of the West Virginia Bar Association, Fairmont,
  December 28–29, 1905*, 106–18. Parkersburg: State Journal Company, 1906.
Anderson, Stanley Judd. *The Kanawha Head Project: A History of Holly River State Park*.
  Utica, Ky.: McDowell Publications, 1993.
Angelo, Ernest. "Activities of the West Virginia Game and Fish Commission." *West
  Virginia Review* 6 (March 1929): 164–66, 258.
Appalachian Land Ownership Task Force. *Who Owns Appalachia? Land Ownership and
  Its Impact*. Lexington: University Press of Kentucky, 1983.
Atkinson, George W. *Bench and Bar of West Virginia*. Charleston: Virginian Law Book
  Company, 1919.
Atkinson, George W., and Alvaro F. Gibbens. *Prominent Men of West Virginia*. Wheeling:
  W. L. Callin, 1890.
Bailey, Kenneth R. "A Judicious Mixture: Negroes and Immigrants in the West Virginia
  Mines, 1880–1917." *West Virginia History* 34 (1973): 141–61.
——. "A Temptation to Lawlessness: Peonage in West Virginia, 1903–1908." *West Virginia
  History* 50 (1991): 25–45.
Barnes, L. Diane. "Avenues to a Market Economy: Harrison County, West Virginia, to
  1860." M.A. thesis, West Virginia University, 1995.
Barns, William Derrick. "The Grange and Populist Movements in West Virginia, 1873–
  1914." Ph.D. diss., West Virginia University, 1946.
——. "Status and Sectionalism in West Virginia, Part II: The Ante-Bellum Settlement
  Pattern from Valley to Valley." *West Virginia History* 34 (1973): 360–81.
——. *The West Virginia State Grange: The First Century, 1873–1973*. Morgantown:
  Morgantown Printing and Binding Company, 1973.

Bartlett, Richard A. *Troubled Waters: Champion International and the Pigeon River Controversy*. Knoxville: University of Tennessee Press, 1995.

Batteau, Allen W. *The Invention of Appalachia*. Tucson: University of Arizona Press, 1990.

Berthoff, Roland. "Celtic Mist Over the South." *Journal of Southern History* 52 (1986): 523–46, with response and rejoinder on 546–50.

Billings, Dwight B., and Kathleen M. Blee. "Agriculture and Poverty in the Kentucky Mountains: Beech Creek, 1850–1910." In *Appalachia in the Making: The Mountain South in the Nineteenth Century*, edited by Mary Beth Pudup, Dwight B. Billings, and Altina L. Waller, 233–69. Chapel Hill: University of North Carolina Press, 1995.

——. "Appalachian Inequality in the Nineteenth Century: The Case of Beech Creek, Kentucky." *Journal of the Appalachian Studies Association* 4 (1992): 113–23.

Billings, Dwight B., Kathleen Blee, and Louis Swanson. "Culture, Family, and Community in Preindustrial Appalachia." *Appalachian Journal* 13 (1986): 154–70.

Blackhurst, W. E. *Riders of the Flood*. 1954. Reprint. Parsons, W.Va.: McClain, 1968.

Bosworth, A. S. *A History of Randolph County, West Virginia*. 1916. Reprint. Parsons, W.Va.: McClain, 1975.

Brashler, Janet. "Before John King Arrived: Early History of the Monongahela National Forest." *Goldenseal* 9 (Winter 1983): 62–64.

Brooks, A. B. "A Constructive Conservation Program." *West Virginia Review* 4 (April 1927): 229–31.

——. *Forestry and Wood Industries*. Vol. 5. Morgantown: West Virginia Geological Survey, 1911.

——. "The Top of West Virginia." *Illustrated Monthly West Virginian* 2 (October–November 1908): 11–17.

Bruce, Thomas. *Heritage of the Trans-Alleghany Pioneers, or, Resources of Central West Virginia*. Baltimore: Nichols, Killam and Maffitt, 1894.

Burckel, Nicholas C. "Publicizing Progressivism: William M. O. Dawson." *West Virginia History* 42 (1981): 222–48.

Bush, Florence Cope. *Dorie: Woman of the Mountains*. Knoxville: University of Tennessee Press, 1992.

Butler, P. H. "Reminiscences," a series of articles published by P. H. Butler during the 1930s in the *Widen News* and reproduced in *Widen: Life and Legend of Clay County People*. Vol. 4, Book 2. Clay, W.Va.: Clay County High School, 1979.

Butterworth, W. "The Largest Hardwood Lumber Plant in the World." *West Virginia Review* 6 (March 1929): 238–40.

Byrne, W. E. R. *Tale of the Elk*. Richwood, W.Va.: Mountain State Press, 1940.

Calhoun, H. M. "A Giant Historic Tree." *West Virginia Wild Life* 8 (1930): 23.

Callahan, James Morton. *History of West Virginia, Old and New*. 3 vols. Chicago: American Historical Society, 1923.

——. *Semi-Centennial History of West Virginia*. Charleston: Semi-Centennial Commission of West Virginia, 1913.

Callahan, Maud F. *Evolution of the Constitution of West Virginia*. Vols. 1–2 of Studies in West Virginia History. Morgantown: West Virginia University, 1909.

Campbell, Carlos C. *Birth of a National Park in the Great Smoky Mountains*. Knoxville: University of Tennessee Press, 1960.

Campbell, John C. *The Southern Highlander and His Homeland*. 1921. Reprint. Lexington: University Press of Kentucky, 1969.

Carnes, Eva Margaret. "The Courthouse Wars." *West Virginia Review*, Part I, 21 (January 1944): 29–31, and Part II, 21 (February 1944): 22–24.

Carpenter, Charles. "Famous West Virginia Trees." *West Virginia Review* 8 (January 1931): 112–14.

Claiborne, J. F. H. "A Trip Through the Piney Woods." Reprinted from the 1841–42 original. *Mississippi Historical Society Publications* 9 (1906): 487–538.

Clark, Christopher. "Household Economy, Market Exchange, and the Rise of Capitalism in the Connecticut Valley, 1800–1860." *Journal of Social History* 13 (1979): 169–89.

———. *The Roots of Rural Capitalism: Western Massachusetts, 1780–1860.* Ithaca: Cornell University Press, 1990.

Clark, Thomas D. *The Greening of the South: The Recovery of Land and Forest.* Lexington: University Press of Kentucky, 1984.

Clarkson, Roy B. *On Beyond Leatherbark: The Cass Saga.* Parsons, W.Va.: McClain, 1990.

———. *Tumult on the Mountains: Lumbering in West Virginia, 1770–1920.* Parsons, W.Va.: McClain, 1964.

Clarkson, Roy B., and Kenneth R. Carvell. "West Virginia's Logging Railroad--Its Past and Present." *Northeastern Logger*, December 1961, 20–21, 62–63.

Clendening, Carl H. "Early Days in the Southern Appalachians." *Southern Lumberman* 143 (December 15, 1931): 101–5.

Clepper, Henry. *Professional Forestry in the United States.* Baltimore: Johns Hopkins Press, 1971.

Cole, J. R. *History of Greenbrier County.* Lewisburg, W.Va.: By the Author, 1917.

Collins, George. "Built to Carry On." *Log Train* 1 (April 1983): 10–15.

Cometti, Elizabeth, and Festus P. Summers, eds. *The Thirty-fifth State: A Documentary History of West Virginia.* Morgantown: West Virginia University Library, 1966.

Conley, Phil. *The West Virginia Encyclopedia.* Charleston: West Virginia Publishing Company, 1929.

Corbin, David Alan. *Life, Work, and Rebellion in the Coal Fields: The Southern West Virginia Miners, 1880–1922.* Urbana: University of Illinois Press, 1981.

Core, Earl L. *Plant Life of West Virginia.* New York: Scholar's Library, 1960.

Cox, Thomas R., Robert S. Maxwell, Phillip Drennon Thomas, and Joseph J. Malone. *This Well-Wooded Land: Americans and Their Forests from Colonial Times to the Present.* Lincoln: University of Nebraska Press, 1985.

Coy, Fred E. Jr., Tom Fuller, Larry G. Meadows, and Don Fig. "Splash Dam Construction in Eastern Kentucky's Red River Drainage Area." *Forest and Conservation History* 36 (1992): 179–84.

Crockett, Maureen. "Doing Time on Kennison Mountain: Pocahontas County's Forgotten Prison." *Goldenseal* 11 (Spring 1985): 38–45.

———. "The Man Who Fed the Animals: Nap Holbrook and the Early Days at Watoga." *Goldenseal* 17 (Summer 1991): 50–57.

Cronon, William. *Nature's Metropolis: Chicago and the Great West.* New York: Norton, 1991.

Crookshanks, Ben. "Nothing but Hardwood: The Meadow River Lumber Company." *Goldenseal* 17 (Winter 1991): 9–13, and photographic essay by *Goldenseal* editors, "Working at the Sawmill: The Johnston and Johnston Photographs of the Meadow River Lumber Company," 14–19.

Cubby, Edwin A. "Timbering Operations in the Tug and Guyandot Valleys in the 1890's." *West Virginia History* 26 (1965): 110–20.

——. "The Transformation of the Tug and Guyandot Valleys: Economic Development and Social Change in West Virginia, 1888–1921." Ph.D. diss., Syracuse University, 1962.

Curry, Richard Orr. *A House Divided: A Study of Statehood Politics and the Copperhead Movement in West Virginia*. Pittsburgh: University of Pittsburgh Press, 1964.

Cuthbert, John. "Riverboat Days on the Little Kanawha River." *Wonderful West Virginia* 54 (January 1991): 2–5.

Daniel, Pete. *The Shadow of Slavery: Peonage in the South, 1901–1969*. New York: Oxford University Press, 1972.

Davis, Henry G. "The Railroads in the Development of West Virginia." In *Semi-Centennial History of West Virginia*, edited by James Morton Callahan, 305–9. Charleston, W.Va.: Semi-Centennial Commission of West Virginia, 1913.

Davis Industrial Edition. *Tucker County Republican*. Reprinted in *West Virginia Hillbilly*, November 23, 1989, 3–11.

Dawkins, John Quincy. "Enemies of the Forest." *Illustrated Monthly West Virginian* 2 (September 1908): 40–41.

Deike, George H. III. *Logging South Cheat: The History of the Snowshoe Resort Lands*. Youngstown, Ohio: Trebco, 1978.

Deverell, William. *Railroad Crossings: Californians and the Railroad, 1850–1910*. Berkeley: University of California Press, 1994.

Dilts, James D. *The Great Road: The Building of the Baltimore and Ohio, the Nation's First Railroad, 1828–1853*. Stanford: Stanford University Press, 1993.

"Disastrous Forest Fires." *Illustrated Monthly West Virginian* 2 (October–November 1908): 4.

Diss Debar, Joseph H. *The West Virginia Hand-Book and Immigrant Guide*. Parkersburg: Gibbens Brothers, 1870.

Dixon, Thomas W. Jr. "The Lumber Industry at Alderson." *Log Train* 6 (1986): 3–13.

Doolittle, Edward S. "On the Circuit in Southern West Virginia." *Green Bag* 12 (1900): 284–86.

Drobney, Jeffrey A. *Lumbermen and Log Sawyers: Life, Labor, and Culture in the North Florida Timber Industry, 1830–1930*. Macon, Ga.: Mercer University Press, 1997.

Dunaway, Wilma A. *The First American Frontier: Transition to Capitalism in Southern Appalachia, 1700–1860*. Chapel Hill: University of North Carolina Press, 1996.

Dunn, Durwood. *Cades Cove: The Life and Death of a Southern Appalachian Community, 1818–1937*. Knoxville: University of Tennessee Press, 1988.

Dunn, Michael J. III. "The Beech Mountain Railroad Company." *West Virginia History* 23 (1962): 79–85.

Einstein, Frank H. "Things Fall Apart in Appalachia Too: Hubert Skidmore's Account of the Transition to Capitalism." *Appalachian Journal* 11 (1983–84): 32–42.

Eller, Ronald D. "Land and Family: An Historical View of Preindustrial Appalachia." *Appalachian Journal* 6 (1979): 83–109.

——. *Miners, Millhands, and Mountaineers: Industrialization of the Appalachian South, 1880–1930*. Knoxville: University of Tennessee Press, 1982.

Elmer, Manuel Conrad. *Timber: America's Magic Resource*. Boston: Christopher, 1961.

Evans, Cerinda W. *Collis Potter Huntington*. Newport News, Va.: Mariner's Museum, 1954.

"The Evolution of the Law Office." *West Virginia Law Quarterly* 1 (1894): 79–80.

Fansler, Homer Floyd. "Echoes of the Past." *Parsons Advocate*, April 9, 1959.

———. "Echoes of the Past: Brooklyn Heights." *Parsons Advocate*, October 30, 1958.

———. "Echoes of the Past: Hambleton, 1908." *Parsons Advocate*, August 16, 1956.

———. "Echoes of the Past: Hendricks, West Virginia." *Parsons Advocate*, November 20, 1958.

———. "Echoes of the Past: Logging Railways and Wrecks." *Parsons Advocate*, December 22, 1960.

———. "Echoes of the Past: Vanishing Villages: Mackeyville." *Parsons Advocate*, September 11, 1958.

———. *History of Tucker County, West Virginia*. Parsons, W.Va.: McClain, 1962.

———. "The Tucker County Seat War." *Parsons Advocate*, April 16, 1959.

Fast, Richard Ellsworth. *The History and Government of West Virginia*. Morgantown: Acme, 1901.

Featherstonhaugh, G. W. *Excursion through the Slave States, from Washington on the Potomac to the Frontier of Mexico; With Sketches of Popular Manners and Geological Notices*. 1884. Reprint. New York: Negro Universities Press, 1968.

"Firebug." *Gateway* [magazine of the Monongahela National Forest] 4 (December 1938): 4–5.

"Fire Trespass Case." *Gateway* 3 (December 1937): 11.

Fischer, David Hackett. *Albion's Seed: Four British Folkways in America*. New York: Oxford University Press, 1989.

"Five Millions Involved." *Southern Lumberman* 52 (July 20, 1907): 24.

Fizer, George A. "The West Virginia and Pittsburgh Railroad." *Log Train* 7 (1987): 3–7.

Flegel, Louise Burner. " 'Durbin Was Quite a Big City': Mabel Burner Remembers." *Goldenseal* 18 (Fall 1992): 27–33.

Ford, Thomas R., ed. *The Southern Appalachian Region: A Survey*. Lexington: University of Kentucky Press, 1962.

"The Forests of West Virginia." *Virginias* 4 (1883): 79–80.

Frame, Nat T. *West Virginia Agriculture and Rural Life from the Close of the Civil War to the End of World War I*. Inwood, W.Va.: West Virginia University Extension and USDA Bureau of Agricultural Economics, n.d.

Friedman, Lawrence M. *A History of American Law*. New York: Simon and Schuster, 1973.

Frome, Michael. *Strangers in High Places*. 1966. Reprint. Knoxville: University of Tennessee Press, 1980.

Frost, William Goodell. "Our Contemporary Ancestors in the Southern Mountains." *Atlantic Monthly* 83 (March 1899): 311–19.

Gilbert, Kenneth, ed. *Mountain Trace*. Book 2. Charleston, W.Va.: Jalamap Publications, 1983.

Gooden, Randall Scott. "The Completion of a Revolution: West Virginia from Statehood through Reconstruction." Ph.D. diss., West Virginia University, 1995.

———. *History of Calhoun County, West Virginia*. Grantsville, W.Va.: Calhoun County Historical and Genealogical Society, 1990.

Goodwyn, Lawrence. *Democratic Promise: The Populist Movement in America*. New York: Oxford University Press, 1976.

Gould, Alan B. " 'Trouble Portfolio' to Secretary of the Interior Walter L. Fisher, 1911–1913." *Forest History* 16 (1973): 4–12.

Gove, William. "The Meadow River Lumber Company: Last of the West Virginia Pioneers." *Northern Logger and Timber Processer* 20 (October 1971): 10–13, 26–29.

Greeley, William B. *Forests and Men*. 1951. Reprint. New York: Arno Press, 1972.

Green, James R. "The Brotherhood of Timber Workers, 1910–1913: A Radical Response to Industrial Capitalism in the Southern U.S.A." *Past and Present* 60 (1973): 161–200.

Hahn, Steven. *The Roots of Southern Populism: Yeoman Farmers and the Transformation of the Georgia Upcountry, 1850–1890*. New York: Oxford University Press, 1983.

Hall, Granville Davisson. *The Rending of Virginia: A History*. Chicago: Mayer and Miller Press, 1902.

Hall, Van Beck. "The Politics of Appalachian Virginia, 1790–1830." In *Appalachian Frontiers: Settlement, Society and Development in the Preindustrial Era*, edited by Robert D. Mitchell, 166–86. Lexington: University Press of Kentucky, 1991.

Hall, William L. "Influences of the National Forests on the South Appalachians." *Journal of Forestry* 17 (1919): 402–7.

Hamer, David. *New Towns in the New World: Images and Perceptions of the Nineteenth-Century Urban Frontier*. New York: Columbia University Press, 1990.

Hanlon, Howard A. *The Ball-Hooters, from the Forests They Felled—Cities Grew*. Prospect, N.Y.: Prospect Books, 1960.

Hart, John Fraser. "Land Rotation in Appalachia." *Geographical Review* 67 (April 1977): 148–66.

Hawkins, Guy Carleton. "Logging for Pulp Wood in the Southern Appalachians." *American Forestry* 16 (1910): 689–94.

Henlein, Paul C. *Cattle Kingdom in the Ohio Valley, 1783–1860*. Lexington: University of Kentucky Press, 1959.

Hennen, John. *The Americanization of West Virginia: Creating a Modern Industrial State, 1916–1925*. Lexington: University Press of Kentucky, 1996.

———. "Benign Betrayal: Capitalist Intervention in Pocahontas County, West Virginia, 1890–1910." *West Virginia History* 50 (1991): 47–62.

Henretta, James A. "Families and Farms: Mentalité in Pre-Industrial America." *William and Mary Quarterly* 35 (1978): 3–32.

Hergert, Herbert L. "The Tannin Extraction Industry in the United States." *Journal of Forest History* 27 (1983): 92–93.

Hickman, Nollie J. *Mississippi Harvest*. University: University of Mississippi Press, 1962.

Hicks, John D. *The Populist Revolt: A History of the Farmers' Alliance and the People's Party*. Minneapolis: University of Minnesota Press, 1931.

Hicks, W. Raymond. "The West Virginia Central and Pittsburgh Railway." *Railway and Locomotive Historical Society Bulletin* 113 (1965): 6–31.

Hodges, Elaine Prater. "Death in Durbin: New Questions about an Old Case." *Goldenseal* 20 (Spring 1994): 20–27.

Hofstadter, Richard. *The Age of Reform: From Bryan to F.D.R.* New York: Knopf, 1955.

———. "The Myth of the Happy Yeoman." *American Heritage* 7 (April 1956): 43–53.

Holmes, Sorrell E., ed. *West Virginia Blue Book, 1989*. Charleston: Jarrett, 1989.

Horn, Stanley F., and Charles W. Crawford. "Perspectives on Southern Forestry: *The Southern Lumberman*, Industrial Forestry, and Trade Associations." *Journal of Forest History* 21 (1977): 19–30.

Horwitz, Morton J. *The Transformation of American Law, 1780–1860*. Cambridge, Mass.: Harvard University Press, 1977.

——. *The Transformation of American Law, 1870–1960: The Crisis of Legal Orthodoxy.* New York: Oxford University Press, 1992.

Hurst, James Willard. *Law and Economic Growth: The Legal History of the Lumber Industry in Wisconsin, 1836–1915.* Cambridge, Mass.: Harvard University Press, 1964.

——. *Law and Social Process in United States History.* Ann Arbor: University of Michigan Law School, 1960.

——. *Law and the Conditions of Freedom in the Nineteenth Century.* Madison: University of Wisconsin Press, 1967.

Huston, James L. "Economic Change and Political Realignment in Antebellum Pennsylvania." *Pennsylvania Magazine of History and Biography* 113 (1989): 347–95.

Inscoe, John C. *Mountain Masters, Slavery, and the Sectional Crisis in Western North Carolina.* Knoxville: University of Tennessee Press, 1989.

Ireland, Robert M. *Little Kingdoms: The Counties of Kentucky, 1850–1891.* Lexington: University Press of Kentucky, 1977.

Item. *West Virginia Bar* 1 (May 1994): 88.

Jackson, Harry F. "Lumbering on Coal River." M.A. thesis, West Virginia University, 1937.

Jensen, Vernon H. *Lumber and Labor.* 1945. Reprint. New York: Arno Press and the New York Times, 1971.

Johnson, Skip. "Bob Withers: Upshur County Logger, Lumber Camp Cook, and Game Warden." *Goldenseal* 5 (October–November 1979): 32–35.

Johnston, David E. *A History of Middle New River Settlements and Continuous Territory.* Huntington, W.Va.: Standard Printing and Publishing Co., 1906.

Judd, Richard W. "Reshaping Maine's Landscape: Rural Culture, Tourism, and Conservation, 1890–1929." *Journal of Forest History* 32 (1988): 180–90.

Julian, Norman. " 'We Liked Big Wood': Recollections of a Wood Hick." *Goldenseal* 10 (Winter 1984): 30–39.

Kahn, Si. "The Government's Private Forests." *Southern Exposure* 2 (Fall 1974): 132–44.

Kennedy, Philip Pendleton. *The Blackwater Chronicle: A Narrative of an Expedition into the Land of Canaan, in Randolph County, Virginia.* New York: Redfield, 1853.

Kephart, George S. "The Pulpwood Drive: A Memoir of Maine in the 1920s." *Journal of Forest History* 20 (1976): 203–9.

Kephart, Horace. *Our Southern Highlanders: A Narrative of Adventure in the Southern Appalachians and a Study of Life among the Mountaineers.* 1913. Reprint. Knoxville: University of Tennessee Press, 1976.

King, John. "Protecting Uncle Sam's Interests: A Year in the Forest Service." *Goldenseal* 9 (Winter 1983): 55–59, 61.

Kirby, Jack Temple. *Rural Worlds Lost: The American South, 1920–1960.* Baton Rouge: Louisiana State University Press, 1987.

Kline, Benjamin F. G. Jr.. "The Nature of the Logging Railroads of West Virginia." *Log Train* 2 (January 1984): 12–15.

——. *"Stemwinders" in the Laurel Highlands: The Logging Railroads of South-Western Pennsylvania.* Book 13 in the series Logging Railroad Era of Lumbering in Pennsylvania. Strasburg, Pa.: By the author, 1973.

Kulikoff, Allan. *The Agrarian Origins of American Capitalism.* Charlottesville: University Press of Virginia, 1992.

——. "Households and Markets: Toward a New Synthesis of American Agrarian History." *William and Mary Quarterly* 50 (1993): 342–55.

———. "The Transition to Capitalism in Rural America." *William and Mary Quarterly* 46 (1989): 120–44.

Lambie, Joseph T. *From Mine to Market: The History of Coal Transportation on the Norfolk and Western Railway.* New York: New York University Press, 1954.

"The Largest Hardwood Lumber Plant in the World." *West Virginia Review* 6 (1929): 238–40.

Leitch, Meridith. "Steps Taken to Preserve Old Up-and-Down Sawmills." *West Virginia Conservation* 14 (1951): 18–19.

Lemon, James T. "Early Americans and Their Social Environment." *Journal of Historical Geography* 6 (1980): 115–31.

Lewin, Jeff L. "The Silent Revolution in West Virginia's Law of Nuisance." *West Virginia Law Review* 90 (Winter 1989–90): 235–353.

Lewis, Charles D. "Government Forests and the Mountain Problem." *Mountain Life and Work* 6 (January 1931): 2–9.

Lewis, Helen Matthews, Linda Johnson, and Donald Askins, eds. *Colonialism in Modern America: The Appalachian Case.* Boone, N.C.: Appalachian Consortium Press, 1978.

Lewis, Ronald L. "Railroads, Deforestation, and the Transformation of Agriculture in the West Virginia Back Counties, 1880–1920." In *Appalachia in the Making: The Mountain State in the Nineteenth Century*, edited by Mary Beth Pudup, Dwight B. Billings, and Altina L. Waller, 297–320. Chapel Hill: University of North Carolina Press, 1995.

Lewis, Ronald L., and John C. Hennen, eds. *West Virginia: Documents in the History of a Rural-Industrial State.* 2d ed. Dubuque, Iowa: Kendall/Hunt, 1996.

Lewis, Virgil A. *How West Virginia Was Made* [Proceedings of the First and Second Wheeling Conventions]. Charleston: News-Mail, 1909.

Lillard, Richard G. *The Great Forest.* New York: Knopf, 1947.

Lincoln, Wayne. "Clarksburg, Weston and Glenville Railroads." *Light Iron and Short Ties* 9 (September 1991): 3–15.

———. "Porter's Creek & Gauley Railroad." *West Virginia Hillbilly*, January 12, 1989, 5, 9, and January 19, 1989, 15.

Lipscomb, J. Roy. "Living in a Mill Town." *Log Train* 8, No. 29 (1988): 3–11.

"Logging on Gauley River, West Virginia." *Virginias* 5 (1884): 23.

"Lumber and Lumbering on Chesapeake & Ohio R'y." *Virginias* 2 (1881): 188; 3 (1882): 10–11; 3 (1882): 28–29.

"Lumbering in the Upper Greenbrier, West Virginia." *Virginias* 6 (1885): 97.

McCreesh, Carolyn D. "The Philadelphia Connection: The Foulke Meadow River Lands in the 18th and 19th Centuries." *West Virginia History* 44 (1983): 289–320.

McDonald, Forrest, and Grady McWhiney. "The Antebellum Southern Herdsman: A Reinterpretation." *Journal of Southern History* 41 (1975): 147–66.

———. "Celtic Origins of Southern Herding Practices." *Journal of Southern History* 51 (1985): 165–82.

McKenzie, Robert Tracy. *One South or Many? Plantation Belt and Upcountry in Civil War–Era Tennessee.* New York: Cambridge University Press, 1994.

———. "Wealth and Income: The Preindustrial Structure of East Tennessee in 1860." *Appalachian Journal* 21 (Spring 1994): 260–79.

McKinney, Gordon. *Southern Mountain Republicans, 1865–1900: Politics and the Appalachian Community.* Chapel Hill: University of North Carolina Press, 1978.

McKinney, Gordon, Edward Cowan, Rodger Cunningham, and Altina Waller. "Culture Wars: David Hackett Fischer's *Albion's Seed*." *Appalachian Journal* 19 (1992): 161–200.

MacMaster, Richard K. "The Cattle Trade in Western Virginia, 1760–1830." In *Appalachian Frontiers: Settlement, Society and Development in the Preindustrial Era*, edited by Robert D. Mitchell, 127–49. Lexington: University Press of Kentucky, 1991.

McMath, Robert C. *American Populism: A Social History, 1877–1898*. New York: Hill and Wang, 1993.

McNeel, William Price. *The Durbin Route: The Greenbrier Division of the Chesapeake & Ohio Railway*. Charleston, W.Va.: Pictorial Histories Publishing Co., 1985.

———. "Lumber Industry in Pocahontas County." In Pocahontas County Historical Society, *History of Pocahontas County, West Virginia*. 1981. Reprint. Pictorial Histories Publishing Company, 1985.

———. "Railroads in Pocahontas County." In Pocahontas County Historical Society. *History of Pocahontas County, West Virginia*. Marlinton, W.Va.: By the Author, 1981.

McNeill, Douglas. *The Last Forest: Tales of the Allegheny Woods*. 1940. Reprint. Parsons, W.Va.: McClain, 1989.

McNeill, Louise. *The Milkweed Ladies*. Pittsburgh: University of Pittsburgh Press, 1988.

McWhiney, Grady. *Cracker Culture: Celtic Ways in the Old South*. Tuscaloosa: University of Alabama Press, 1988.

Mann, Ralph. "Diversity in the Antebellum Appalachian South: Four Farm Communities in Tazewell County, Virginia." In *Appalachia in the Making: The Mountain South in the Nineteenth Century*, edited by Mary Beth Pudup, Dwight B. Billings, and Altina L. Waller, 132–62. Chapel Hill: University of North Carolina Press, 1995.

———. "Mountains, Land, and Kin Networks: Burkes Garden, Virginia, in the 1840s and 1850s." *Journal of Southern History* 58 (1992): 411–34.

Marquess, E. Lawrence. "The West Virginia Venture: Empire Out of Wilderness." *West Virginia History* 14 (1952): 5–27.

Marquis, Albert Nelson. *Who's Who in West Virginia*. Vol. 1. Chicago: A. N. Marquis, 1939.

Martin, Joseph. *A New and Comprehensive Gazetteer of Virginia and the District of Columbia*. Charlottesville: J. Martin, 1835.

Marx, Leo. *The Machine in the Garden: Technology and the Pastoral Ideal in America*. New York: Oxford University Press, 1964.

Maury, M. F., and William M. Fontaine. *Resources of West Virginia*. Wheeling: Register Company, 1876.

Maxwell, Claude W. "Minear's Mill: The First Sawmill West of the Mountains." *West Virginia Review* 5 (March 1928): 220.

Maxwell, Hu. *The History of Randolph County, West Virginia*. 1898. Reprint. Parsons, W.Va.: McClain, 1961.

———. *History of Tucker County, West Virginia*. 1884. Reprint. Kingwood, W.Va.: Preston, 1971.

Maxwell, Robert S., and Robert D. Baker. *Sawdust Empire: The Texas Lumber Industry, 1830–1940*. College Station: Texas A&M University Press, 1983.

Men of West Virginia. 2 vols. Chicago: Biographical Publishing Company, 1903.

Merrill, Michael. "Cash Is Good to Eat: Self-Sufficiency and Exchange in the Rural Economy of the United States." *Radical History Review* 4 (Winter 1977): 42–71.

Miller, F. Thornton. *Juries and Judges versus the Law: Virginia's Provincial Legal Perspective, 1783–1828*. Charlottesville: University Press of Virginia, 1994.

Miller, Tom D., et al. "Who Owns West Virginia?" Reprint from *Huntington* (W.Va.) *Herald-Advertiser*. Huntington: Huntington Publishing Company, 1974.

Mitchell, Robert D. *Commercialism and the Frontier: Perspectives on the Early Shenandoah Valley*. Charlottesville: University Press of Virginia, 1977.

——, ed. *Appalachian Frontiers: Settlement, Society, and Development in the Preindustrial Era*. Lexington: University Press of Kentucky, 1991.

Moore, Barrington Jr. *Social Origins of Dictatorship and Democracy: Lord and Peasant in the Making of the Modern World*. Boston: Beacon Press, 1966.

"More Peonage Cases." *Southern Lumberman* 52 (November 30, 1907): 49.

Murphy, James Marion. "Transportation on the Little Kanawha River in Gilmer County." M.A. thesis, West Virginia University, 1950.

Myers, Sylvester. *Myers's History of West Virginia*. Vol. 1. Wheeling, W.Va.: Wheeling News Lithograph Company, 1915.

Nash, Roderick. *Wilderness and the American Mind*. New Haven: Yale University Press, 1967.

Nelson, Arnold E., Ozella Nelson, and Rosemary Smith. *Haven in the Hardwood: The History of Pickens, West Virginia*. Parsons, W.Va.: McClain, 1971.

Nelson, Bill. "The Big Mill Story." *West Virginia Hillbilly*, Part 1, February 23, 1989, 14–15; Part 2, March 2, 1989, 22; Part 3, March 9, 1989, 8–9; Part 4, March 16, 1989, 14, 23; Part 5, March 23, 1989, 17.

Newton, Milton. "Cultural Preadaptation and the Upland South." In *Man and Cultural Heritage: Papers in Honor of Fred B. Kniffen*, edited by H. J. Walker and W. G. Haag, 143–54. Baton Rouge: Louisiana State University Press, 1974.

Noe, Kenneth. " 'Appalachia's' Civil War Genesis: Southwest as Depicted by Northern and European Writers, 1825–1865." *West Virginia History* 50 (1991): 91–108.

——. *Southwest Virginia's Railroad: Modernization and the Sectional Crisis*. Urbana: University of Illinois Press, 1994.

Nordin, Dennis Sven. *Rich Harvest: A History of the Grange, 1867–1900*. Jackson: University of Mississippi Press, 1974.

Novak, William J. *The People's Welfare: Law and Regulation in Nineteenth-Century America*. Chapel Hill: University of North Carolina Press, 1996.

Oliverio, Jean E. *Footprints in the Soil and Reflections on the Water: Thirty Years of Soil and Water Conservation in West Virginia*. Parsons, W.Va.: McClain, 1972.

Otto, John Solomon. "The Decline of Forest Farming in Southern Appalachia." *Journal of Forest History* 27 (1983): 18–27.

——. "The Migration of the Southern Plain Folk: An Interdisciplinary Synthesis." *Journal of Southern History* 51 (1985): 183–200.

——. *The Southern Frontiers, 1607–1860: The Agricultural Evolution of the Colonial and Antebellum South*. Westport, Conn.: Greenwood Press, 1989.

Otto, J. S., and N. E. Anderson. "Slash-and-Burn Cultivation in the Highlands South: A Problem in Comparative Agricultural History." *Comparative Studies in Society and History* 24 (January 1982): 131–47.

"Our Greatest Forest Fire." *Illustrated Monthly West Virginian* 2 (December 1908): 37.

Owsley, Frank L. *Plain Folk of the Old South*. Baton Rouge: Louisiana State University Press, 1949.

Palaszynski, Edmund W., and William McNeil. "The Greenbrier Tannery at Marlinton." *Log Train* 2, No. 2 (1983): 8–12.

Pepper, Charles M. *The Life and Times of Henry Gassaway Davis, 1823–1916*. New York: Century, 1920.

Pessen, Edward. "How Different from Each Other Were the Antebellum North and South?" *American Historical Review* 85 (1980): 1119–49, and Forum in same issue 1150–66.

Peyton, J. Lewis. *Memoir of John Howe Peyton*. Staunton, Va.: A. B. Blackburn, 1894.

Pinkett, Harold T. *Gifford Pinchot: Private and Public Forester*. Urbana: University of Illinois Press, 1970.

"Pleads Guilty to the Charge of Peonage." *Southern Lumberman* 52 (July 20, 1907): 28.

Polk, Noel, ed. *Mississippi's Piney Woods: A Human Perspective*. Jackson: University of Mississippi Press, 1986.

Post, Melville Davisson. *Dwellers in the Hills*. New York: G. P. Putnam's Sons, 1901.

———. *The Strange Schemes of Randolph Mason*. 1896. Reprint. New York: Arno Press, 1976.

Price, Andrew. "The Williams River Country." *Fayette Journal*, June 28, 1906.

Pudup, Mary Beth. "The Boundaries of Class in Preindustrial Appalachia." *Journal of Historical Geography* 15 (1989): 139–62.

———. "The Limits of Subsistence: Agriculture and Industry in Central Appalachia." *Agricultural History* 64 (1990): 61–89.

———. "Social Class and Economic Development in Southeast Kentucky, 1820–1880." In *Appalachian Frontiers: Settlement, Society, and Development in the Preindustrial Era*, edited by Robert D. Mitchell, 235–60. Lexington: University Press of Kentucky, 1991.

Pudup, Mary Beth, Dwight B. Billings, and Altina L. Waller, eds. *Appalachia in the Making: The Mountain South in the Nineteenth Century*. Chapel Hill: University of North Carolina Press, 1995.

Pyne, Stephen J. *Fire in America: A Cultural History of Wildland and Rural Fire*. Princeton: Princeton University Press, 1982.

Raine, John. "The West Virginia Lumber Industry." *West Virginia Review* 4 (April 1927): 226–28.

Ramella, Richard. "On Bower's Ridge: Family Life in Wyoming County." *Goldenseal* 19 (Fall 1993): 36–45.

Rasmussen, Barbara. *Absentee Landowning and Exploitation in West Virginia, 1760–1920*. Lexington: University Press of Kentucky, 1994.

Recknagel, Arthur B. *Forestry: A Study of Its Origin, Application, and Significance in the United States*. New York: Knopf, 1929.

Rehder, John B. "The Scotch-Irish and English in Appalachia." In *To Build in a New Land: Ethnic Landscapes in North America*, edited by Allen G. Noble, 95–118. Baltimore: Johns Hopkins University Press, 1992.

Reid, John Phillip. *An American Judge: Marmaduke Dent of West Virginia*. New York: New York University Press, 1968.

———. "Henry Brannon and Marmaduke Dent: The Shapers of West Virginia Law, Part I." *West Virginia Law Review* 65 (1962): 19–37.

———. "Henry Brannon and Marmaduke Dent: The Shapers of West Virginia Law, Part II." *West Virginia Law Review* 65 (1963): 99–126.

Reiger, John F. *American Sportsmen and the Origins of Conservation*. New York: Winchester Press, 1975.

Repess, Carolyn Collett. *Beverly, West Virginia: A Pictorial History from 1753 to 1908*. Baltimore: Sprint Print, 1986.

Rice, Donald L. *Bicentennial History of Randolph County, West Virginia, 1787–1987.* Elkins, W.Va.: Randolph County Historical Society, 1987.

Rice, Harvey Mitchell. *The Life of Jonathan M. Bennett: A Study of the Virginias in Transition.* Chapel Hill: University of North Carolina Press, 1943.

Rice, Otis K. *The Allegheny Frontier: West Virginia Beginnings, 1730–1830.* Lexington: University Press of Kentucky, 1970.

——. *A History of Greenbrier County.* Parsons, W.Va.: McClain Printing Company for the Greenbrier Historical Society, 1986.

Rice, Otis K., and Stephen W. Brown. *West Virginia: A History.* 2d ed. Lexington: University Press of Kentucky, 1993.

Ried, H. *The Virginian Railway.* Milwaukee: Kalmbach, 1961.

Riggleman, Homer F. *A West Virginia Mountaineer Remembers.* Parsons, W.Va.: McClain, 1980.

Ritter, William H. "Early Days in West Virginia." *Southern Lumberman* 167 (December 15, 1943): 167–68.

Rodd, Thomas Whitney. "Tracing West Virginia's Constitution." *West Virginia Public Interest Law Report,* Summer 1982, 12–21.

Roeber, A. G. *Faithful Magistrates and Republican Lawyers: Creators of Virginia Legal Culture, 1680–1810.* Chapel Hill: University of North Carolina Press, 1981.

Ross, Thomas Richard. *Henry Gassaway Davis: An Old-Fashioned Biography.* Parsons, W.Va.: McClain, 1994.

Rostow, W. W. *The Stages of Economic Growth: A Non-Communist Manifesto.* Cambridge: Cambridge University Press, 1961.

Rothenberg, Winifred Barr. *From Market-Places to a Market Economy: The Transformation of Rural Massachusetts, 1750–1850.* Chicago: University of Chicago Press, 1992.

Rothstein, Morton. "The Antebellum South as a Dual Economy: A Tentative Hypothesis." *Agricultural History* 41 (1967): 373–82.

Royall, Anne. *Sketches of History, Life, and Manners in the United States, by a Traveller.* New Haven: By the Author, 1826.

"Rumbarger Affairs." *Southern Lumberman* 52 (November 30, 1907): 49.

Salstrom, Paul. "Appalachia's Informal Economy and the Transition to Capitalism." *Journal of Appalachian Studies* 2 (1996): 213–33.

——. *Appalachia's Path to Dependency: Rethinking a Region's Economic History, 1730–1940.* Lexington: University Press of Kentucky, 1994.

Sargent, C. S. "Statistics of the Lumber Industry in the Virginias during the Tenth Census." *Virginias* 3 (1882): 121.

Sarvis, Will. "An Appalachian Forest: Creation of the Jefferson National Forest and Its Effects on the Local Community." *Forest and Conservation History* 37 (1993): 169–78.

Saylor, Robert B. *The Railroads of Pennsylvania.* University Park: Bureau of Business Research, Pennsylvania State University, 1964.

Schwartz, Gary T. "Tort Law and the Economy in Nineteenth-Century America: A Reinterpretation." *Yale Law Review* 90 (1981): 1717–75.

Shapiro, Henry D. *Appalachia on Our Mind: The Southern Mountains and Mountaineers in the American Consciousness, 1870–1920.* Chapel Hill: University of North Carolina Press, 1978.

Sharp, George W. "The Work of the West Virginia Game and Fish Commission." *West Virginia Review* 2 (February 1925): 170, 184.

Shaw, J. G. "Richwood: A Thriving and Prosperous Young City." *West Virginia State Weekly*, April 1, 1911, 6–10.

Shea, John. "Our Pappies Burned the Woods." *American Forestry* 46 (April 1940): 159–62.

Shirey, M. R. "Agrarian Conditions in West Virginia Following the Civil War." *West Virginia Review* 12 (October 1934): 10–11.

Silver, James W. "The Hardwood Producers Come of Age." *Journal of Southern History* 23 (1957): 427–53.

Simon, Richard M. "Development of Underdevelopment: The Coal Industry and Its Effect on the West Virginia Economy." Ph.D. diss., University of Pittsburgh, 1978.

———. "Uneven Development and the Case of West Virginia: Going Beyond the Colonialism Model." *Appalachian Journal* 8 (1981): 165–86.

Sitton, Thad. *Backwoodsmen: Stockmen and Hunters along a Big Thicket River Valley.* Norman: University of Oklahoma Press, 1995.

Skidmore, Hubert. *Heaven Came So Near.* Garden City, N.Y.: Doubleday, Doran, 1938.

———. *I Will Lift Up Mine Eyes.* Garden City, N.Y.: Doubleday, Doran, 1936.

———. *River Rising!* Garden City, N.Y.: Doubleday, Doran, 1939.

Sklar, Martin J. *The Corporate Reconstruction of American Capitalism, 1890–1916: The Market, the Law, and Politics.* New York: Cambridge University Press, 1988.

Slotkin, Richard. *Regeneration through Violence: The Mythology of the American Frontier, 1600–1860.* Middletown, Conn.: Wesleyan University Press, 1973.

Smith, Kenneth L. *Sawmill: The Story of Cutting the Last Great Virgin Forest East of the Rockies.* Fayetteville: University of Arkansas Press, 1986.

Soltow, Lee. "Land Speculation in West Virginia in the Early Federal Period: Randolph County as a Specific Case." *West Virginia History* 44 (1983): 111–34.

"The Southern Appalachian Reserve." *Southern Lumberman* 47 (February 10, 1905): 16–17.

Spence, Robert Y. *The Land of the Guyandot: A History of Logan County.* Detroit: Harlo Press, 1976.

Speranza, Gino C. "Forced Labor in West Virginia." *Outlook* 74 (June 13, 1903): 407–10.

Starcher, Mark. "Where Shall It Be Located?" *Switchback* 3 (January 1993): 8–9.

Starkey, Edith Kimmell. "Over the Mountain: Timbering at Braucher." *Goldenseal* 13 (Summer 1987): 34–39.

Stealey, John Edmund III. "Notes on the Ante-Bellum Cattle Industry from the McNeill Family Papers." *Ohio History* 75 (1966): 38–47, 70–72.

Stephenson, Steven L., ed. *Upland Forests of West Virginia.* Parsons, W.Va.: McClain, 1993.

Stover, John F. *History of the Baltimore and Ohio Railroad.* West Lafayette: Purdue University Press, 1987.

Strother, David Hunter. "The Mountains, Part VII." *Harper's Monthly* 46 (1873): 675–76.

———. "The Virginia Canaan." *Harper's Magazine* 8 (1855): 18–36.

———. *Virginia Illustrated: Containing a Visit to the Virginia Canaan, and the Adventures of Porte Crayon and His Cousins.* New York: Harper & Brothers, 1871.

Summers, Festus P. *Johnson Newlon Camden, A Study in Individualism.* New York: G. P. Putnam's Sons, 1937.

Teets, Jo Ann Sereno. *From This Green Glade: A History of Terra Alta, West Virginia.* Terra Alta, W.Va.: By the Author, 1978.

Teter, Don. "Elkins." *Tygart Valley Press*, February 15, 1978.

——. *Goin' Up Gandy: A History of the Dry Fork Region of Randolph and Tucker Counties, West Virginia*. Parsons, W.Va.: McClain, 1977.

——. "Moving the County Seat from Beverly to Elkins." *Tygart Valley Press*, February 1, 1978.

——. "Past." *Tygart Valley Press*, January 4, 1978.

Thoenen, Eugene D. *History of the Oil and Gas Industry in West Virginia*. Charleston, W.Va.: Education Foundation, 1964.

Thomas, Samuel W. *Dawn Comes to the Mountains*. Louisville, Ky.: George Rogers Clark Press, 1981.

Thompson, George B. *A History of the Lumber Business at Davis, West Virginia, 1886–1924*. Parsons, W.Va.: McClain, 1974.

——. "Woods Force Superintendent Viering Tells Tale of Horror." *Parsons Advocate*, November 20, 1973.

Thorndale, William, and William Dollarhide. *Map Guide to the U.S. Federal Censuses, 1790–1920*. Baltimore: Genealogical Publishing Company, 1987.

Thornton, J. Mills III. "The Ethic of Subsistence and the Origins of Southern Secession." *Tennessee Historical Quarterly* 48 (1989): 67–85.

Tillson, Albert H. Jr. *Gentry and Common Folk: Political Culture on a Virginia Frontier, 1740–1789*. Lexington: University Press of Kentucky, 1991.

Tudiver, Sari Lubitsch. "Political Economy and Culture in Central Appalachia, 1790–1977." Ph.D. diss., University of Michigan, 1984.

Turner, Charles Wilson. *Chessie's Road*. Richmond: Garrett and Massie, 1956.

Turner, Frederick Jackson. "The Significance of the Frontier in American History." *Annual Report of the American Historical Association for the Year 1893*, 199–227. Indianapolis: Bobbs-Merrill Reprint Series in History H-214.

Turner, William Patrick Jr. "From Bourbon to Liberal: The Life and Times of John T. McGraw, 1856–1920." Ph.D. diss., West Virginia University, 1960.

Vandervort, J. W. "The Supreme Court of West Virginia," Part 1, *Green Bag* 12 (1900): 187–93; Part 2, 12 (1900): 234–44; Part 3, 12 (1900): 292–302.

Verhoeff, Mary. *The Kentucky River Navigation*. Filson Club Publication 28. Louisville, Ky.: John P. Morton, 1917.

Vinson, Z. T. "Railway Corporations and the Juries." *Minutes of the West Virginia Bar Association*. 17th Annual Meeting. Clarksburg, February 12–13, 1902, 42–51.

Virginia and West Virginia Digest. Vol. 16. St. Paul: West, 1970.

Virginias 2 (September 1881): 131.

Walker, Laurence C. *The Southern Forest: A Chronicle*. Austin: University of Texas Press, 1991.

Waller, Altina L. *Feud: Hatfields, McCoys, and Social Change in Appalachia, 1860–1900*. Chapel Hill: University of North Carolina Press, 1988.

Walls, David S., and Dwight Billings. "The Sociology of Southern Appalachia." *Appalachian Journal* 5 (1977): 131–44.

Warden, William E. Jr. "Engine Smoke in the Mountains of West Virginia: The Story of the Buffalo Creek and Gauley Railroad." In *Hickory and Lady Skippers: Life and Legend of Clay County People*. Vol. 4, book 2 (Clay County High School, 1979).

——. *West Virginia Logging Railroads*. Lynchburg, Va.: TLC Publishing, 1994.

Waugh, Jack. "Lumbering before Pinchot: The Short, Loud Death of the Canaan Valley." *American Heritage* 42 (February–March 1991): 93–94.

Weise, Robert. "Big Stone Gap and the New South, 1880–1890." In *The Edge of the South: Life in Nineteenth-Century Virginia*, edited by Edward L. Ayers and John C. Willis, 173–93. Charlottesville: University Press of Virginia, 1991.

West Virginia Bar Association. Minutes. In *Proceedings of the West Virginia Bar Association*. Wheeling, 1888.

——. *Report of the 12th Annual Meeting of the West Virginia State Bar Association*. Morgantown, November 3–4, 1897.

——. *Report of the 13th Annual Meeting of the West Virginia State Bar Association*. Charleston, January 17–18, 1899.

——. *Report of the 16th Annual Meeting of the West Virginia State Bar Association*. Parkersburg, February 4–5, 1901.

West Virginia Central and Pittsburgh Railway Company. New York: Privately printed, 1899.

West Virginia Central and Pittsburgh Railway Company. 1899. Reprint. Parsons, W.Va.: McClain, 1981.

"W.Va. Central and Pittsburgh R.R." *Virginias* 2 (June 1881): 85.

West Virginia Central Railway: The New Route to the Sea. New York: West Virginia Central Railway, 1974.

"West Virginia Natural Resource Commission." *Illustrated Monthly West Virginian* 2 (October–November 1908): 42–44.

West Virginia Reports. St. Paul: West, 1879–1916.

West Virginia State Gazetteer and Business Directory, 1891–92. Vol. 4. Detroit: R. L. Polk, 1892.

West Virginia State Gazetteer and Business Dirctory, 1902–03. Vol. 8. Detroit: R. L. Polk, 1902.

West Virginia State Gazetteer and Business Directory, 1906–07. Vol. 10. Detroit: R. L. Polk, 1906.

West Virginia State Gazetteer and Business Directory, 1914–1915. Vol. 14. Detroit: R. L. Polk, 1914.

West Virginia State Gazetteer and Business Directory, 1923. Vol. 19. Detroit: R. L. Polk, 1923.

Wickline, W. W. Jr. "The Iron Mountain and Greenbrier Railroad, Early Splash Dams of the Anthony Creek Area, Timbering, and Related History." *Journal of the Greenbrier Historical Society* 1 (September 1965): 11–16.

"Widen: An Appalachian Empire." *Hickory and Lady Slippers: Life and Legend of Clay County People*. Vol. 4, book 2 (1979), published by Clay County (W.Va.) High School.

Widner, Ralph R. "West Virginia: If Trees Could Cuss." In *Forests and Forestry in the American States*, edited by Ralph R. Widner, 313–21. Washington, D.C.: National Association of State Foresters, 1968.

Wilhelm, Eugene J. "Animal Drives: A Case Study in Historical Geography." *Journal of Geography* 66 (1967): 327–34.

Willey, Waitman T. *An Inside View of the Formation of West Virginia*. Wheeling, W.Va.: News Publishing Company, 1901.

Williams, Charles Richard, ed., *Diary and Letters of Rutherford Birchard Hayes*. Vol. 2. Columbus: Ohio Archaeological and Historical Society, 1922.

Williams, John Alexander. "Class, Section, and Culture in Nineteenth-Century West Virginia Politics." In *Appalachia in the Making: The Mountain South in the Nineteenth*

Century, edited by Mary Beth Pudup, Dwight B. Billings, and Altina L. Waller, 210–32. Chapel Hill: University of North Carolina Press, 1995.

——. "The New Dominion and the Old: Ante-Bellum and Statehood Politics as the Background of West Virginia's 'Bourbon Democracy.'" *West Virginia History* 33 (1973): 317–407.

——. *West Virginia: A History*. New York: Norton, 1976.

——. *West Virginia and the Captains of Industry*. Morgantown: West Virginia University Library, 1976.

Williams, Michael. *Americans and Their Forests: A Historical Geography*. Cambridge: Cambridge University Press, 1989.

Wilson, Darlene. "The Felicitous Convergence of Mythmaking and Capital Accumulation: John Fox Jr. and the Formation of An(Other) Almost-White American Underclass." *Journal of Appalachian Studies* 1 (1995): 5–44.

Wooster, Ralph A. *Politicians, Planters and Plain Folk: Courthouse and Statehouse in the Upper South, 1850–1860*. Knoxville: University of Tennessee Press, 1975.

Workman, Michael E. "Political Culture and the Coal Economy in the Upper Monongahela Region, 1776–1933." Ph.D. diss., West Virginia University, 1995.

"Ye Mighty Men." *Gateway* [Monongahela National Forest Newsletter] 2 (April 1937): 2.

corporations, 124; and Social Darwinism, 124; as ideal judge, 128

Braucher, W.Va., 91

Bretz, W.Va., 72

Brooklyn Heights, W.Va., 206–7

Brooks, A. B., 239, 267, 273, 277, 289–90

Brotherhood of Timber Workers, 162

Brown, A. B., 10–11

Brown, James H., 111

Brown, Joe, 208

Bryan, William Jennings, 245

Buckhannon, W.Va., 68–69

Burner, C. L. "Bud," 204

Burner, Elmer, 207

Burner, Emma, 207

Butler, P. H., 153, 156, 167, 258

"Cabin Creek Wreck," 149–50

Caldwell, W.Va., 98, 274–75

Camden, Johnson Newlon, 58, 62, 63, 67, 68, 69, 71, 76, 214, 243

Camden-on-Gauley, W.Va., 68, 69, 182, 192

Cameron, J. M., 88

Cameron, Simon, 74

Camp, E. H., 92

Campbell, John E., 246

Canaan Valley, 16, 148, 264

Carlisle, John S., 55, 57, 215

Cass, Joseph K., 99

Cass, W.Va., 78, 98, 99, 139, 154, 155, 162, 163, 169, 185, 191, 193, 194, 203, 207

Cayton, William M., 219

Central West Virginia Fire Protection Association, 288

Chambers, Charles C., 12

Champion Fibre Company, 10, 12

Charleston, W.Va., 51, 73, 104, 111, 156, 167, 177

Cheat Mountain, 139, 141, 147, 169, 182

Cheat River, 78, 217, 273

Cherry River, 97, 263

Cherry River Boom and Lumber Company, 95–98, 156, 163, 266

Chesapeake and Ohio Railroad. See Railroads–companies

Clarke-McNary Act, 288

Clarksburg, W.Va., 52, 55, 67, 68

Coal and Coke Railroad. See Railroads–companies

Coal and Iron Railroad. See Railroads–companies

Coal River, 59

Colio, John, 183

Condon, Emily, 88

Condon-Lane Boom and Lumber Company, 88–89

Conservation:

—and U.S. government agencies: Soil Conservation Service, 270; Civilian Conservation Commission, 290; Works Projects Administration, 290

—and West Virginia law: early conservation legislation, 278–80; impediments to enforcement, 279–82, 285; class bias of, 280; traditional practices, 283–85. See also Law–and industrial transition in West Virginia

—and West Virginia state agencies: Natural Resource Commission, 273; Fish Commission, 278–80; Fish and Game Commission, 280–82; Conservation Commission, 286–87; Game and Fish Commission, 289; Forest and Park Commission, 290

Cornwell, John J., 289

Corrick, Lorenzo Dow, 223

Couch v. Chesapeake and Ohio, 126

Covington, Va., 78, 98, 259, 275

Cranberry River, 97, 291

Crane and Company, 39, 60

Craver, Joseph and Sophia, 196

Crescent Lumber Company, 75, 88

Crickard, Patrick, 232

Croft Lumber Company, 157

Cumberland Daily News, 171

Cunningham, Dan, 176–79

Cupp, Will E., 220

Curtin Lumber Company, 156

Dailey, C. Wood, 230, 232, 234

Davis, Henry Gassaway, 45, 67, 70, 71, 73, 74, 76, 78, 92, 186, 189, 193, 199, 213, 214, 224–26, 229–33, 238

Greenbrier River, 32, 34, 39, 73, 75, 98–99, 167, 182, 274

Greenbrier River Lumber Company, 88

Greenbrier Valley Democrat, 275

Griffith Lumber Company, 69

Guyandotte River, 39, 60, 315 (n. 45)

Hall, Granville D., 56

Hambleton, W.Va., 189, 190, 195

Hamilton et al. v. Tucker County Court et al., 221–22

Hamilton Leather Company, 223

Hammonds, Edn, 315 (n. 67)

Hammonds, Jesse, 284

Hansford, Lloyd, 281

Harper, Riley, 223

Harrison, Nathaniel, 216

Harrison, William A., 111

Hatcher, John H., 178

Hatfield, Elias, 179, 180

Hatfield-McCoy Feud, 223

Hawks, James, 183

Hayes, Rutherford B., 55

Haymond, Alpheus F., 104, 113

Heaster, Emmett, 156

Hendricks, W.Va., 72, 184, 189–93, 195–96, 206

Hinton, W.Va., 243, 274, 275

Hoffman, John S., 113

Hoke, John, 230

Hollingsworth, Levi, 88

Holt, Homer A., 113, 122

"Hoodoo" engine. See Railroads

Horton, W.Va., 73, 152–53, 157, 193, 195, 265

Hosterman Lumber Company, 146

Houston, W. H., 177, 178

Howell, Clark, 92

Hubbard, Henry B., 237–38

Huling Lumber Company, 189

Huntersville, W.Va., 77, 197–98, 237

Huntington, Collis P., 59

Huttonsville, W.Va., 74, 231

Industrial Workers of the World, 162, 163

Ingalls, Melville E., 59, 78

Inter-Mountain, 227

Interstate Commerce Act of 1887, 243

"Ironheaded" industrialists, 8, 212, 224, 225, 309 (n. 1)

Iskra, John, 171

Jefferson, Peter, 16

Jefferson, Thomas, 247, 248

Jenkins, John B., 223

Jenningston, W.Va., 147–49

"Jes in frum Caynane," 186–87

Johnson, Okey, 104, 113

Jones, S. A., 11

Julian, Carzza, and Company, 167

Junior Order of American Mechanics, 163

Kaler, Solomon W., 222

Kanawha Ring, 213, 214

Kanawha River, 38, 51, 60, 277–78, 315 (n. 45)

Keller, Benjamin F., 180

Kennedy, Philip Pendleton, 7

Kildow, J. Ed, 231

Kimmell, J. W., 91

King, Abraham, 184

King, Henry C., 86–87

Kingwood, W.Va., 276

Kinsport, James, 92

Kline, George W., 149

Knapp's Creek, 167

Knights of Pythias, 220

Lane, Martin, 232–33

Laneville, W.Va., 207

Lansburgh, Max, 87

Lary, Dan, 183

Lashley, C. G., 222

Laurel River, 149

Laurel River Lumber Company, 148, 149

Law:

—and industrial transition in West Virginia: expanding capitalist economy, 105–29 passim; judicial subsidies to business, 107–10, 115, 117–19; judicial subsidies to lumber industry, 108, 118–19; New Court, 110, 114–29; Old Court, 110–14, 129; Supreme Court of Appeals, 110–29 passim; problems of judicial system, 111;

locomotives killing stock, 115–16; judicial subsidies to railroads, 115–18, 122–29; locomotives causing fires, 116–17; "reasonable use" doctrine, 117, 127; "legal positivism," 118; riparian rights, 118–19; conflicting philosophies of judges on supreme court of appeals, 119–29 [see also Brannon, Henry; Dent, Marmaduke H.]; circuit courts and "jury nullification," 127–28; "Boarding House Law," 174; Yost Law (Prohibition), 206. See also Supreme Court of Appeals—pivot decisions of West Virginia
—and Virginia tradition: evolution, 105, 114; judicial subsidies to business, 109–10; "country over court," 110; juries as "shield of liberty," 110; influence on West Virginia law, 110–14, 129; and accidents involving locomotives, 115–16; Featherstone Act of 1908, 116
Leading Creek, 227
Lead Mine, W.Va., 18
Leadsville, W.Va., 71
Leatherwood Lumber Company, 75
Letcher, John, 54
Lewis, Thomas, 16
Lewisburg, W.Va., 274–75
Lidgerwood aerial skidder, 143–45
Lilly, J. C., 176, 178
Little Blackwater River, 93
Little Kanawha Navigation Company, 43–44
Little Kanawha River, 43, 216, 278, 315 (n. 45)
Little Kanawha River Lumber Company, 60
Little River Lumber Company, 10, 13
Lucas, Daniel B., 113
Ludwig, Fred "the German," 171
Luke, John, 284–85
Luke, Thomas, 137
Luke, William, 77, 98
Luke, Md., 77
Luke family, 98–99
Lumber industry, 6, 9, 11; log drives and rafting, 37–44; Coal and Lumber Agency, 64, 66; band mills, 82, 92–100,

152; absentee ownership, 85–87, 89–92, 313 (n. 56); land speculation and acquisition, 85–89; milling centers, 92–100 [see also Cass, W.Va.; Davis, W.Va.; Rainelle, W.Va.; Richwood, W.Va.]; organization of, 100–102; West Virginia Lumberman's Association, 163; music in lumber towns, 195–96
—capitalist values: and wood hicks, 203; liquor and violent behavior, 203–9; opponents of speakeasies, 203–9; and courts, 205
—commercial development and: in backcounties, 185–202; milltowns as commercial centers, 186–89, 191–98, 201–2; banks, 192–93, 202–3; professional services, 193–94; utilities, 193–94; newspapers, 200–201
—labor force: independent and transitory, 133, 161; in mills, 150–55; recruitment of local farmers, 155–61; native born, 165–67; ethnic mix, 165–84; African Americans, 167, 174, 182, 184; Italians, 167–70, 175–84; imported, 168–70; agencies and contractors, 168–70, 175, 182; Austrians, 170–74; labor stealing, 171–74; debt peonage, 174–82, 306 (n. 21); nativism among, 181–84; social conflict, 182–84
—lumber companies: Babcock Lumber and Boom Company, 93, 149, 171, 174, 253; Beaver Creek Lumber Company, 93, 96; Blackwater Boom and Lumber Company, 92, 93, 266; C. Crane and Company, 39, 60; Cherry River Boom and Lumber Company, 95–98, 156, 163, 266; Condon-Lane Boom and Lumber Company, 88–89, 233; Crescent Lumber Company, 75, 88; Croft Lumber Company, 157; Curtin Lumber Company, 156; Deer Creek Lumber Company, 156; Denman and Ritter Lumber Company, 92; Elk River Coal and Lumber Company, 74, 88; Gauley Lumber Company, 69; Greenbrier River Lumber Company, 88; Griffith Lumber Company, 69; Hosterman Lumber Company, 146; Huling Lumber Company, 189; Laurel River

ginia Conservation Commission of 1908, 165; "Boarding House Law," 174; Yost Law (prohibition), 206; West Virginia Reform Law of 1909, 286
— politics. *See* Political parties and factions in West Virginia
— state conservation agencies: Department of Agriculture, 241, 264; Geological Survey, 267, 276; Natural Resource Commission, 273; Fish Commission, 278–80; Fish and Game Commission, 280; Conservation Commission, 286; Game and Fish Commission, 289; Forest and Park Commission, 290
West Virginia and Pittsburgh Railroad. *See* Railroads — companies
West Virginia Audubon Society, 288
West Virginia Bar Association, 121, 122, 126, 280
West Virginia Central and Pittsburgh Railroad. *See* Railroads — companies
West Virginia Federation of Labor, 163
West Virginia Fish and Game Protection Association, 288
"The West Virginia Hills," 184
West Virginia Pulp and Paper Company, 77, 78, 80, 94, 98–100, 137, 139, 147, 162, 169, 183, 191, 204, 253, 274, 275, 284
Wheeling, W.Va., 51, 52, 55, 56, 111
Wheeling Intelligencer, 55, 222
Wheeling Register, 58, 69, 239
Whig Party, 56, 212
White, Albert B., 176, 287–88

White, Benjamin, 216
White, C. S., 279
White, I. C., 286
White, Scott, 208, 268
Whitehair, Joshua, 259
White House Conference of Governors (1908), 286
White Sulphur Springs, W.Va., 34, 259
Whitmer, Robert F., 189, 233
Whitmer, W.Va., 208–9, 268
Whitmer Lumber Company, 233
Widen, W.Va., 74
Wilderness, 15–16, 293 (n. 3). *See also* Deforestation
Willdell, W.Va., 266
Willey, Waitman T., 215, 242–43
Williams, H. E., 273
Williams River, 96, 162, 266, 273, 284, 291
Wilson, Benjamin, Jr., 104
Wilson, E. Willis, 243
Wilson, William G., 232
Winterburn, W.Va., 78
Withers, Bob, 156
Wolfe, S. M., 179
Woods, Samuel, 104, 113
Woodsmen of America, 162
Wriston, Emory N., 263–64

Yeager, C. A., 202
Yellow Poplar Lumber Company, 60
Yokum, Humbolt, 230

Zaylor, Andrew, 171–74